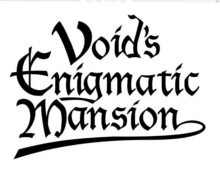

5

DISCARDED

HeeEun Kim
JiEun Ha

Yen
Press

Void's Enigmatic Mansion

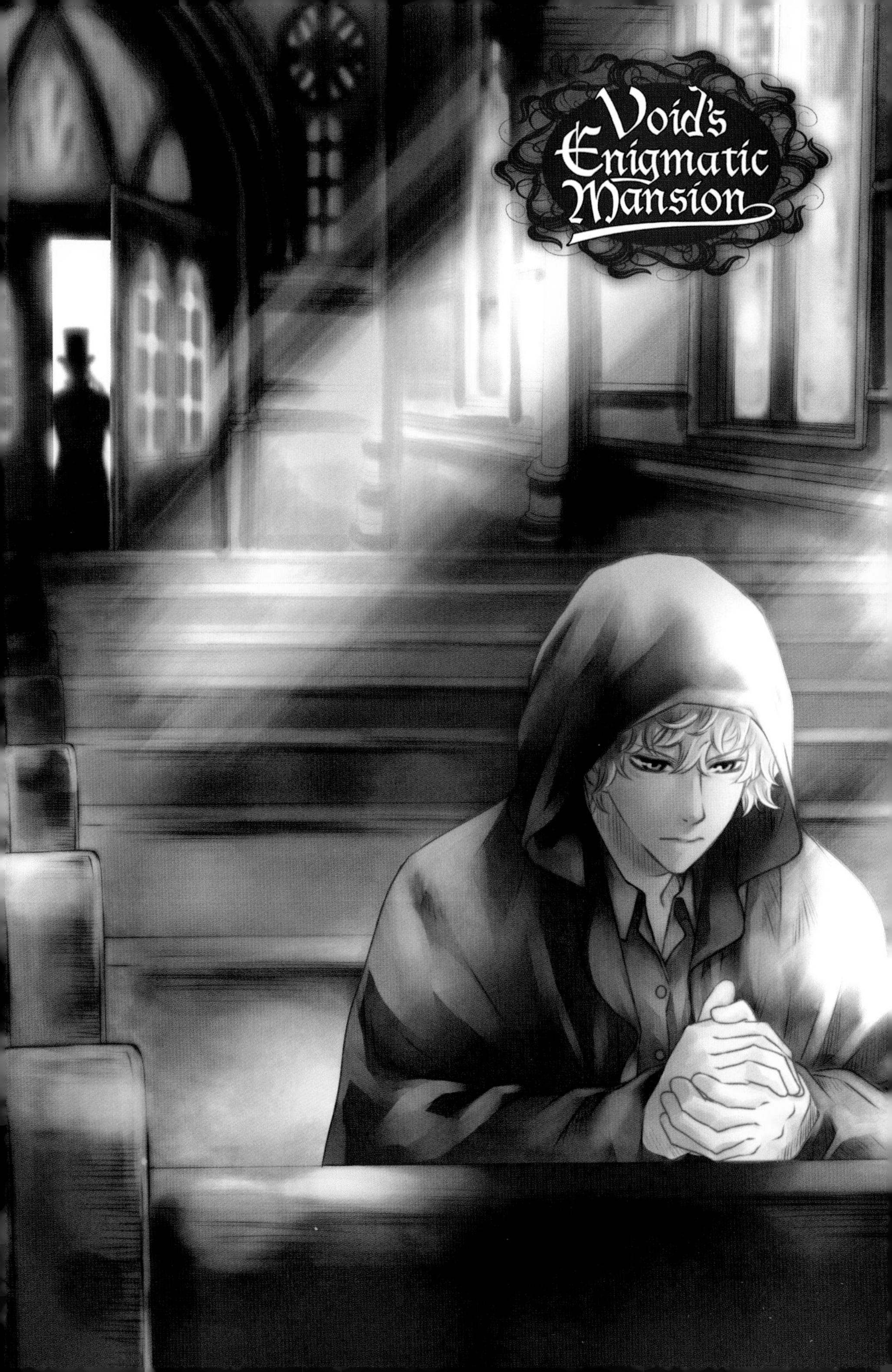
Void's
Enigmatic
Mansion

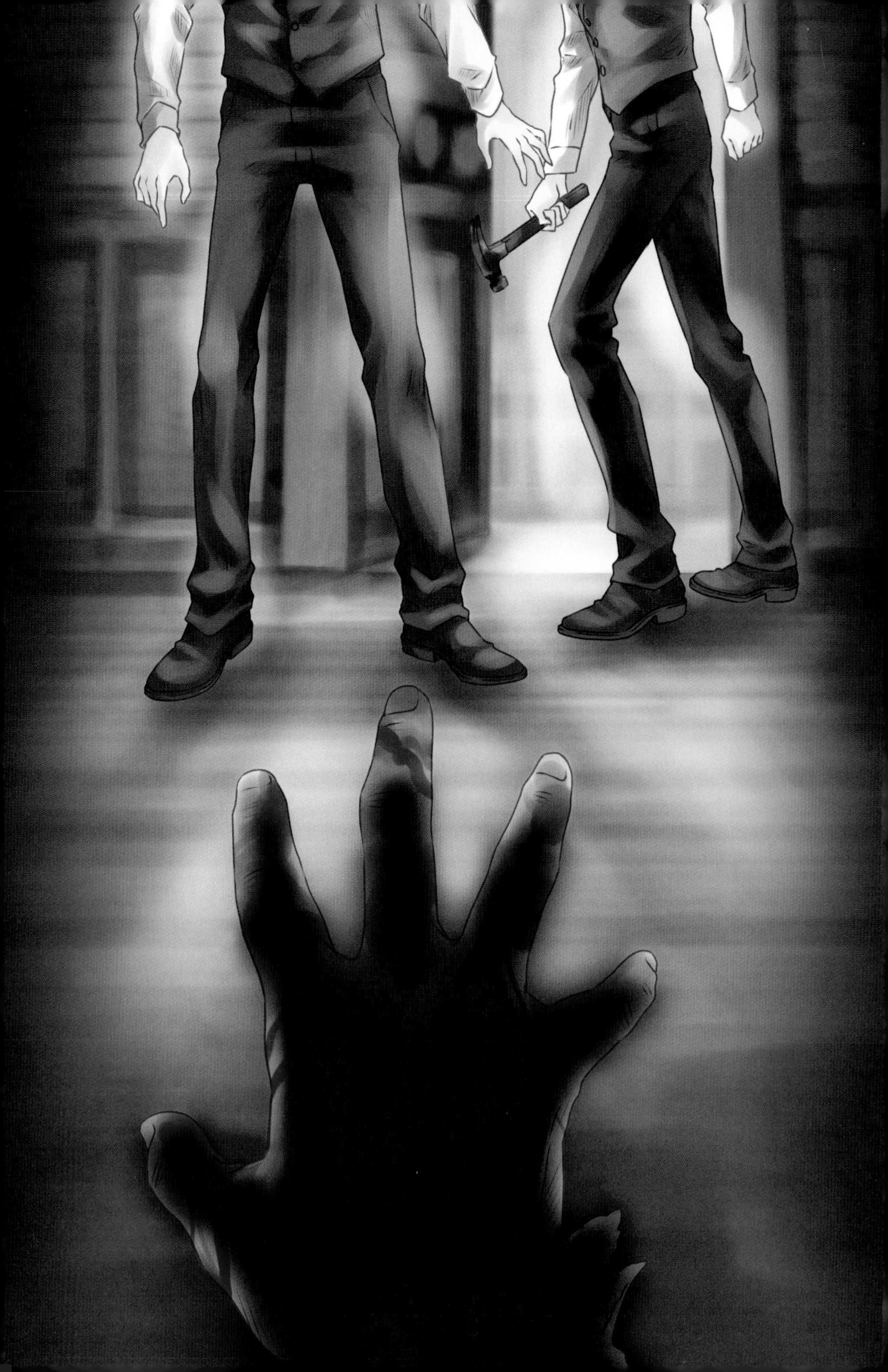

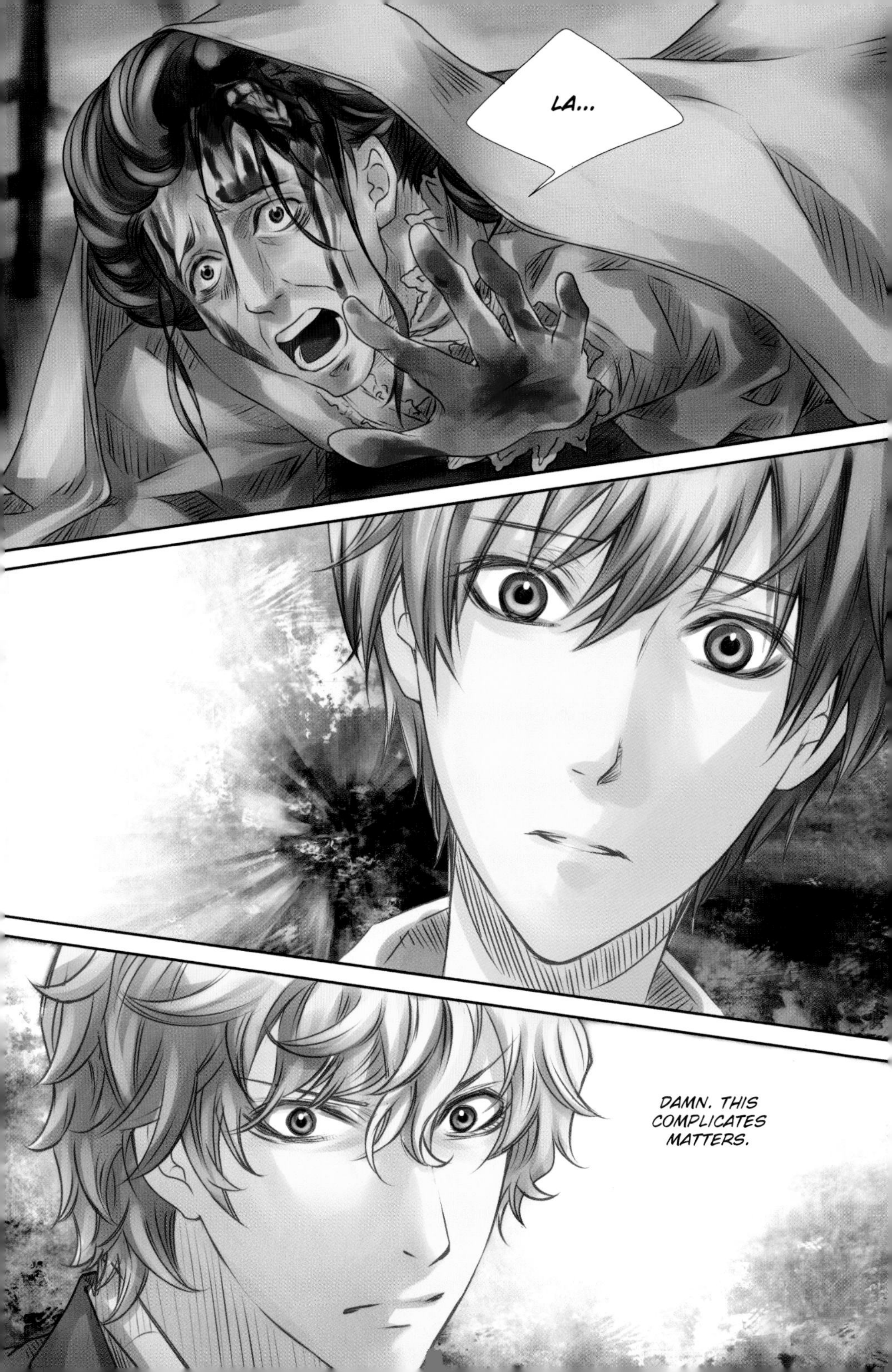
LA...
DAMN. THIS COMPLICATES MATTERS.

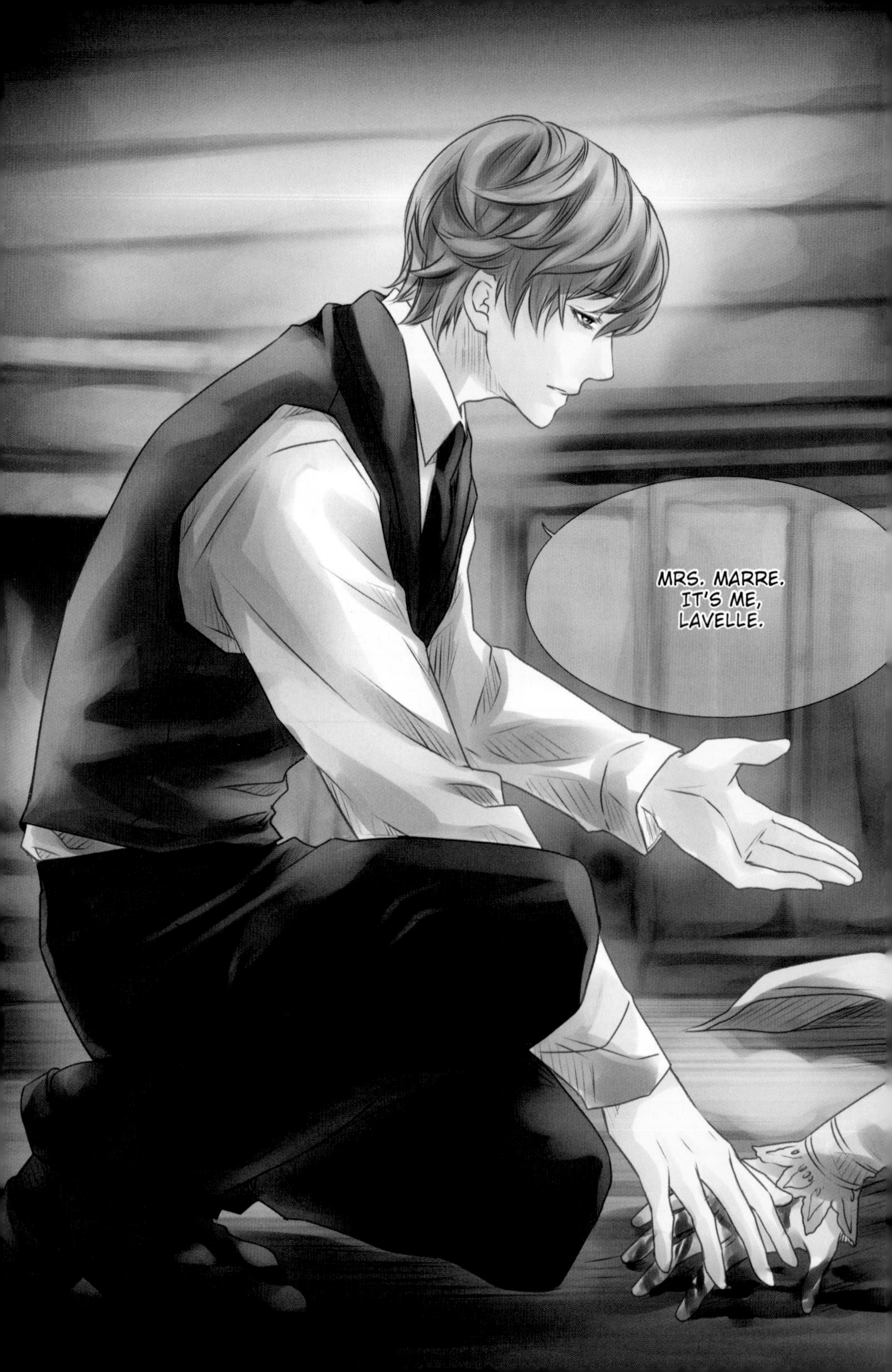
MRS. MARRE. IT'S ME, LAVELLE.

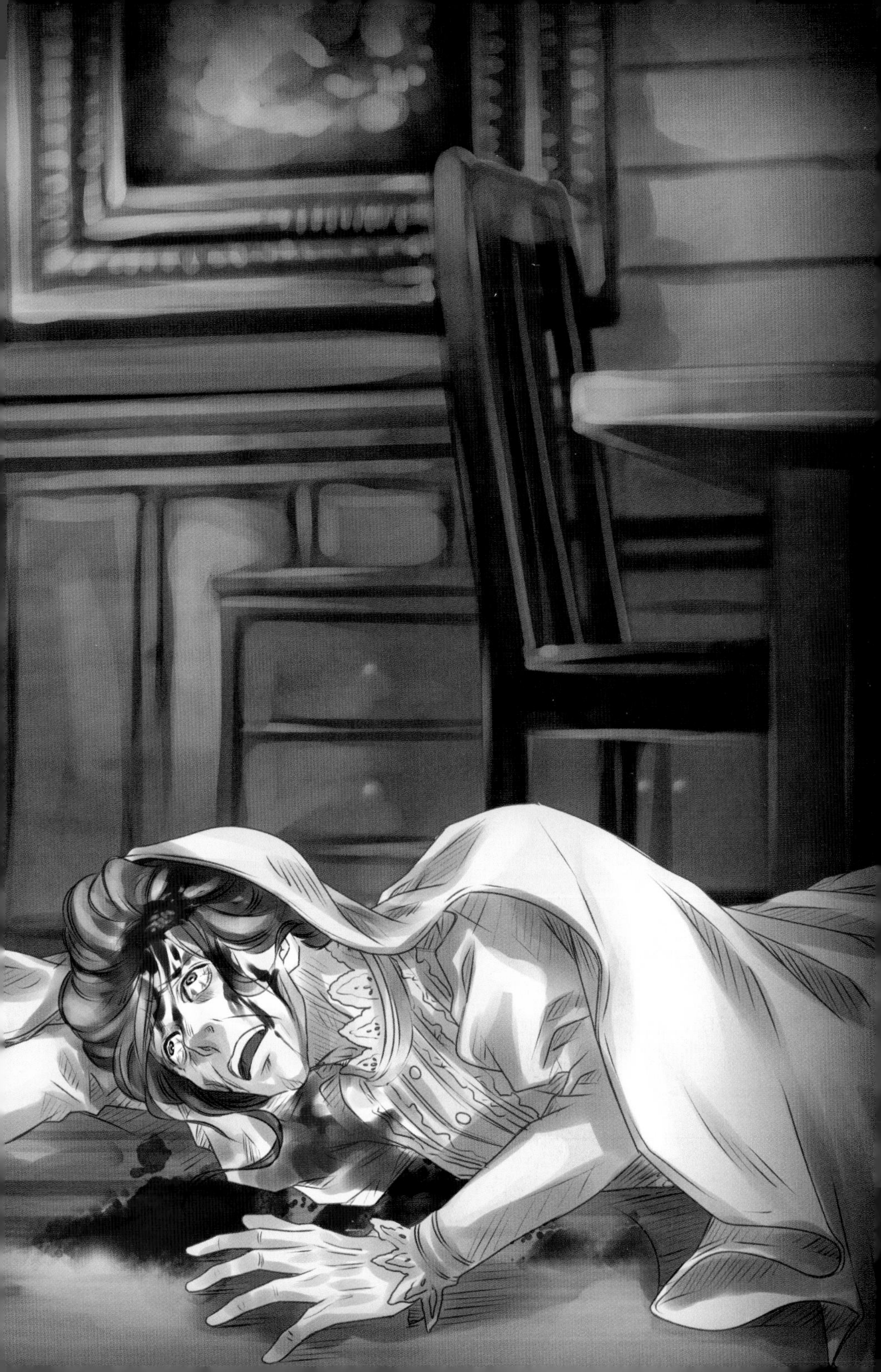

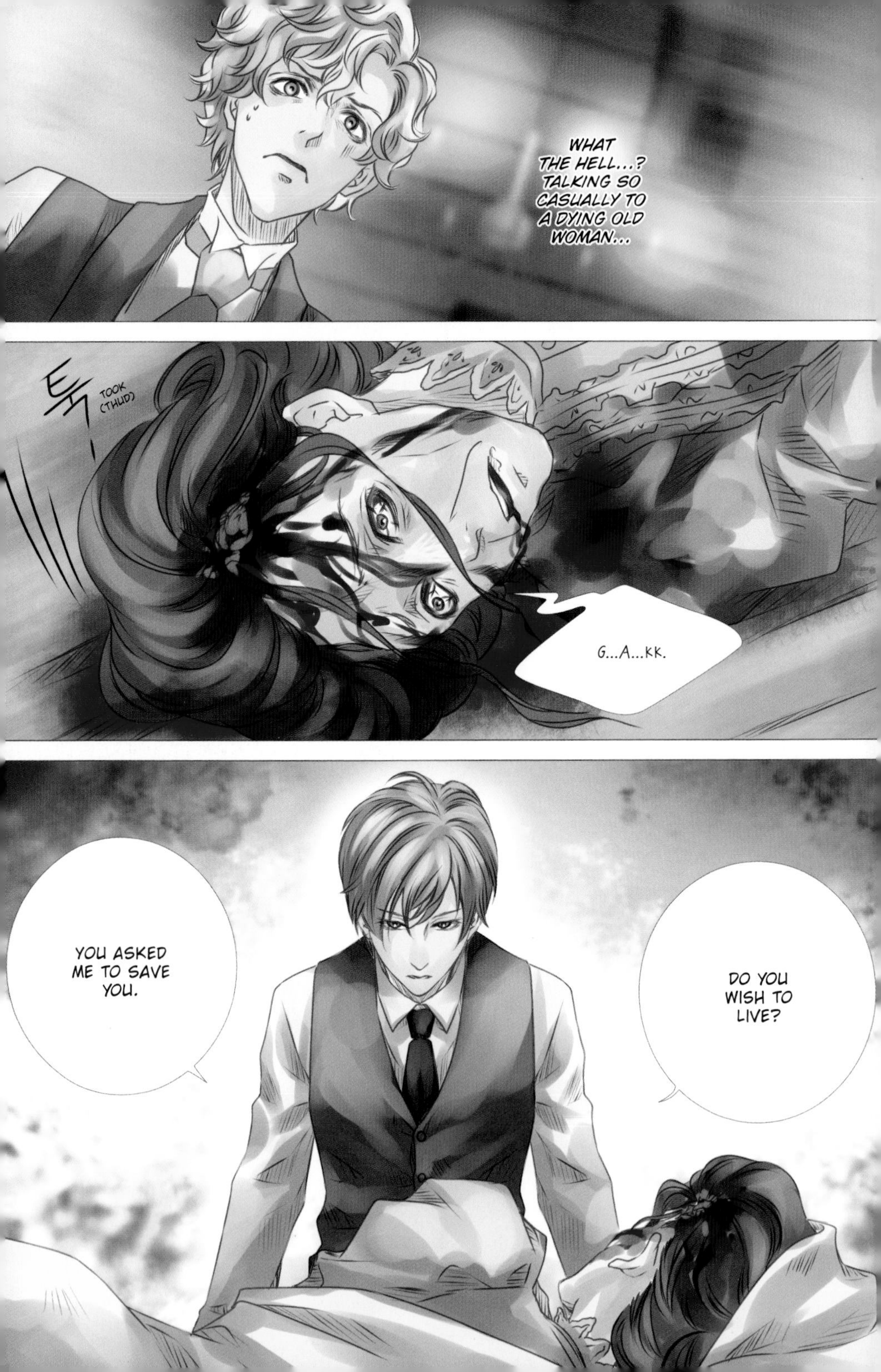
WHAT THE HELL...? TALKING SO CASUALLY TO A DYING OLD WOMAN...
툭
TOOK (THUD)
G...A...KK.
DO YOU WISH TO LIVE?
YOU ASKED ME TO SAVE YOU.

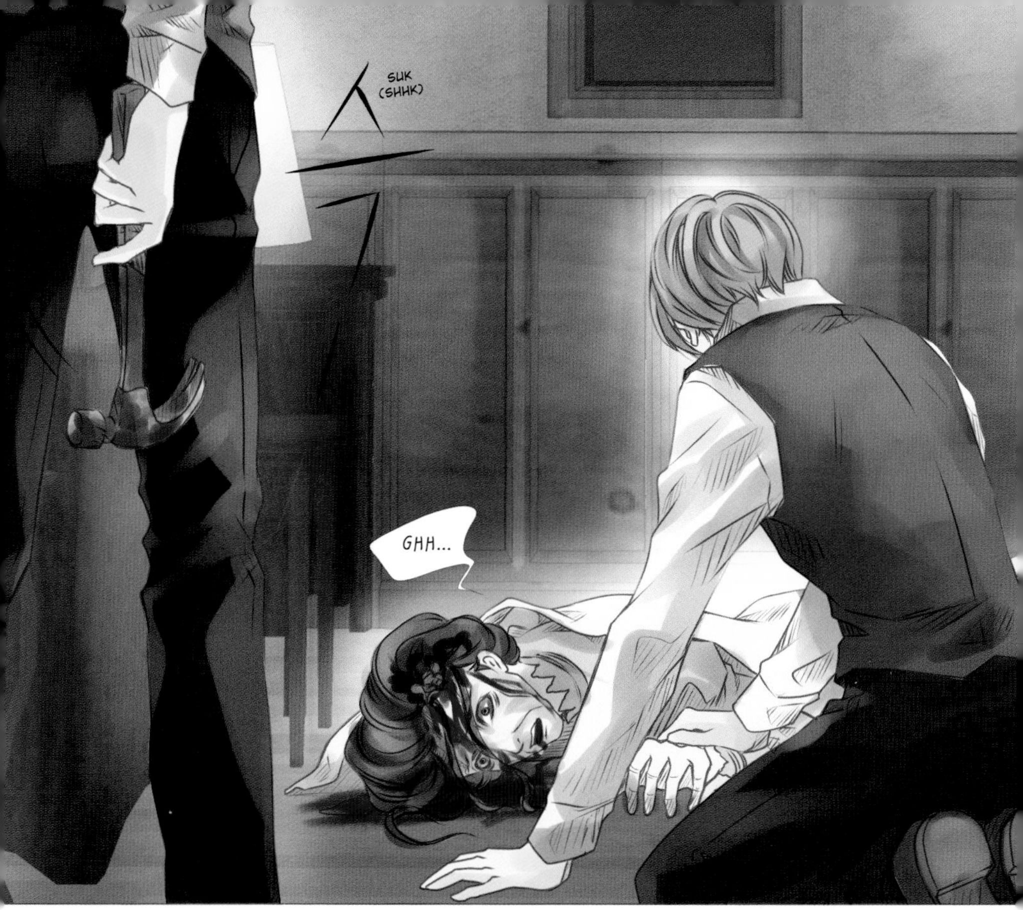
SUK
(SHHK)
GHH...

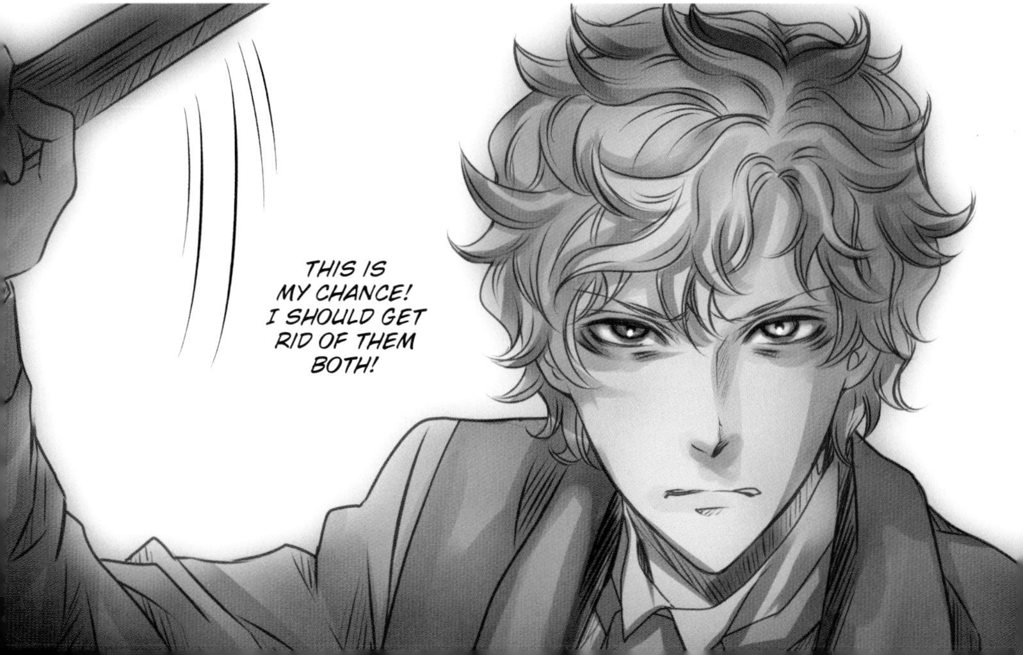
THIS IS MY CHANCE! I SHOULD GET RID OF THEM BOTH!

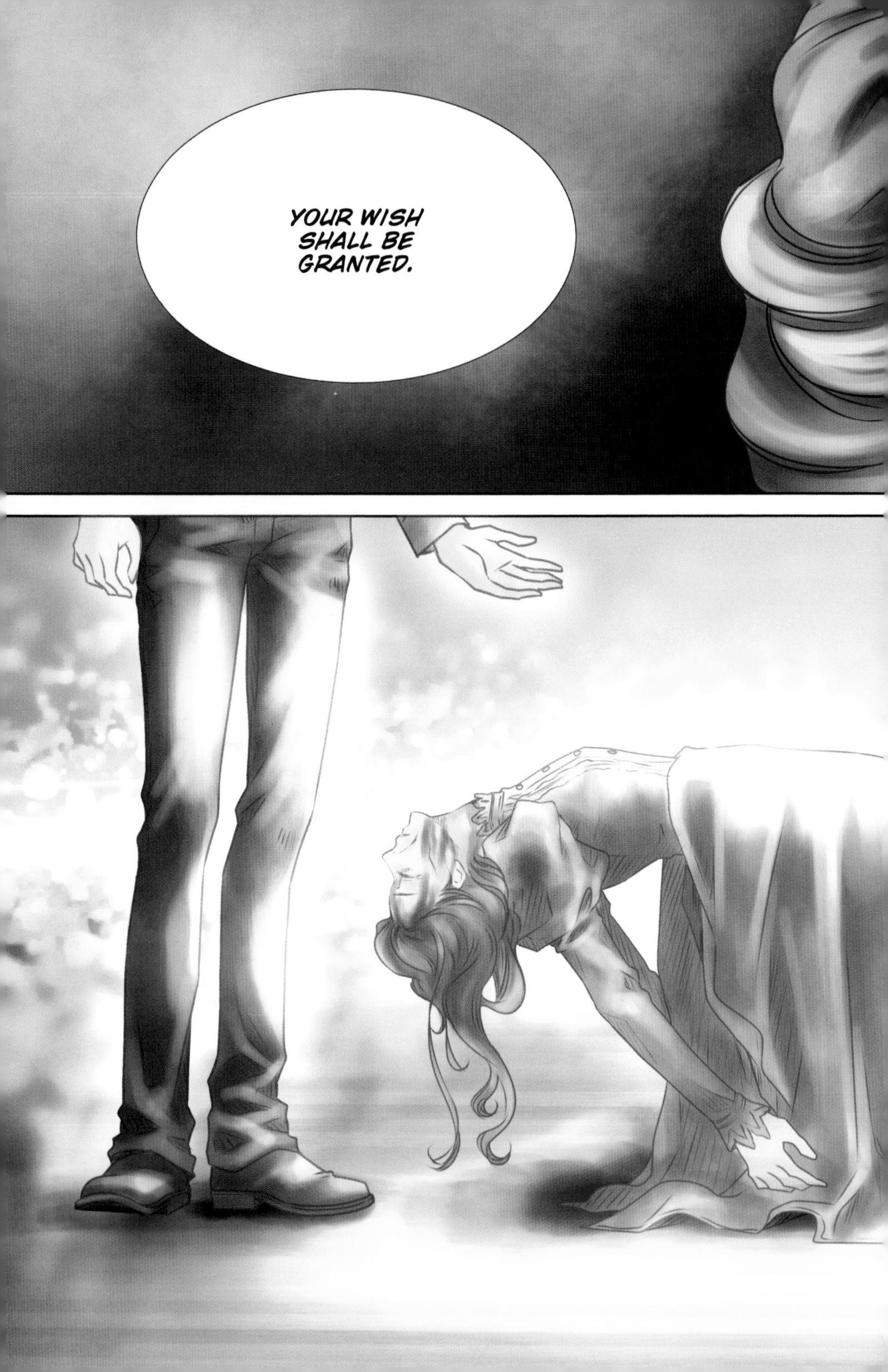
YOUR WISH SHALL BE GRANTED.

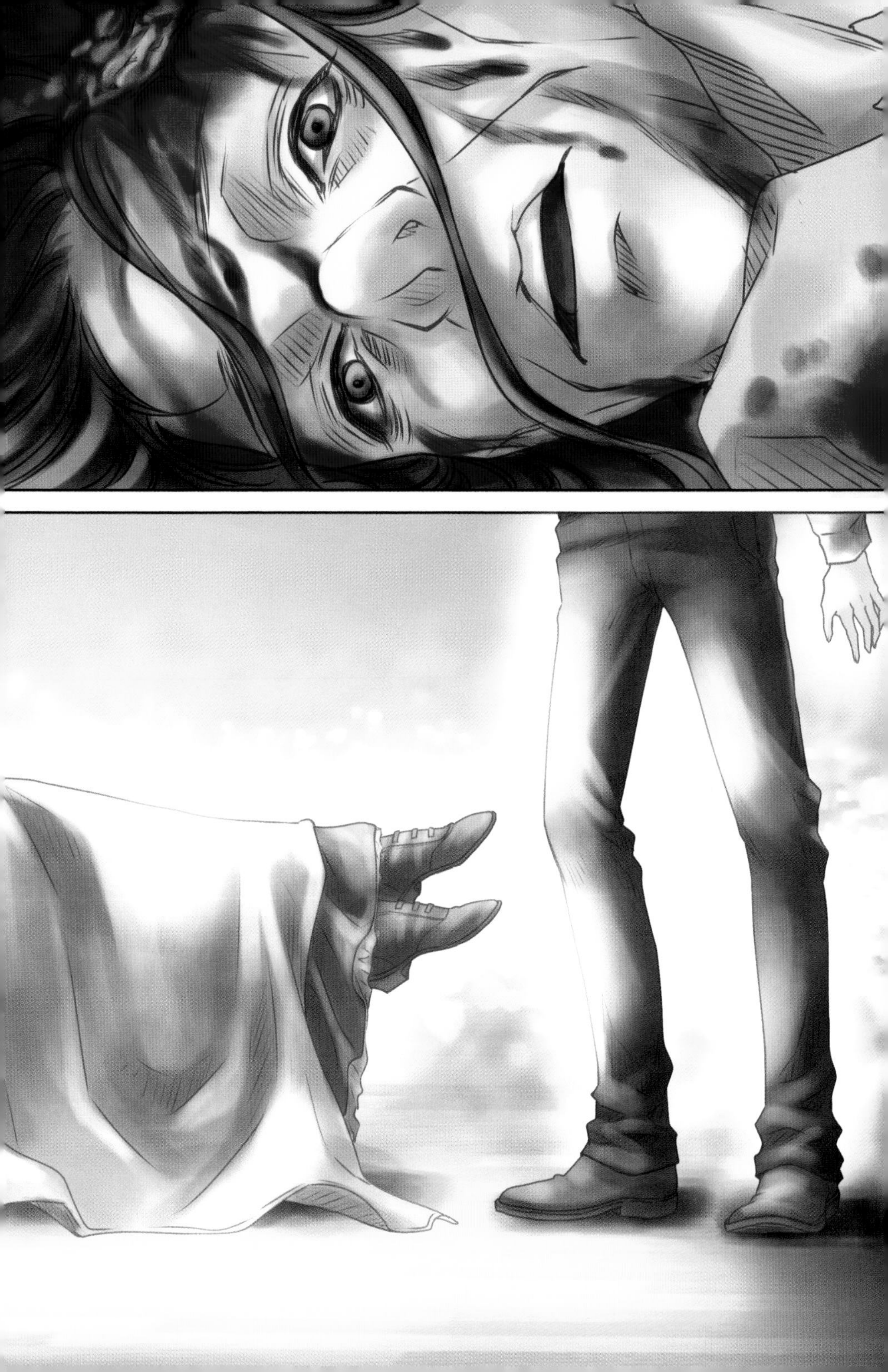

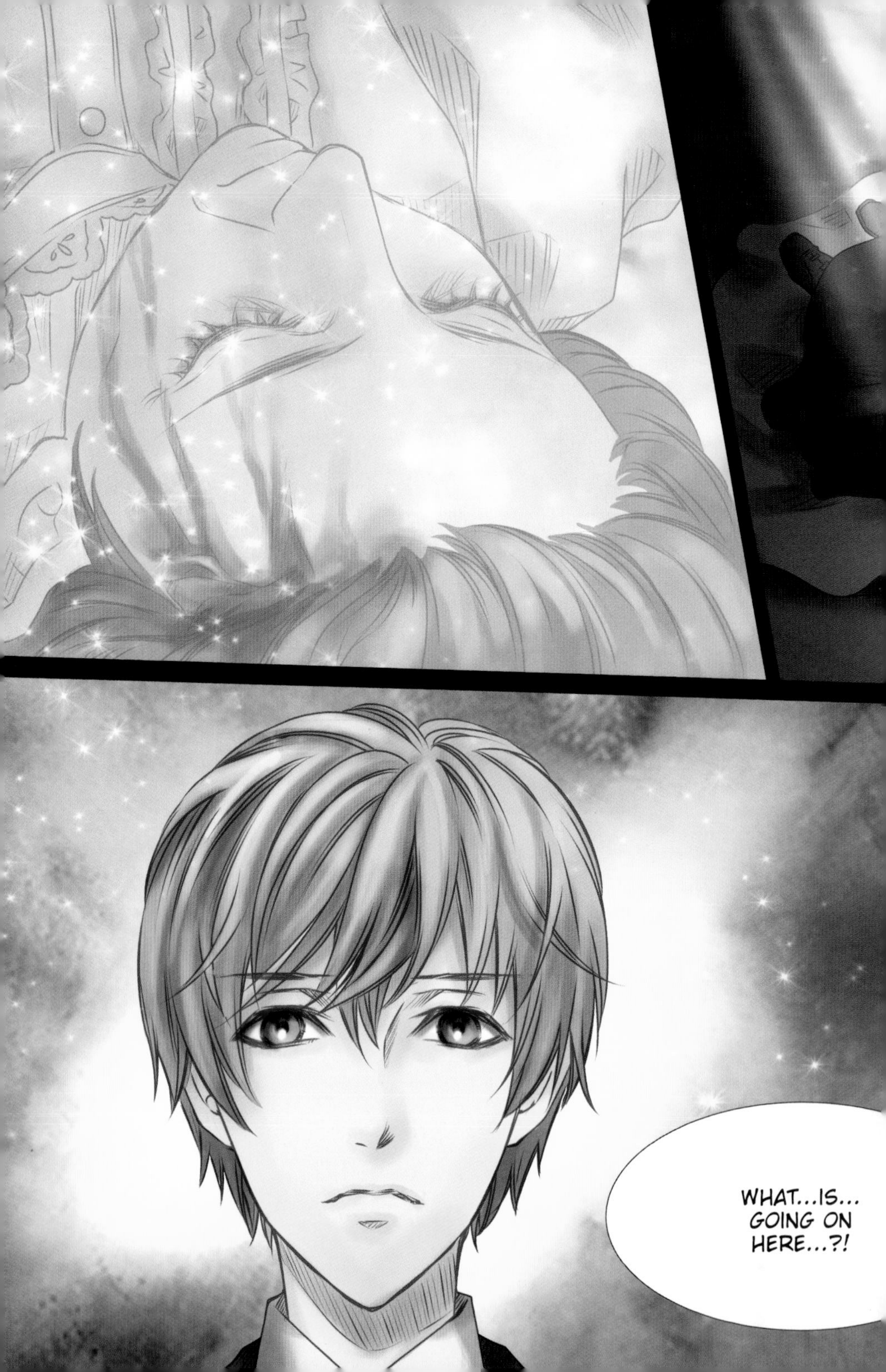
WHAT...IS... GOING ON HERE...?!

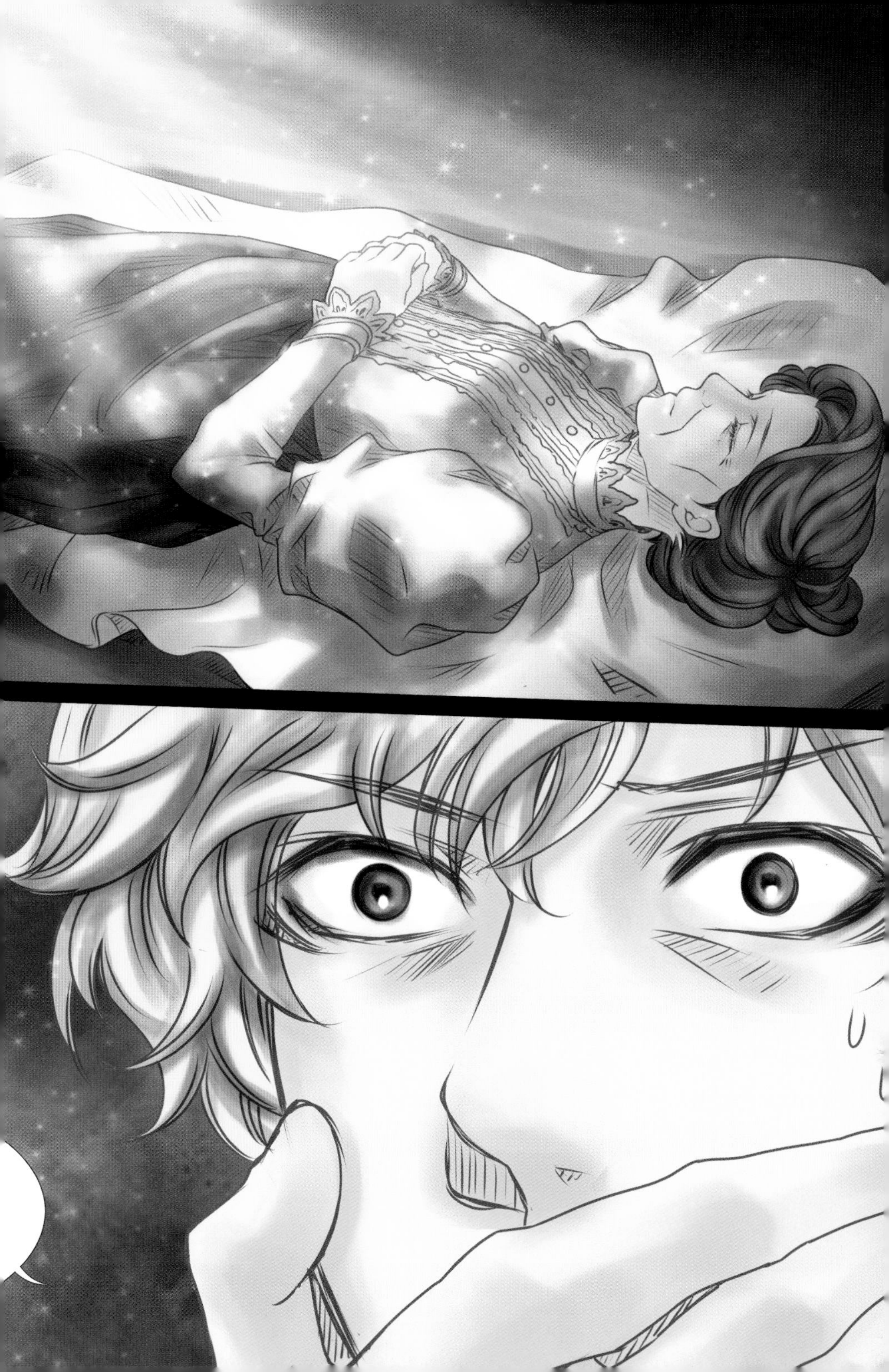

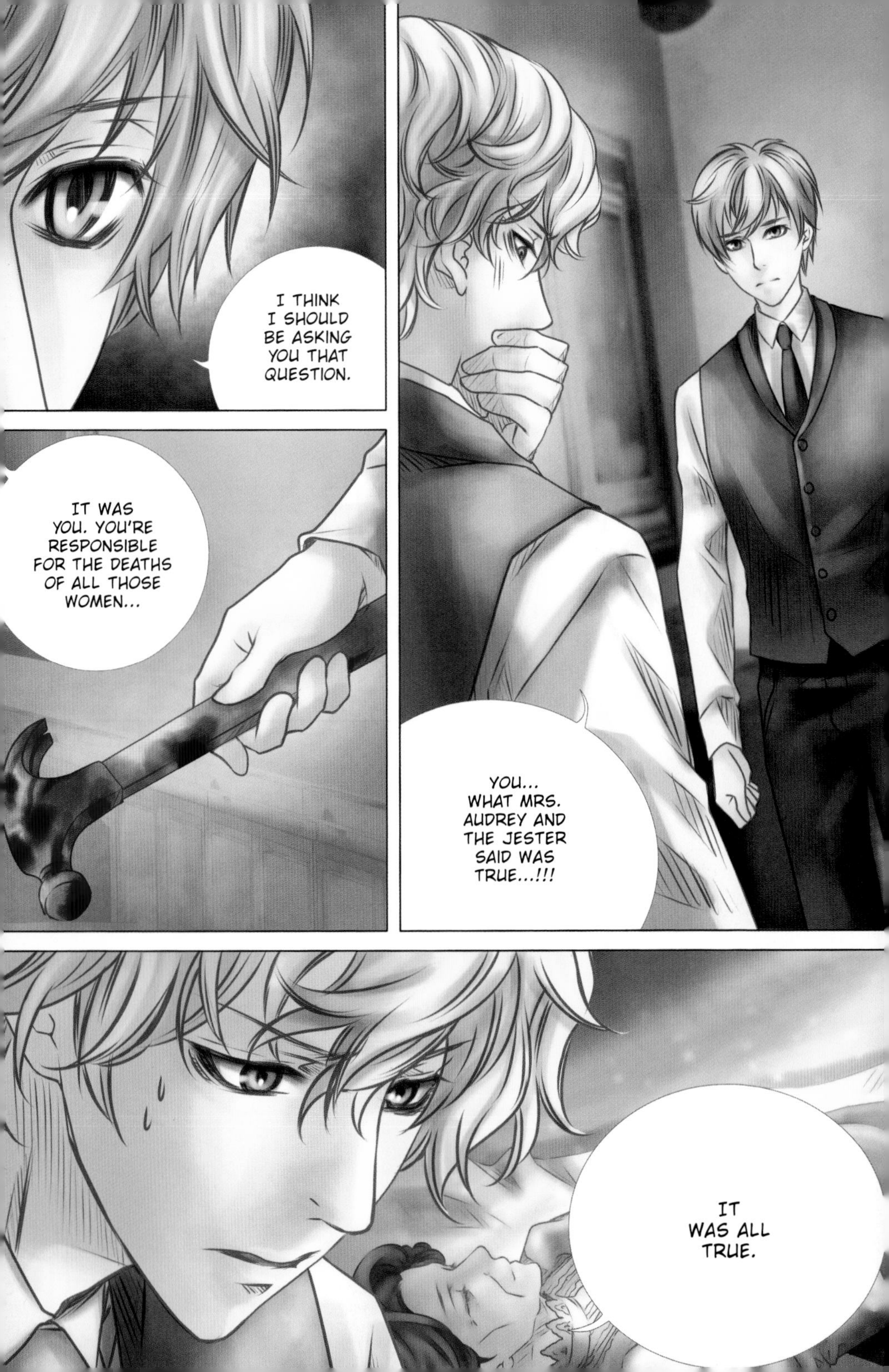
I THINK I SHOULD BE ASKING YOU THAT QUESTION.
IT WAS YOU. YOU'RE RESPONSIBLE FOR THE DEATHS OF ALL THOSE WOMEN...
YOU... WHAT MRS. AUDREY AND THE JESTER SAID WAS TRUE...!!!
IT WAS ALL TRUE.

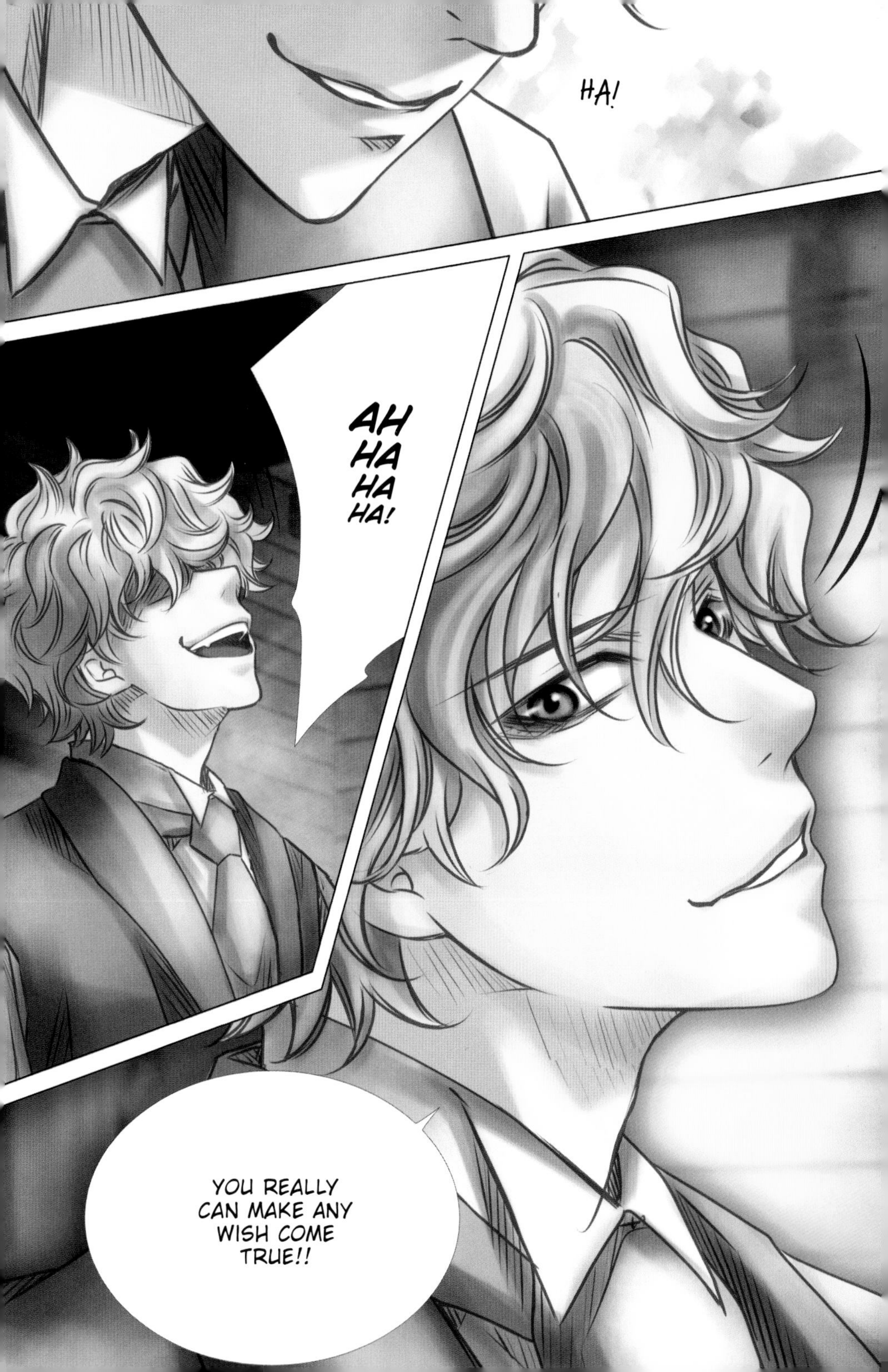
HA!
AH HA HA HA!
YOU REALLY CAN MAKE ANY WISH COME TRUE!!

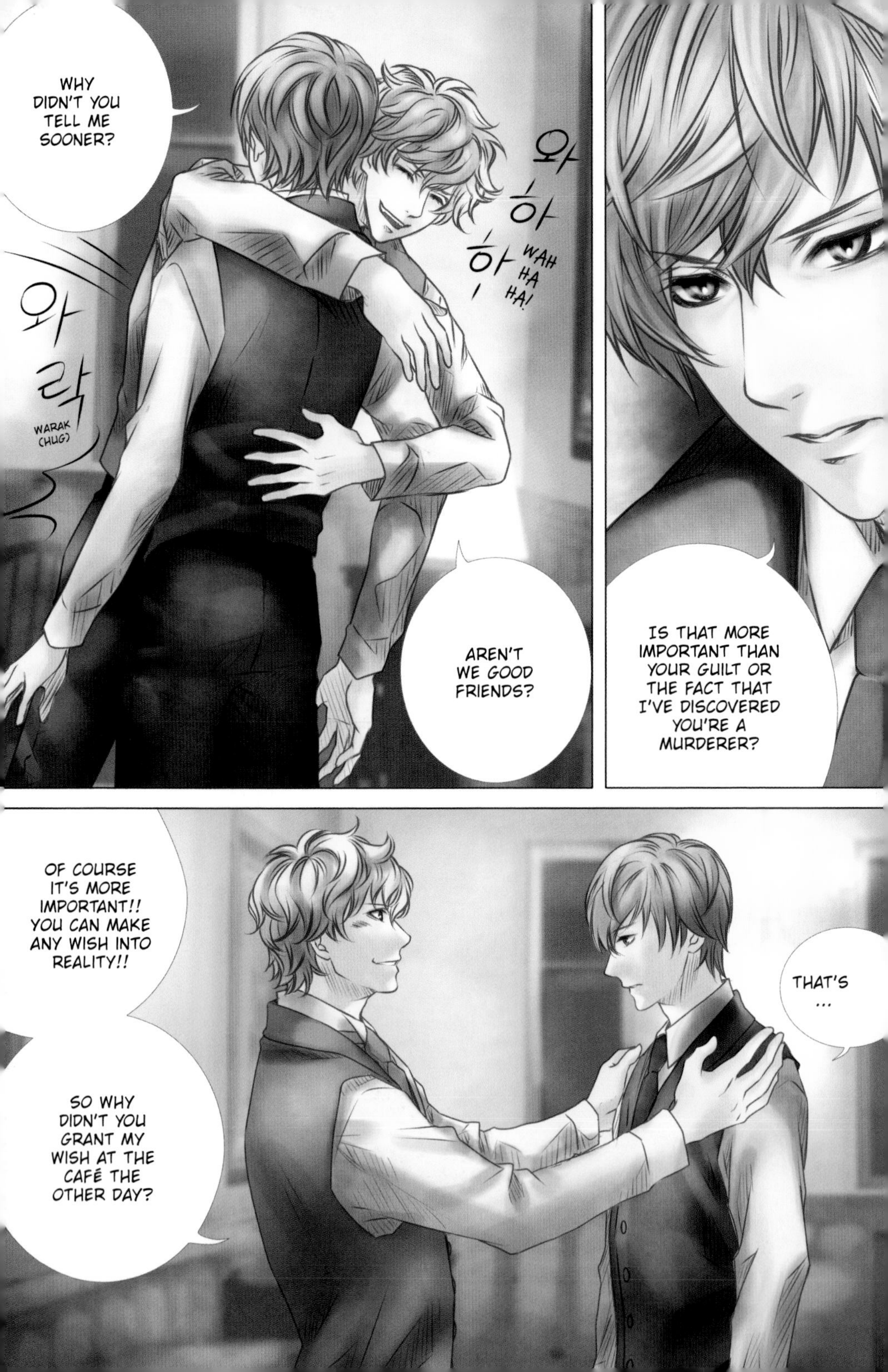
WHY DIDN'T YOU TELL ME SOONER?
와락
WARAK (HUG)
와하하!
WAH HA HA!
AREN'T WE GOOD FRIENDS?
IS THAT MORE IMPORTANT THAN YOUR GUILT OR THE FACT THAT I'VE DISCOVERED YOU'RE A MURDERER?
OF COURSE IT'S MORE IMPORTANT!! YOU CAN MAKE ANY WISH INTO REALITY!!
SO WHY DIDN'T YOU GRANT MY WISH AT THE CAFÉ THE OTHER DAY?
THAT'S ...

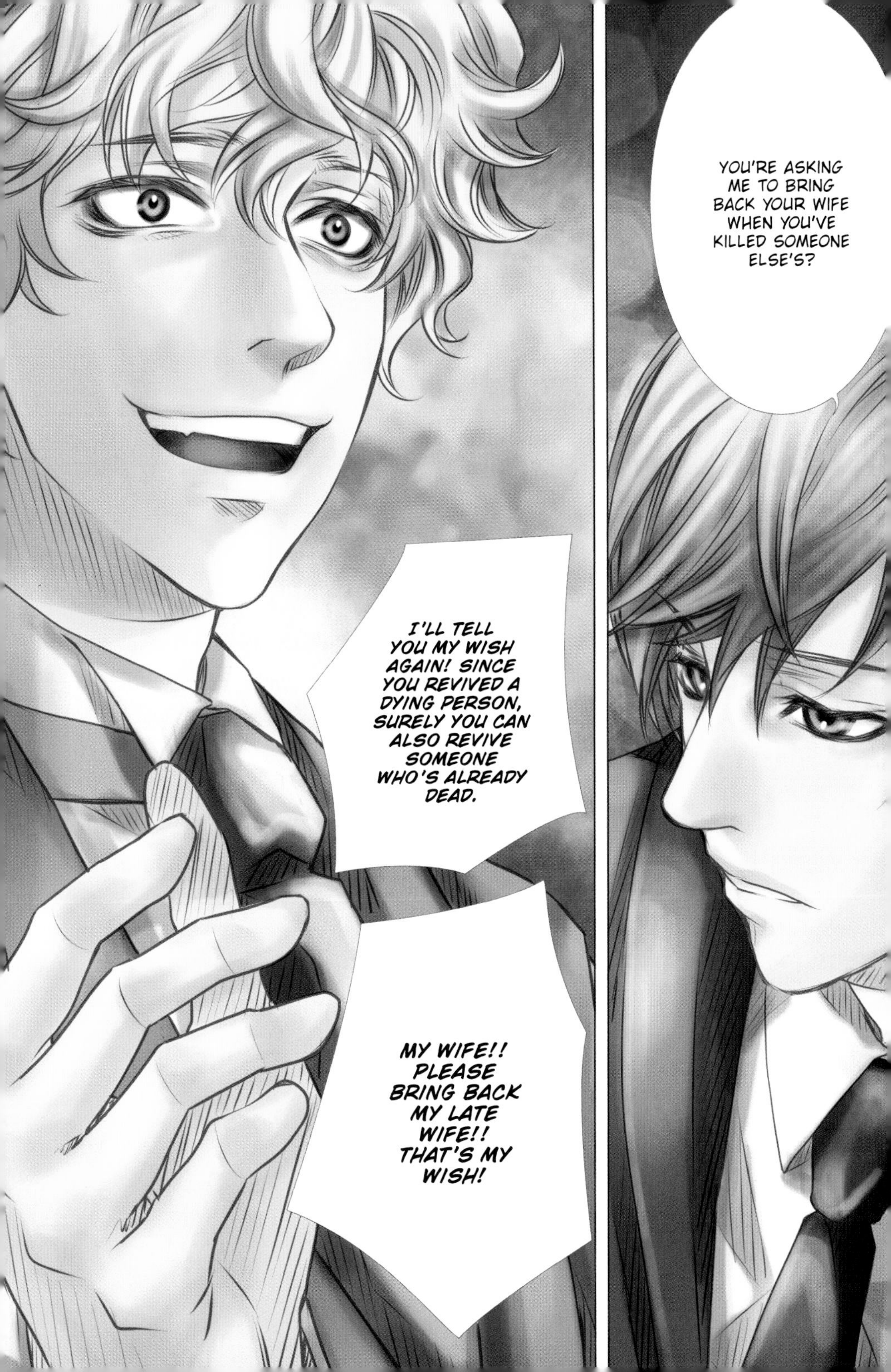
I'LL TELL YOU MY WISH AGAIN! SINCE YOU REVIVED A DYING PERSON, SURELY YOU CAN ALSO REVIVE SOMEONE WHO'S ALREADY DEAD.
MY WIFE!! PLEASE BRING BACK MY LATE WIFE!! THAT'S MY WISH!
YOU'RE ASKING ME TO BRING BACK YOUR WIFE WHEN YOU'VE KILLED SOMEONE ELSE'S?

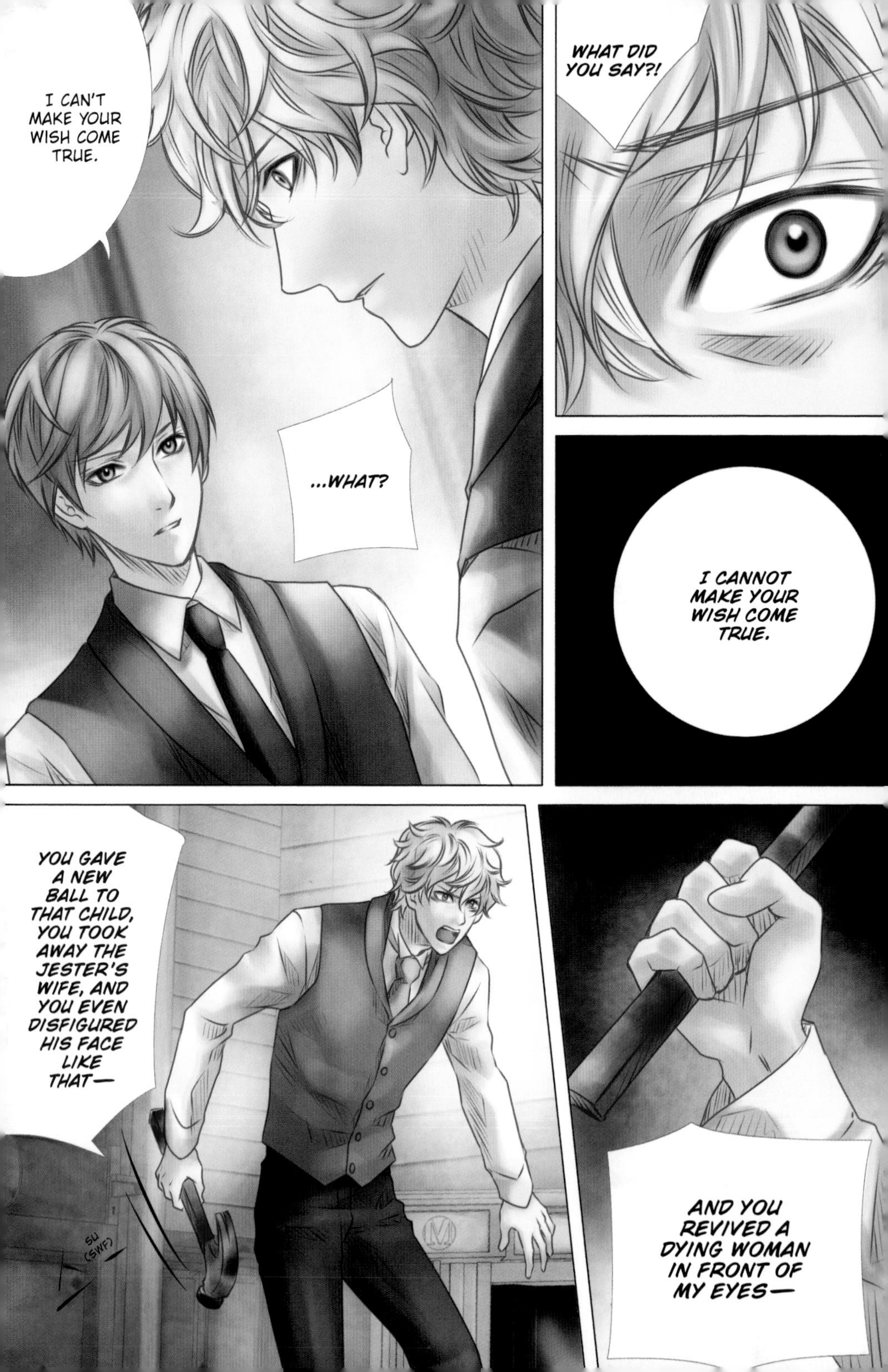
I CAN'T MAKE YOUR WISH COME TRUE.
...WHAT?
WHAT DID YOU SAY?!
I CANNOT MAKE YOUR WISH COME TRUE.
YOU GAVE A NEW BALL TO THAT CHILD, YOU TOOK AWAY THE JESTER'S WIFE, AND YOU EVEN DISFIGURED HIS FACE LIKE THAT—
SU (SWF)
AND YOU REVIVED A DYING WOMAN IN FRONT OF MY EYES—

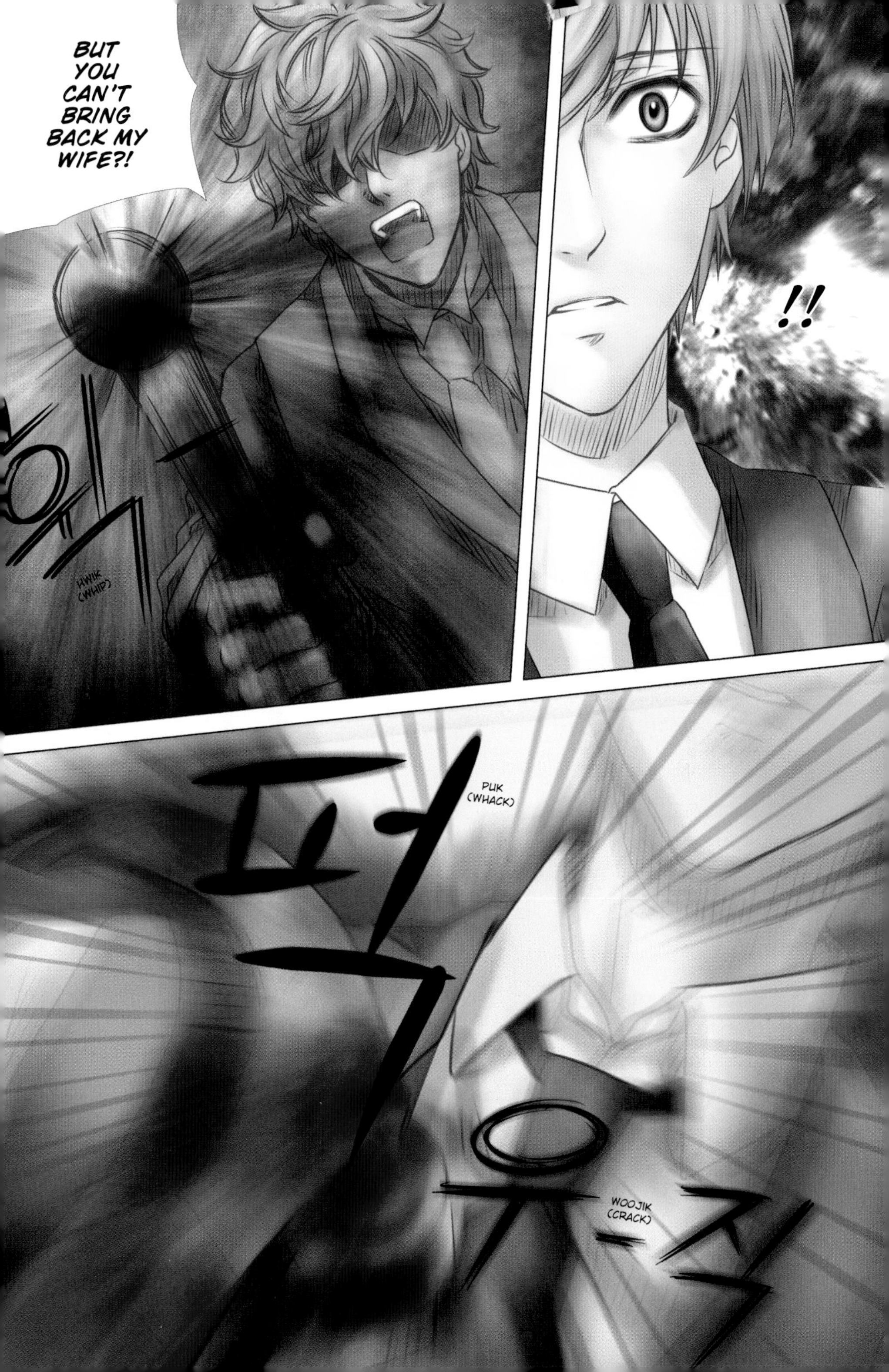

BUT YOU CAN'T BRING BACK MY WIFE?!
HWIK (WHIP)
!!
PUK (WHACK)
WOOJIK (CRACK)

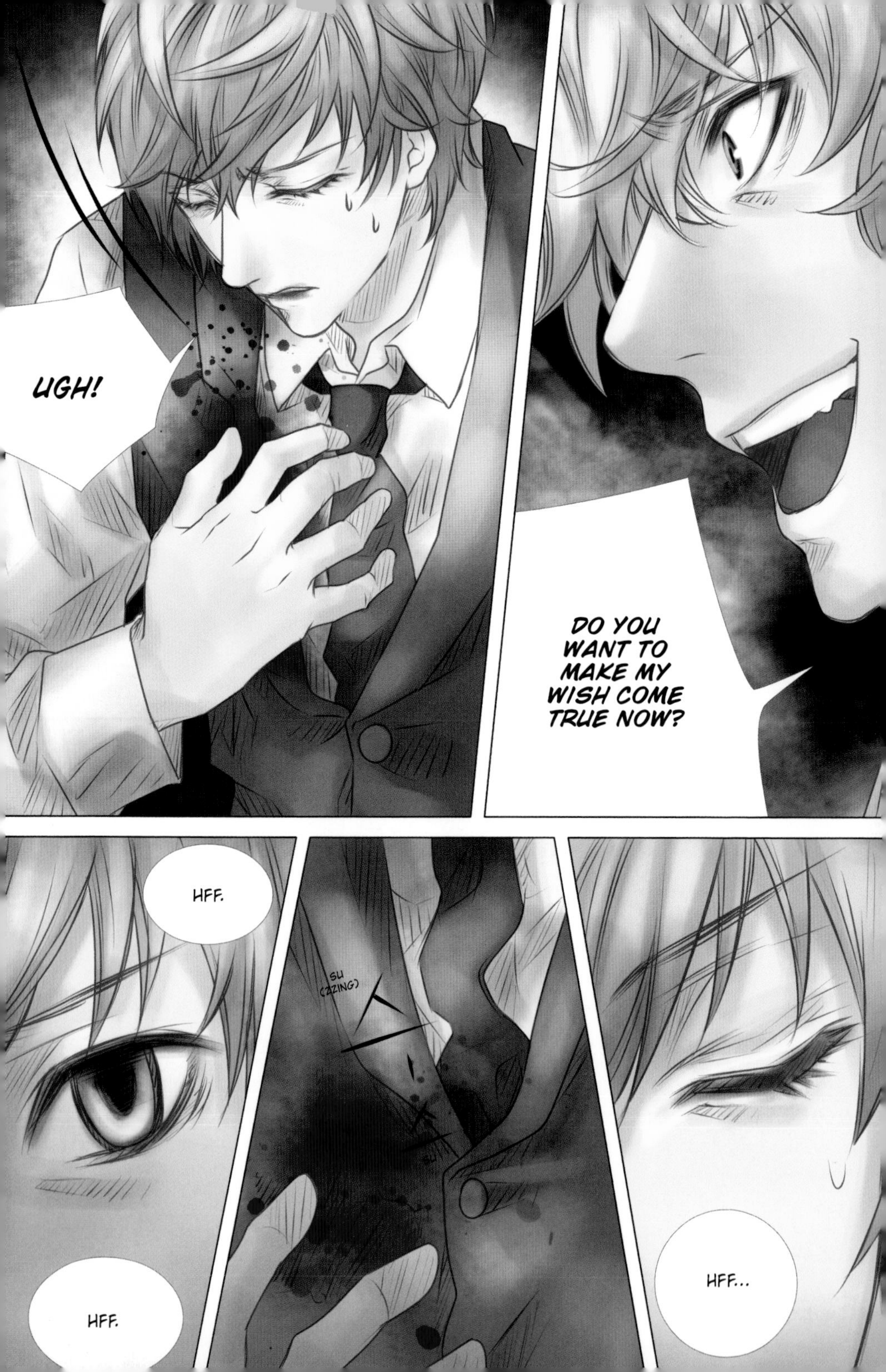
DO YOU WANT TO MAKE MY WISH COME TRUE NOW?
UGH!
HFF...
SU (ZZING)
HFF.
HFF.

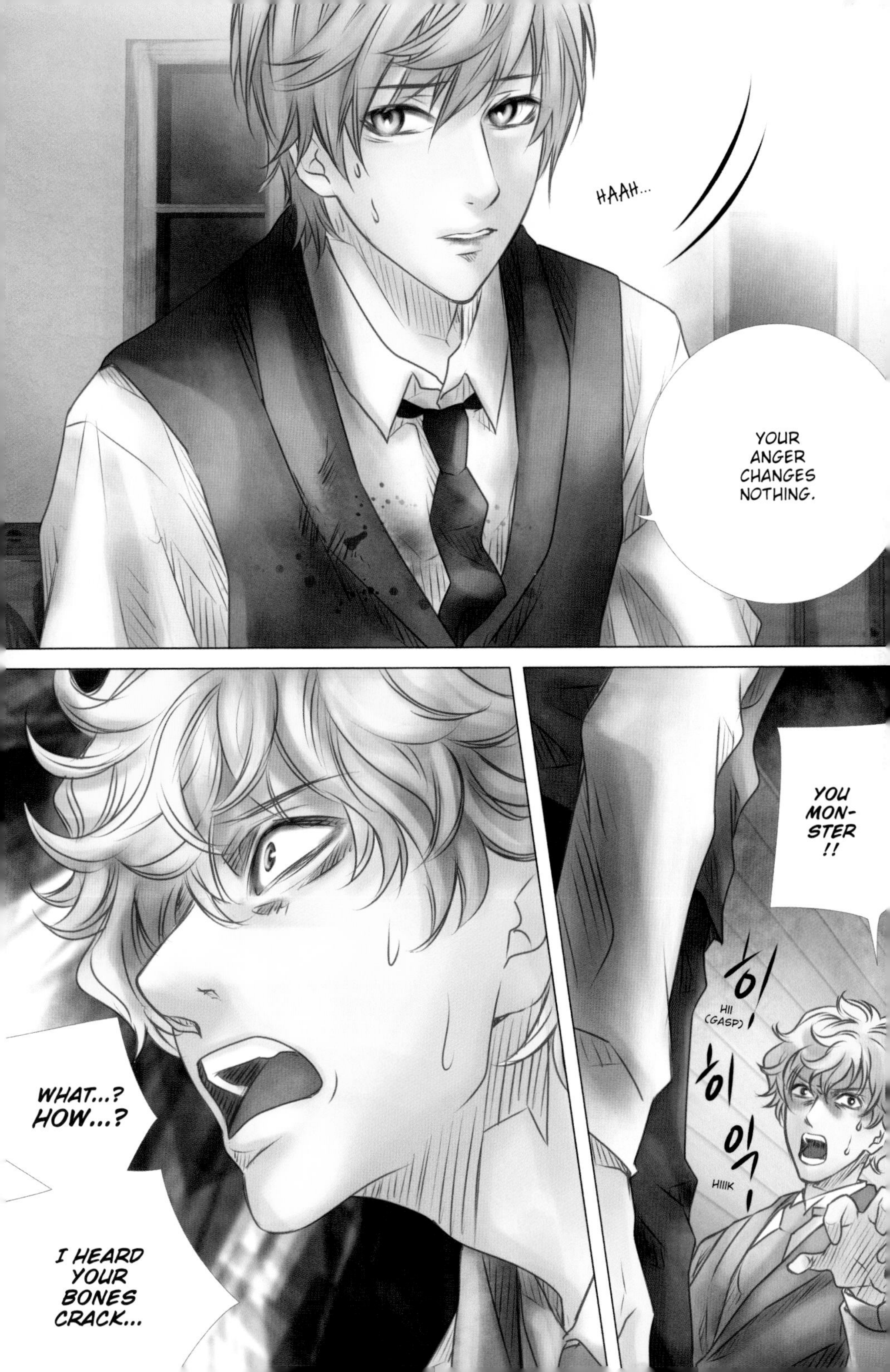
HAAH...
YOUR ANGER CHANGES NOTHING.
YOU MON-STER !!
히
HII (GASP)
히익
HIIIK
WHAT...? HOW...?
I HEARD YOUR BONES CRACK...

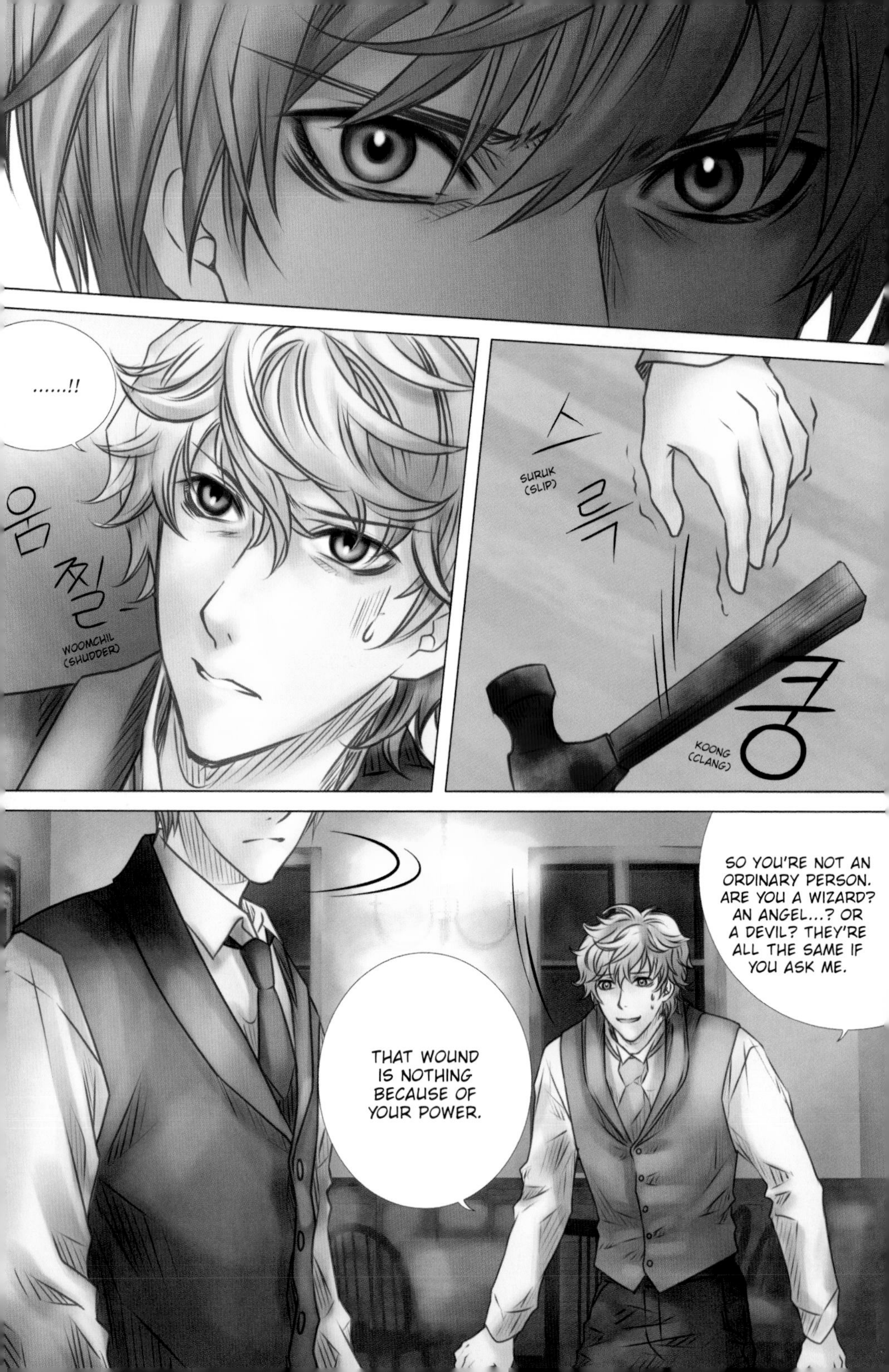
......!!
움찔
WOOMCHIL (SHUDDER)
스륵
SURUK (SLIP)
쿵
KOONG (CLANG)
SO YOU'RE NOT AN ORDINARY PERSON. ARE YOU A WIZARD? AN ANGEL...? OR A DEVIL? THEY'RE ALL THE SAME IF YOU ASK ME.
THAT WOUND IS NOTHING BECAUSE OF YOUR POWER.

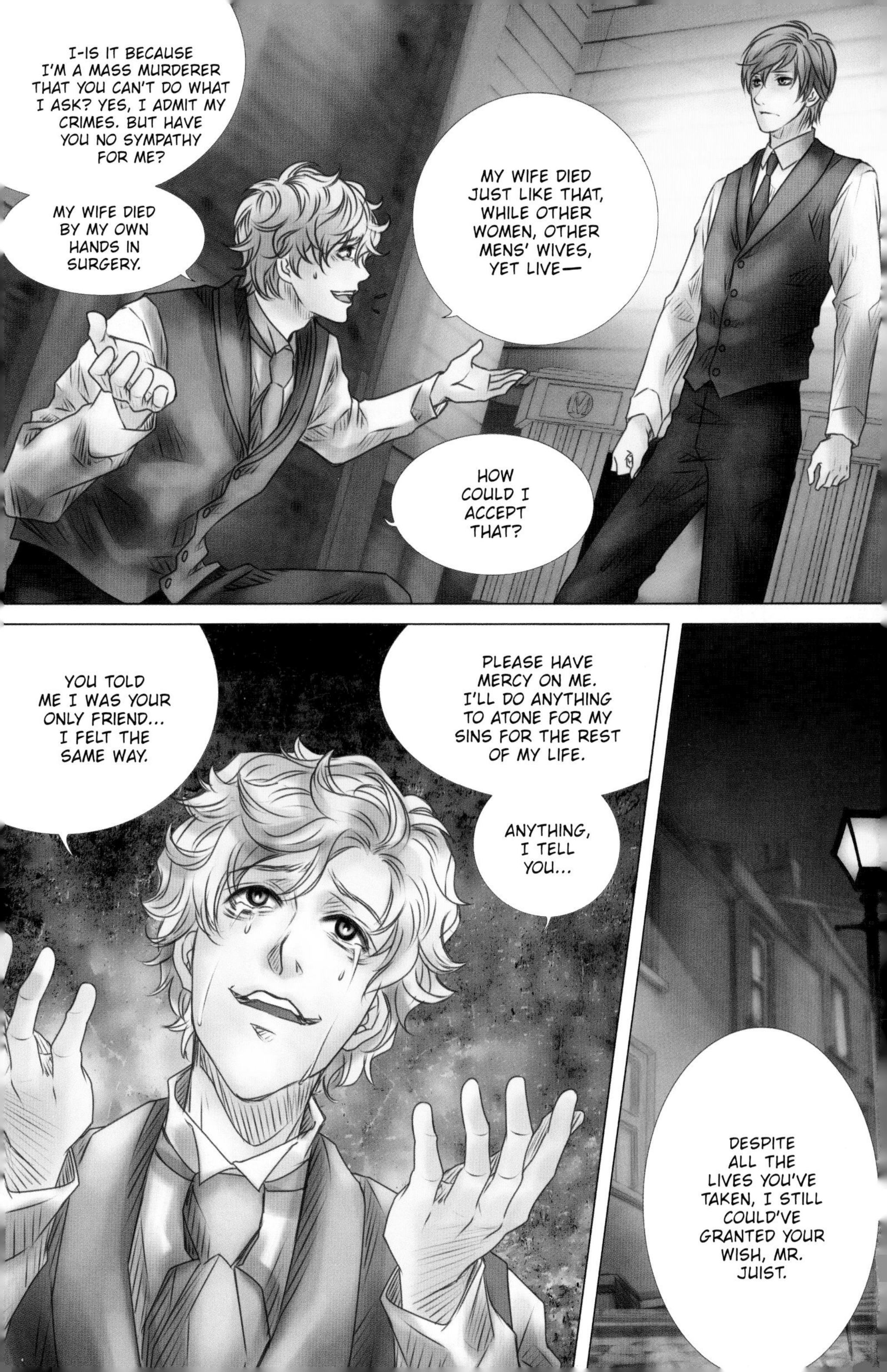
I-IS IT BECAUSE I'M A MASS MURDERER THAT YOU CAN'T DO WHAT I ASK? YES, I ADMIT MY CRIMES. BUT HAVE YOU NO SYMPATHY FOR ME?
MY WIFE DIED BY MY OWN HANDS IN SURGERY.
MY WIFE DIED JUST LIKE THAT, WHILE OTHER WOMEN, OTHER MENS' WIVES, YET LIVE—
HOW COULD I ACCEPT THAT?
YOU TOLD ME I WAS YOUR ONLY FRIEND... I FELT THE SAME WAY.
PLEASE HAVE MERCY ON ME. I'LL DO ANYTHING TO ATONE FOR MY SINS FOR THE REST OF MY LIFE.
ANYTHING, I TELL YOU...
DESPITE ALL THE LIVES YOU'VE TAKEN, I STILL COULD'VE GRANTED YOUR WISH, MR. JUIST.

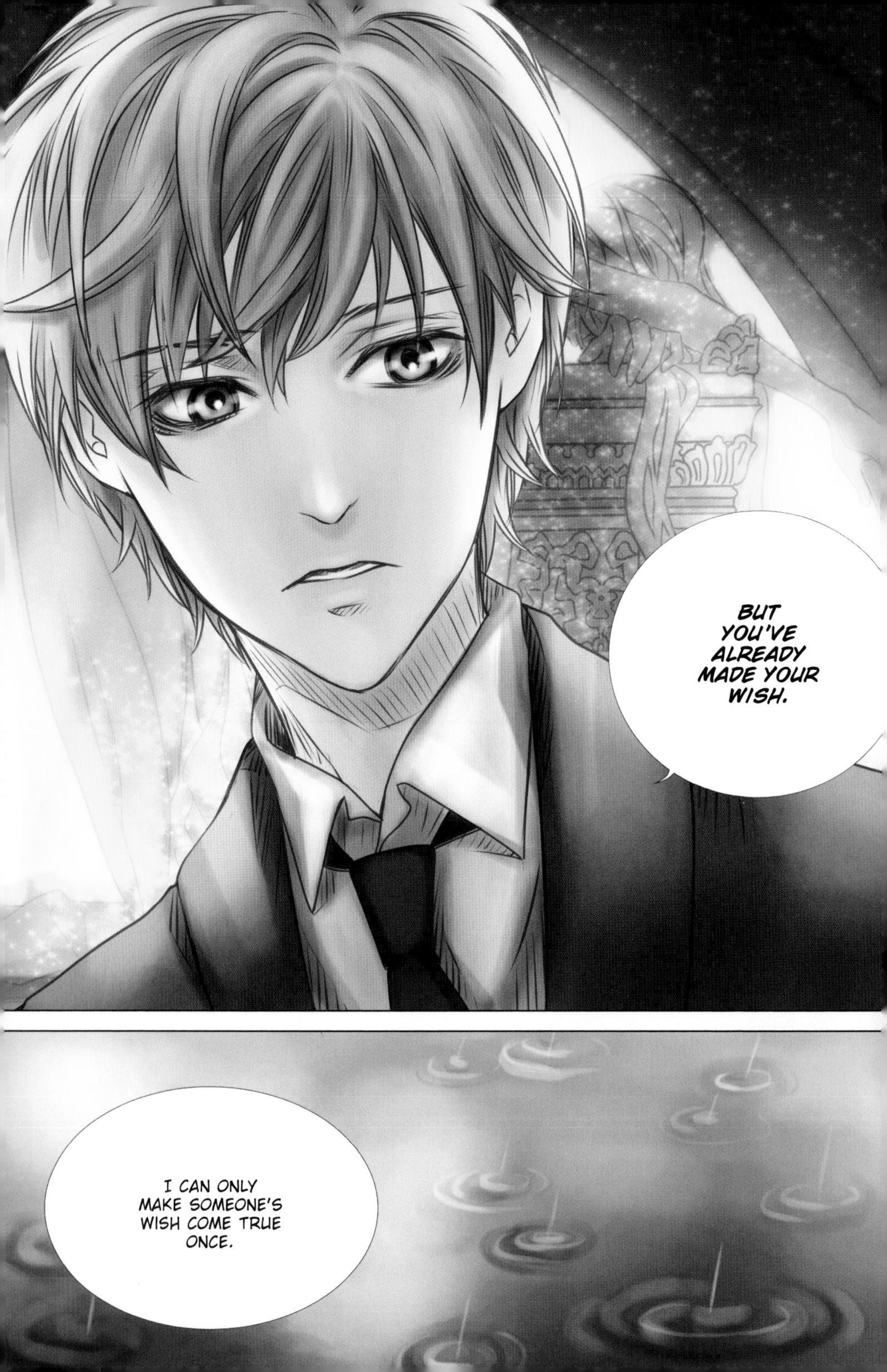
BUT YOU'VE ALREADY MADE YOUR WISH.
I CAN ONLY MAKE SOMEONE'S WISH COME TRUE ONCE.

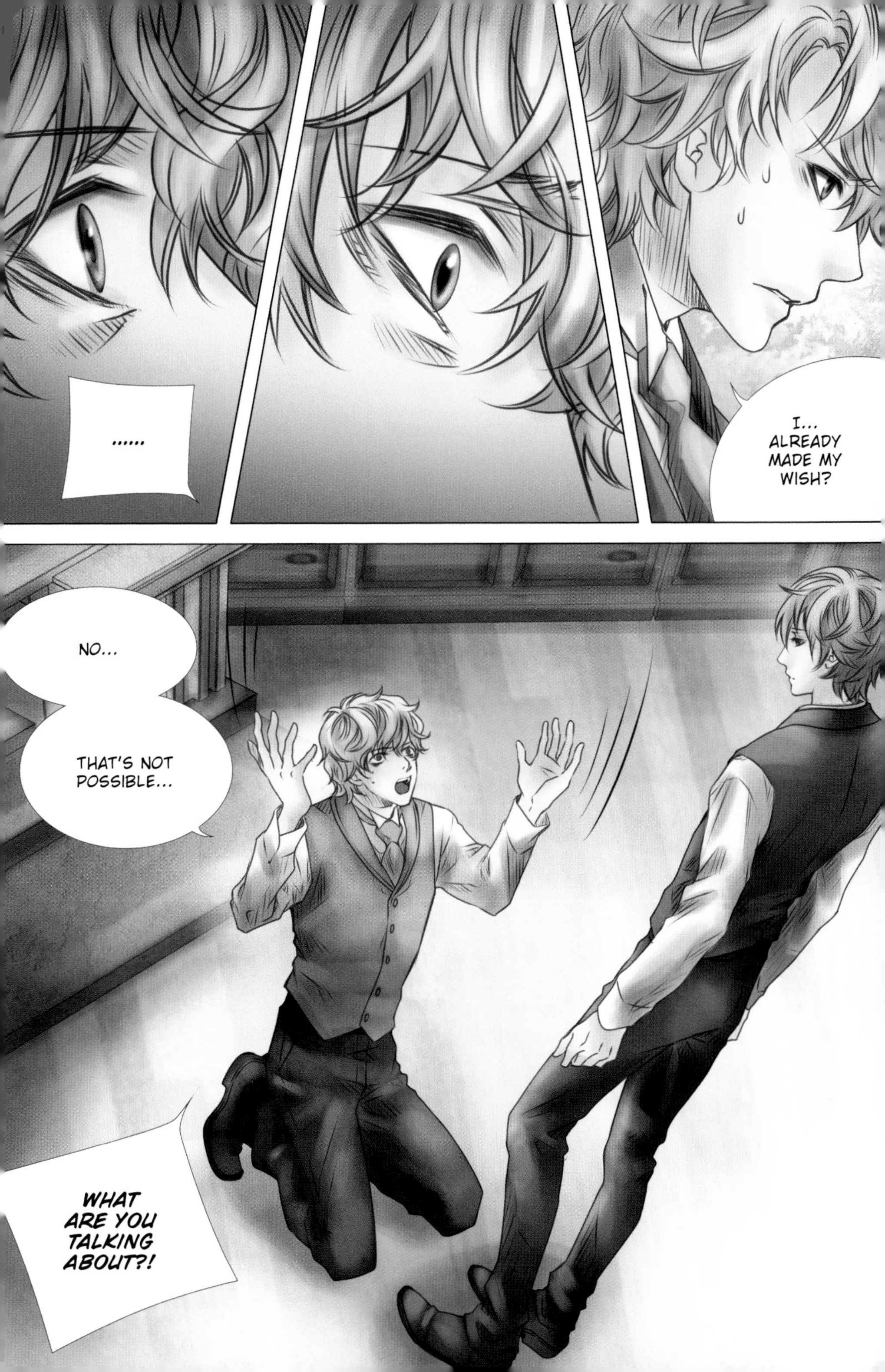
......
I... ALREADY MADE MY WISH?
NO...
THAT'S NOT POSSIBLE...
WHAT ARE YOU TALKING ABOUT?!

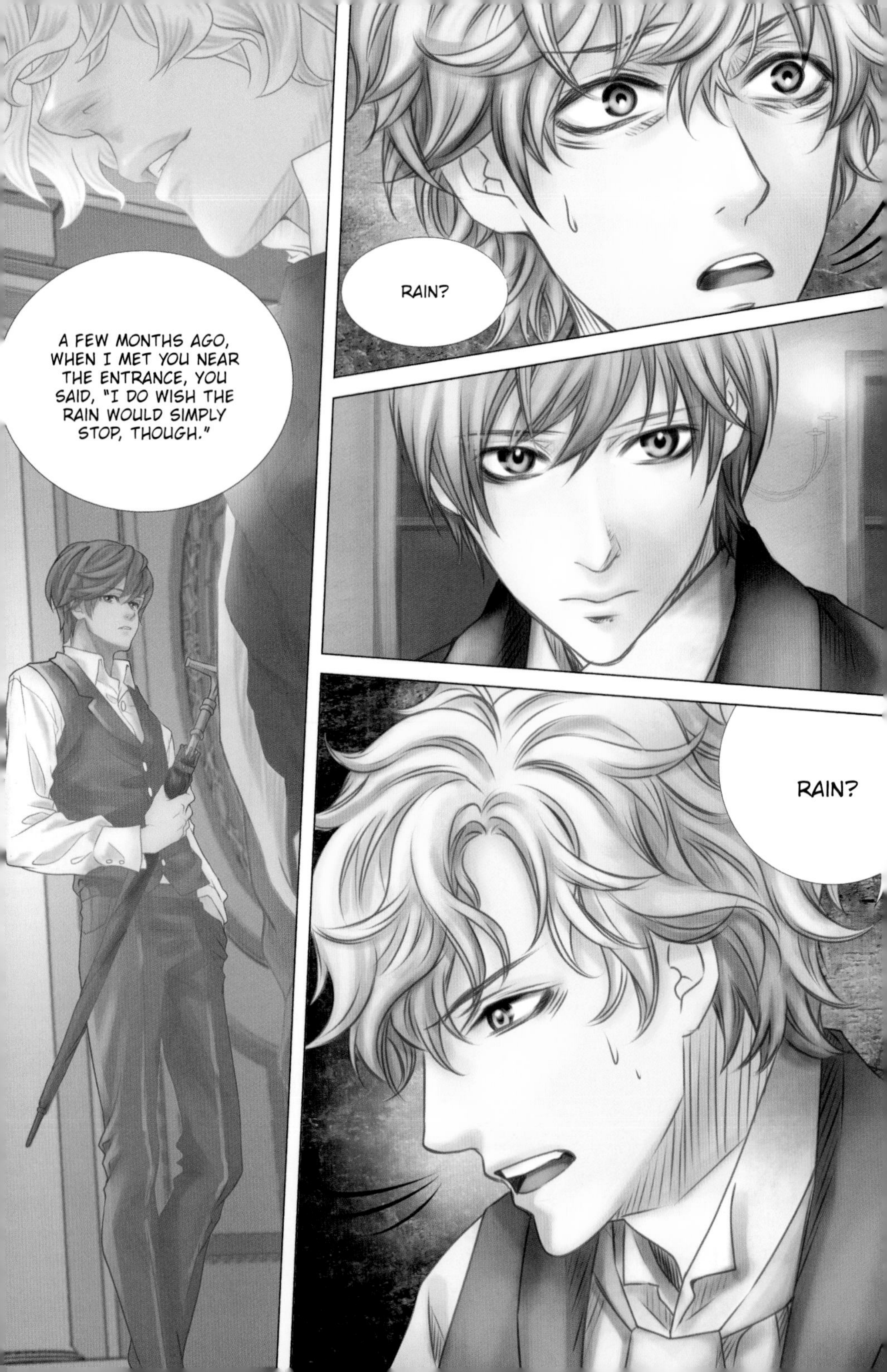
A FEW MONTHS AGO, WHEN I MET YOU NEAR THE ENTRANCE, YOU SAID, "I DO WISH THE RAIN WOULD SIMPLY STOP, THOUGH."
RAIN?
RAIN?

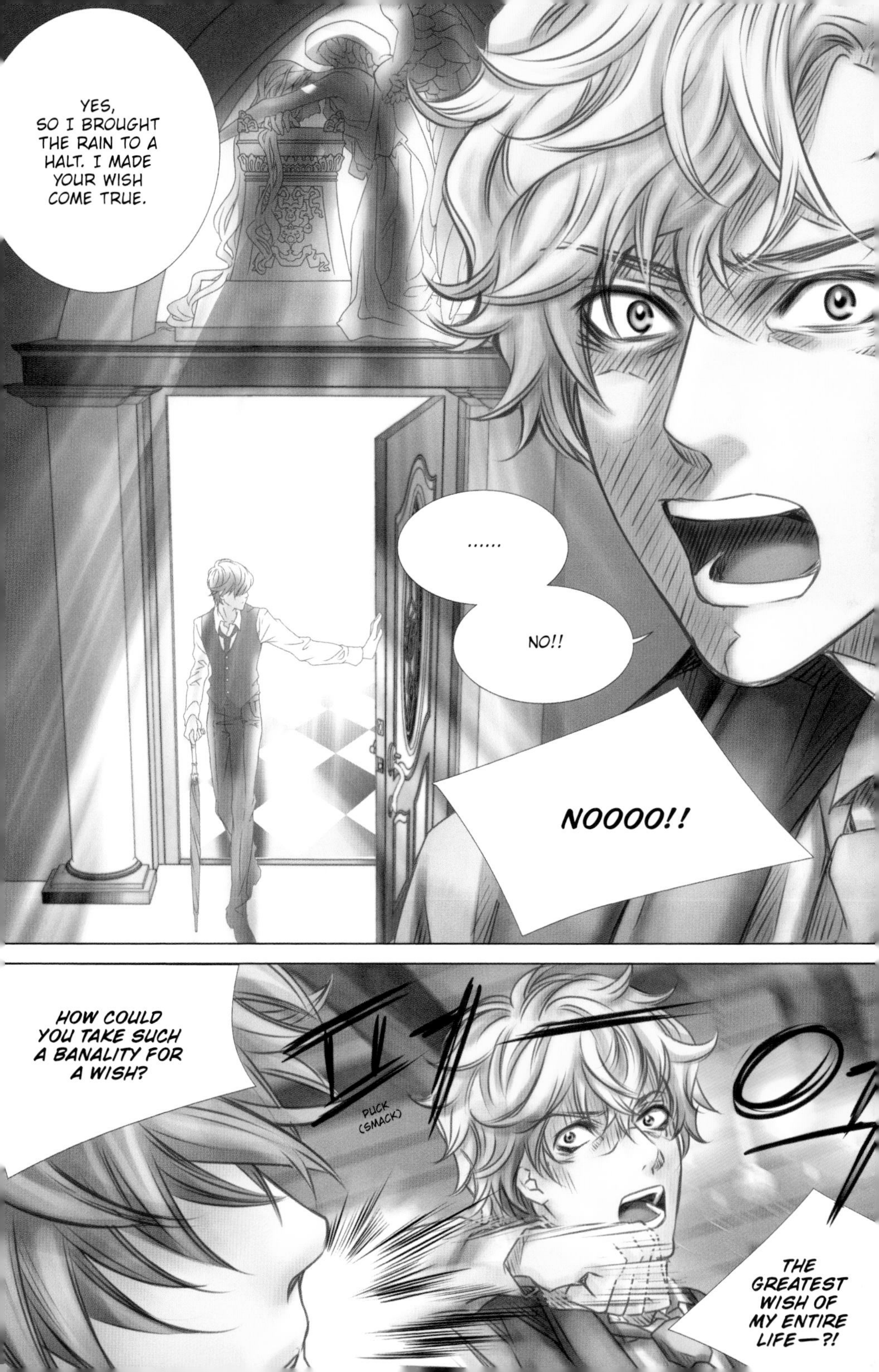
YES, SO I BROUGHT THE RAIN TO A HALT. I MADE YOUR WISH COME TRUE.
......
NO!!
NOOOO!!
HOW COULD YOU TAKE SUCH A BANALITY FOR A WISH?
PUCK (SMACK)
THE GREATEST WISH OF MY ENTIRE LIFE—?!

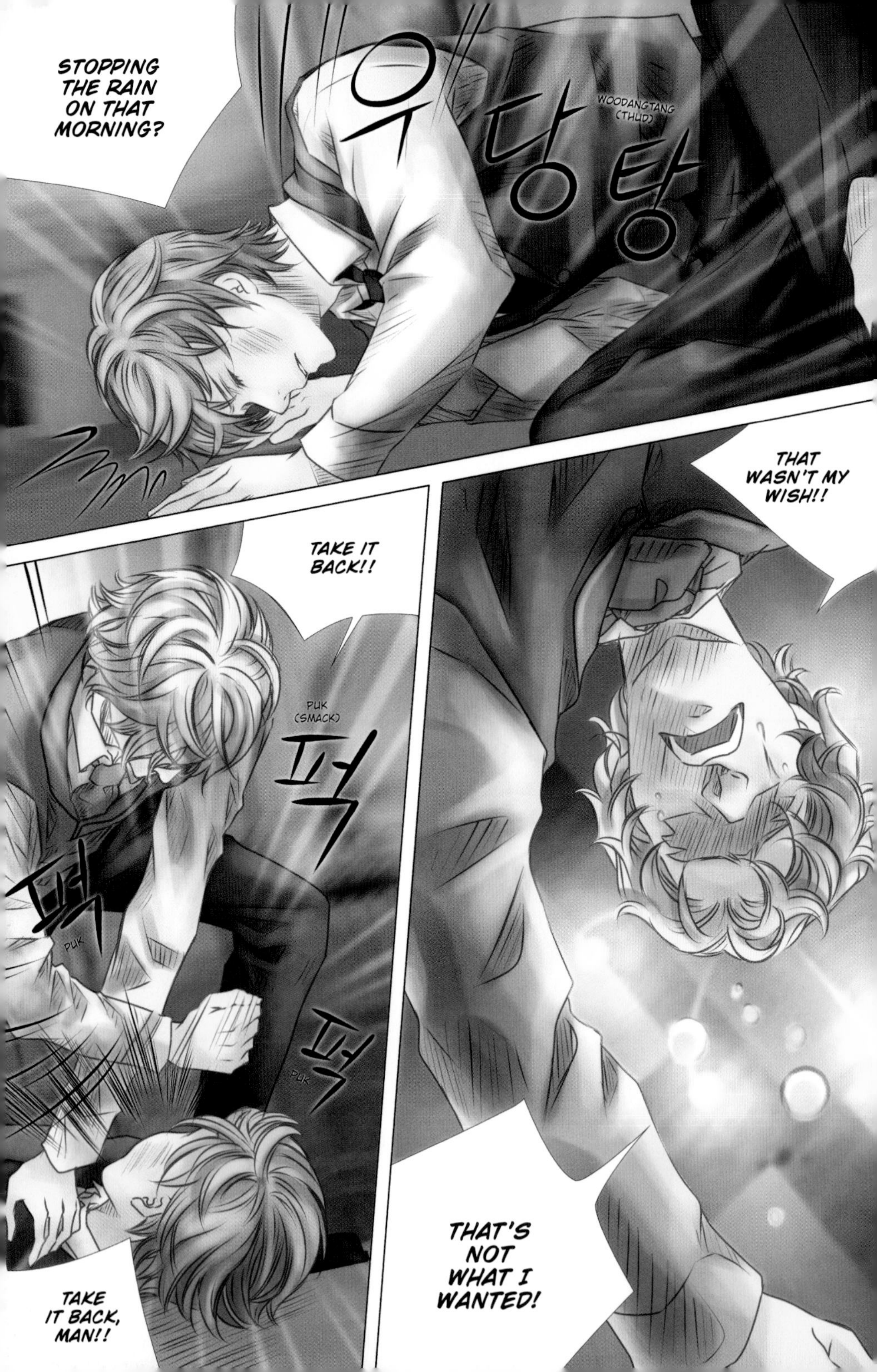
STOPPING THE RAIN ON THAT MORNING?
우당탕
WOODANGTANG (THUD)
THAT WASN'T MY WISH!!
TAKE IT BACK!!
퍽
PUK (SMACK)
퍽
PUK
퍽
PUK
THAT'S NOT WHAT I WANTED!
TAKE IT BACK, MAN!!

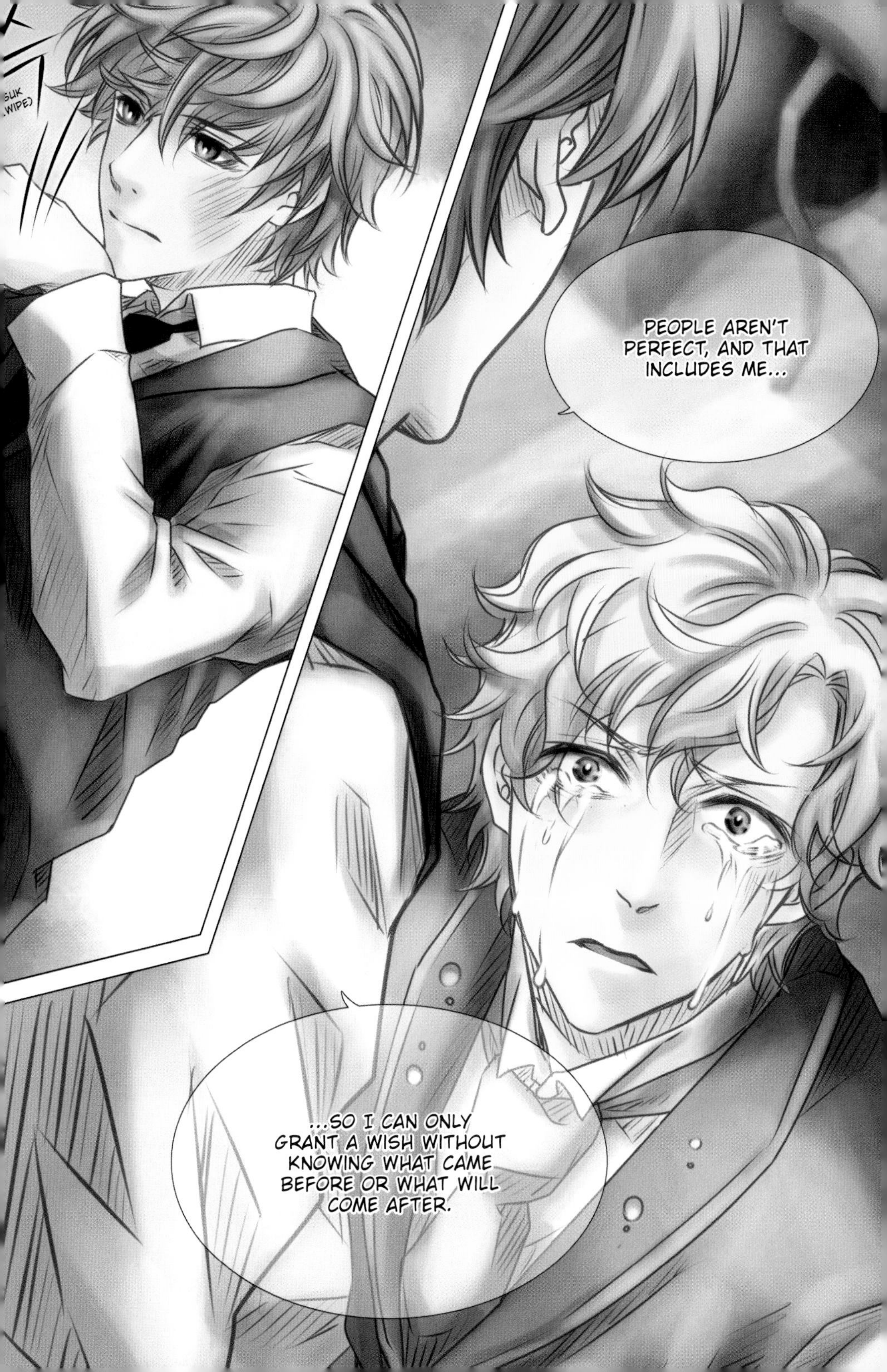
SUK
WIPE)
PEOPLE AREN'T PERFECT, AND THAT INCLUDES ME...
...SO I CAN ONLY GRANT A WISH WITHOUT KNOWING WHAT CAME BEFORE OR WHAT WILL COME AFTER.

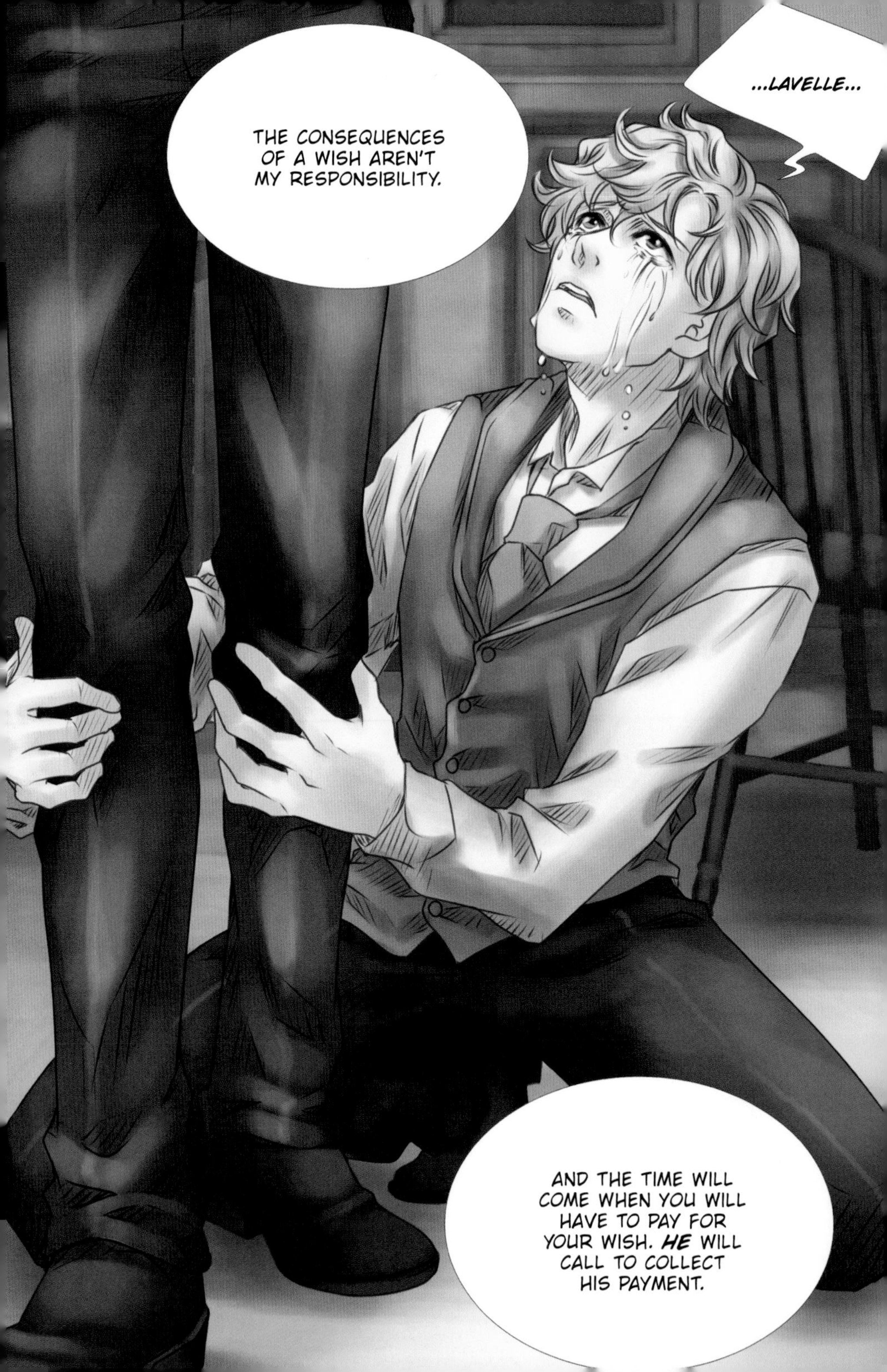
THE CONSEQUENCES OF A WISH AREN'T MY RESPONSIBILITY.
...LAVELLE...
AND THE TIME WILL COME WHEN YOU WILL HAVE TO PAY FOR YOUR WISH. *HE* WILL CALL TO COLLECT HIS PAYMENT.

톡 투 둑
TOOK   TOO TOOK
(DRIP)

뚝벅
TUBOK
(TMP)

뚝벅
TUBOK

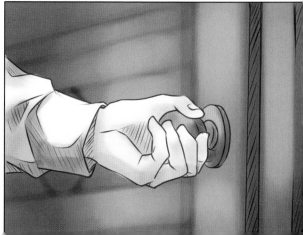

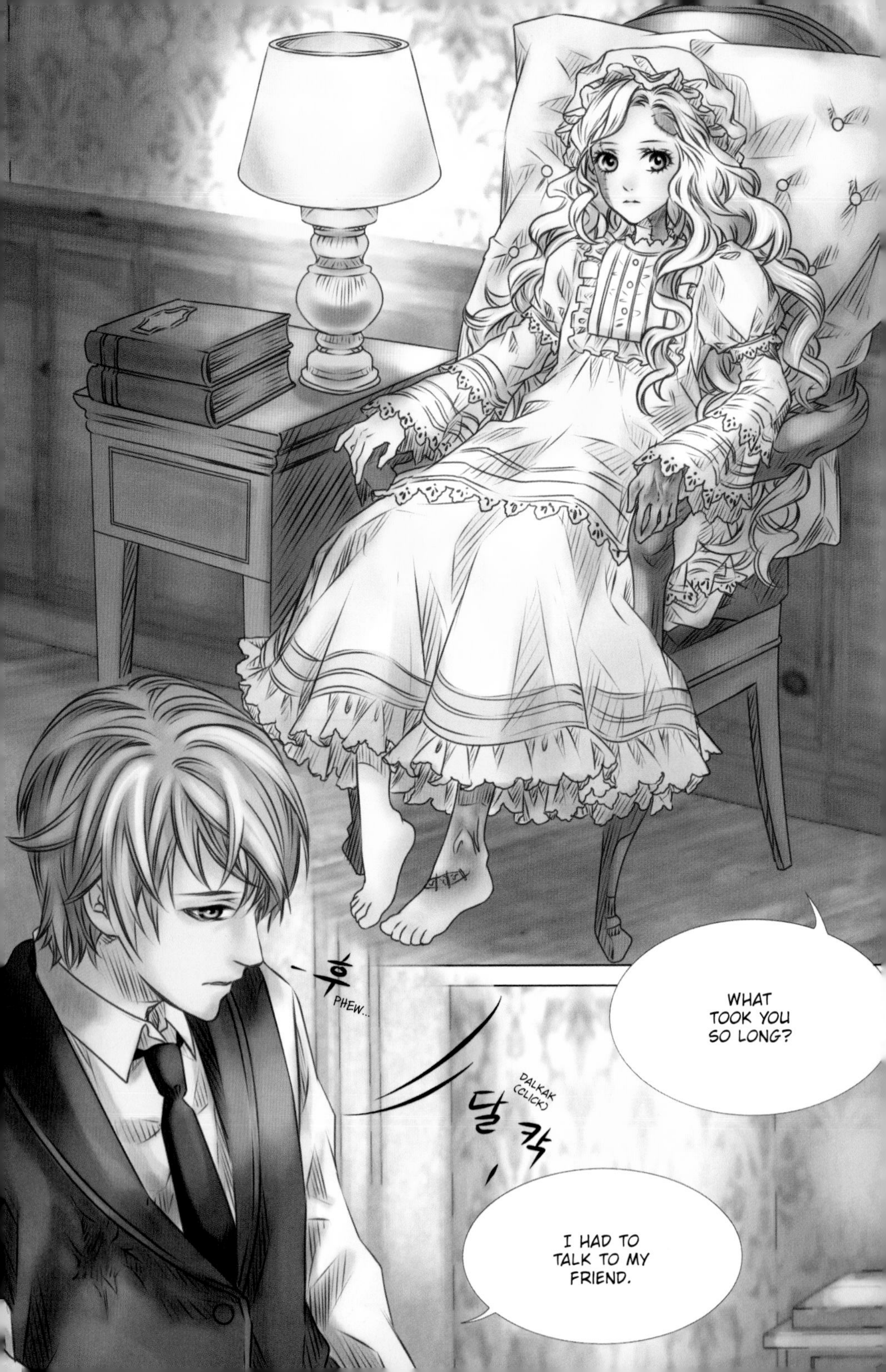

후
PHEW...
WHAT TOOK YOU SO LONG?
달칵
DALKAK (CLICK)
I HAD TO TALK TO MY FRIEND.

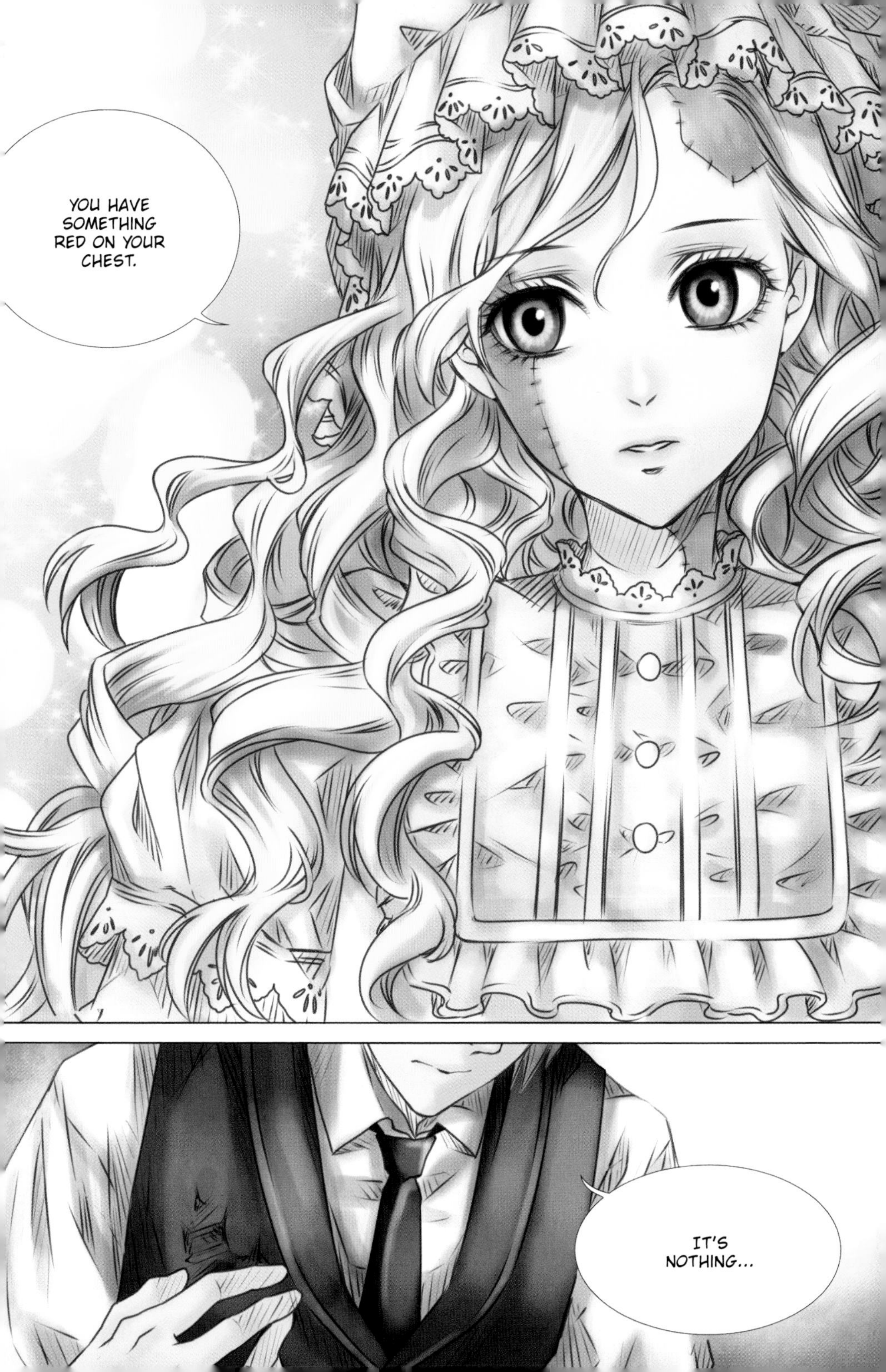
YOU HAVE SOMETHING RED ON YOUR CHEST.
IT'S NOTHING...

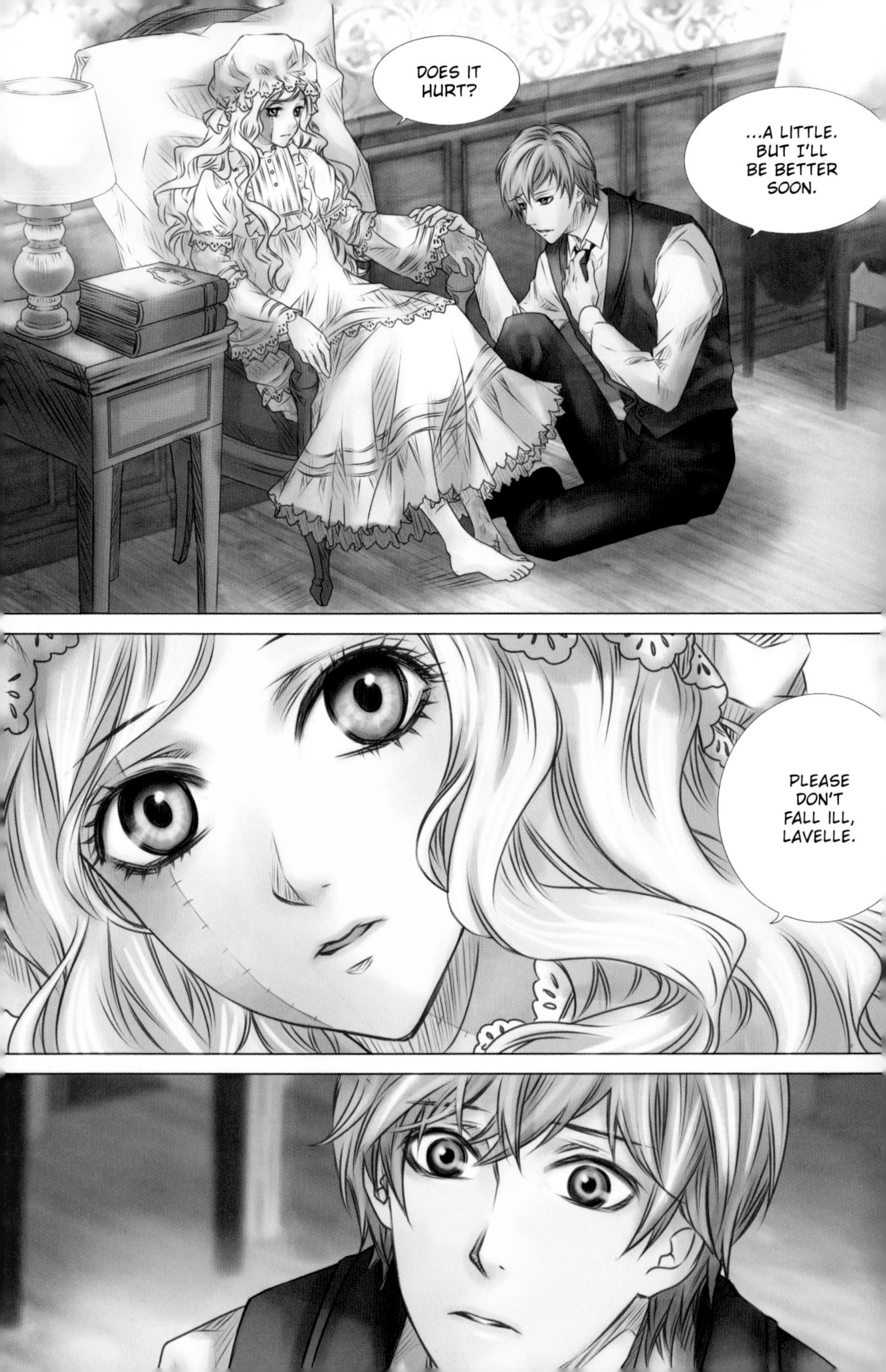
DOES IT HURT?
...A LITTLE. BUT I'LL BE BETTER SOON.
PLEASE DON'T FALL ILL, LAVELLE.

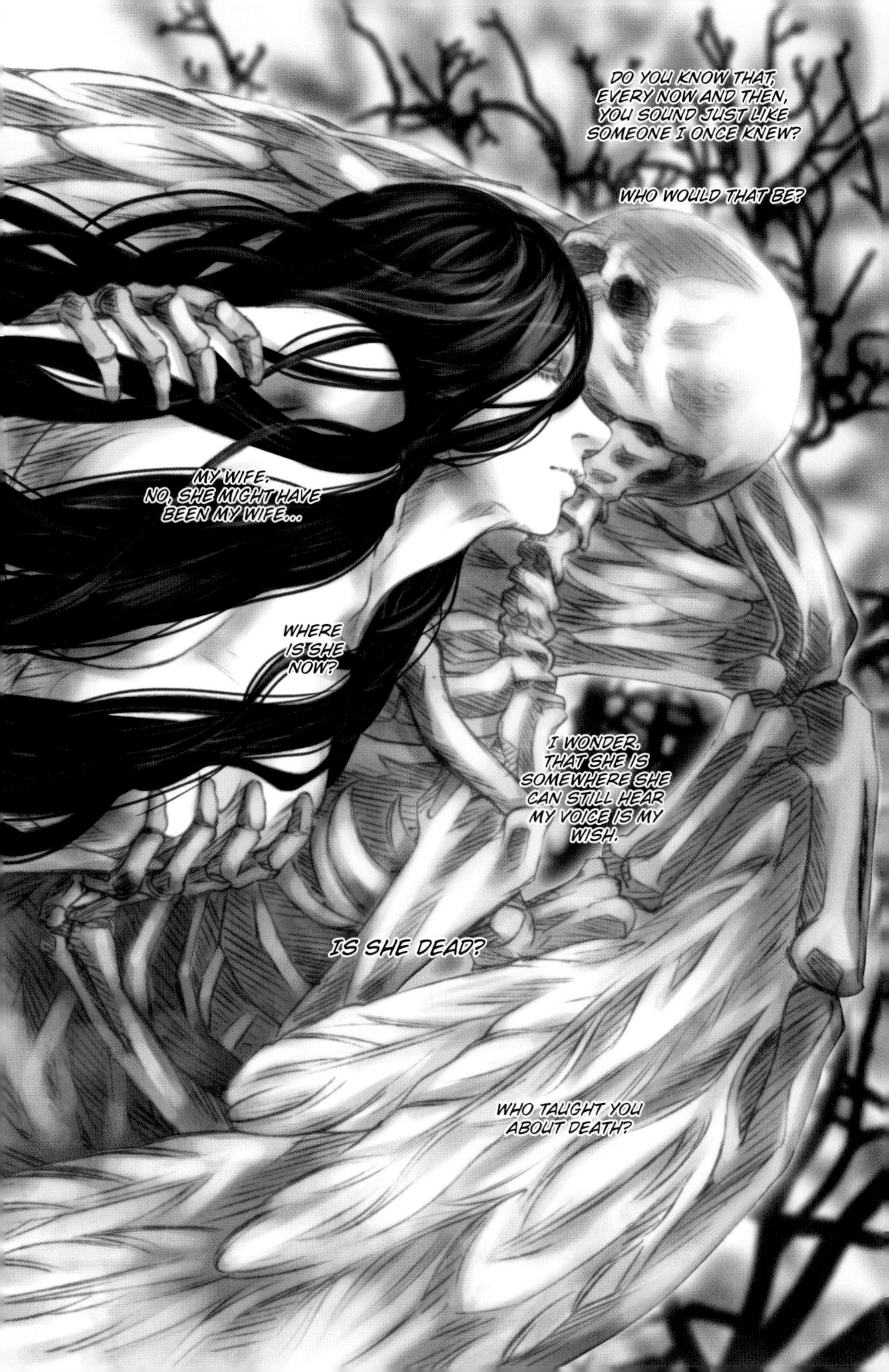
DO YOU KNOW THAT, EVERY NOW AND THEN, YOU SOUND JUST LIKE SOMEONE I ONCE KNEW?
WHO WOULD THAT BE?
MY WIFE. NO, SHE MIGHT HAVE BEEN MY WIFE...
WHERE IS SHE NOW?
I WONDER. THAT SHE IS SOMEWHERE SHE CAN STILL HEAR MY VOICE IS MY WISH.
IS SHE DEAD?
WHO TAUGHT YOU ABOUT DEATH?

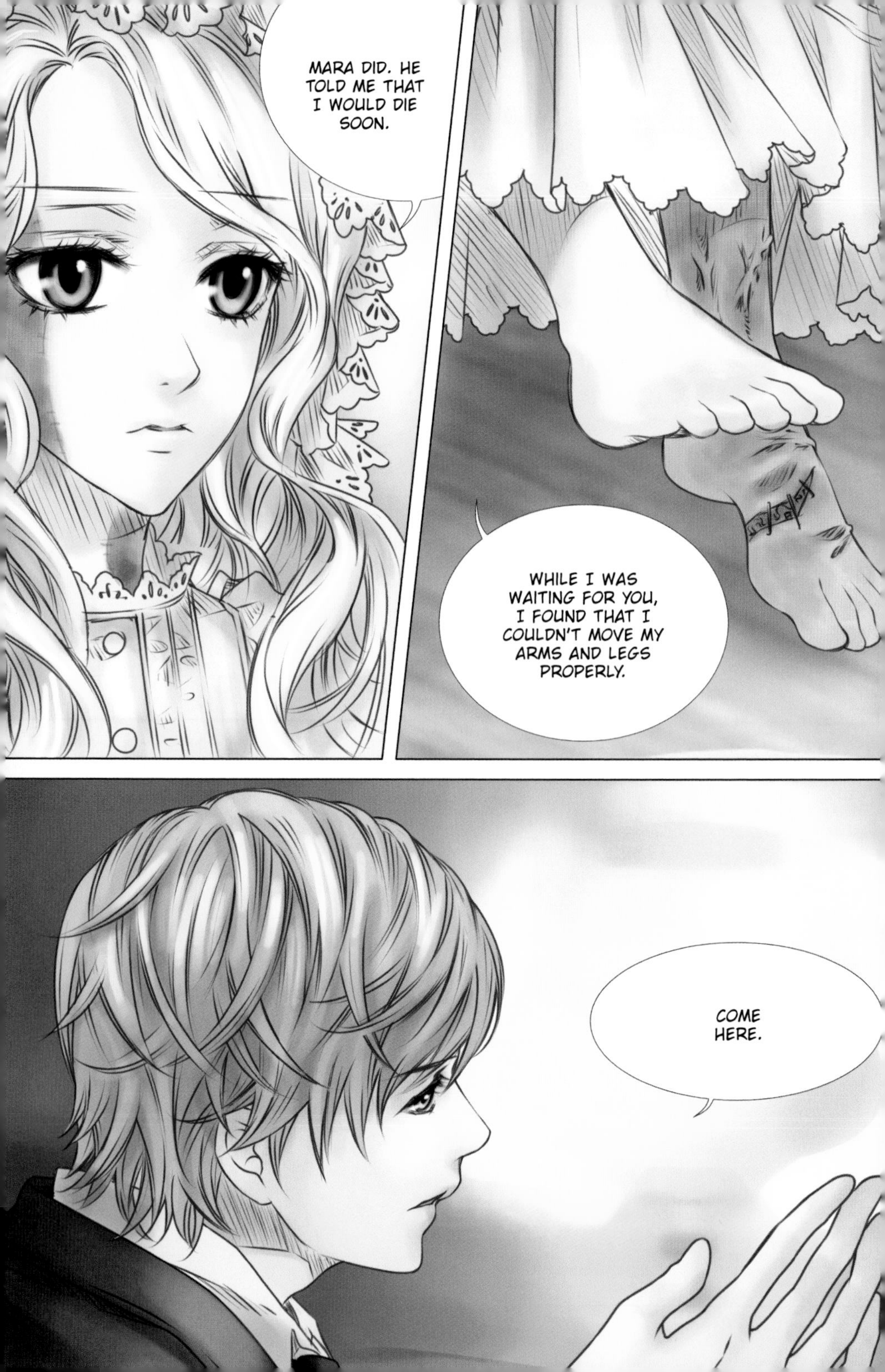
MARA DID. HE TOLD ME THAT I WOULD DIE SOON.
WHILE I WAS WAITING FOR YOU, I FOUND THAT I COULDN'T MOVE MY ARMS AND LEGS PROPERLY.
COME HERE.

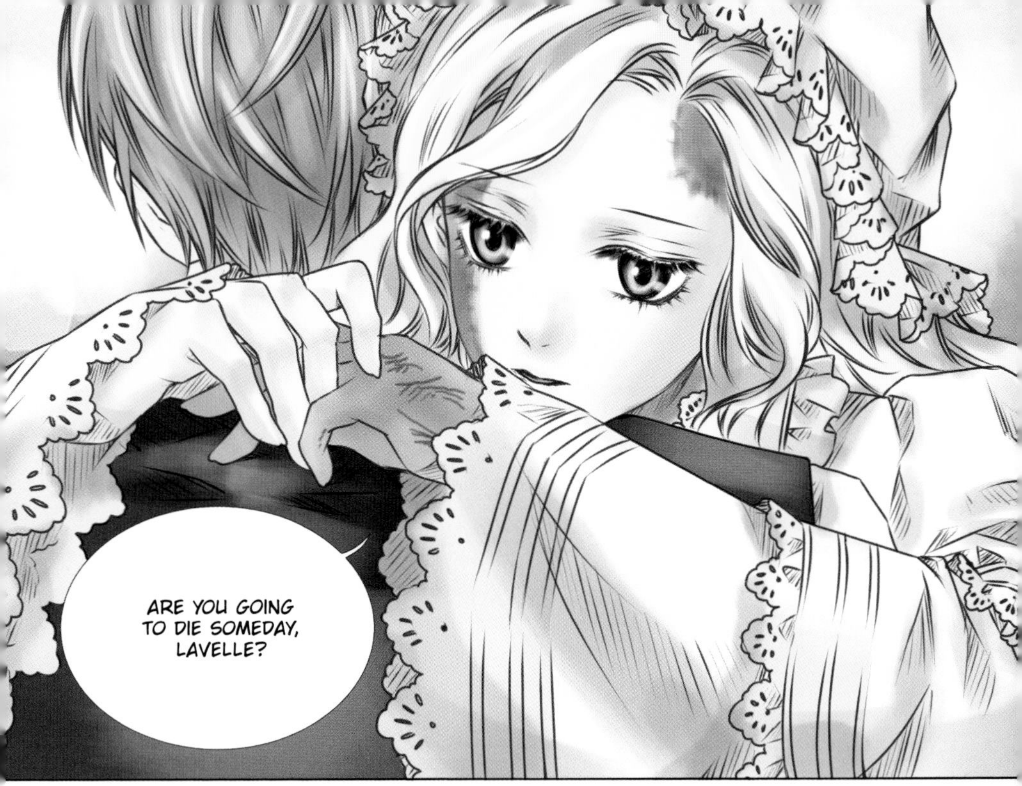
ARE YOU GOING TO DIE SOMEDAY, LAVELLE?

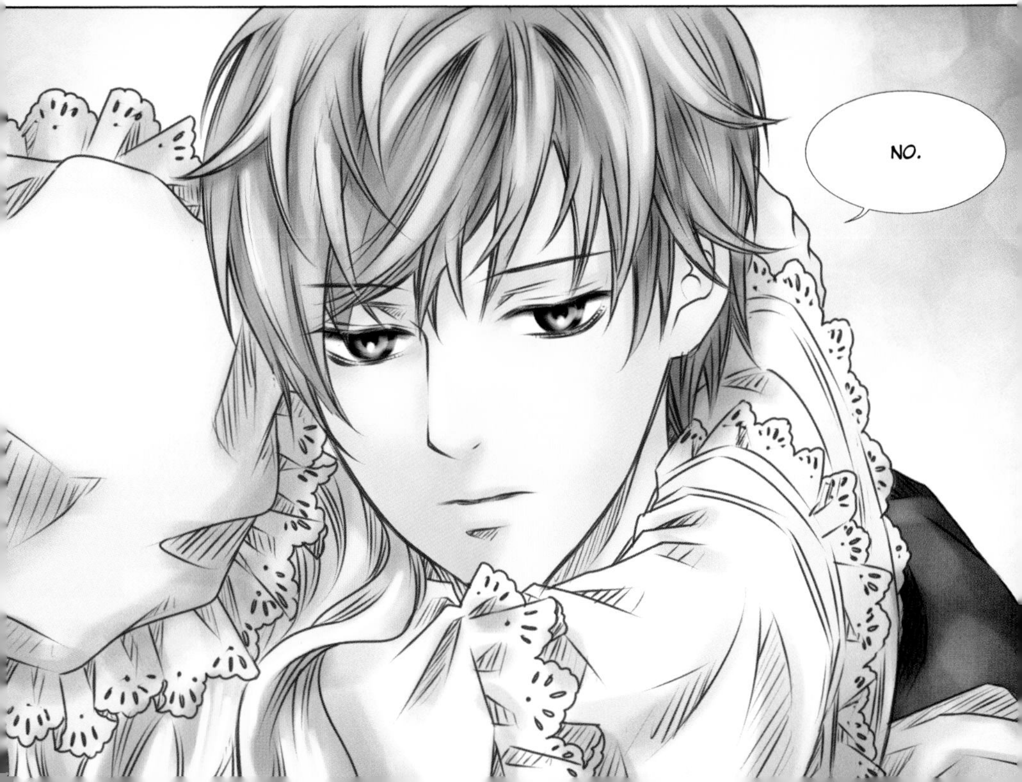
NO.

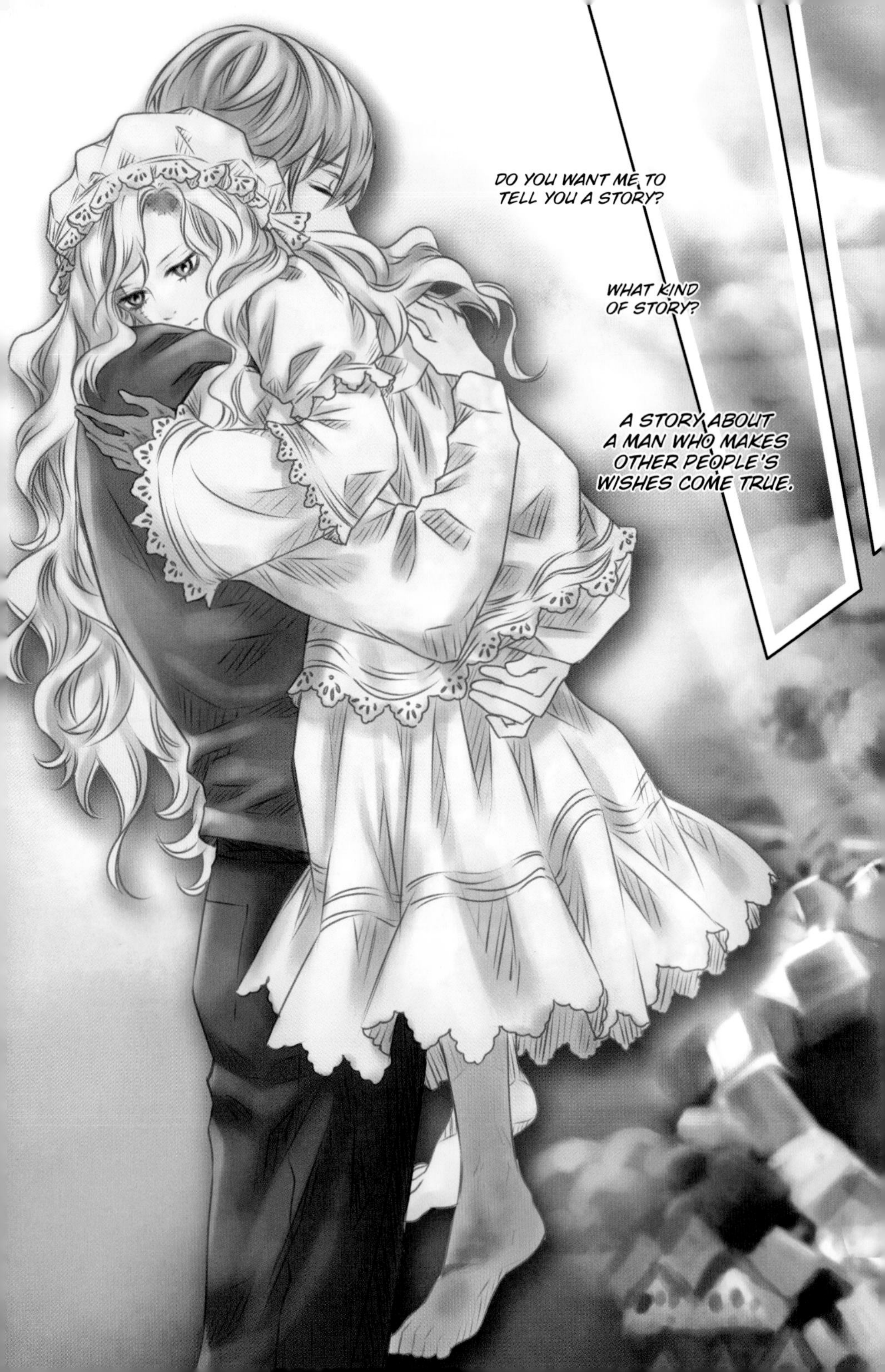
DO YOU WANT ME TO TELL YOU A STORY?
WHAT KIND OF STORY?
A STORY ABOUT A MAN WHO MAKES OTHER PEOPLE'S WISHES COME TRUE.

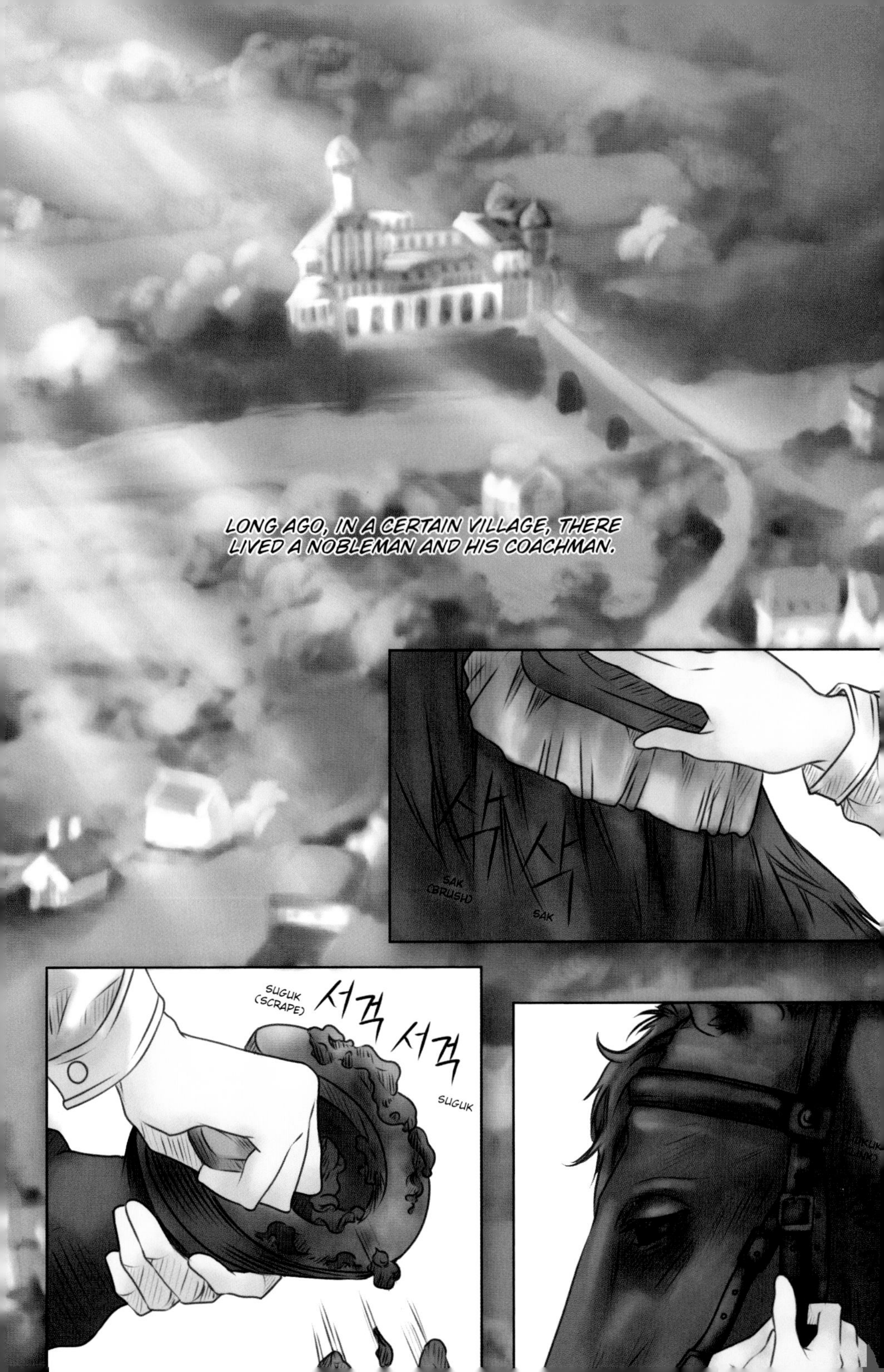
LONG AGO, IN A CERTAIN VILLAGE, THERE LIVED A NOBLEMAN AND HIS COACHMAN.
삭 삭
SAK (BRUSH)
SAK
SUGUK (SCRAPE)
서걱 서걱
SUGUK

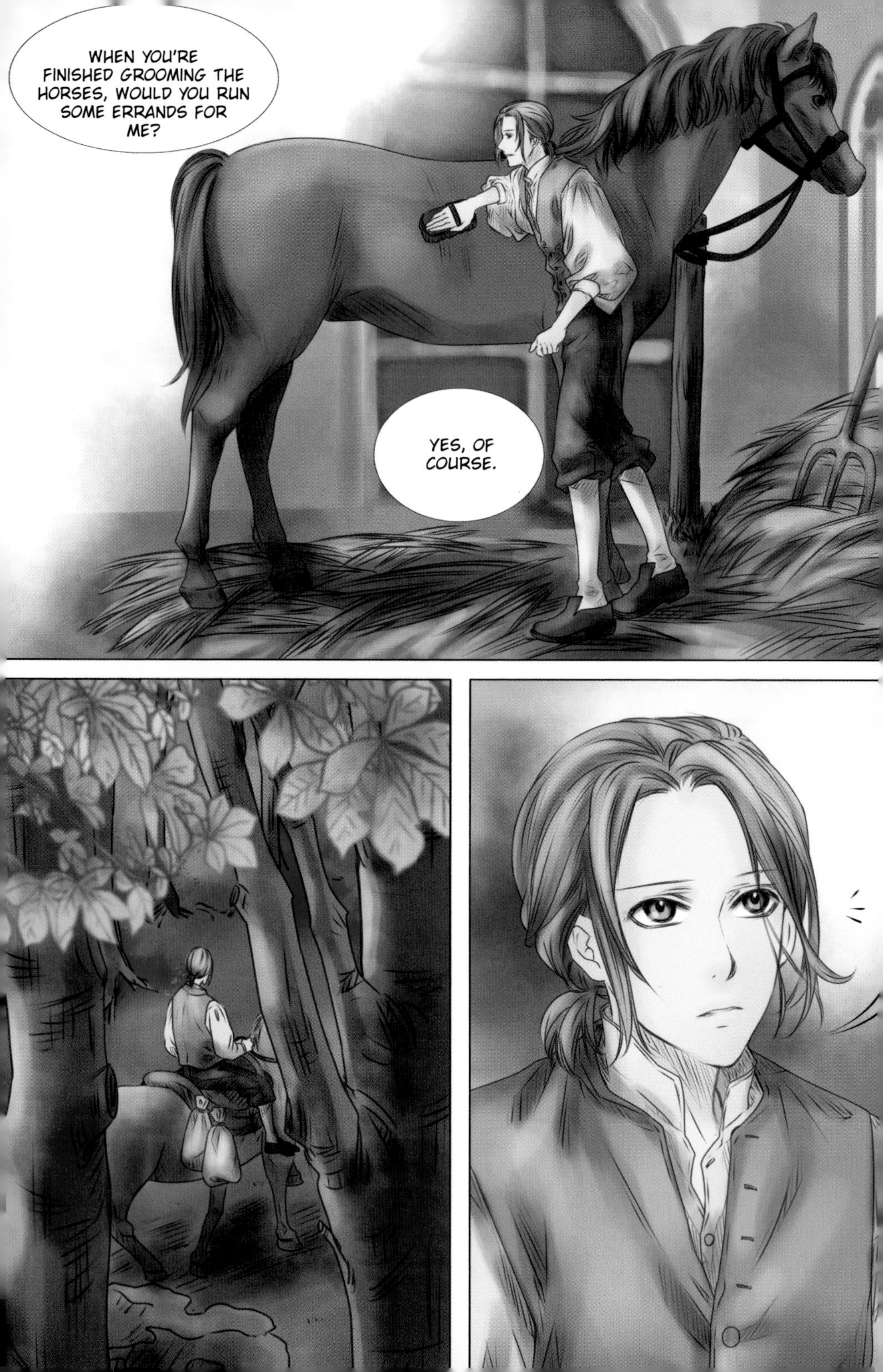
WHEN YOU'RE FINISHED GROOMING THE HORSES, WOULD YOU RUN SOME ERRANDS FOR ME?
YES, OF COURSE.

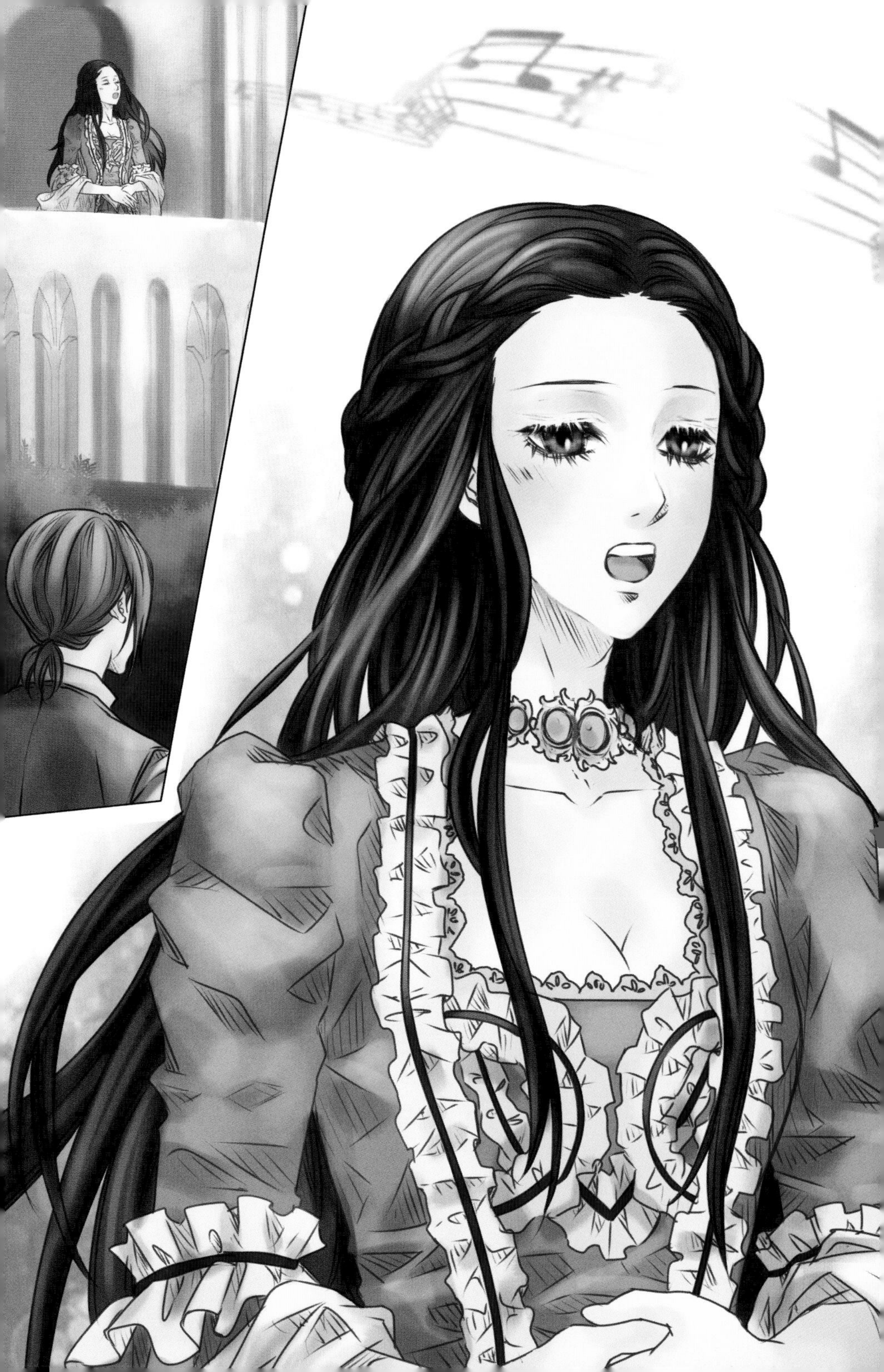

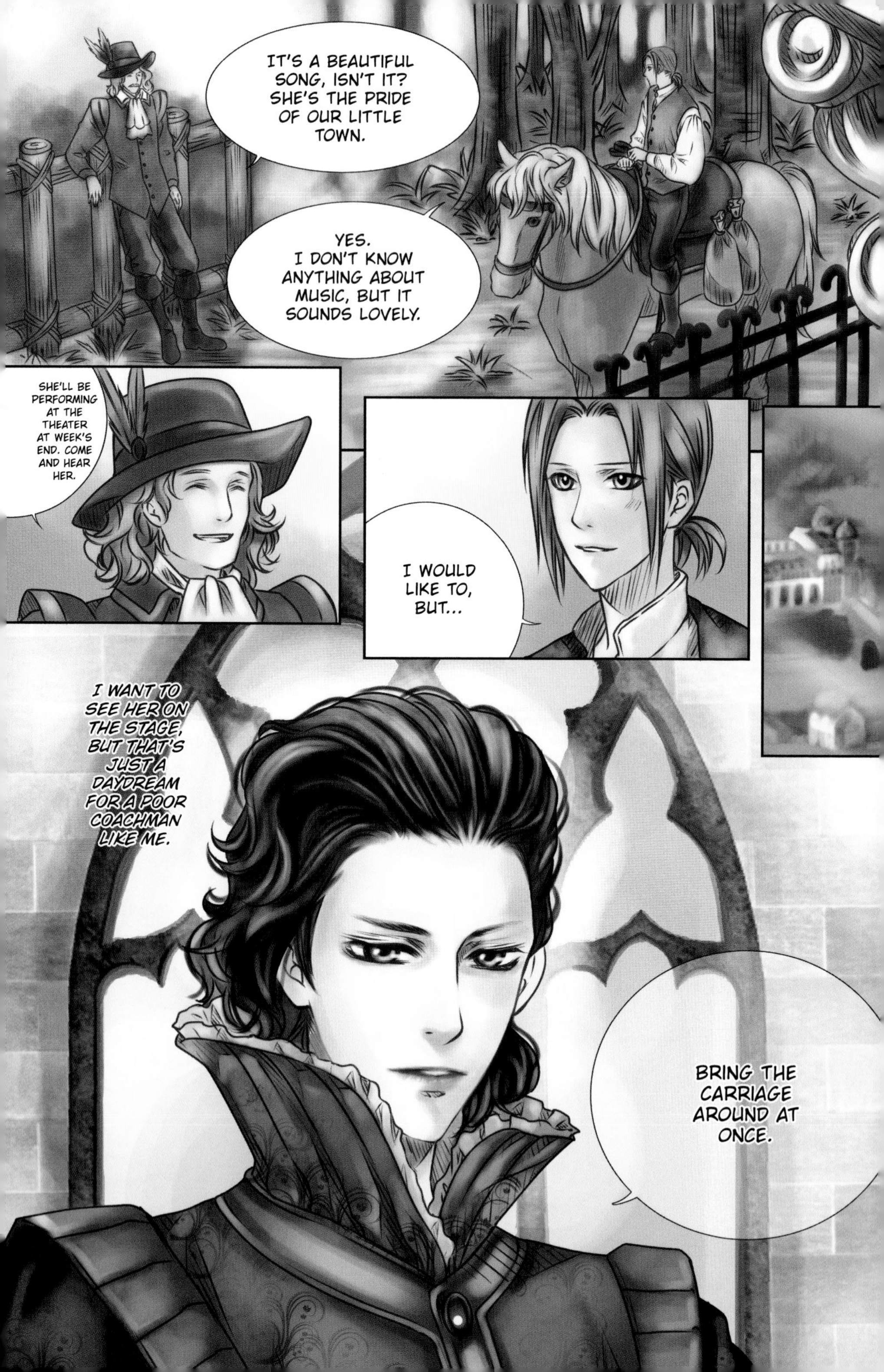
IT'S A BEAUTIFUL SONG, ISN'T IT? SHE'S THE PRIDE OF OUR LITTLE TOWN.
YES. I DON'T KNOW ANYTHING ABOUT MUSIC, BUT IT SOUNDS LOVELY.
SHE'LL BE PERFORMING AT THE THEATER AT WEEK'S END. COME AND HEAR HER.
I WOULD LIKE TO, BUT...
I WANT TO SEE HER ON THE STAGE, BUT THAT'S JUST A DAYDREAM FOR A POOR COACHMAN LIKE ME.
BRING THE CARRIAGE AROUND AT ONCE.

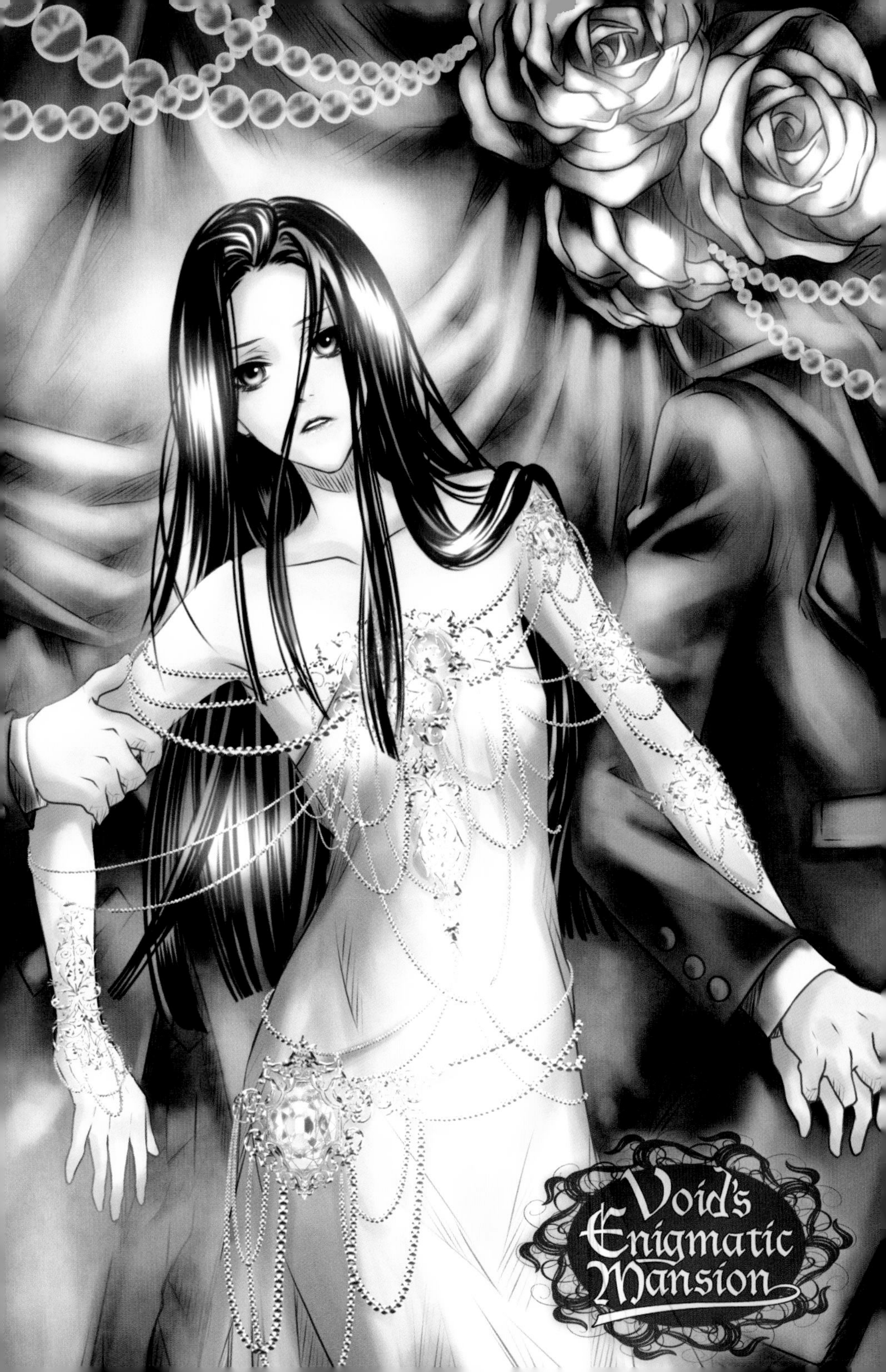
Void's Enigmatic Mansion

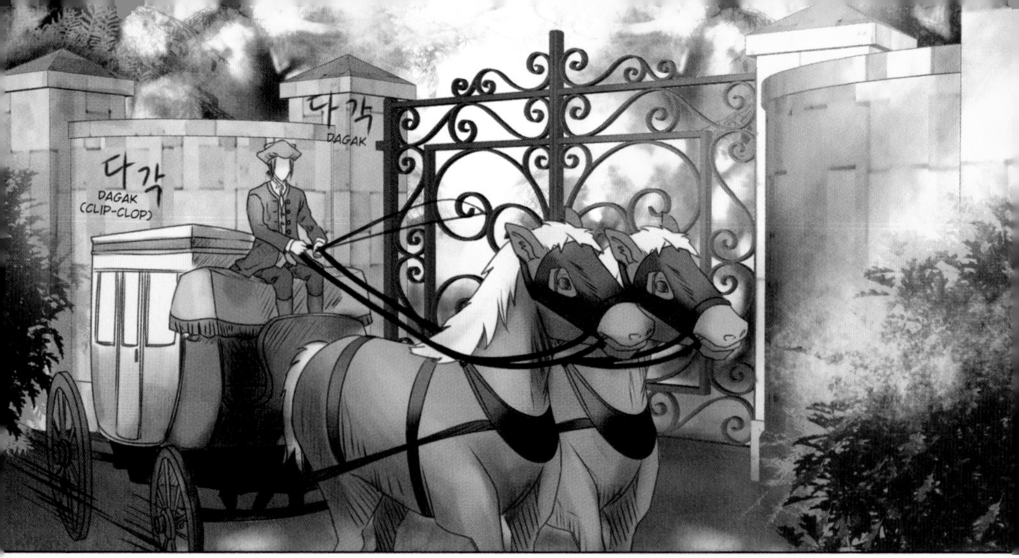
다각
DAGAK
다각
DAGAK
(CLIP-CLOP)

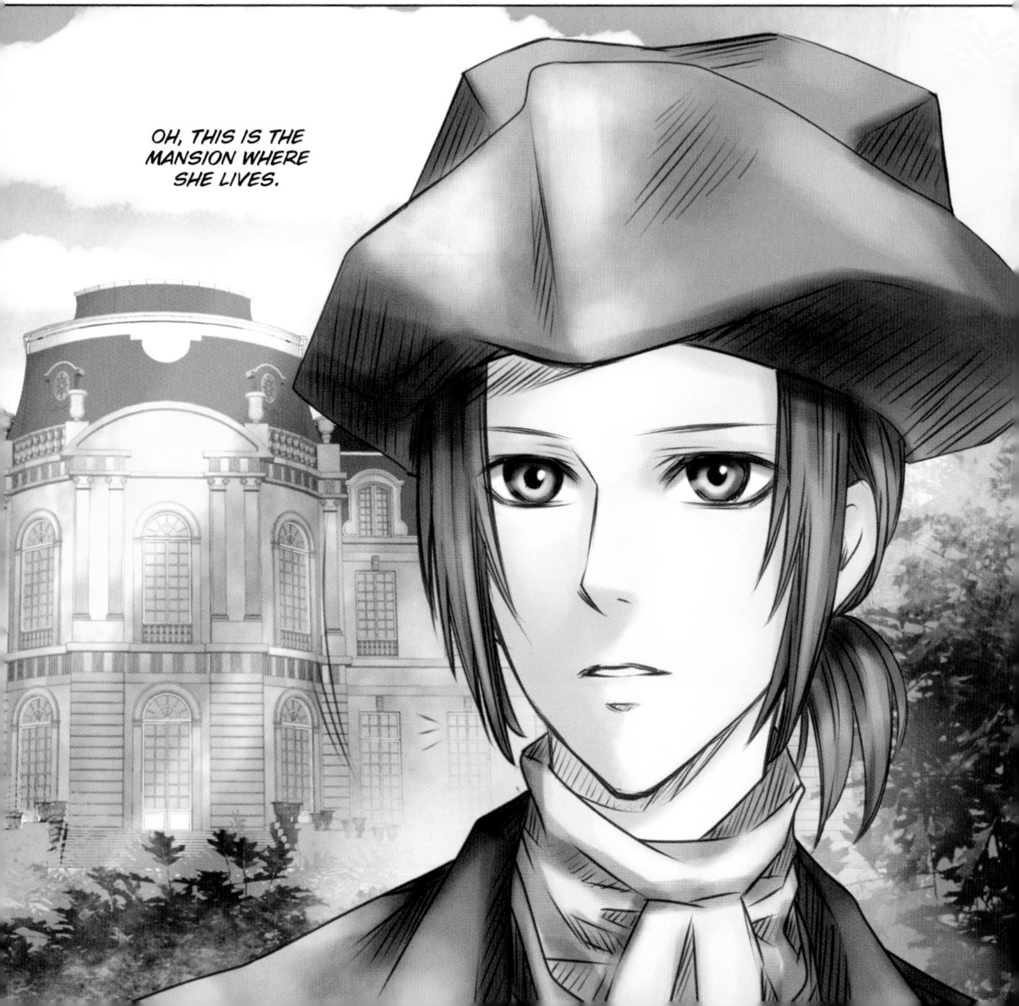
OH, THIS IS THE
MANSION WHERE
SHE LIVES.

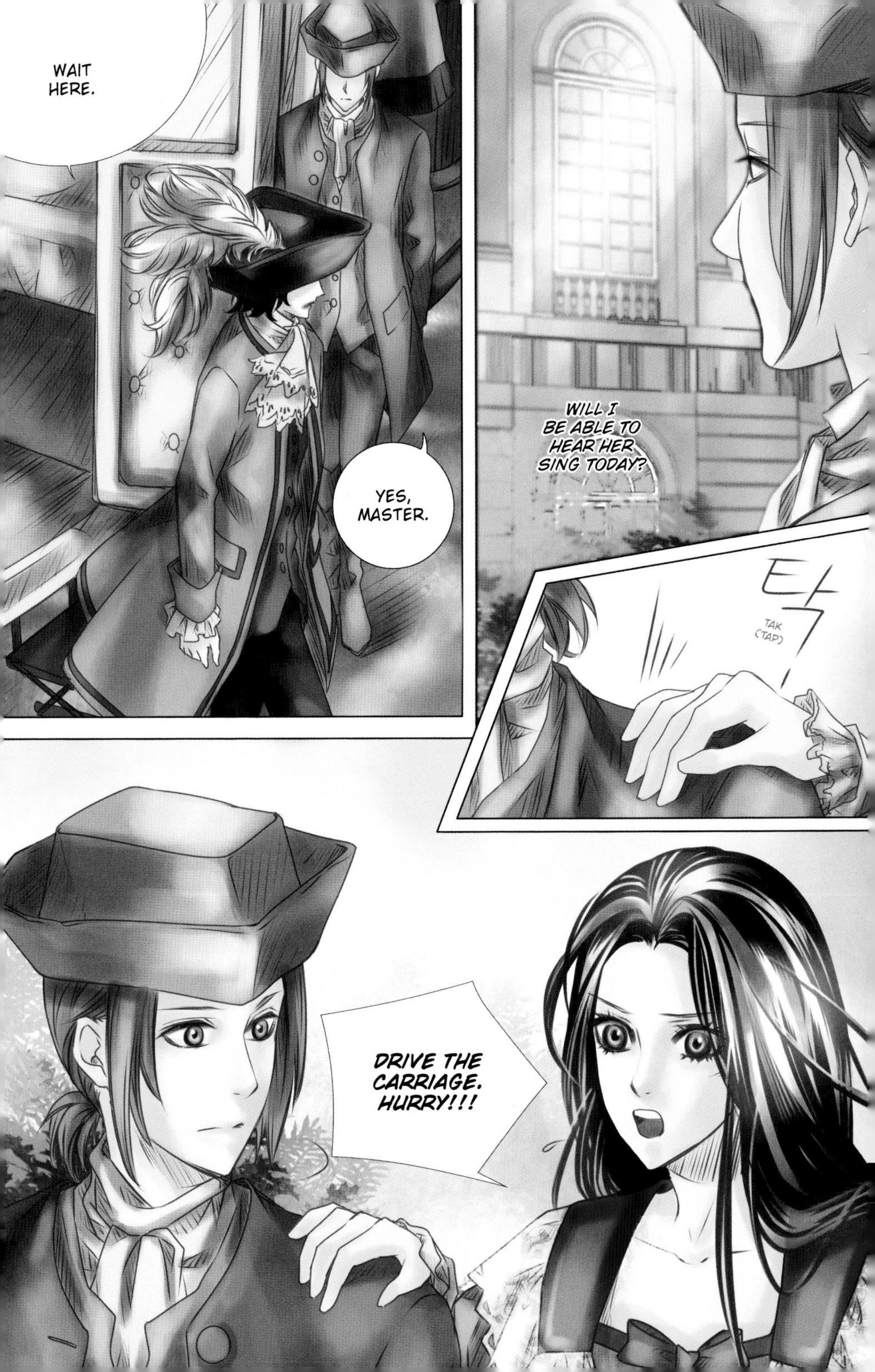
WAIT HERE.
YES, MASTER.
WILL I BE ABLE TO HEAR HER SING TODAY?
타
TAK (TAP)
DRIVE THE CARRIAGE. HURRY!!!

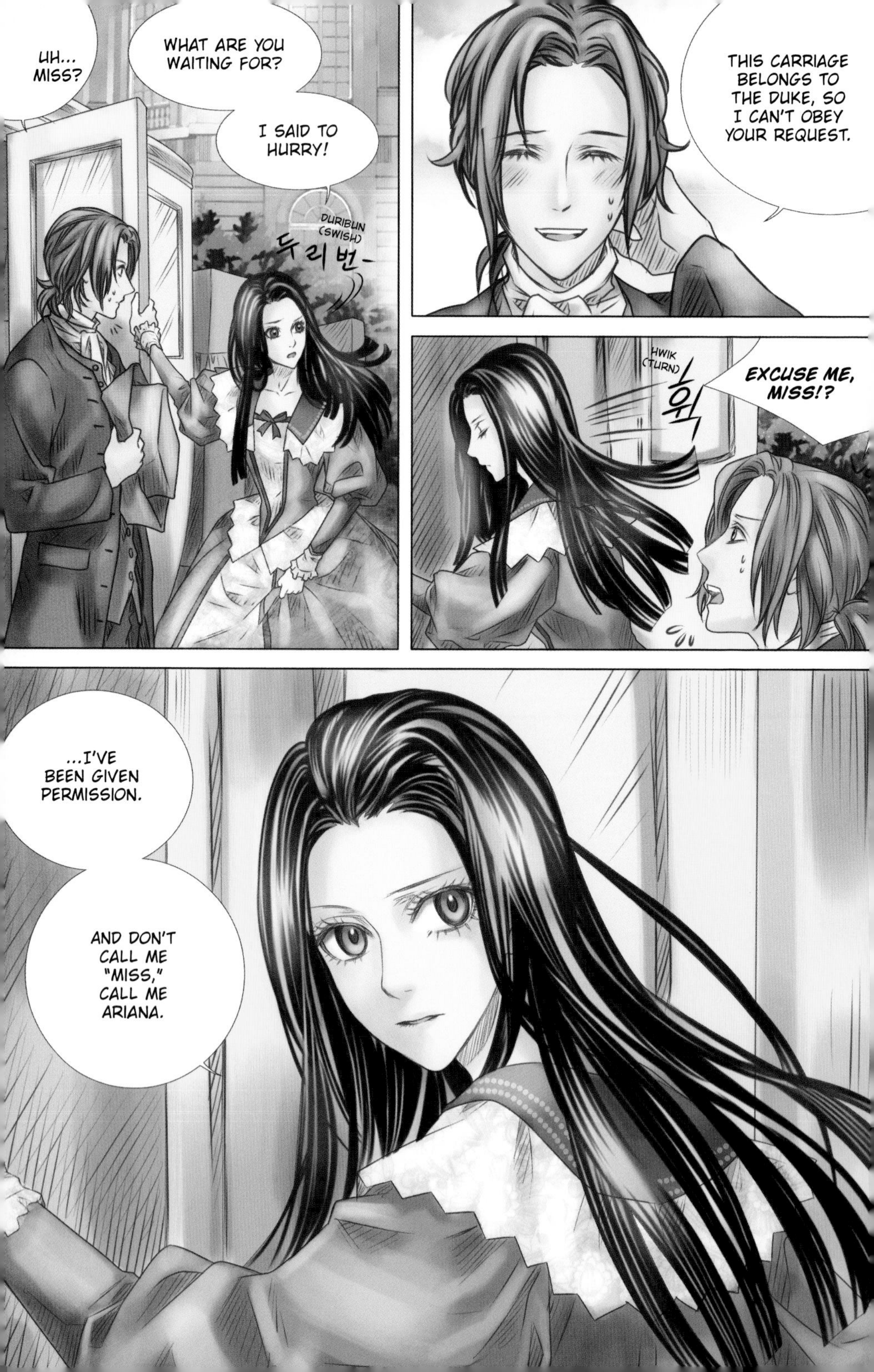
UH... MISS?
WHAT ARE YOU WAITING FOR?
I SAID TO HURRY!
DURIBUN (SWISH)
두리번
THIS CARRIAGE BELONGS TO THE DUKE, SO I CAN'T OBEY YOUR REQUEST.
HWIK (TURN)
EXCUSE ME, MISS!?
...I'VE BEEN GIVEN PERMISSION.
AND DON'T CALL ME "MISS," CALL ME ARIANA.

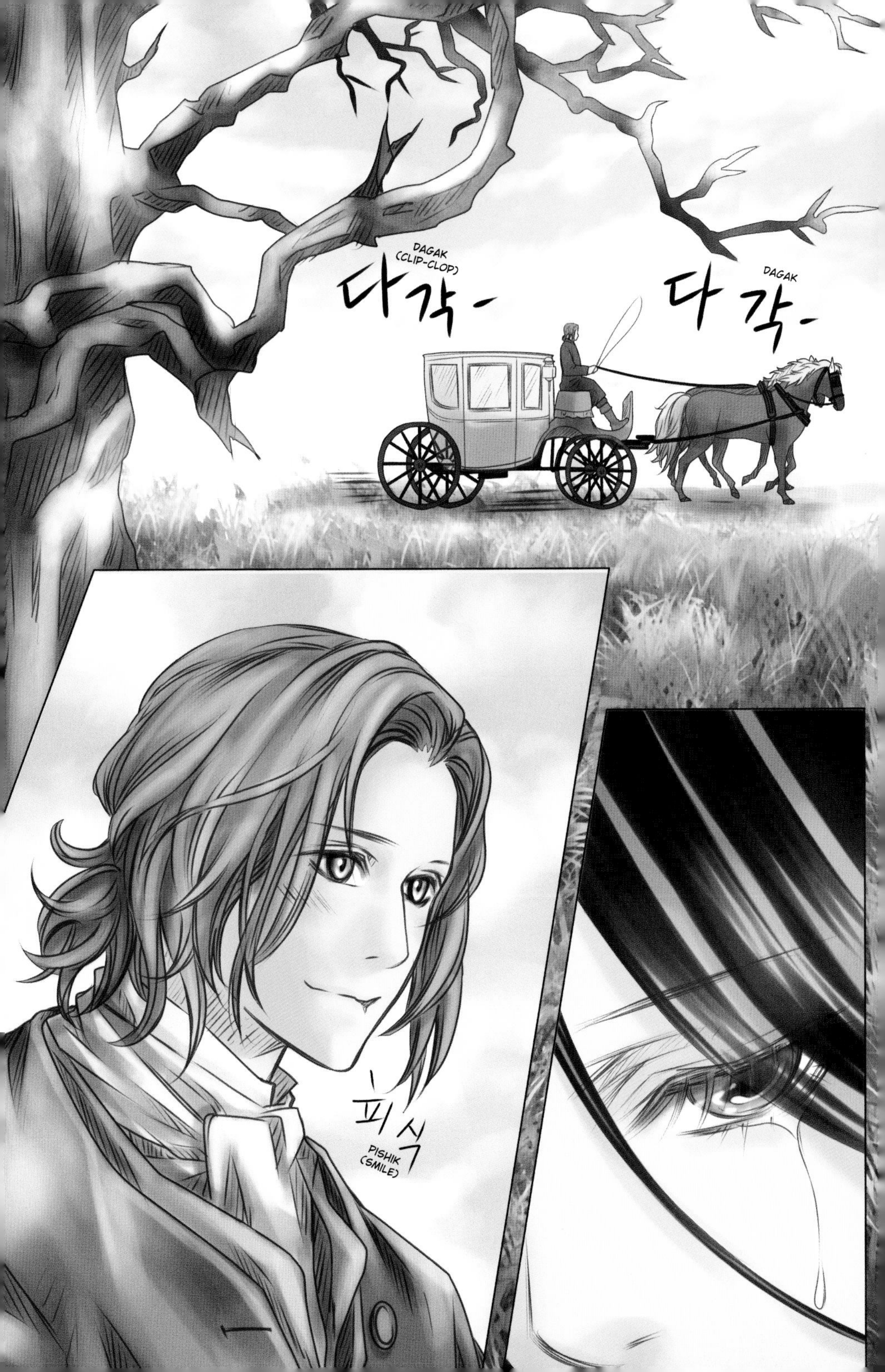
DAGAK
(CLIP-CLOP)
다각-
DAGAK
다각-
피식
PISHIK
(SMILE)

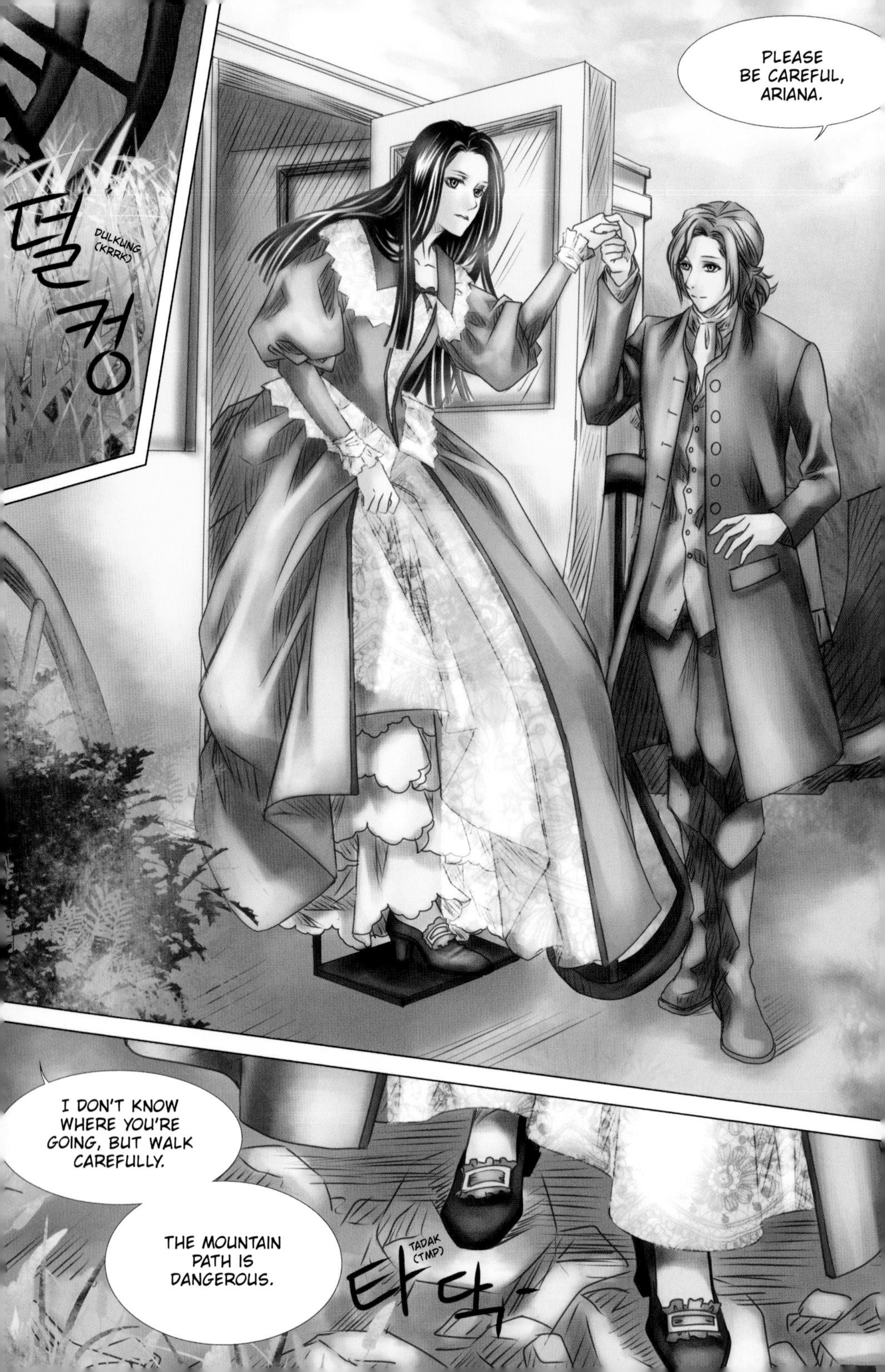

PLEASE BE CAREFUL, ARIANA.
덜컹
DULKUNG (KRRK)
I DON'T KNOW WHERE YOU'RE GOING, BUT WALK CAREFULLY.
THE MOUNTAIN PATH IS DANGEROUS.
타닥-
TADAK (TMP)

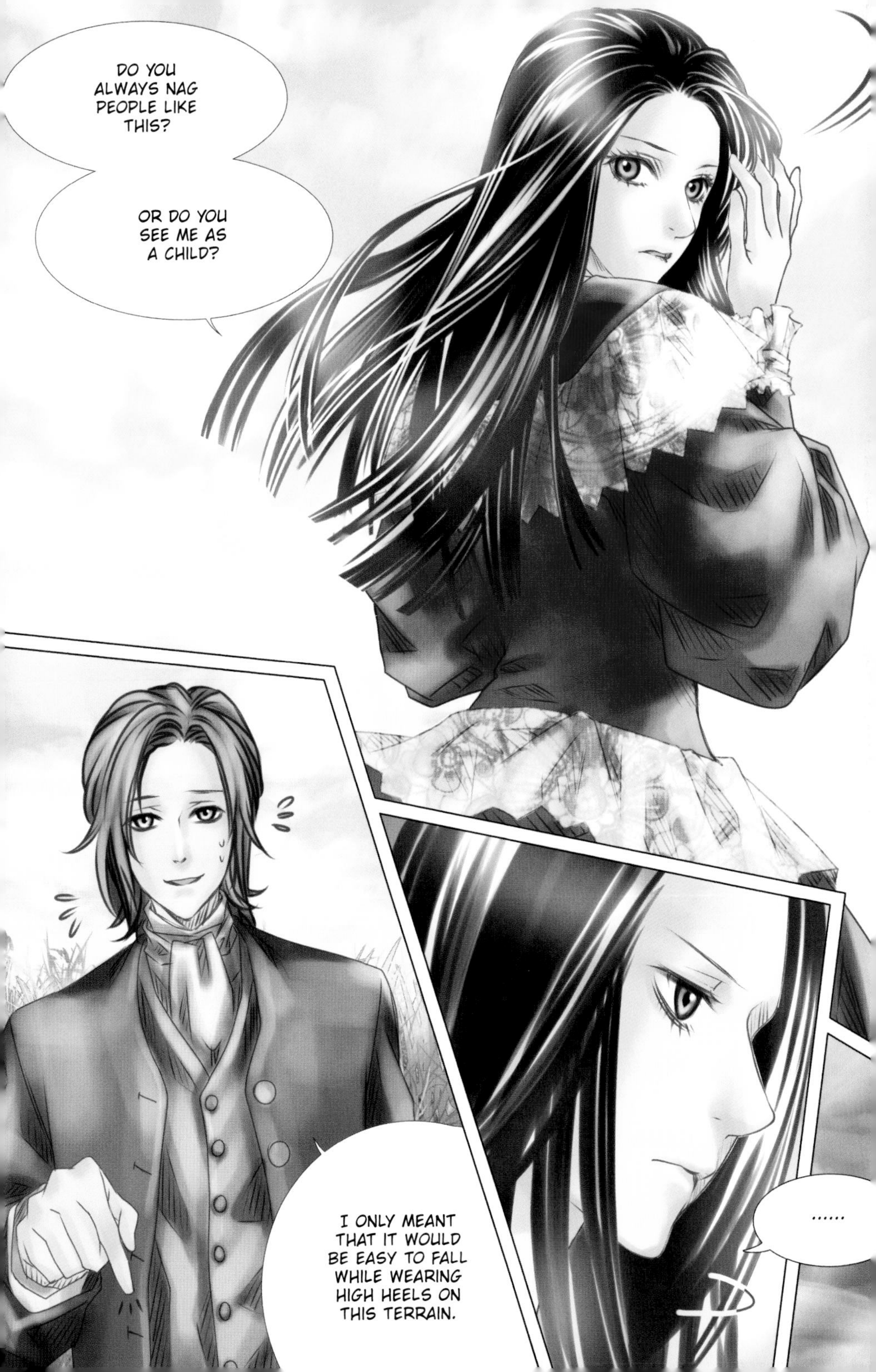
DO YOU ALWAYS NAG PEOPLE LIKE THIS?
OR DO YOU SEE ME AS A CHILD?
I ONLY MEANT THAT IT WOULD BE EASY TO FALL WHILE WEARING HIGH HEELS ON THIS TERRAIN.
......

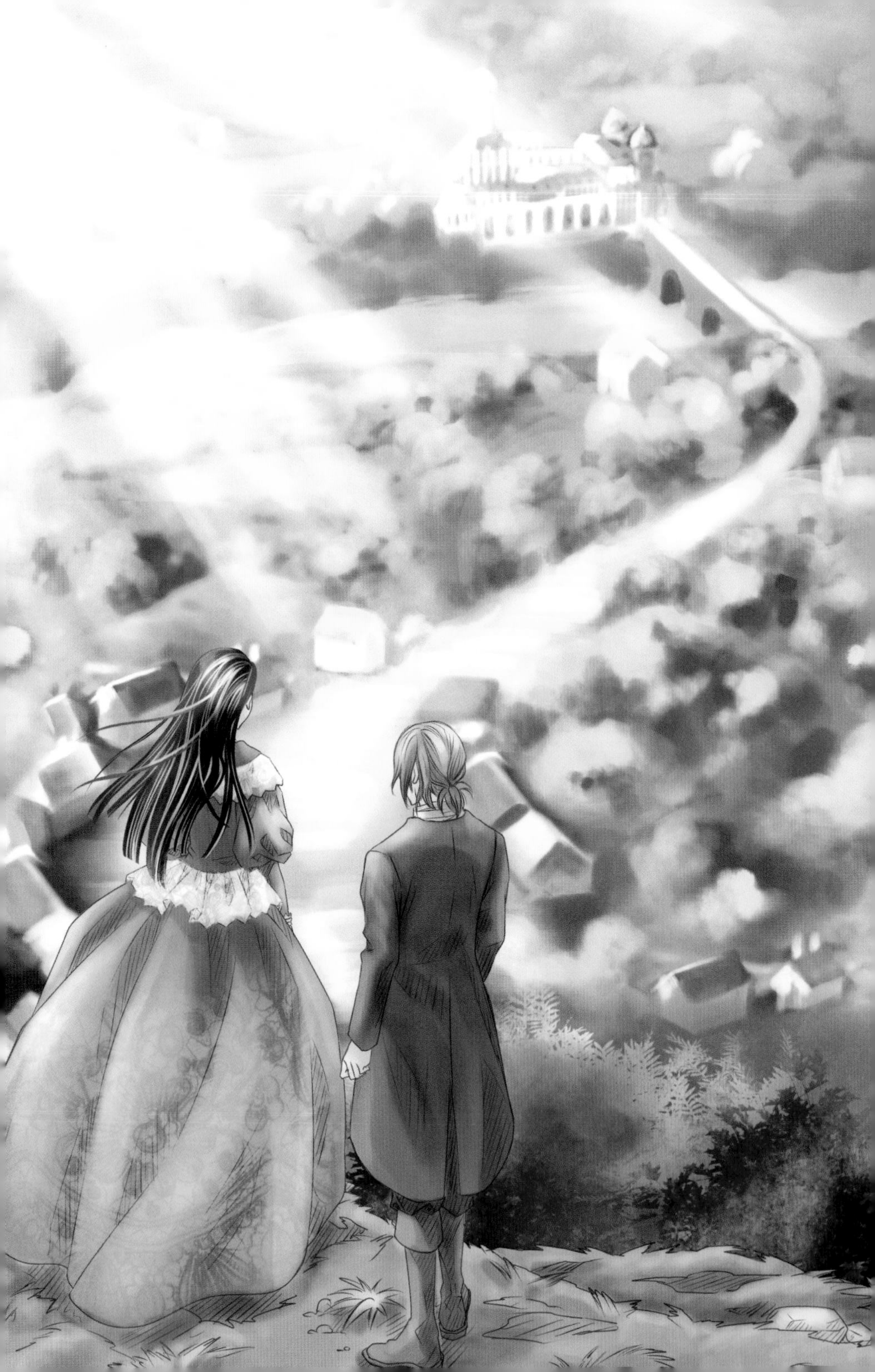

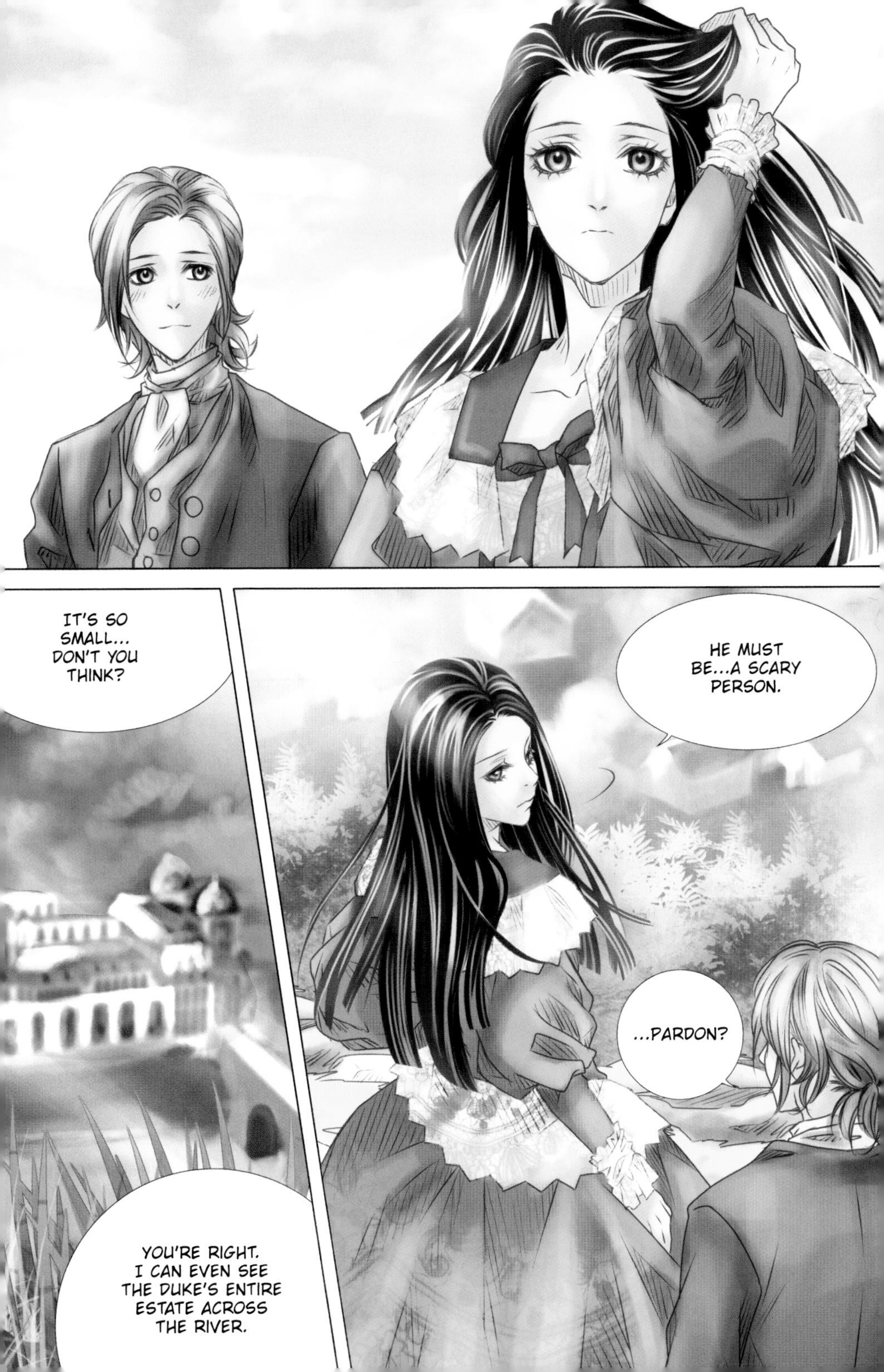
IT'S SO SMALL... DON'T YOU THINK?
YOU'RE RIGHT. I CAN EVEN SEE THE DUKE'S ENTIRE ESTATE ACROSS THE RIVER.
HE MUST BE...A SCARY PERSON.
...PARDON?

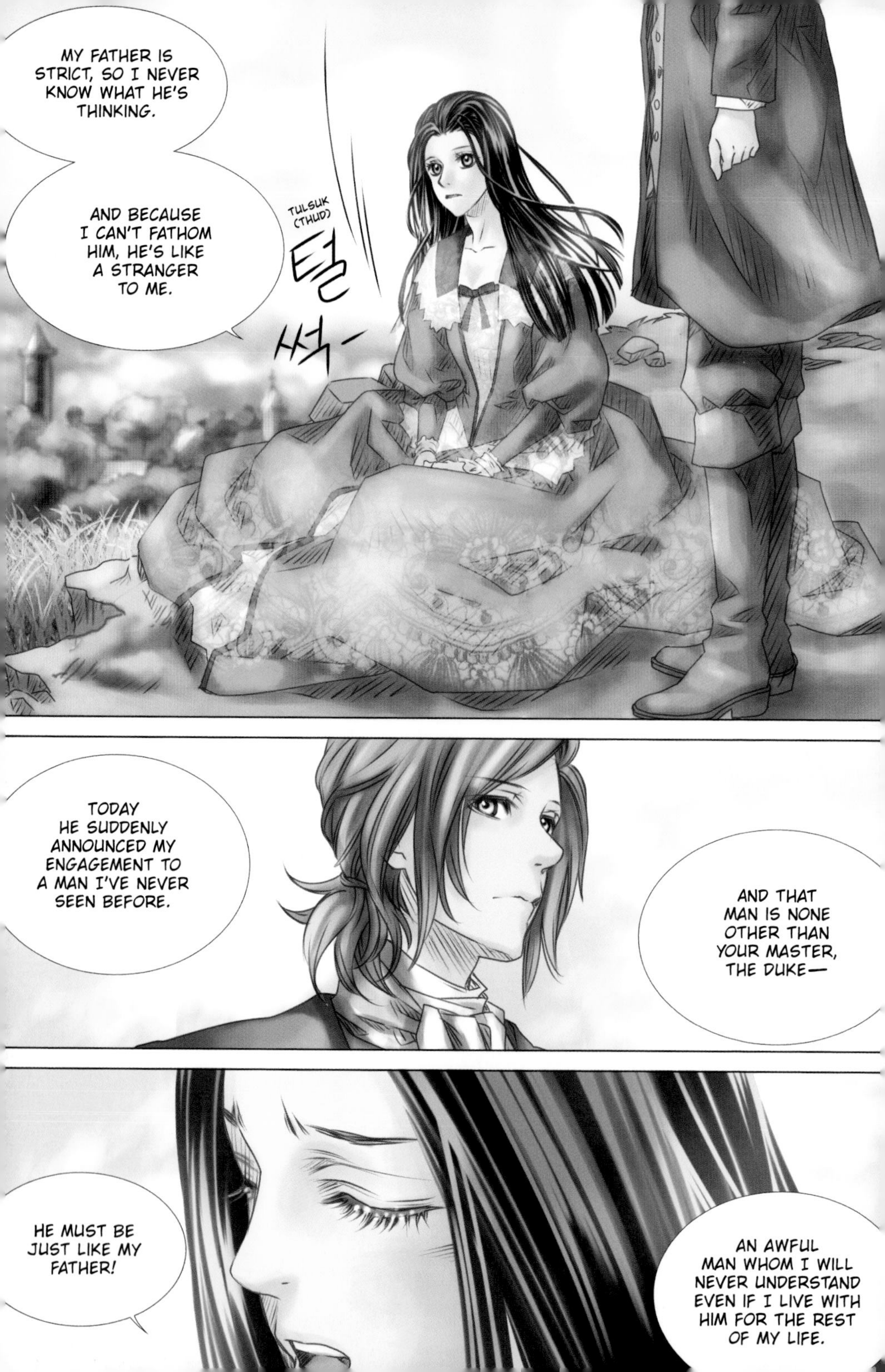
MY FATHER IS STRICT, SO I NEVER KNOW WHAT HE'S THINKING.
AND BECAUSE I CAN'T FATHOM HIM, HE'S LIKE A STRANGER TO ME.
TULSUK (THUD)
털
썩
TODAY HE SUDDENLY ANNOUNCED MY ENGAGEMENT TO A MAN I'VE NEVER SEEN BEFORE.
AND THAT MAN IS NONE OTHER THAN YOUR MASTER, THE DUKE—
HE MUST BE JUST LIKE MY FATHER!
AN AWFUL MAN WHOM I WILL NEVER UNDERSTAND EVEN IF I LIVE WITH HIM FOR THE REST OF MY LIFE.

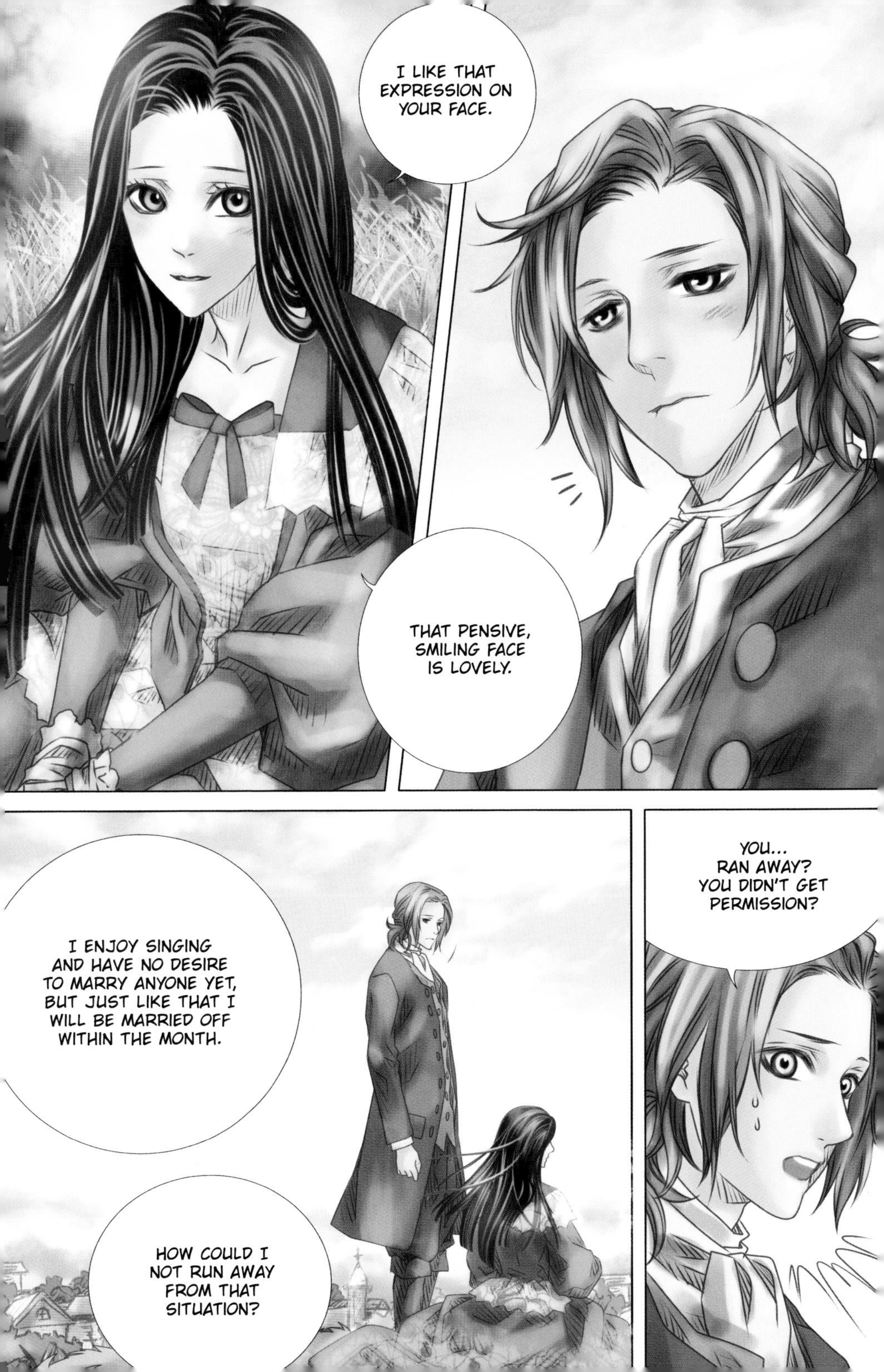
I LIKE THAT EXPRESSION ON YOUR FACE.
THAT PENSIVE, SMILING FACE IS LOVELY.
I ENJOY SINGING AND HAVE NO DESIRE TO MARRY ANYONE YET, BUT JUST LIKE THAT I WILL BE MARRIED OFF WITHIN THE MONTH.
HOW COULD I NOT RUN AWAY FROM THAT SITUATION?
YOU... RAN AWAY? YOU DIDN'T GET PERMISSION?

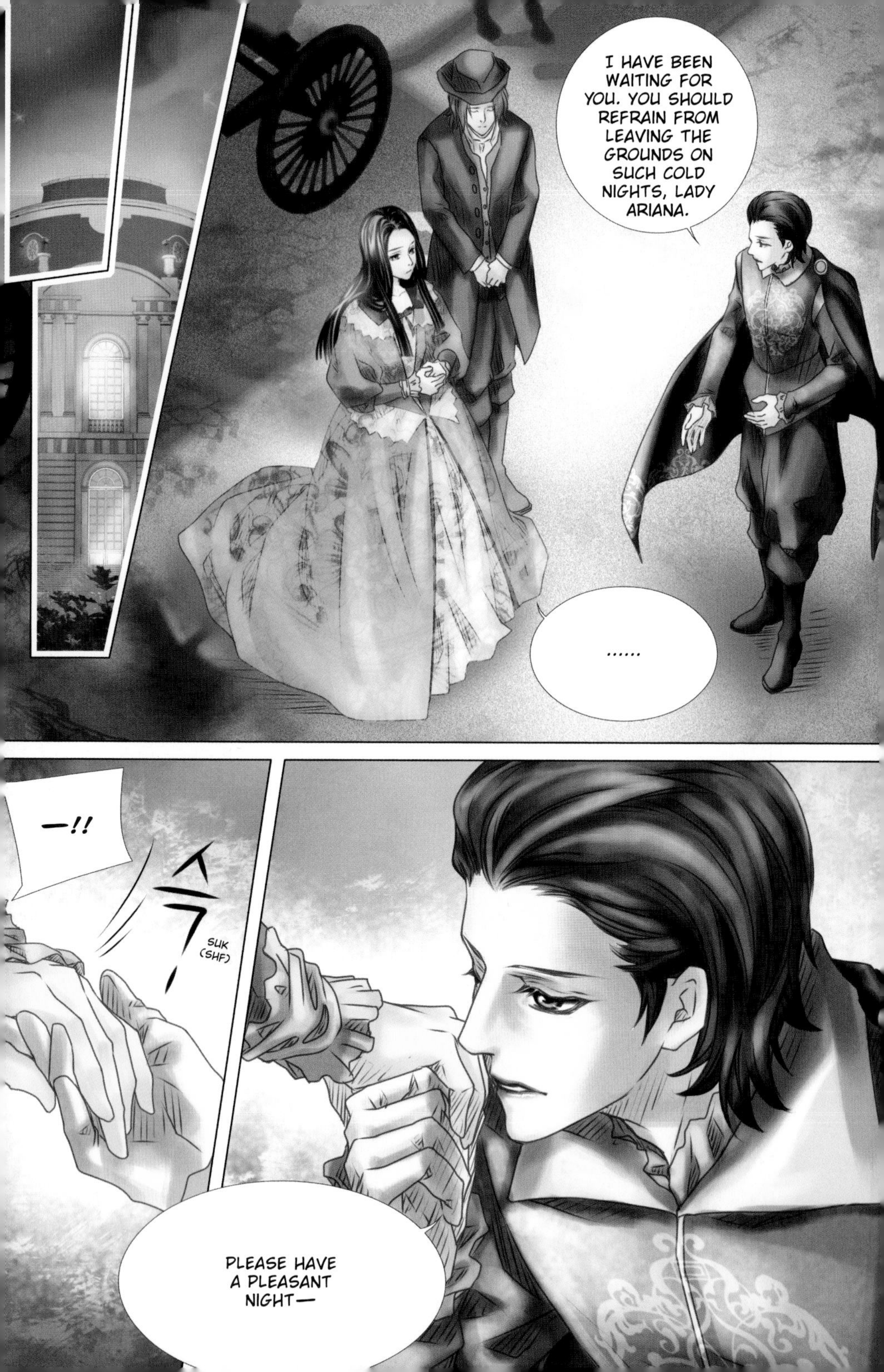
I HAVE BEEN WAITING FOR YOU. YOU SHOULD REFRAIN FROM LEAVING THE GROUNDS ON SUCH COLD NIGHTS, LADY ARIANA.
......
—!!
SUK (SHF)
PLEASE HAVE A PLEASANT NIGHT—

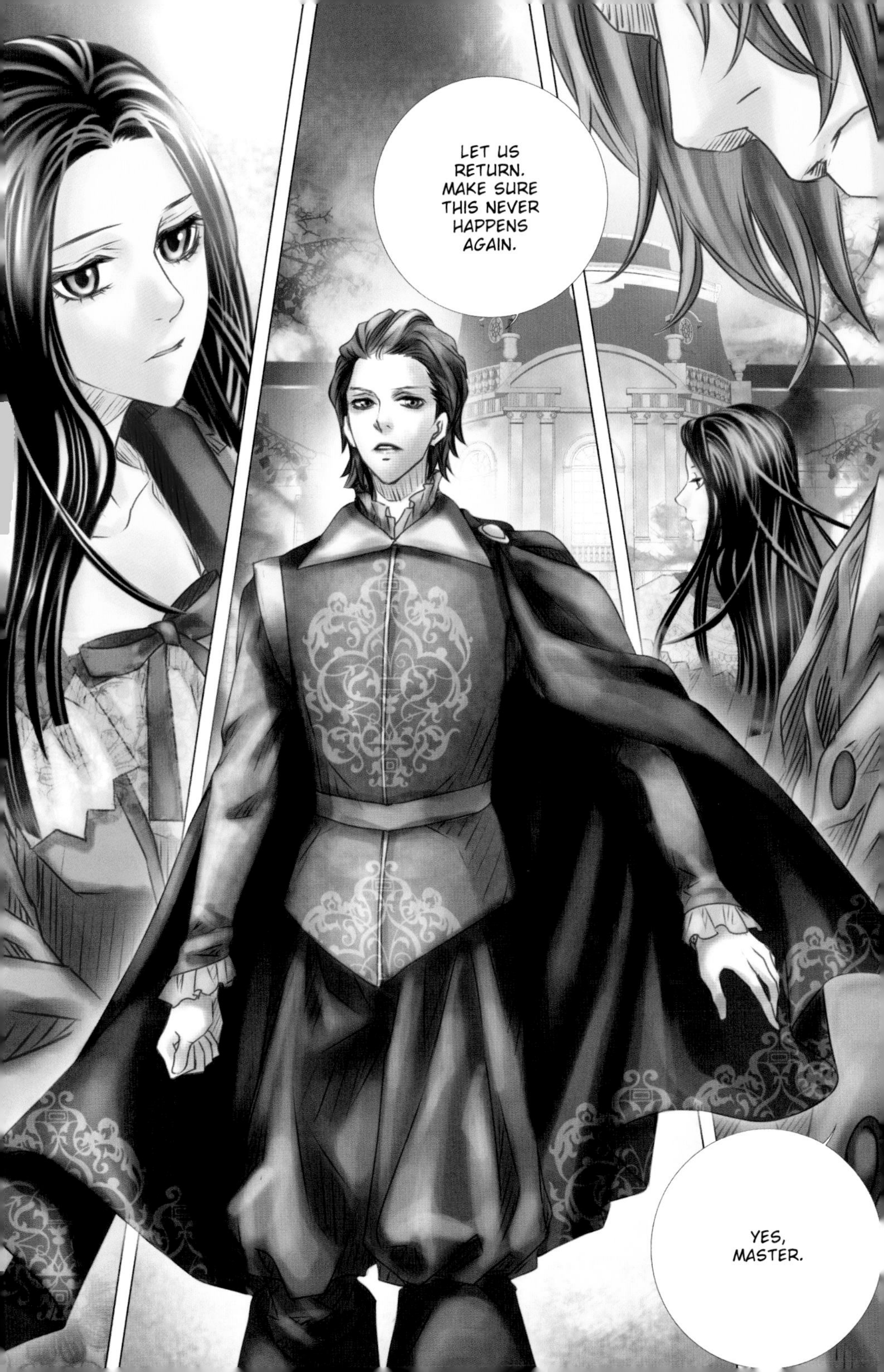
LET US RETURN. MAKE SURE THIS NEVER HAPPENS AGAIN.
YES, MASTER.

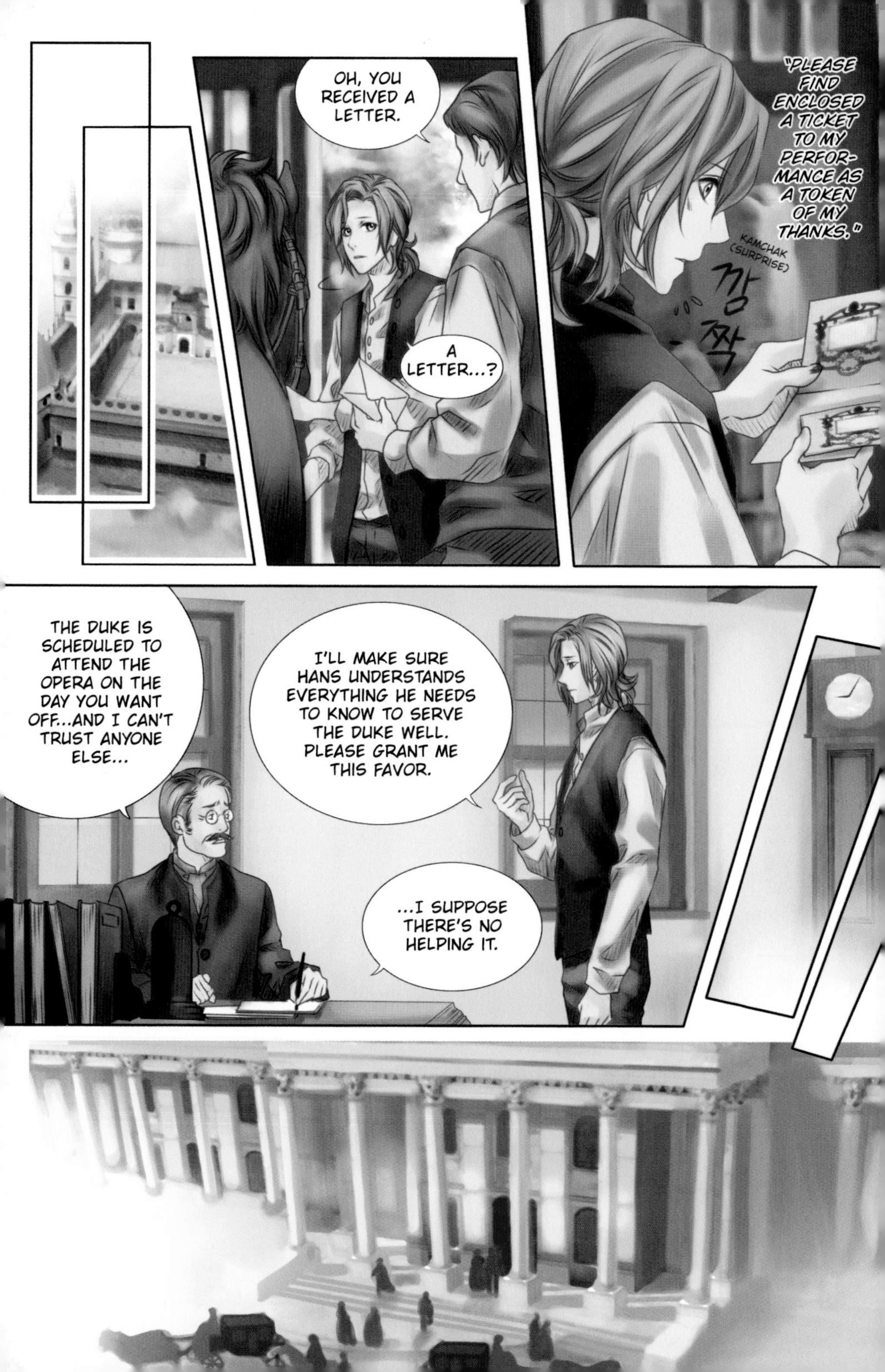
OH, YOU RECEIVED A LETTER.
A LETTER...?
"PLEASE FIND ENCLOSED A TICKET TO MY PERFORMANCE AS A TOKEN OF MY THANKS."
KAMCHAK (SURPRISE)
깜짝
THE DUKE IS SCHEDULED TO ATTEND THE OPERA ON THE DAY YOU WANT OFF...AND I CAN'T TRUST ANYONE ELSE...
I'LL MAKE SURE HANS UNDERSTANDS EVERYTHING HE NEEDS TO KNOW TO SERVE THE DUKE WELL. PLEASE GRANT ME THIS FAVOR.
...I SUPPOSE THERE'S NO HELPING IT.

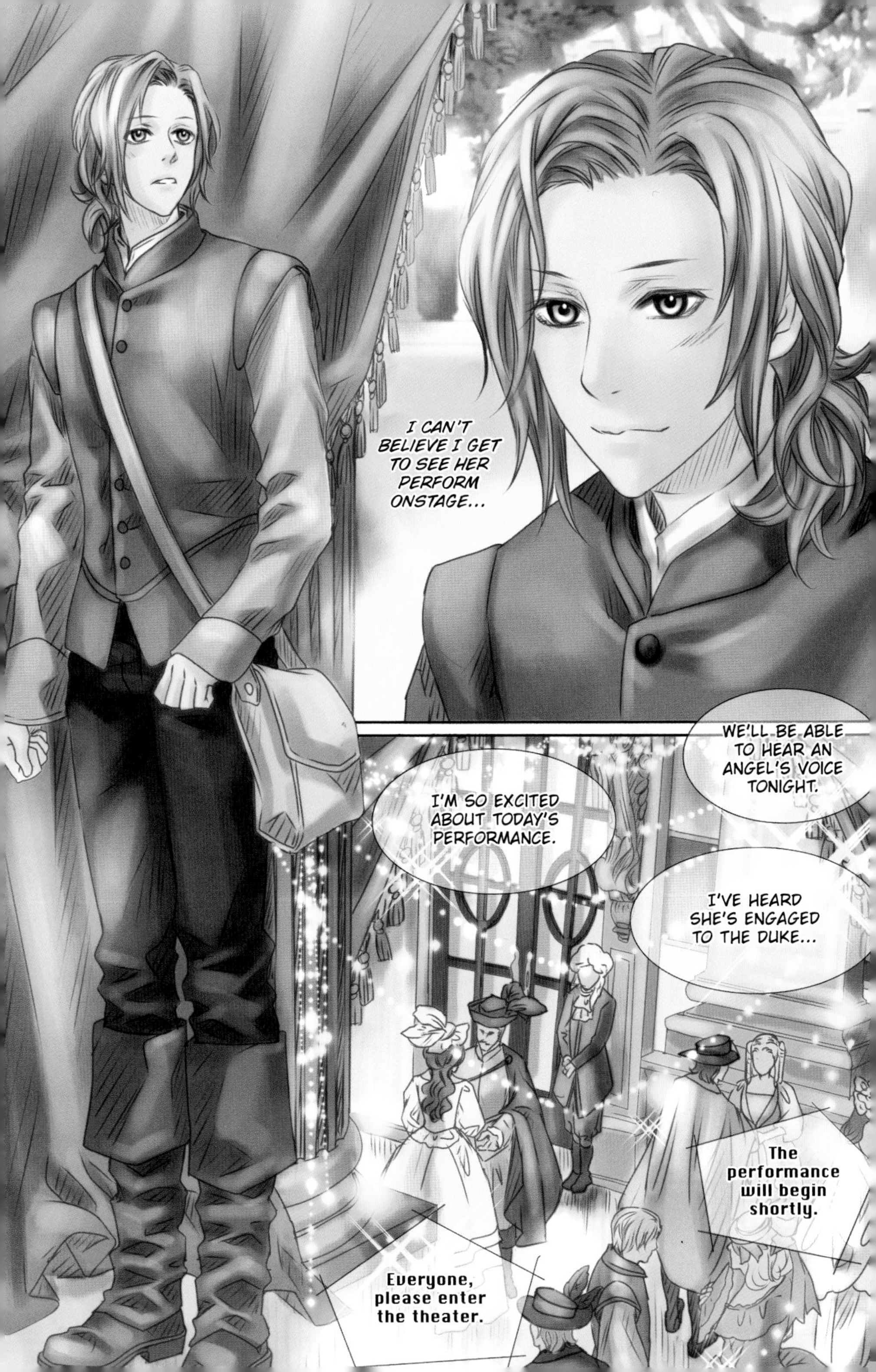

I CAN'T BELIEVE I GET TO SEE HER PERFORM ONSTAGE...
WE'LL BE ABLE TO HEAR AN ANGEL'S VOICE TONIGHT.
I'M SO EXCITED ABOUT TODAY'S PERFORMANCE.
I'VE HEARD SHE'S ENGAGED TO THE DUKE...
The performance will begin shortly.
Everyone, please enter the theater.

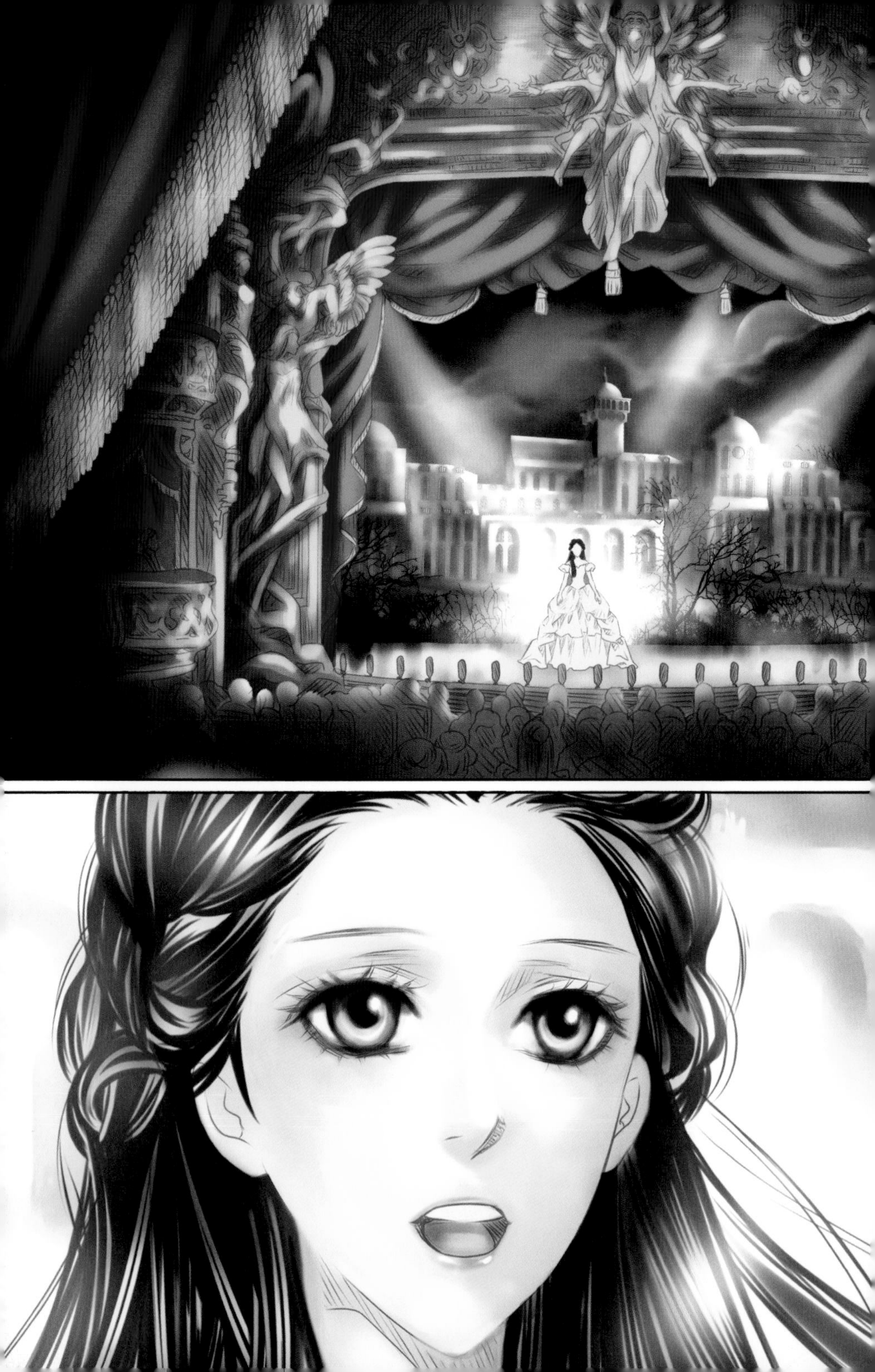

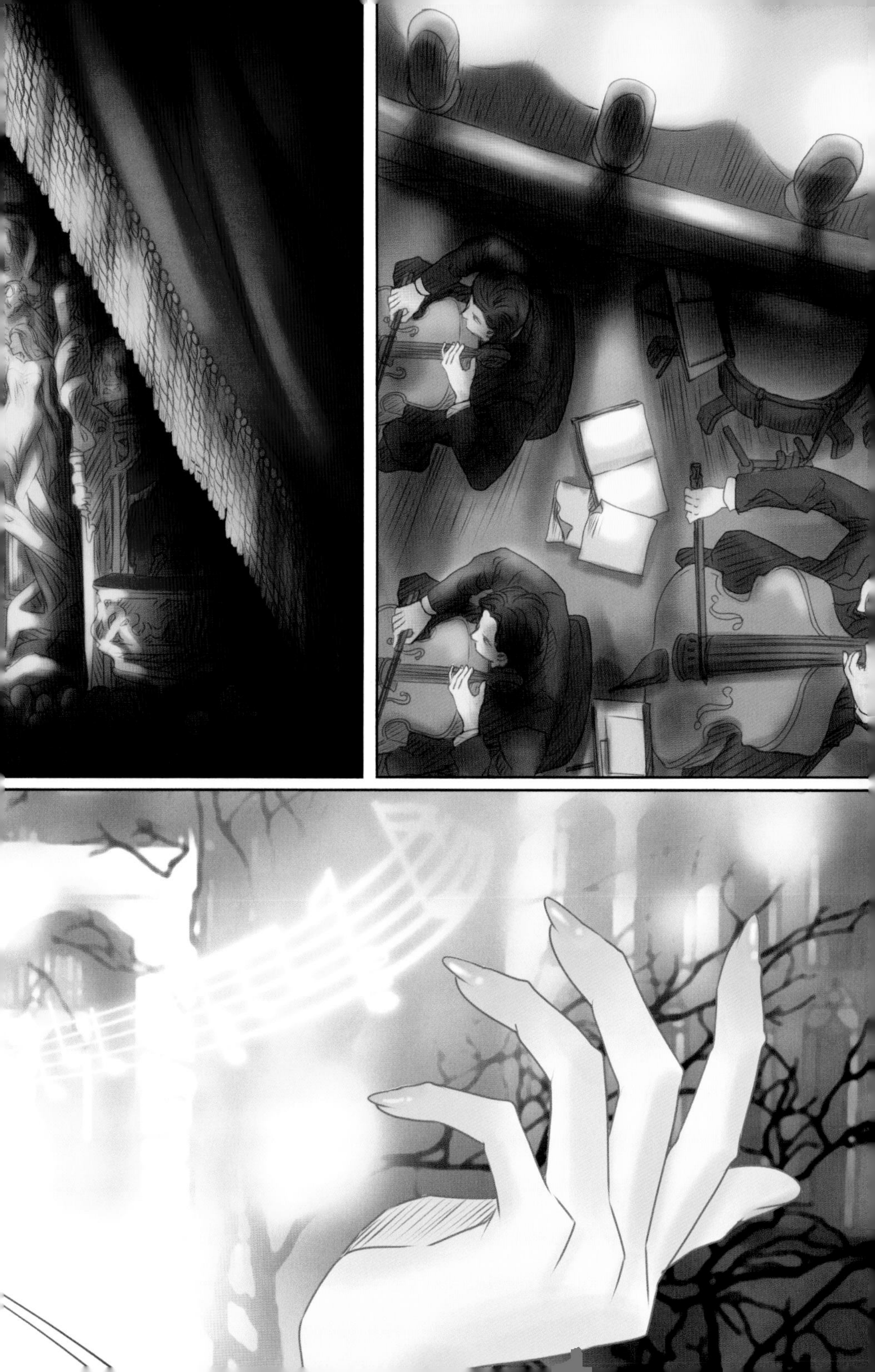

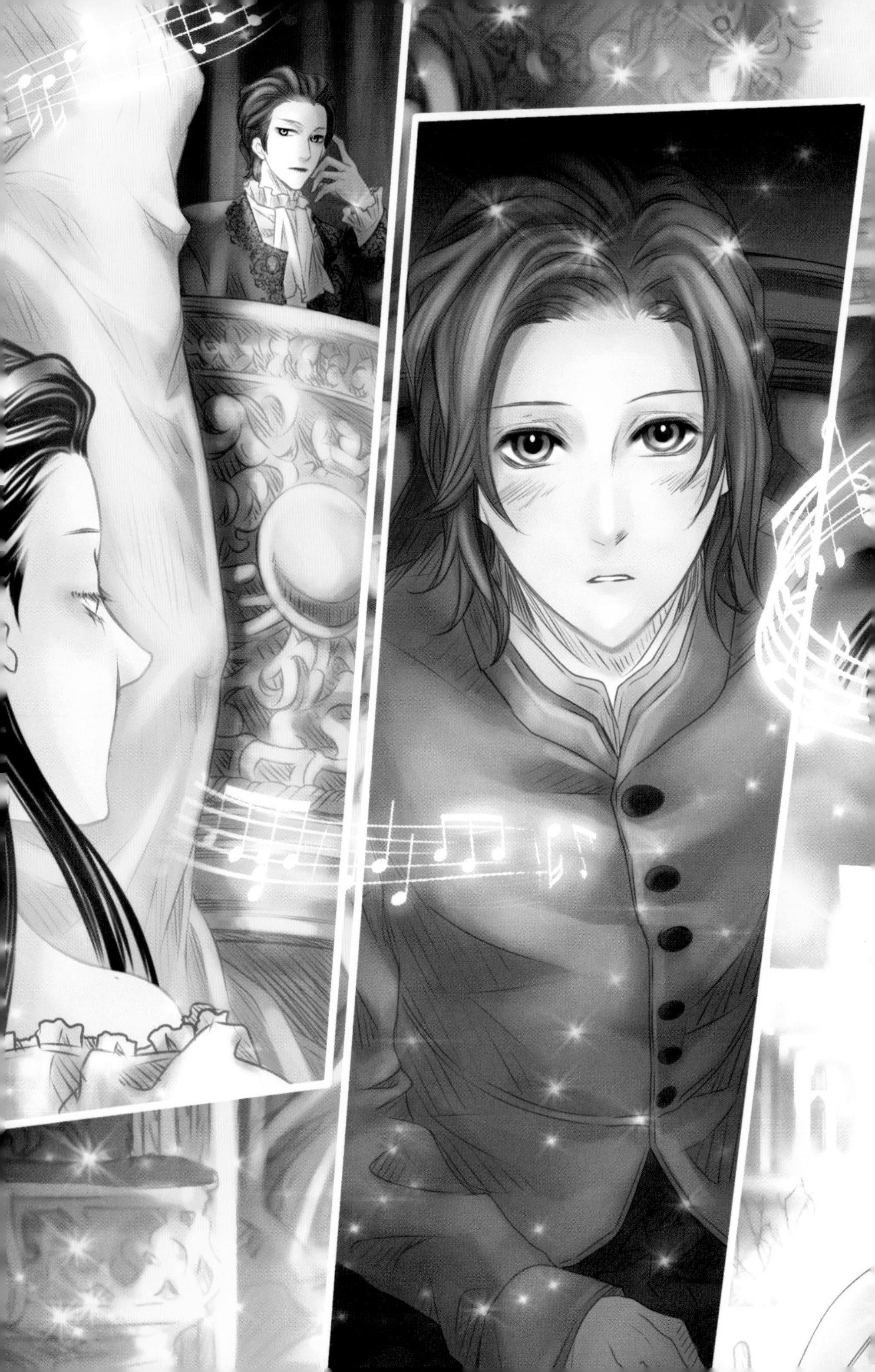

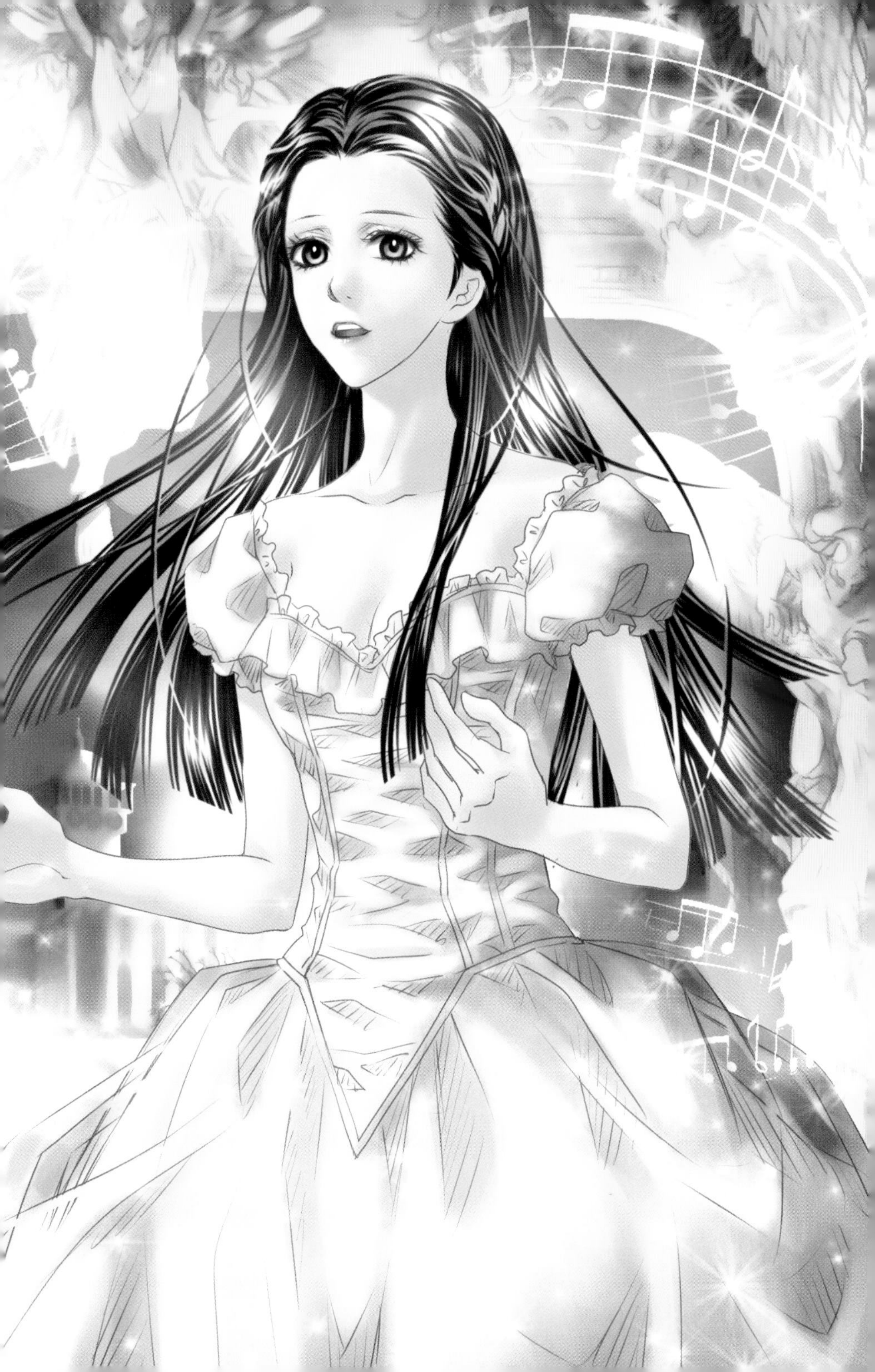

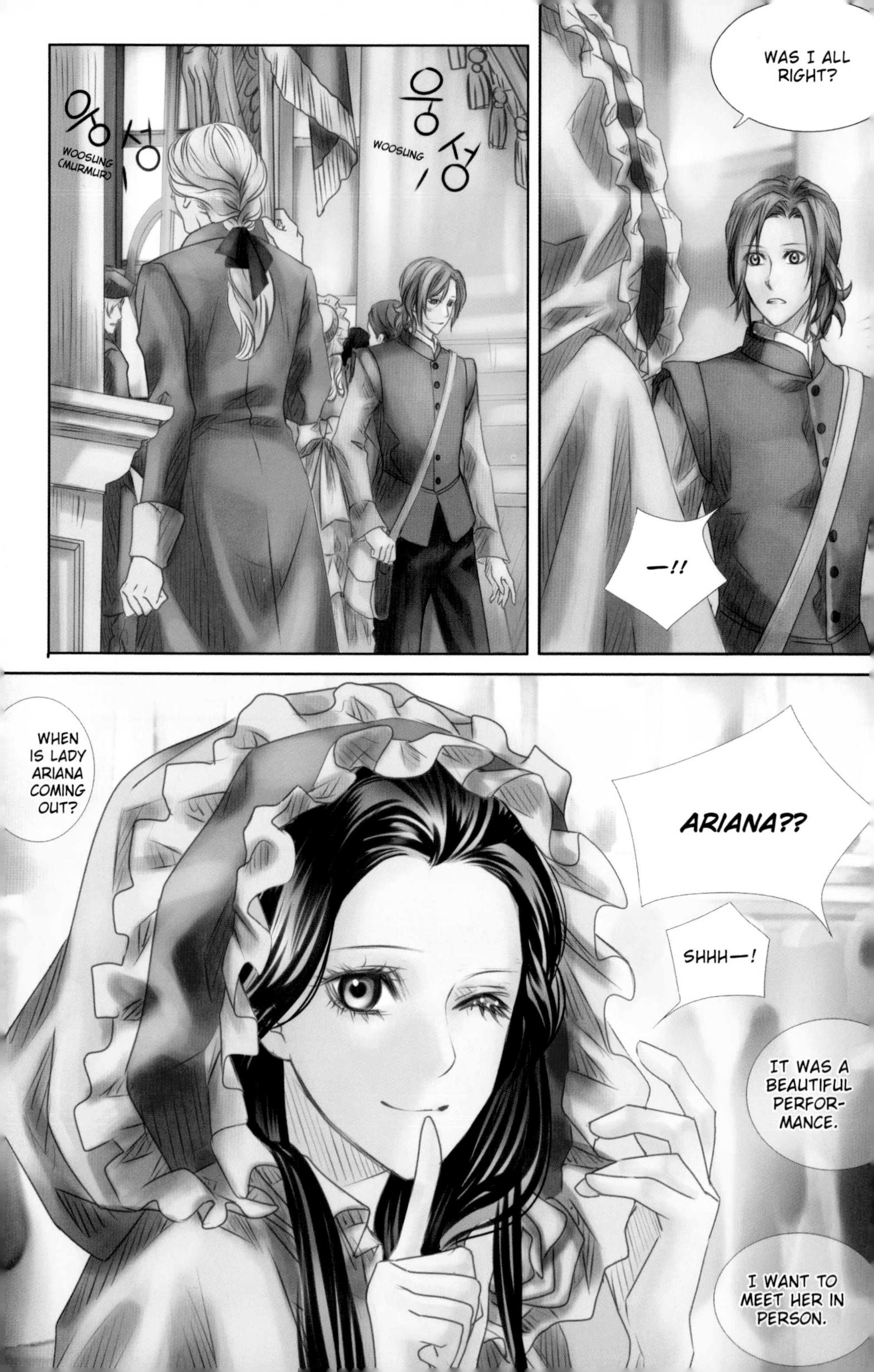

웅성
WOOSUNG
웅성
WOOSUNG (MURMUR)
WAS I ALL RIGHT?
—!!
ARIANA??
WHEN IS LADY ARIANA COMING OUT?
SHHH—!
IT WAS A BEAUTIFUL PERFOR-MANCE.
I WANT TO MEET HER IN PERSON.

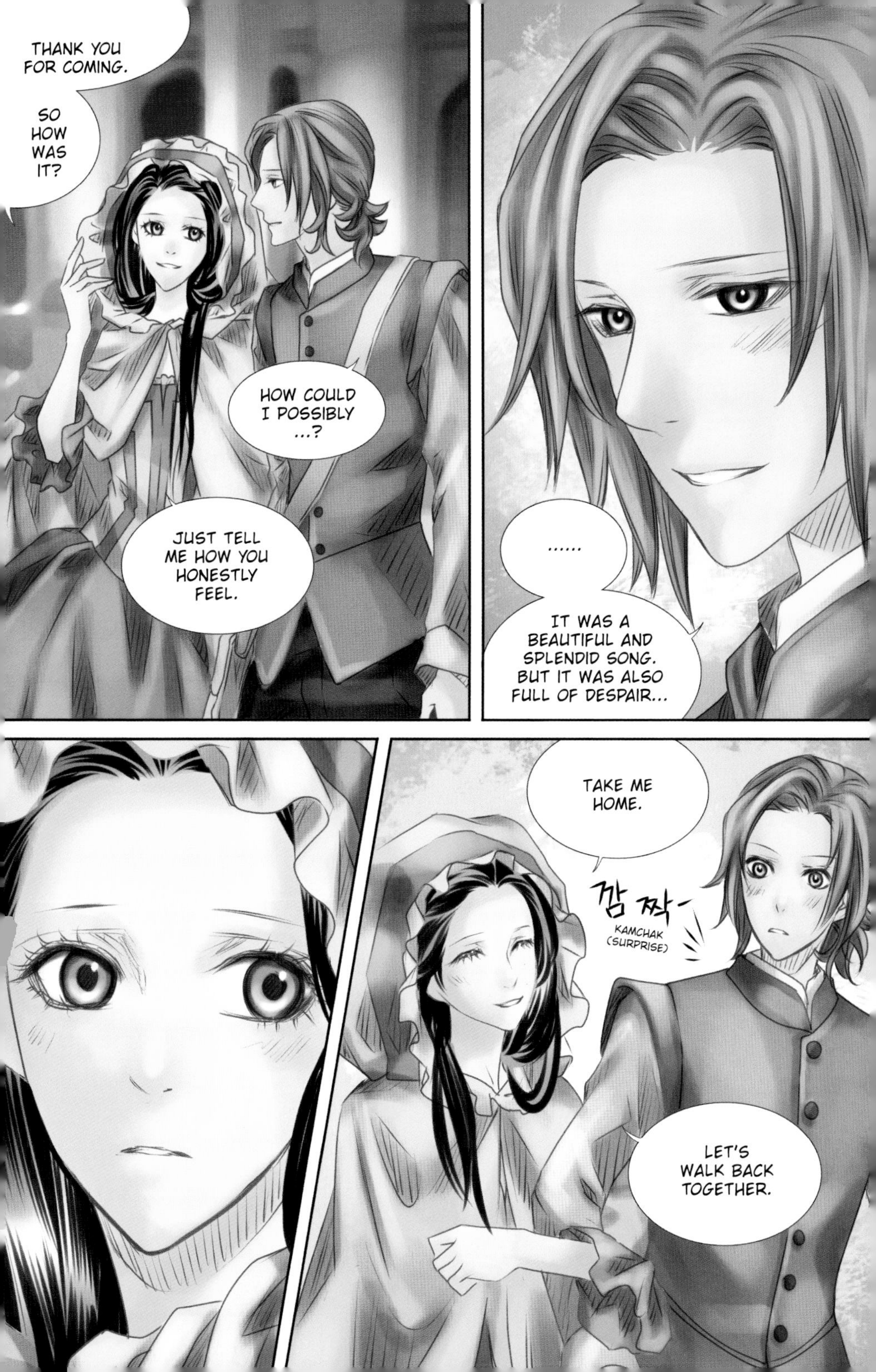
THANK YOU FOR COMING.
SO HOW WAS IT?
HOW COULD I POSSIBLY ...?
JUST TELL ME HOW YOU HONESTLY FEEL.
......
IT WAS A BEAUTIFUL AND SPLENDID SONG. BUT IT WAS ALSO FULL OF DESPAIR...
TAKE ME HOME.
깜짝
KAMCHAK (SURPRISE)
LET'S WALK BACK TOGETHER.

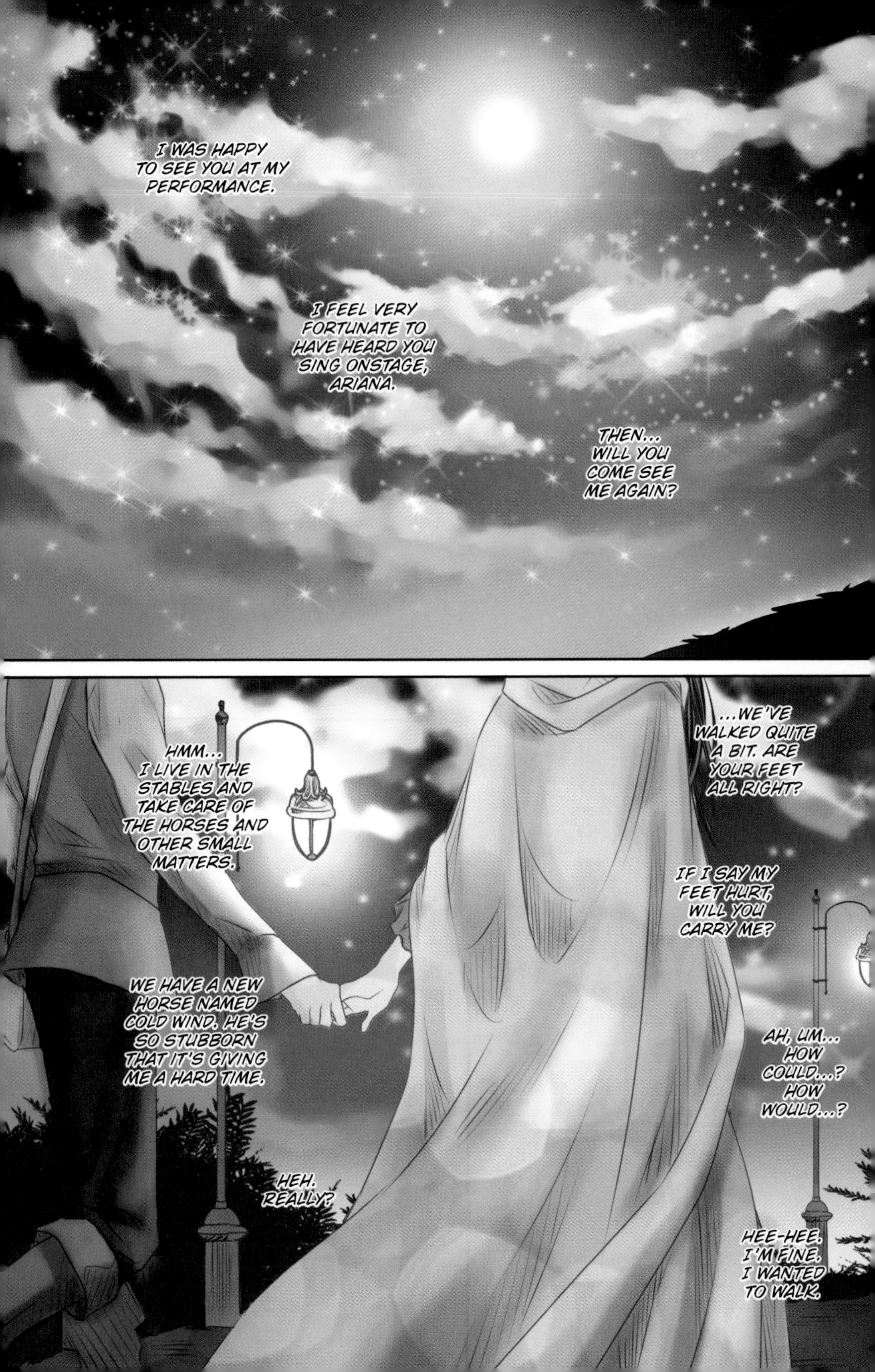
I WAS HAPPY TO SEE YOU AT MY PERFORMANCE.
I FEEL VERY FORTUNATE TO HAVE HEARD YOU SING ONSTAGE, ARIANA.
THEN... WILL YOU COME SEE ME AGAIN?
...WE'VE WALKED QUITE A BIT. ARE YOUR FEET ALL RIGHT?
HMM... I LIVE IN THE STABLES AND TAKE CARE OF THE HORSES AND OTHER SMALL MATTERS.
IF I SAY MY FEET HURT, WILL YOU CARRY ME?
WE HAVE A NEW HORSE NAMED COLD WIND. HE'S SO STUBBORN THAT IT'S GIVING ME A HARD TIME.
AH, UM... HOW COULD...? HOW WOULD...?
HEH. REALLY?
HEE-HEE. I'M FINE. I WANTED TO WALK.

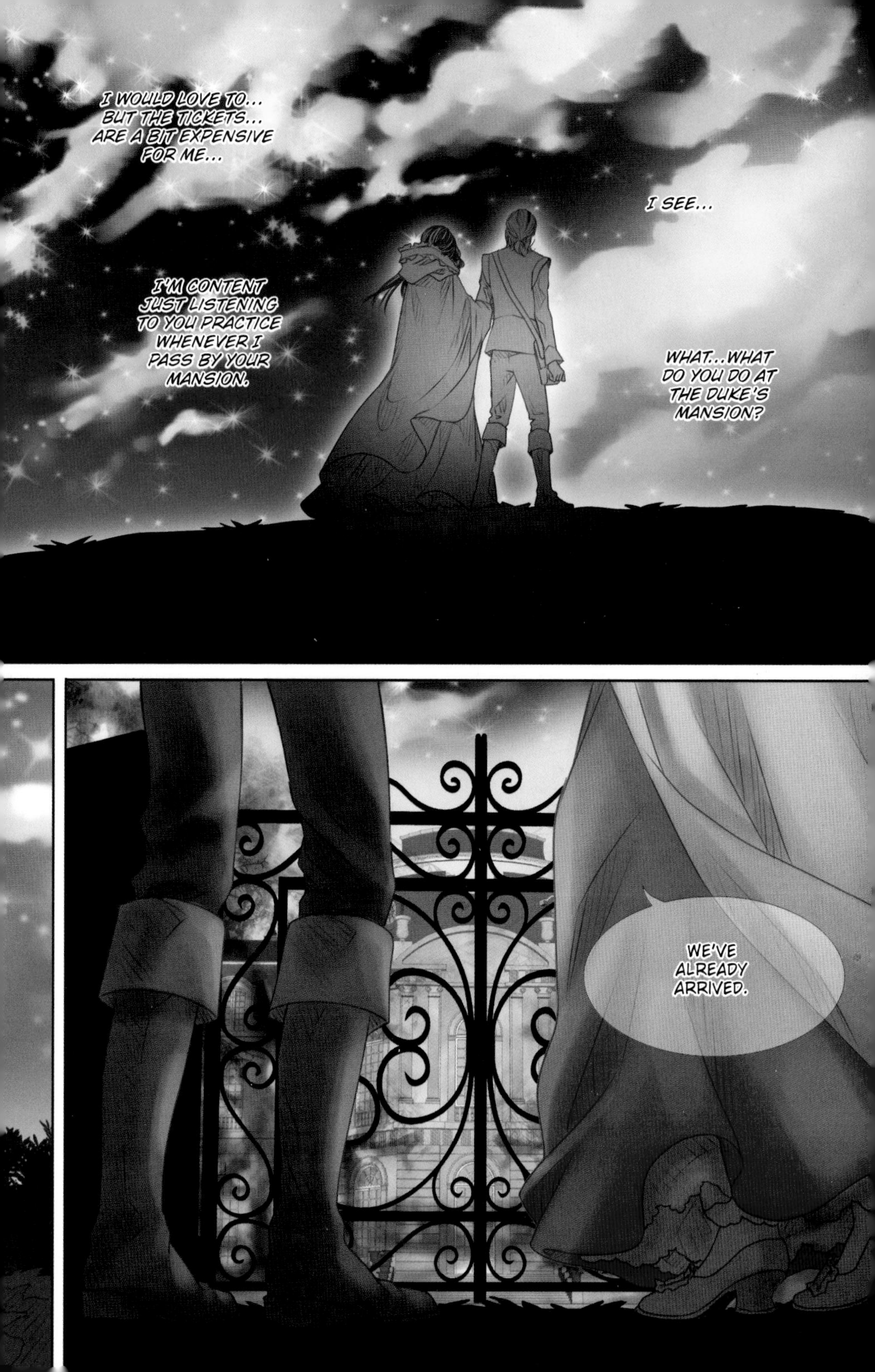
I SEE...
I WOULD LOVE TO... BUT THE TICKETS... ARE A BIT EXPENSIVE FOR ME...
WHAT...WHAT DO YOU DO AT THE DUKE'S MANSION?
I'M CONTENT JUST LISTENING TO YOU PRACTICE WHENEVER I PASS BY YOUR MANSION.
WE'VE ALREADY ARRIVED.

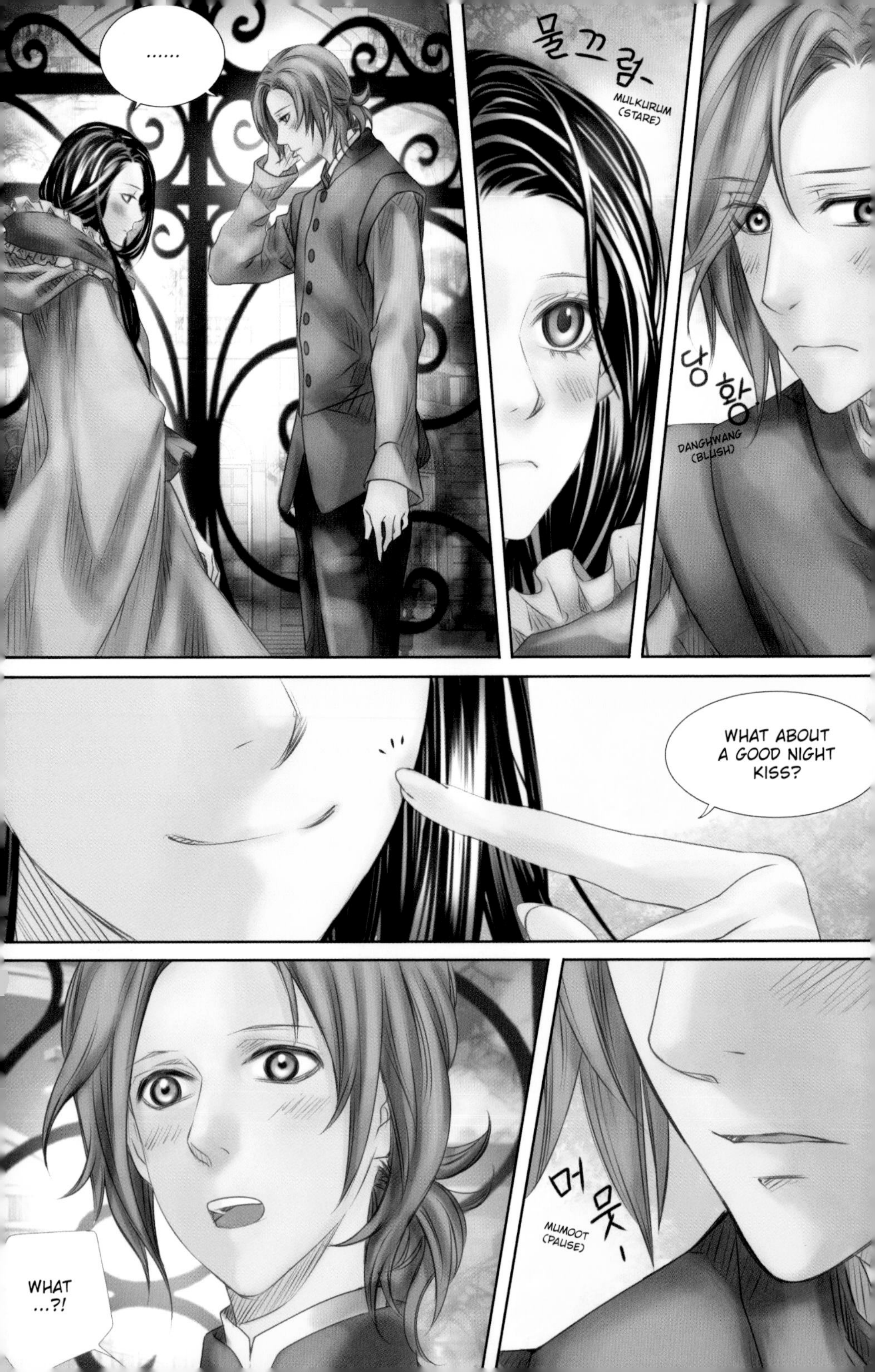
......
물끄럼
MULKURUM
(STARE)
당황
DANGHWANG
(BLUSH)
WHAT ABOUT A GOOD NIGHT KISS?
WHAT ...?!
머뭇
MUMOOT
(PAUSE)

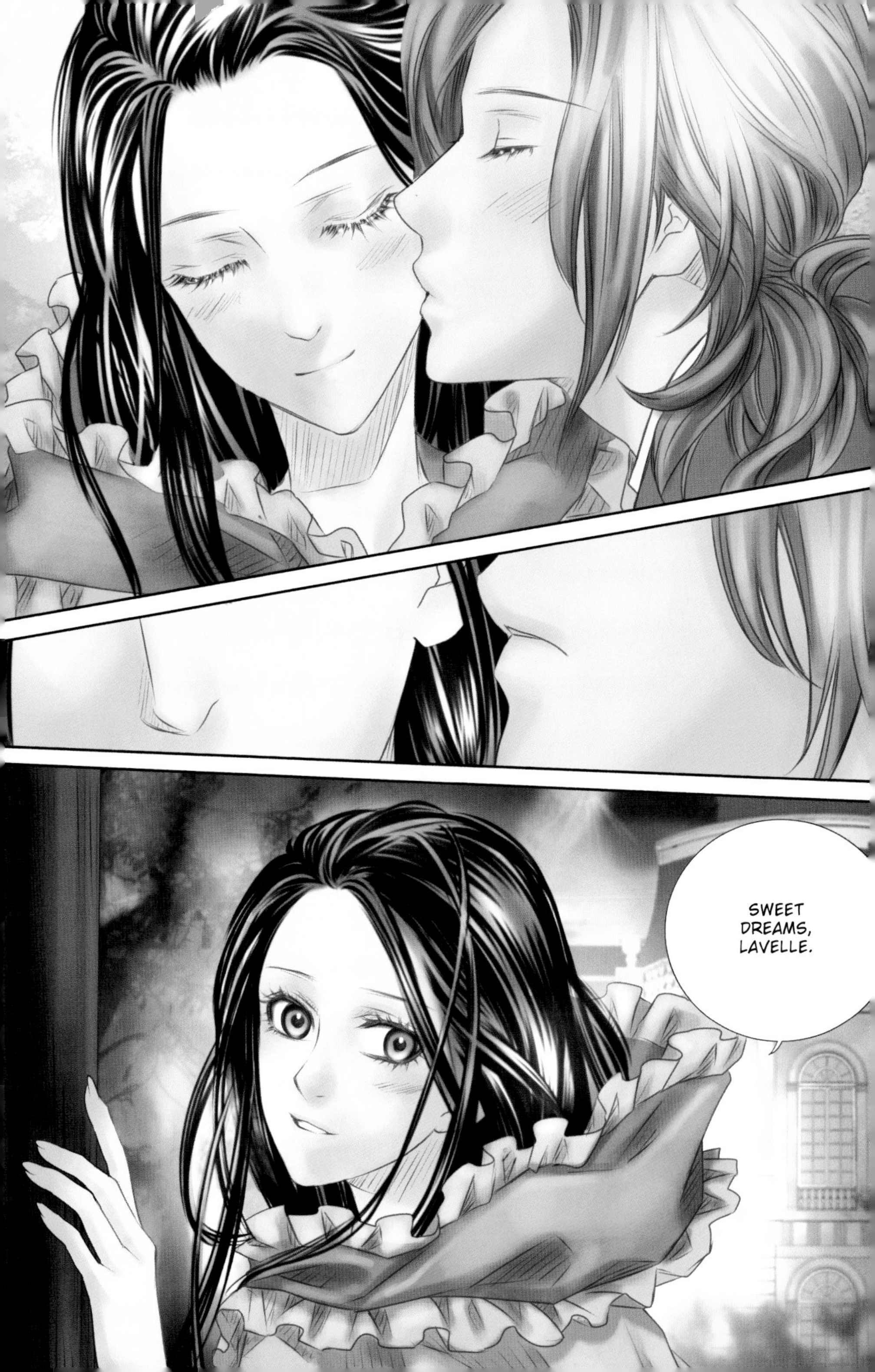
SWEET DREAMS, LAVELLE.

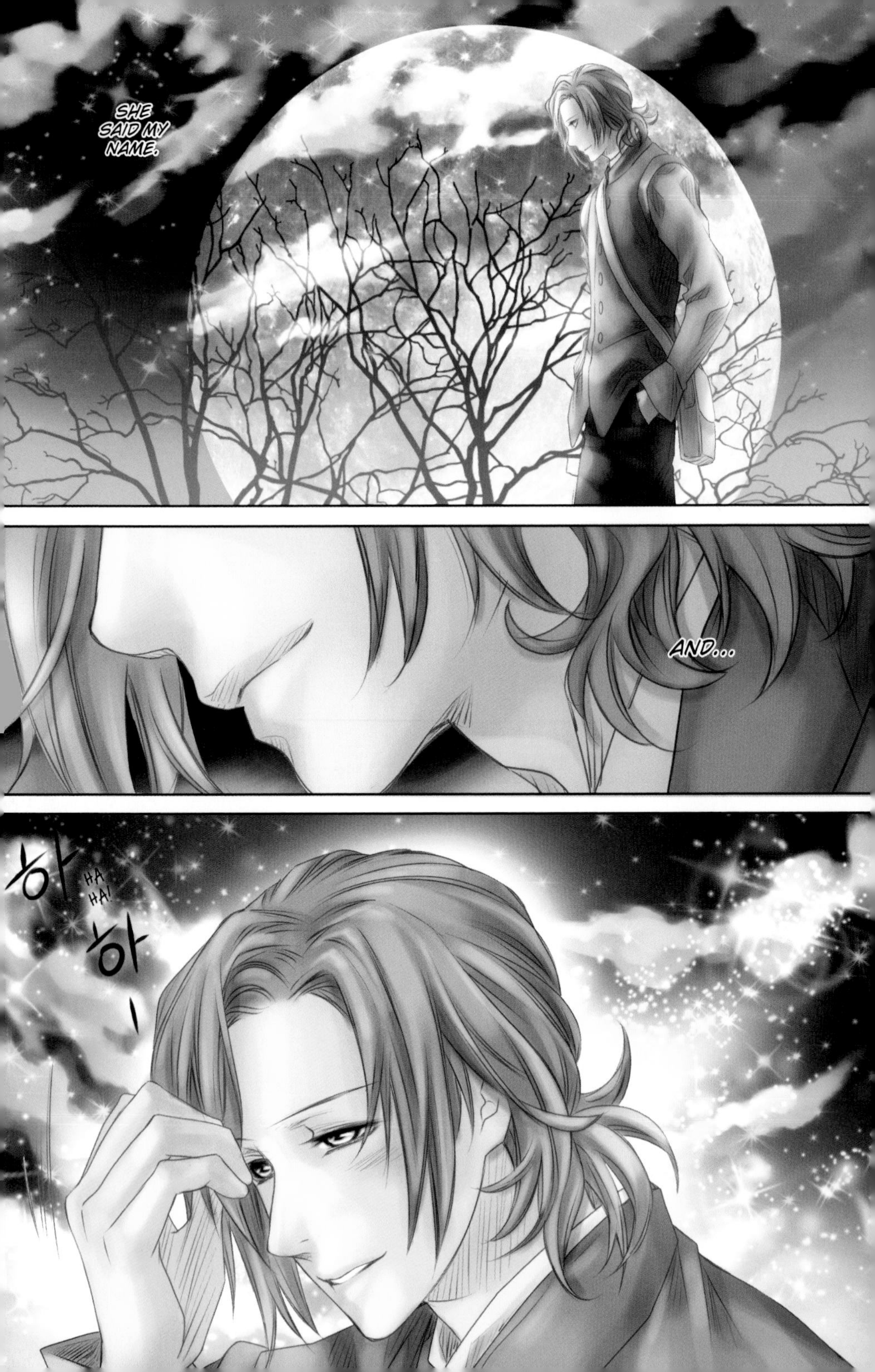
SHE SAID MY NAME.
AND...
하하-
HA HA!

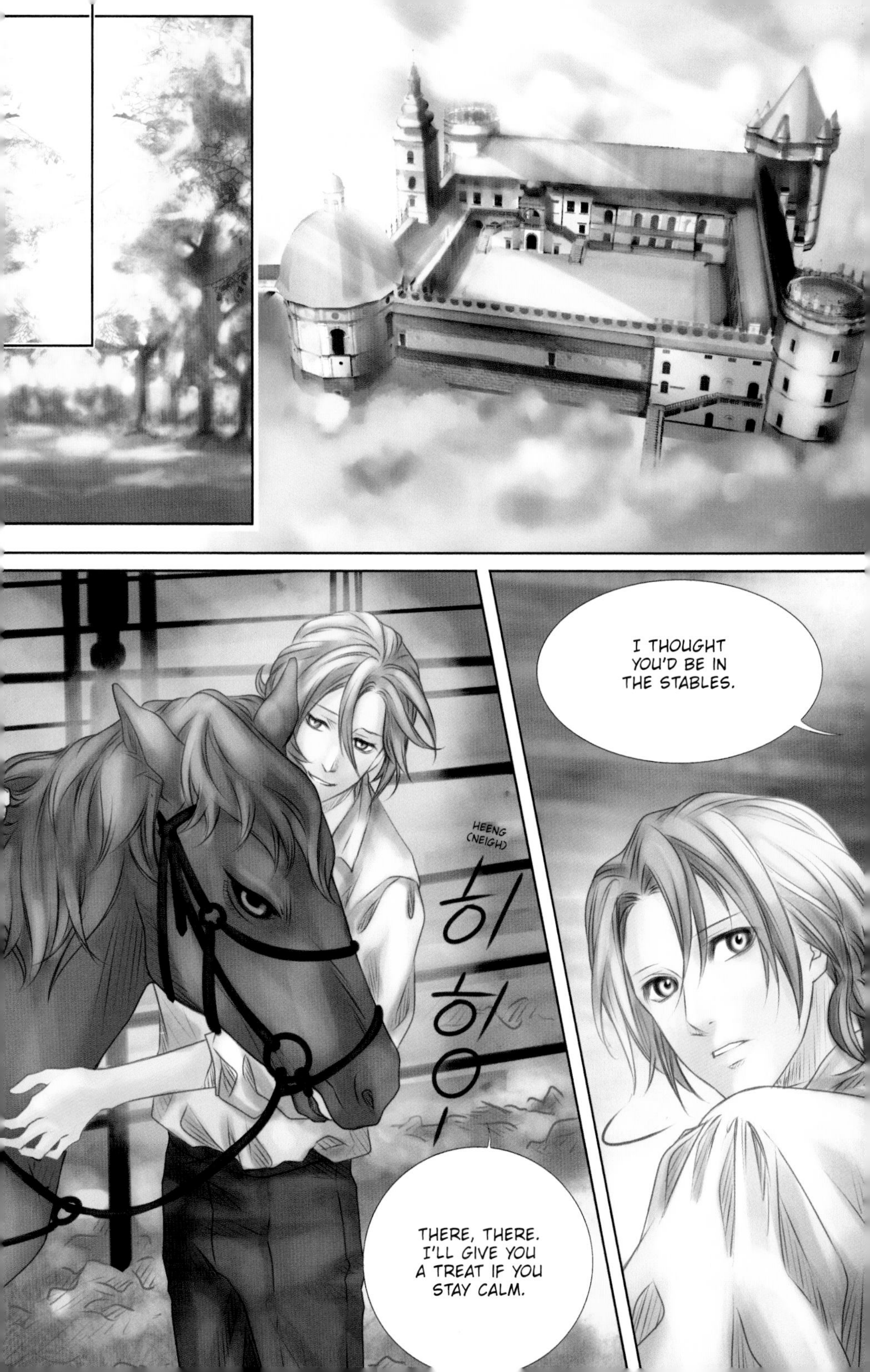
I THOUGHT YOU'D BE IN THE STABLES.
HEENG (NEIGH)
히히이-
THERE, THERE. I'LL GIVE YOU A TREAT IF YOU STAY CALM.

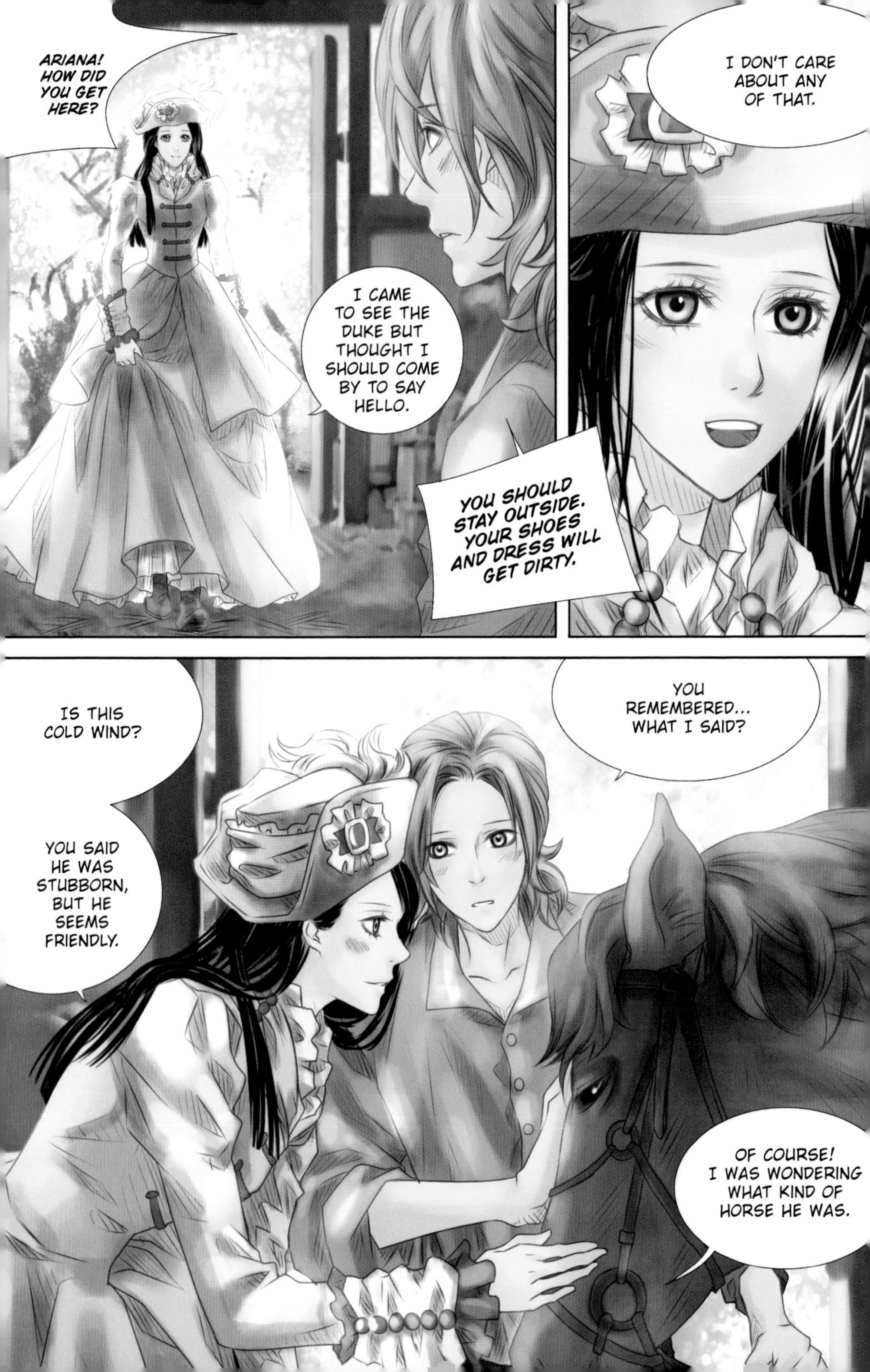
ARIANA! HOW DID YOU GET HERE?
I CAME TO SEE THE DUKE BUT THOUGHT I SHOULD COME BY TO SAY HELLO.
YOU SHOULD STAY OUTSIDE. YOUR SHOES AND DRESS WILL GET DIRTY.
I DON'T CARE ABOUT ANY OF THAT.
IS THIS COLD WIND?
YOU SAID HE WAS STUBBORN, BUT HE SEEMS FRIENDLY.
YOU REMEMBERED... WHAT I SAID?
OF COURSE! I WAS WONDERING WHAT KIND OF HORSE HE WAS.

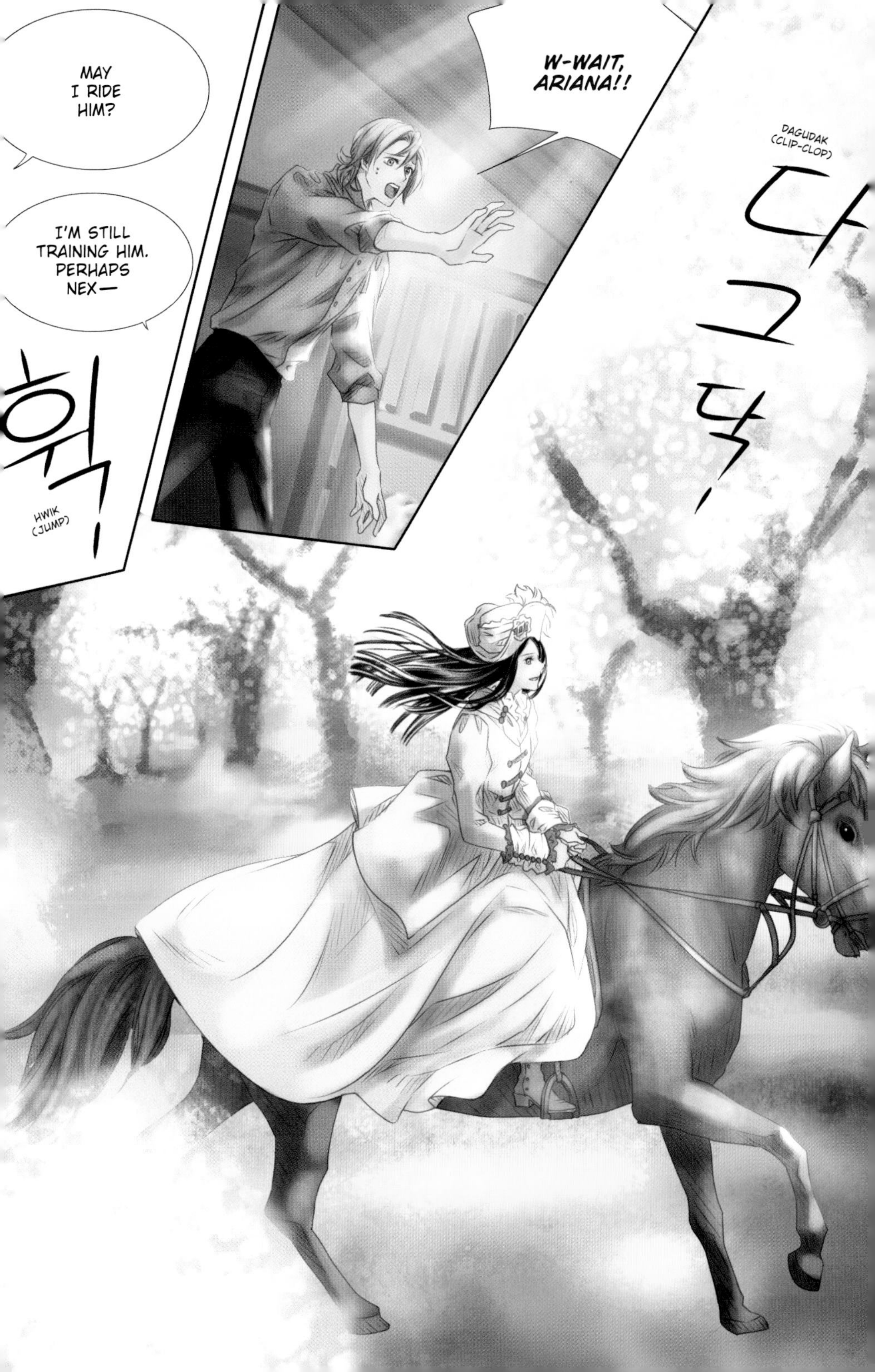

MAY I RIDE HIM?
I'M STILL TRAINING HIM. PERHAPS NEX—
훽!
HWIK (JUMP)
W-WAIT, ARIANA!!
다그닥!
DAGUDAK (CLIP-CLOP)

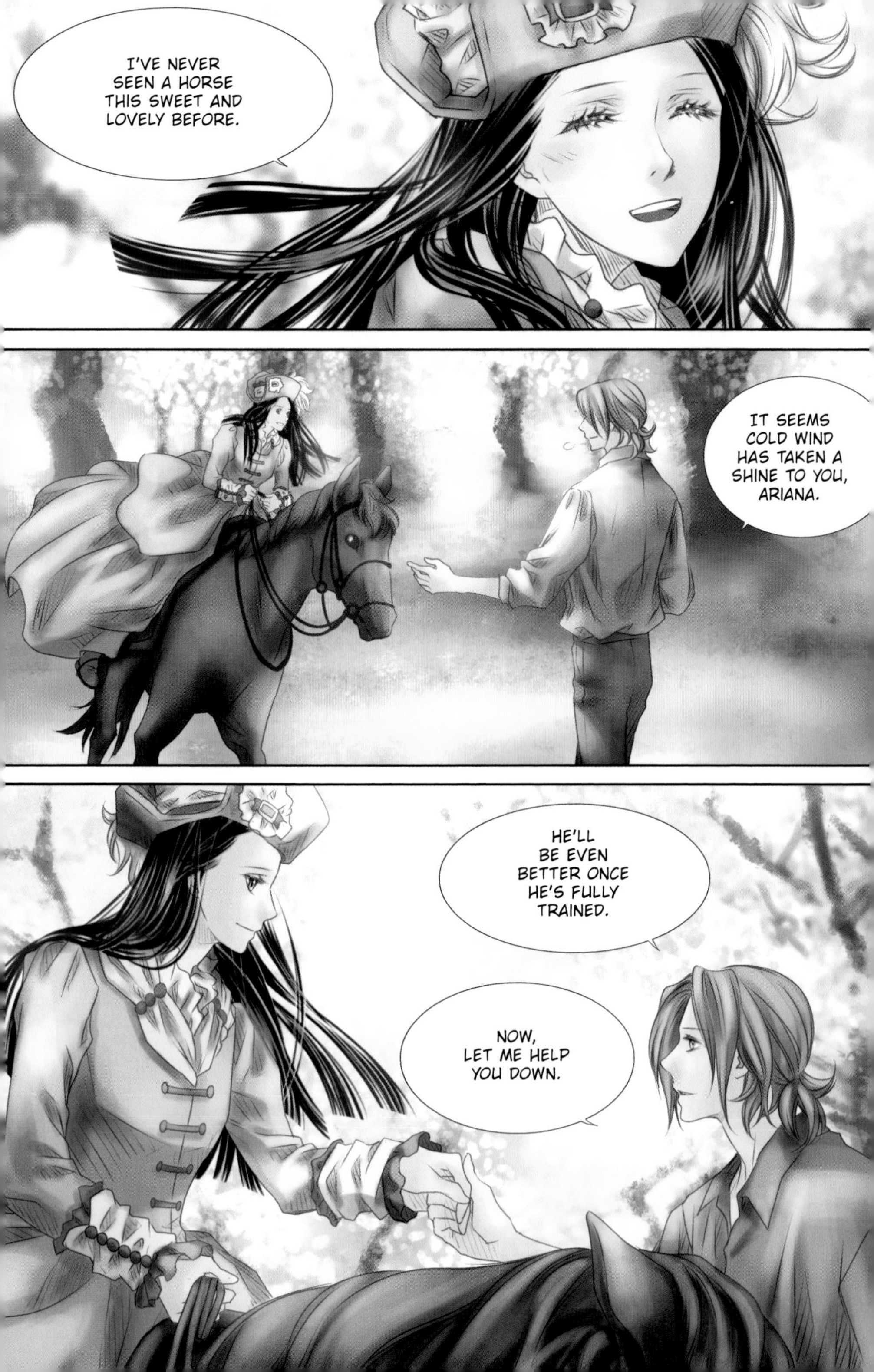
I'VE NEVER SEEN A HORSE THIS SWEET AND LOVELY BEFORE.
IT SEEMS COLD WIND HAS TAKEN A SHINE TO YOU, ARIANA.
HE'LL BE EVEN BETTER ONCE HE'S FULLY TRAINED.
NOW, LET ME HELP YOU DOWN.

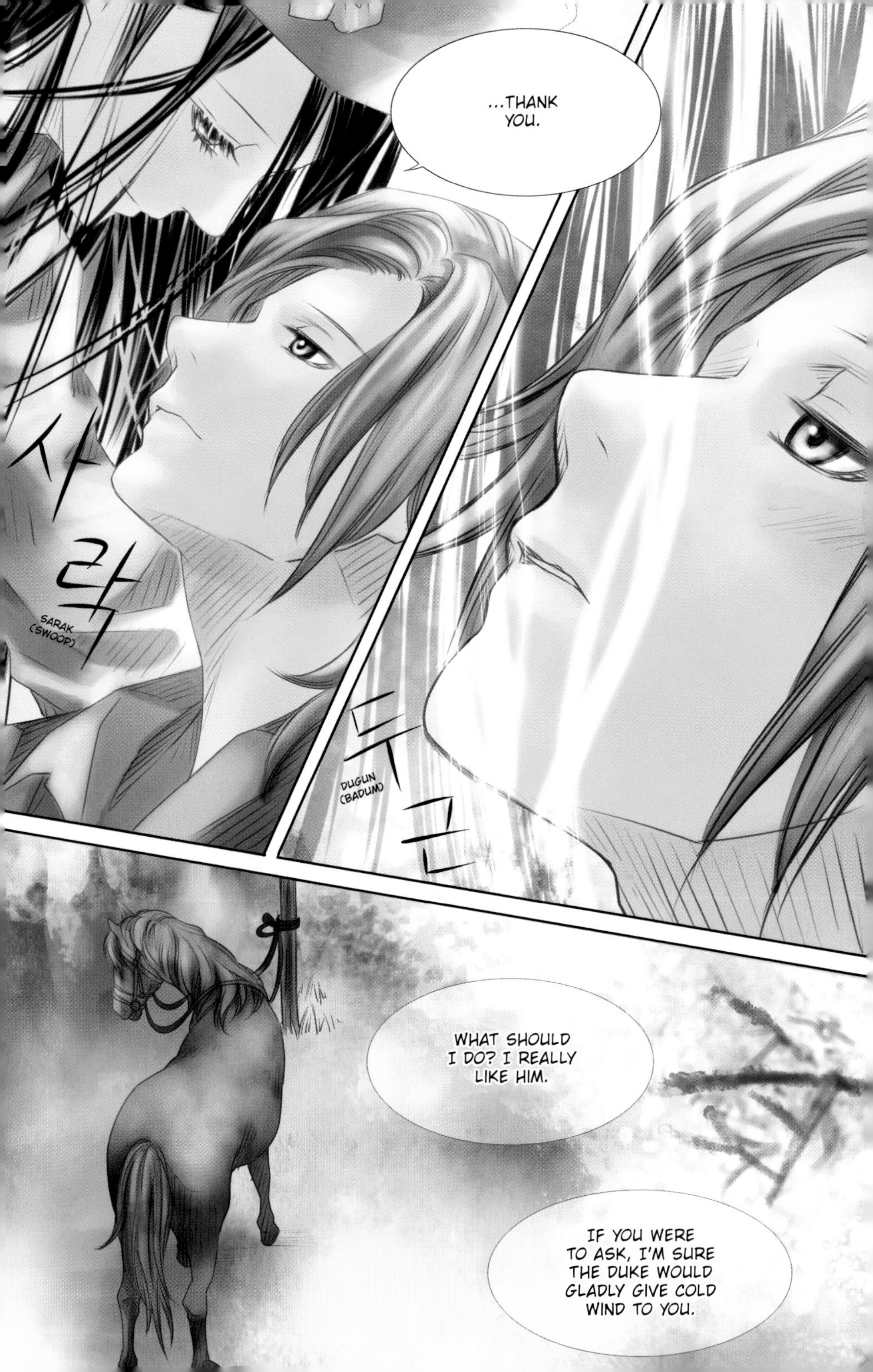
...THANK YOU.
SARAK (SWOOP)
DUGUN (BADUM)
WHAT SHOULD I DO? I REALLY LIKE HIM.
IF YOU WERE TO ASK, I'M SURE THE DUKE WOULD GLADLY GIVE COLD WIND TO YOU.

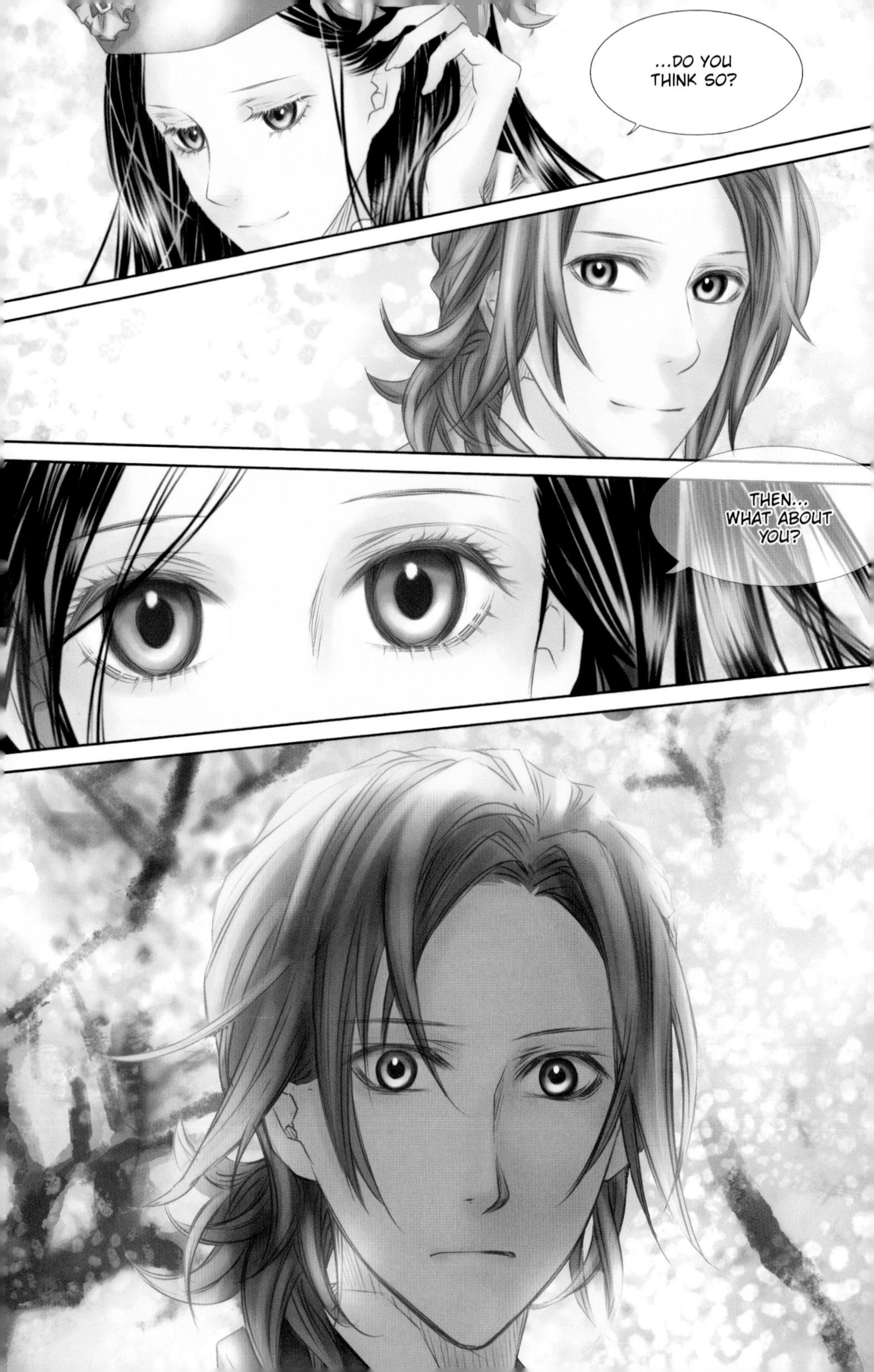
...DO YOU THINK SO?
THEN... WHAT ABOUT YOU?

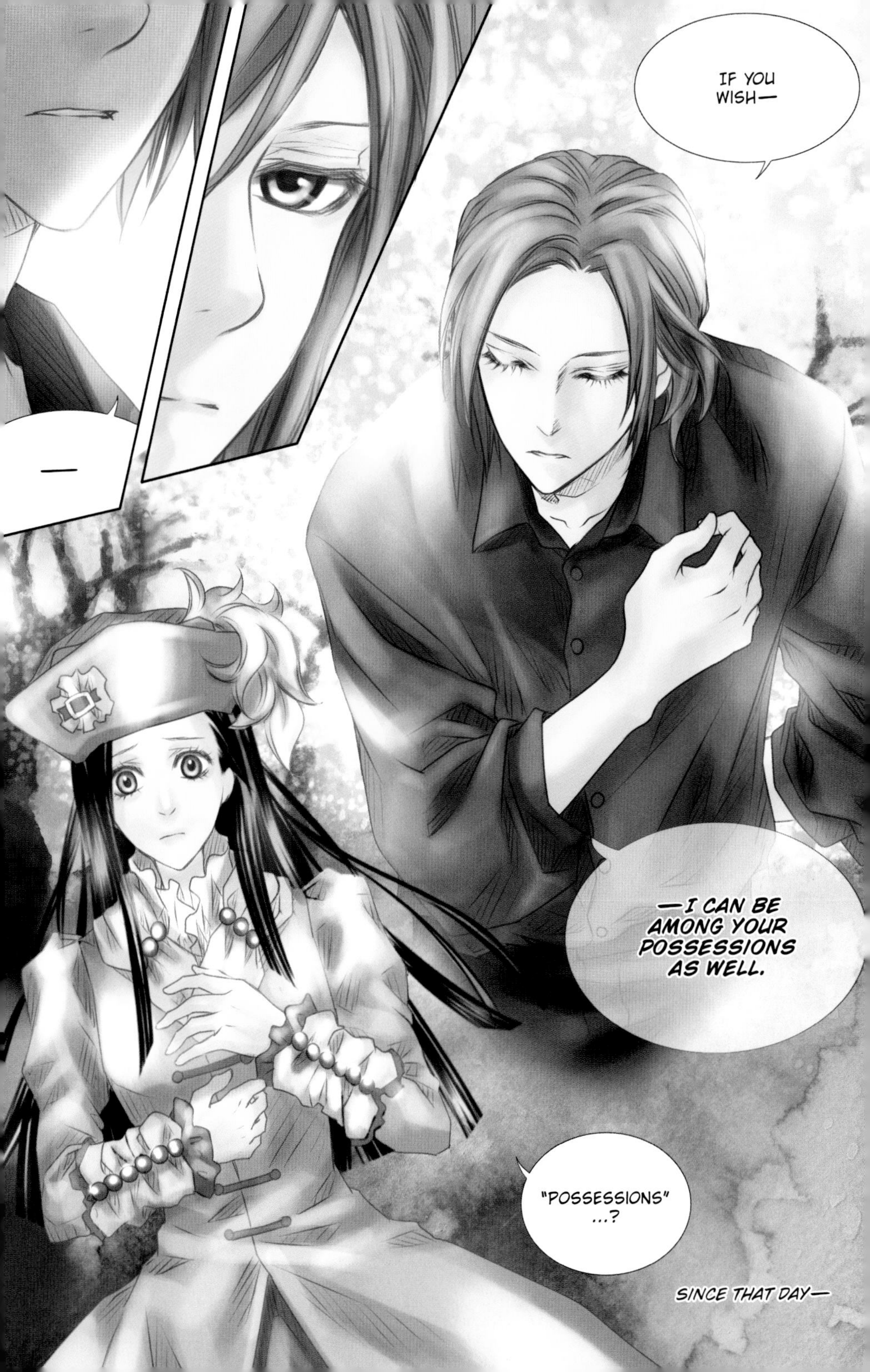
IF YOU WISH—
—
—I CAN BE AMONG YOUR POSSESSIONS AS WELL.
"POSSESSIONS" ...?
SINCE THAT DAY—

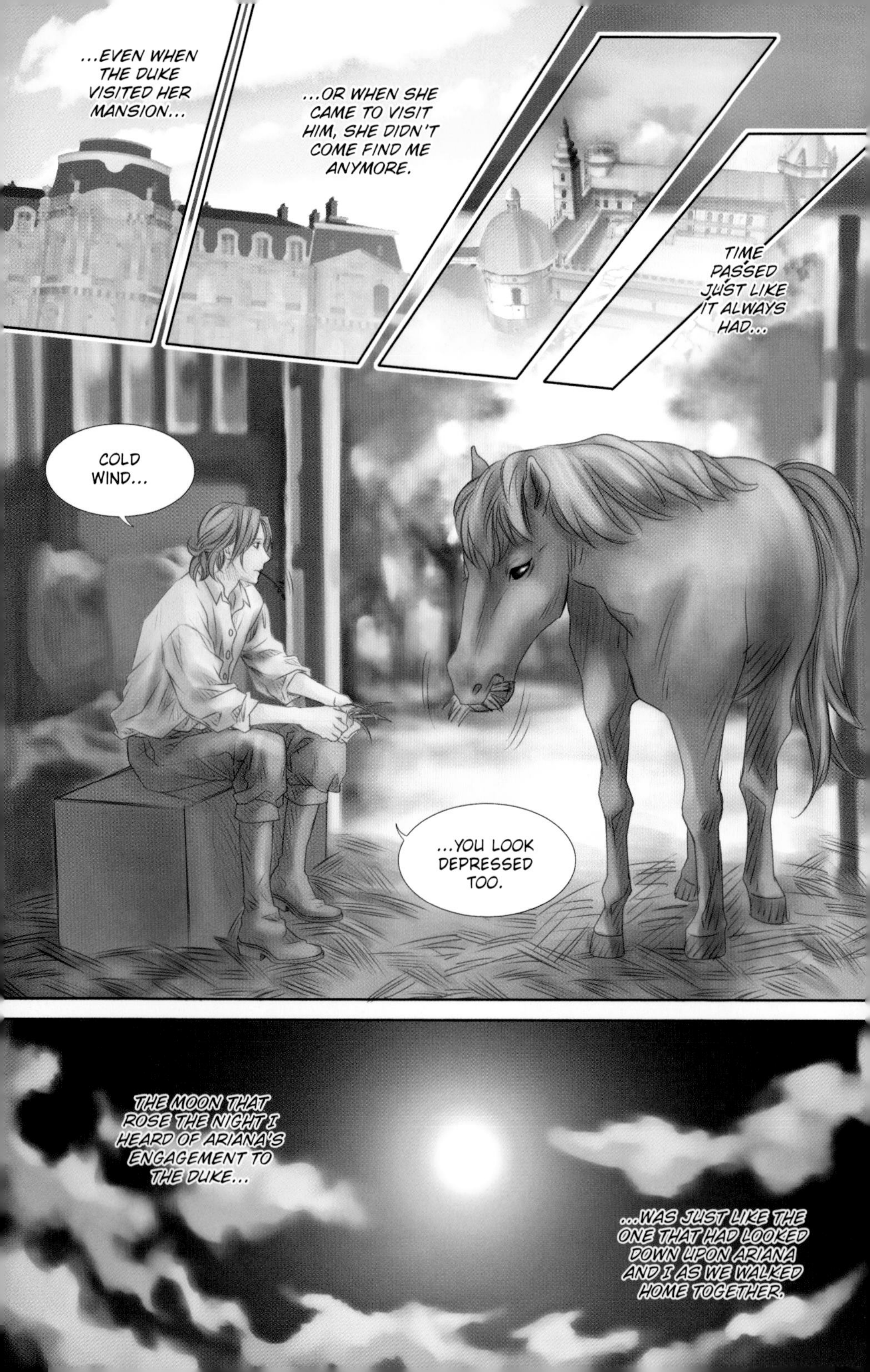
...EVEN WHEN THE DUKE VISITED HER MANSION...
...OR WHEN SHE CAME TO VISIT HIM, SHE DIDN'T COME FIND ME ANYMORE.
TIME PASSED JUST LIKE IT ALWAYS HAD...
COLD WIND...
...YOU LOOK DEPRESSED TOO.
THE MOON THAT ROSE THE NIGHT I HEARD OF ARIANA'S ENGAGEMENT TO THE DUKE...
...WAS JUST LIKE THE ONE THAT HAD LOOKED DOWN UPON ARIANA AND I AS WE WALKED HOME TOGETHER.

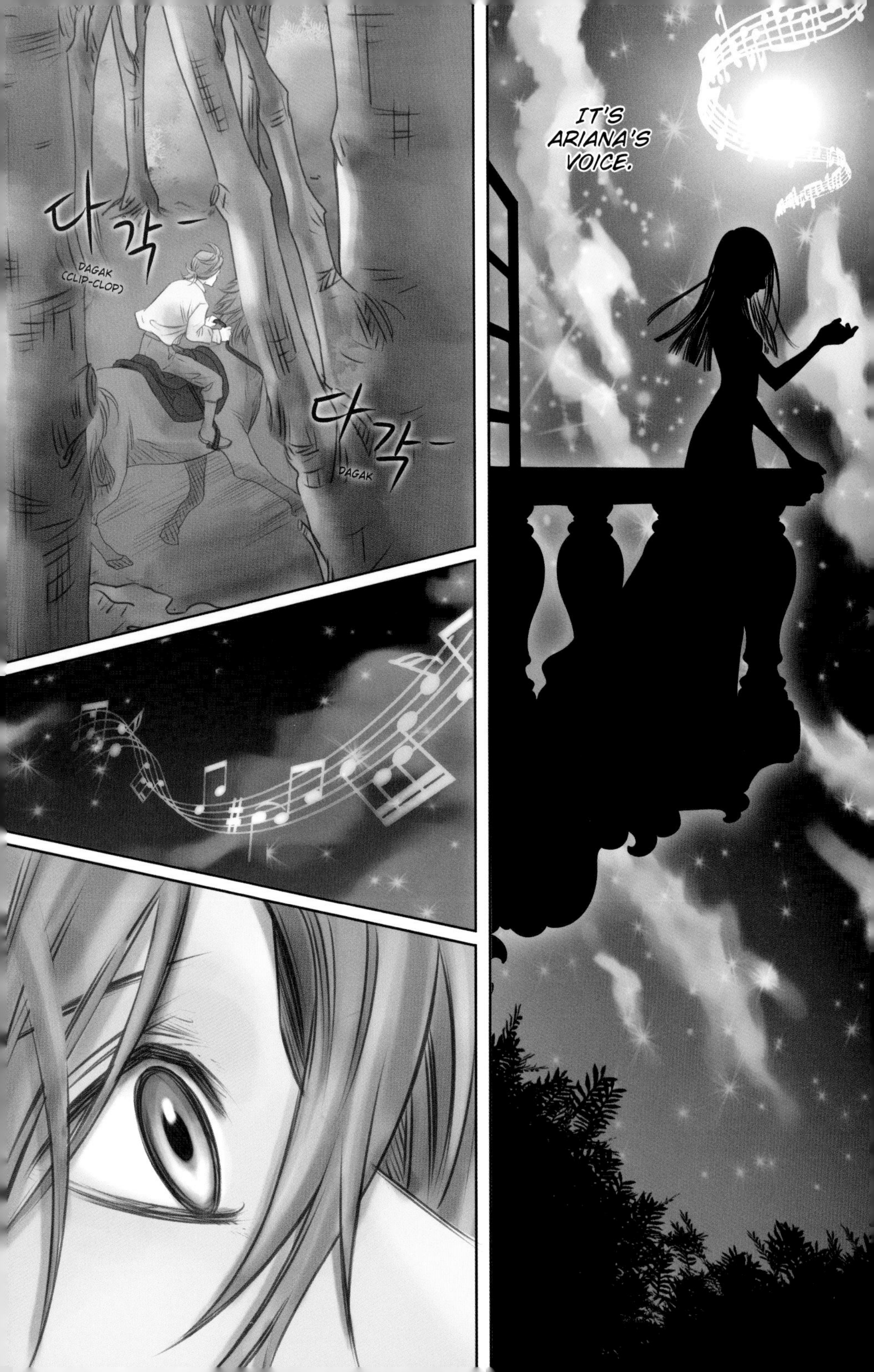
다각 —
DAGAK (CLIP-CLOP)
다각 —
DAGAK
IT'S ARIANA'S VOICE.

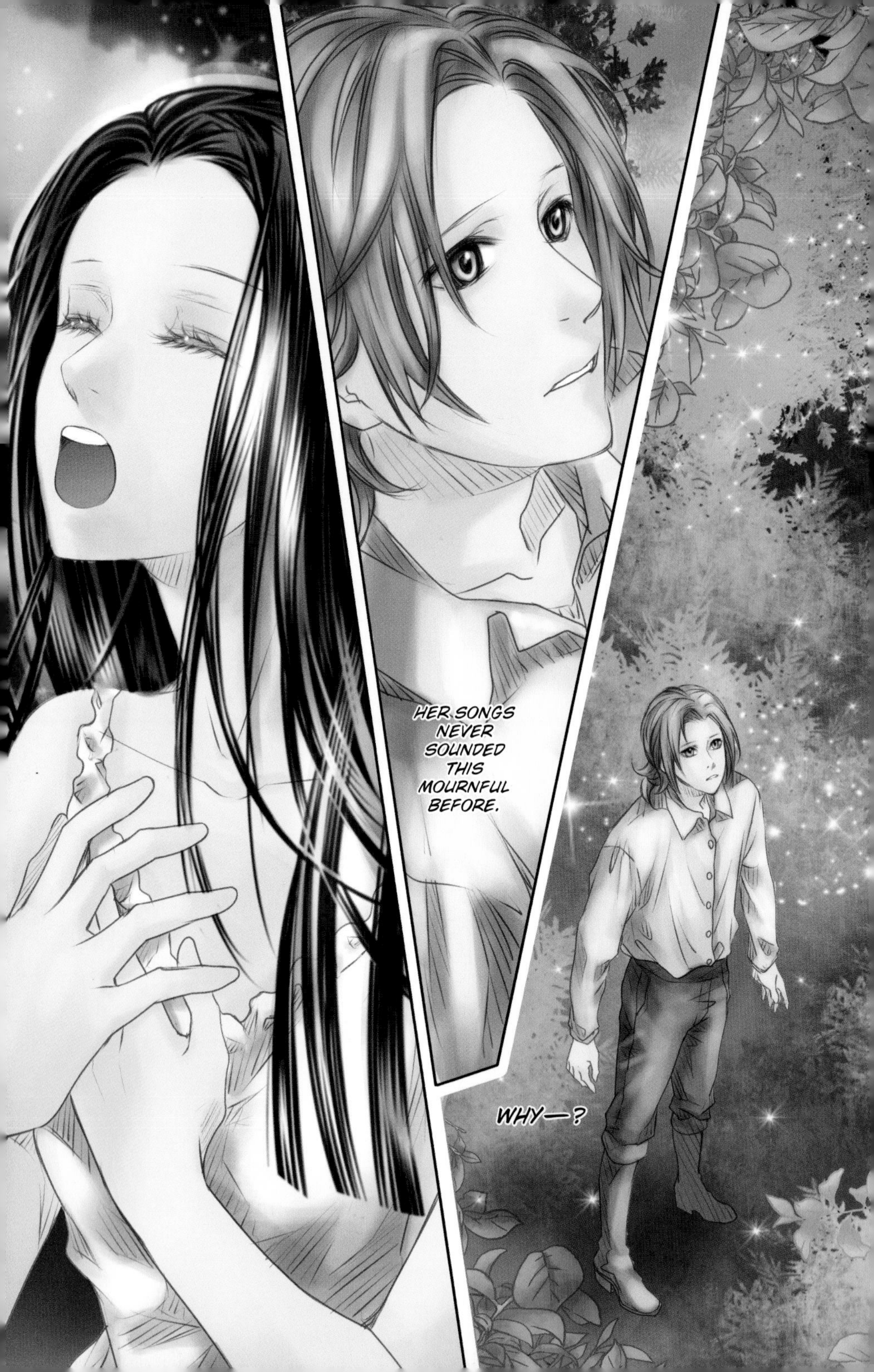
HER SONGS NEVER SOUNDED THIS MOURNFUL BEFORE.
WHY—?

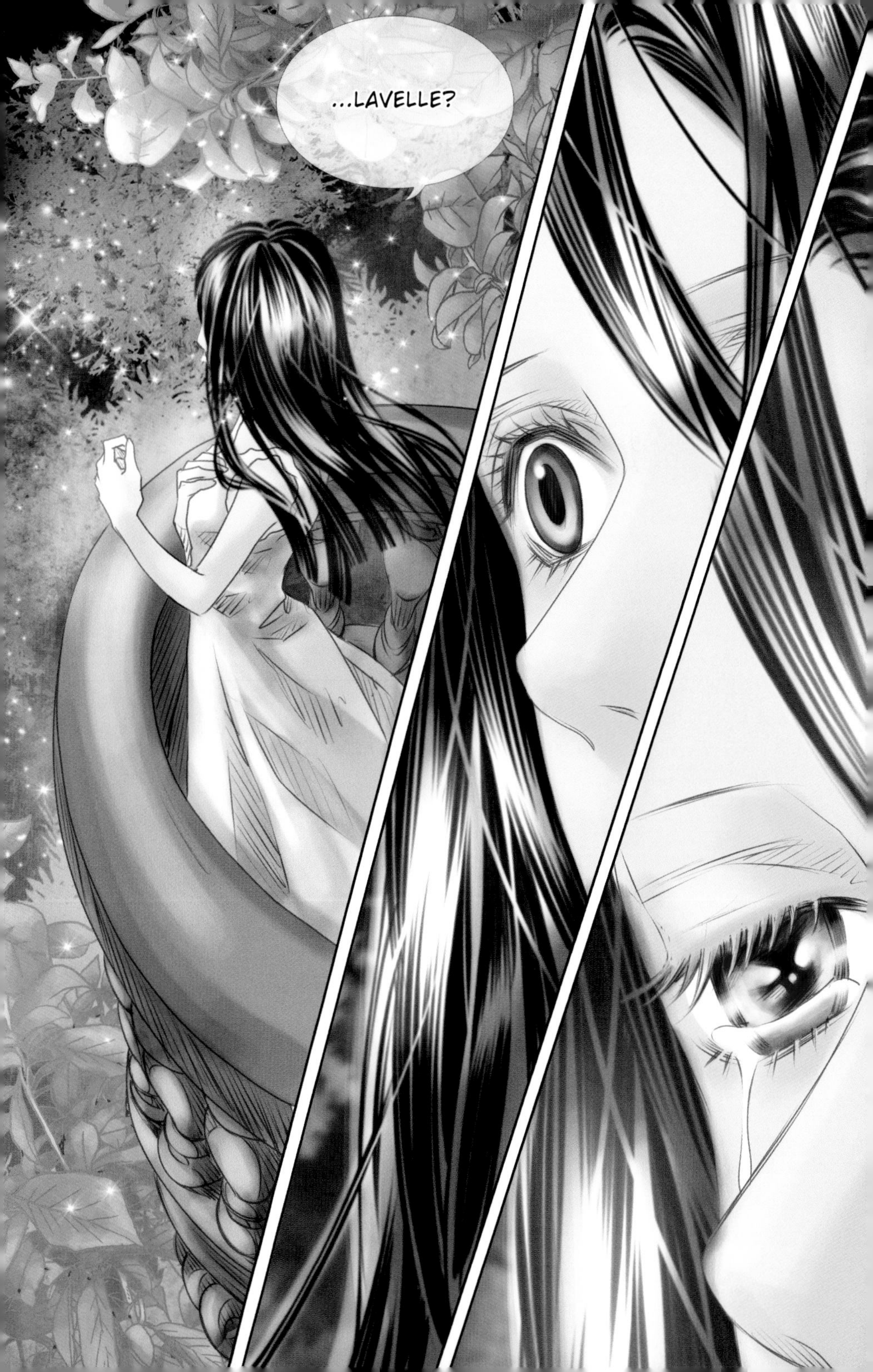
...LAVELLE?

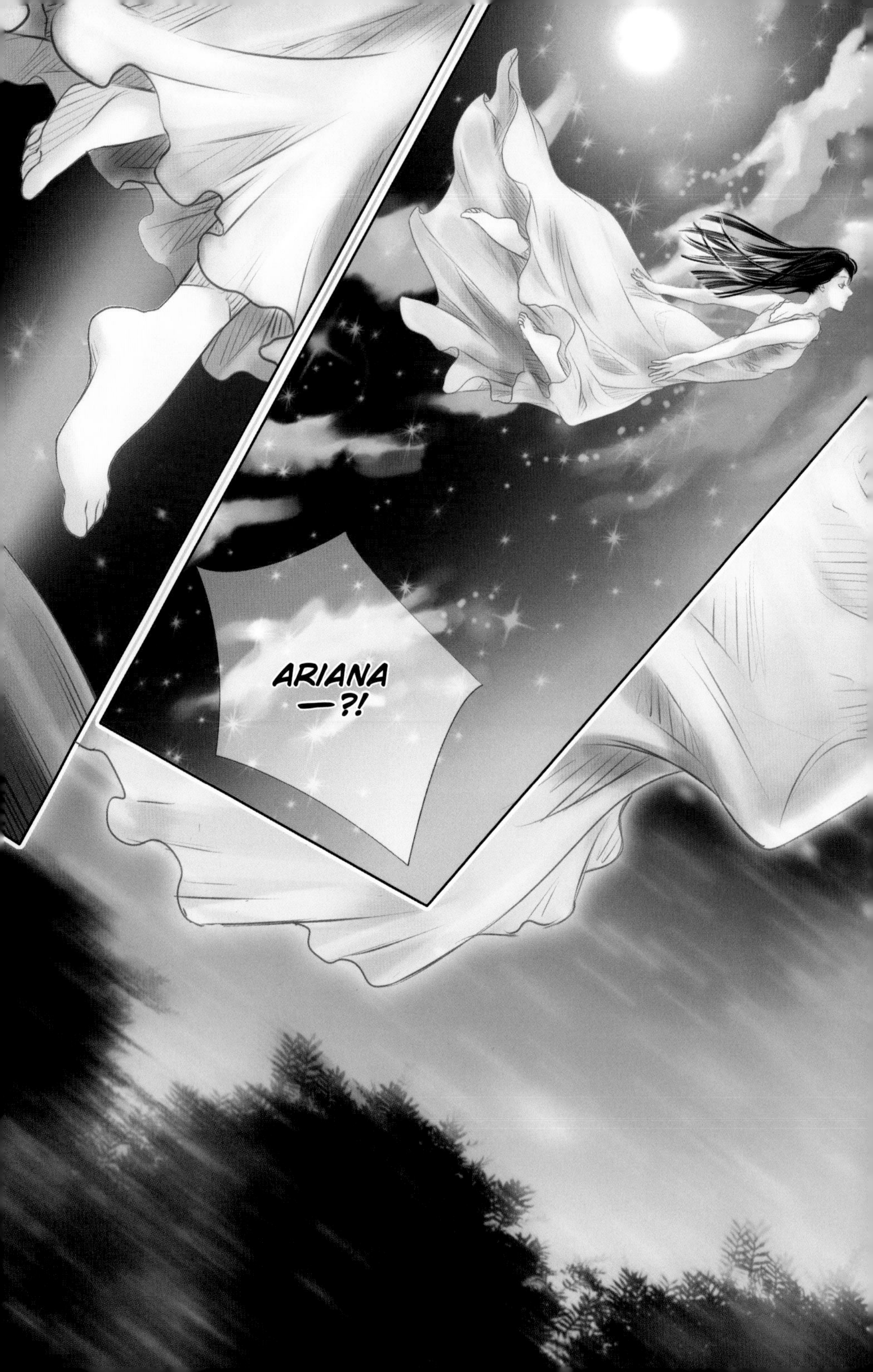
ARIANA —?!

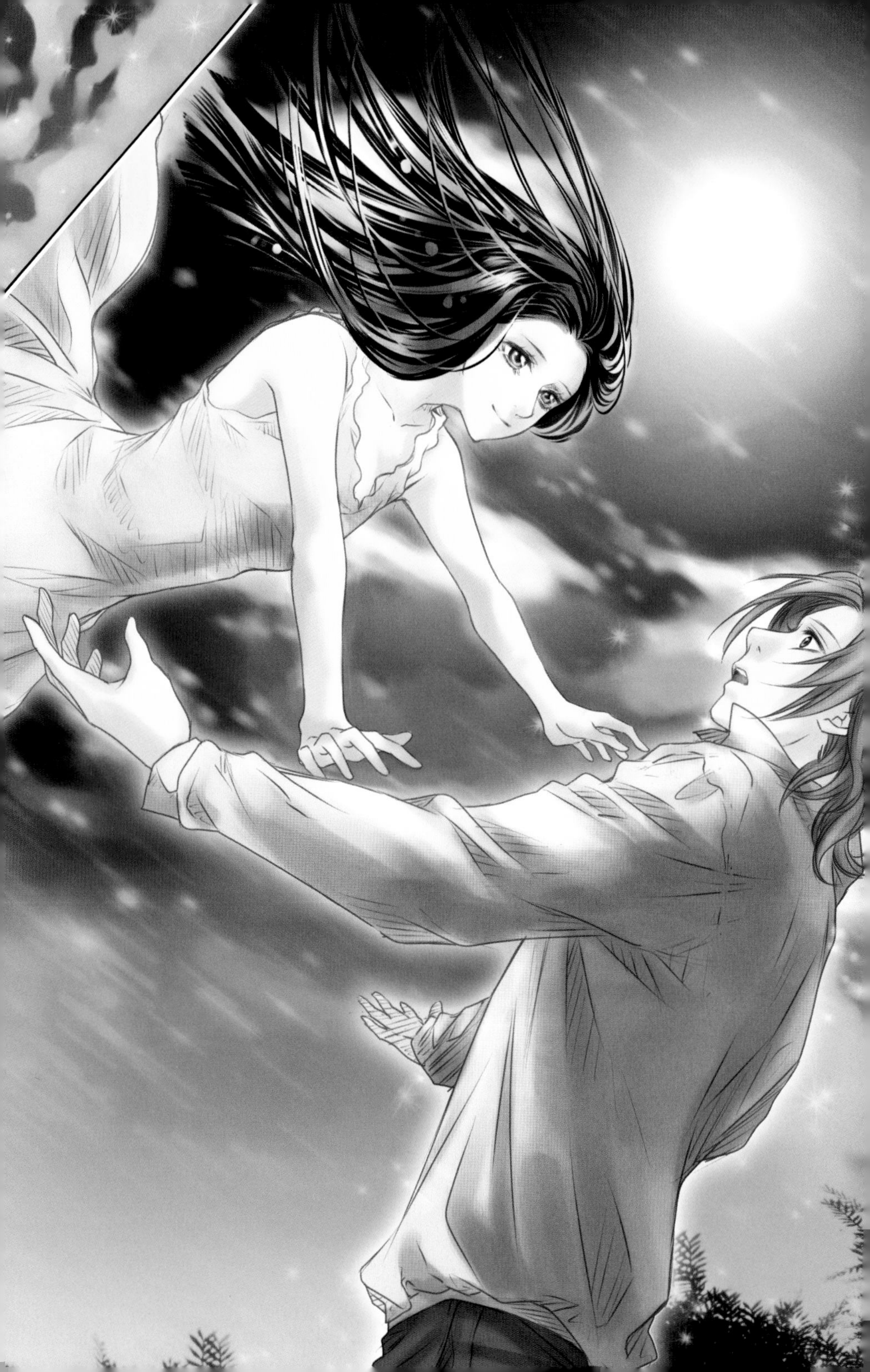

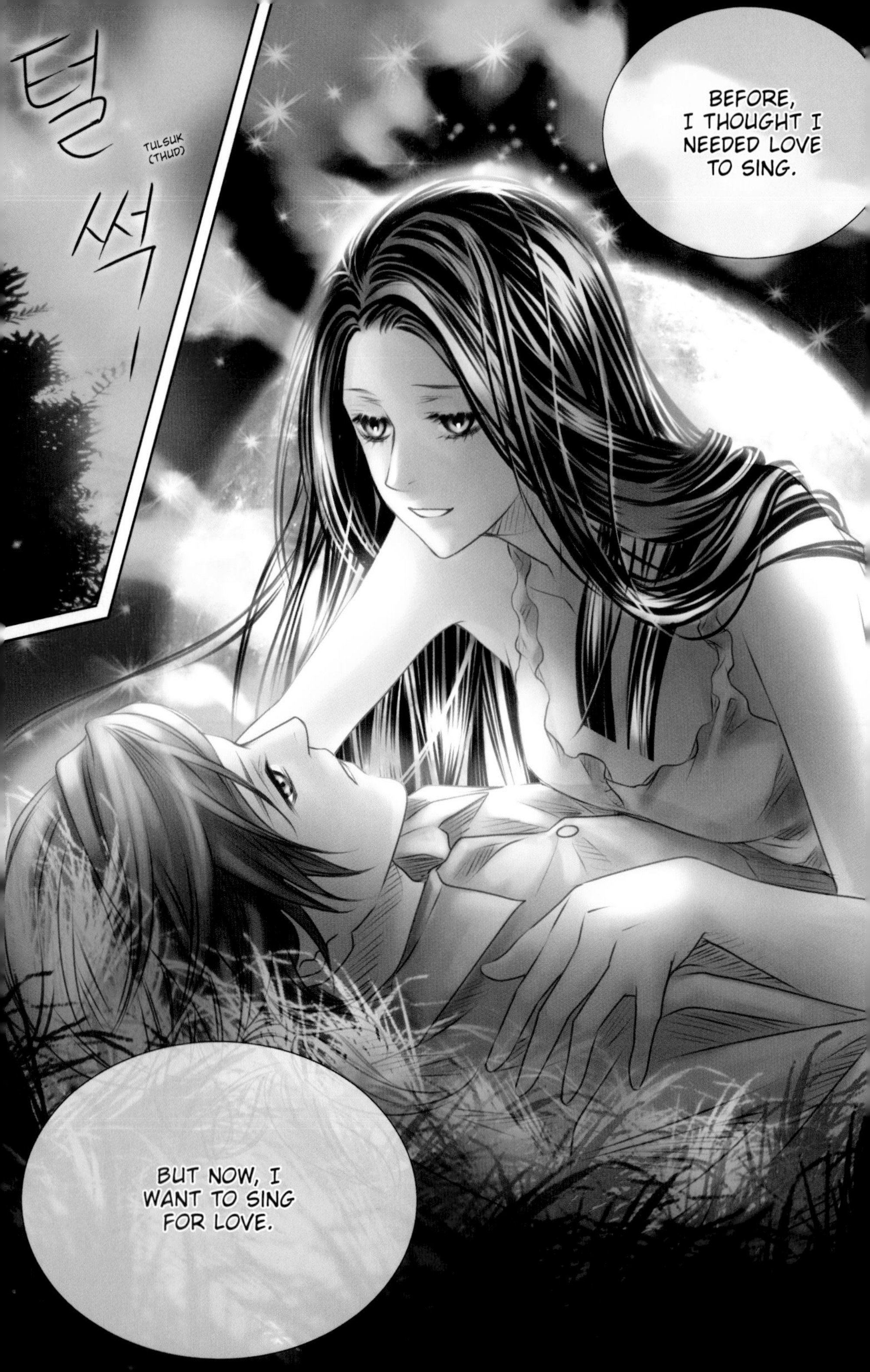
털썩
TULSUK (THUD)
BEFORE, I THOUGHT I NEEDED LOVE TO SING.
BUT NOW, I WANT TO SING FOR LOVE.

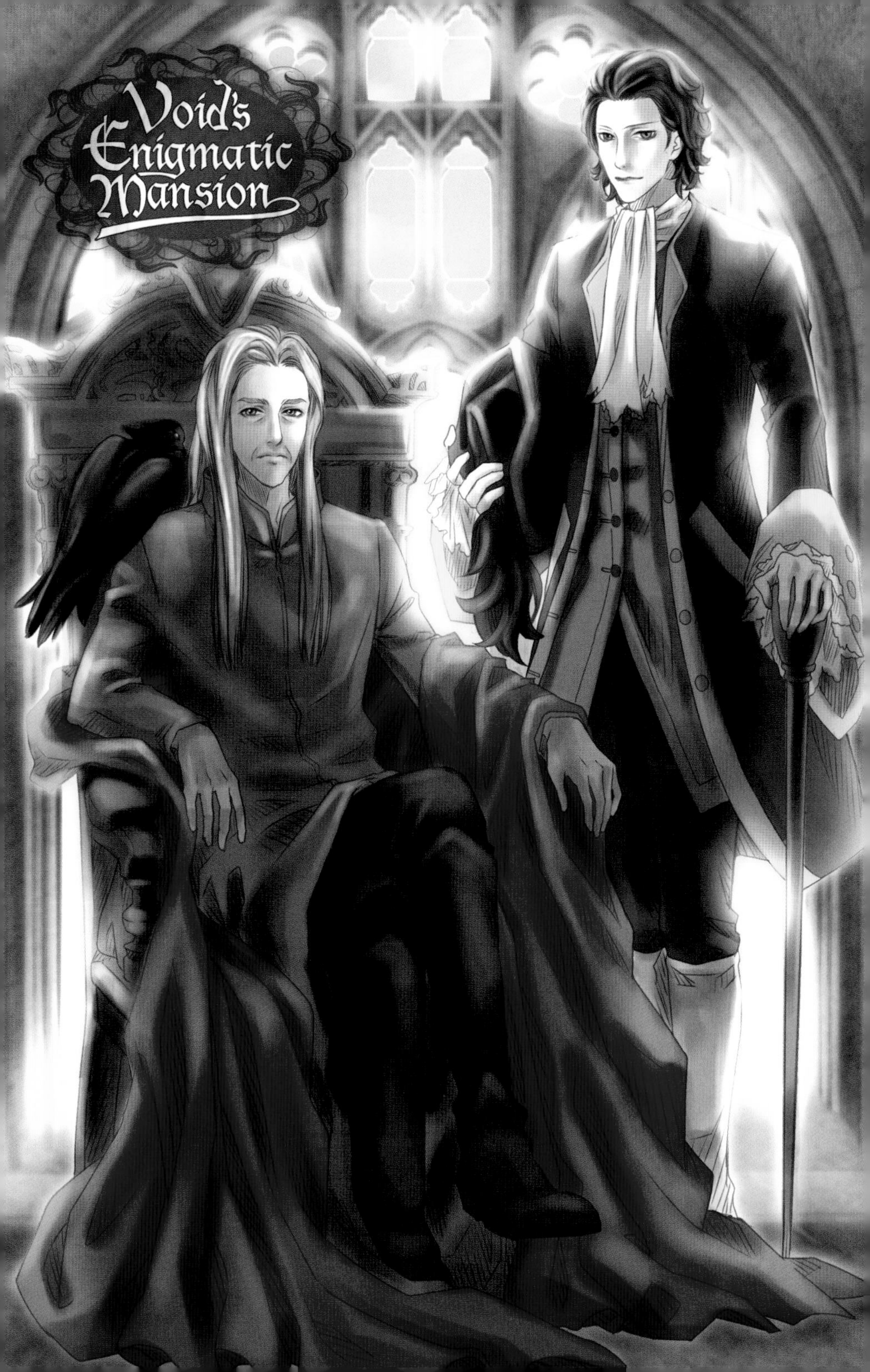
Void's Enigmatic Mansion

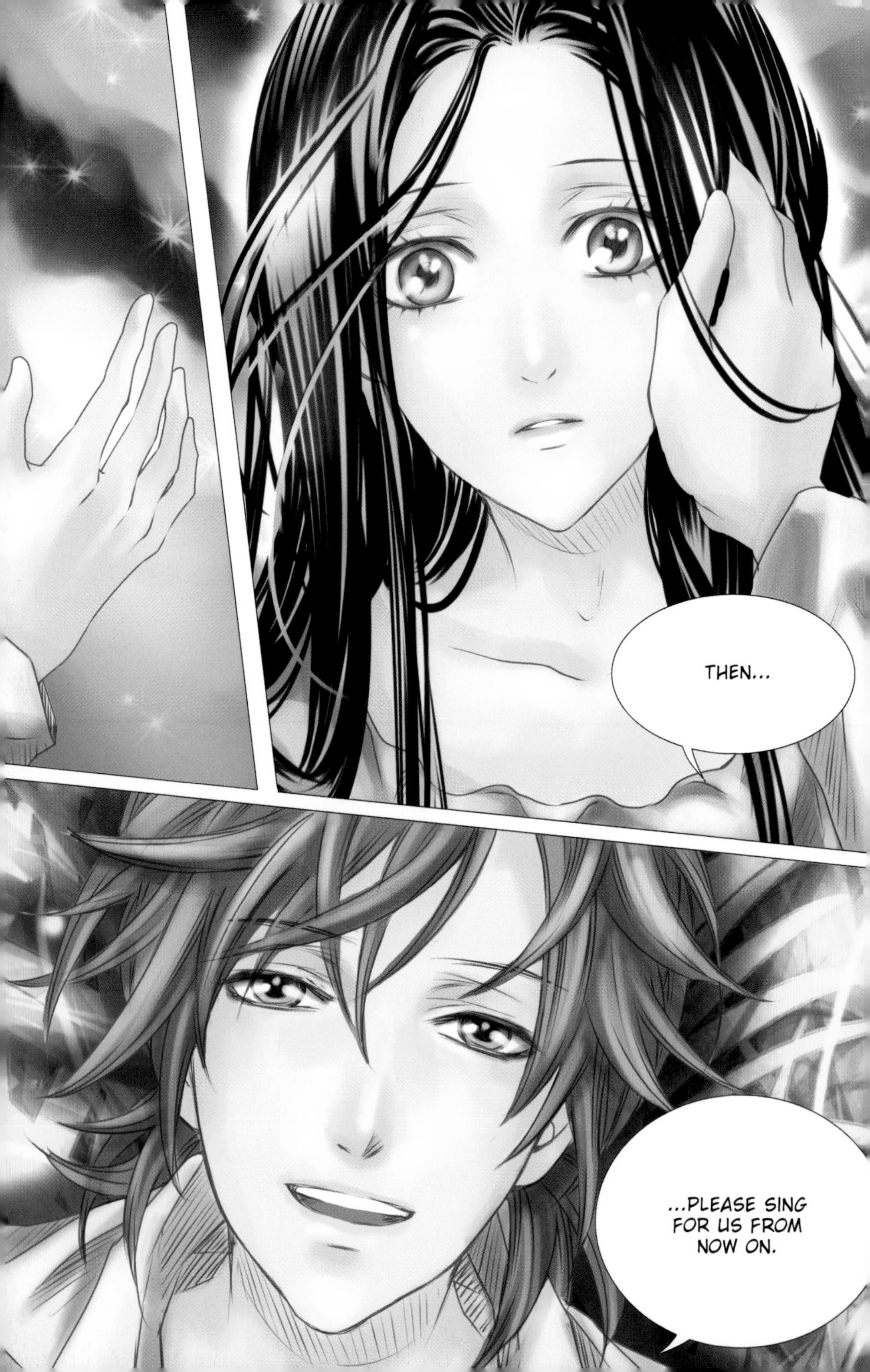
THEN...
...PLEASE SING FOR US FROM NOW ON.

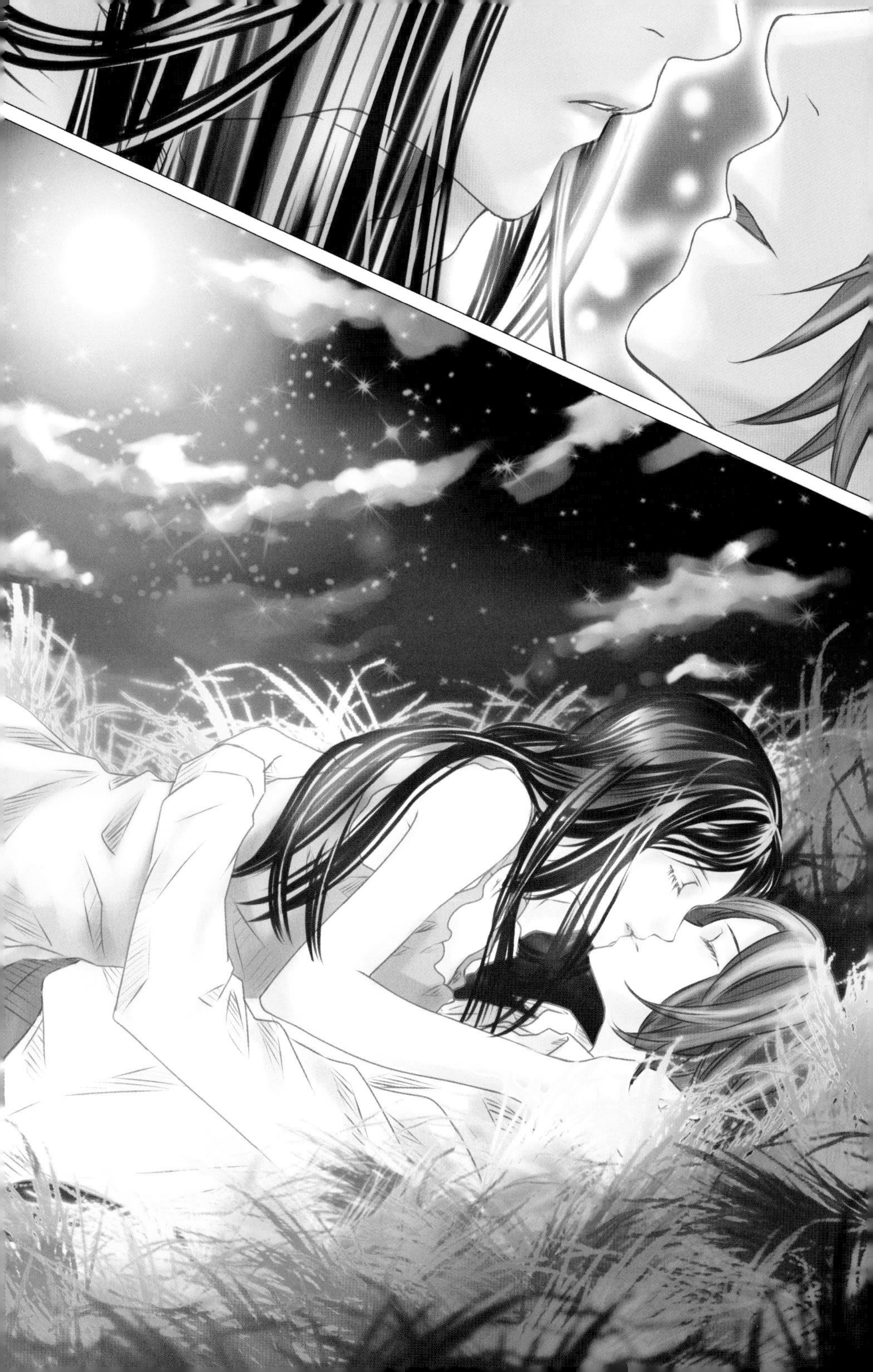

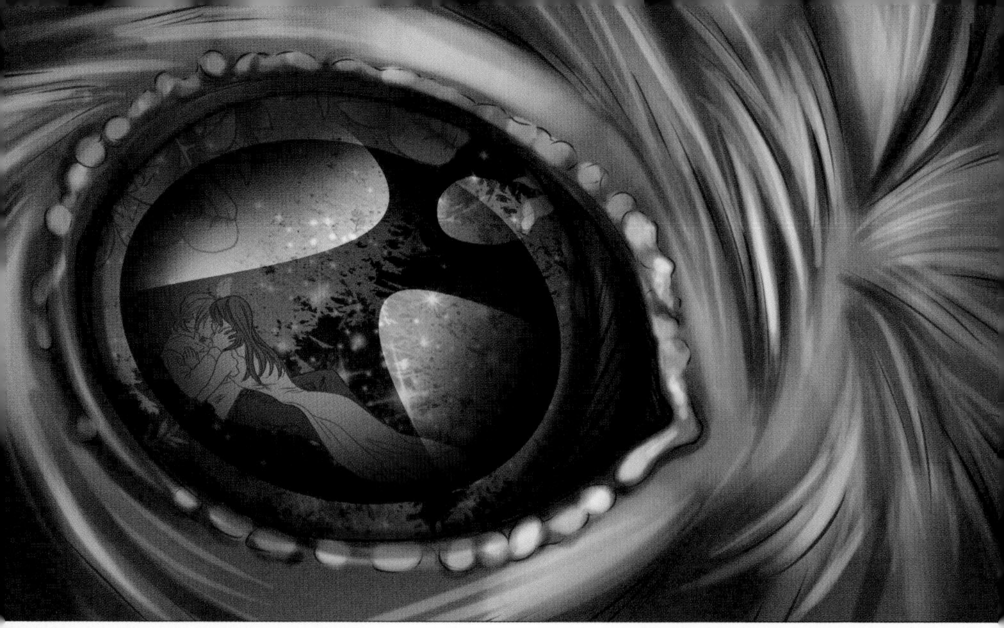

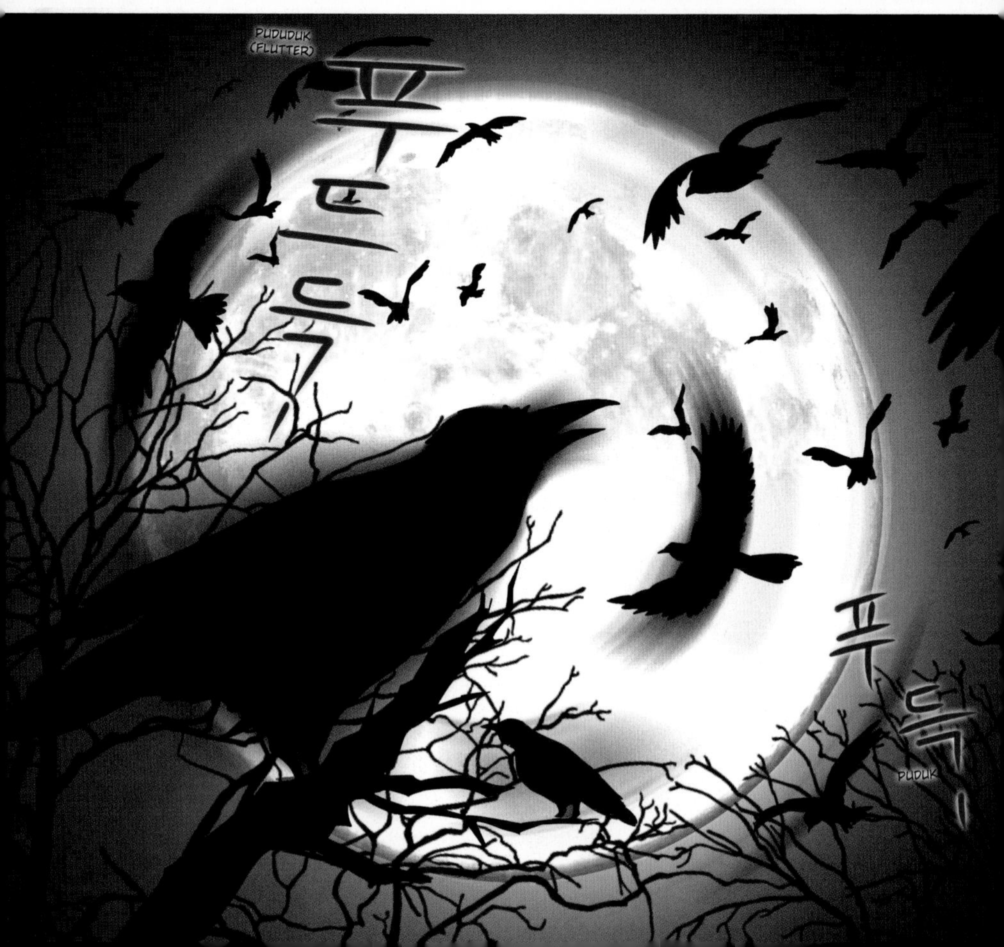
PUDUDUK (FLUTTER)
PUDUK

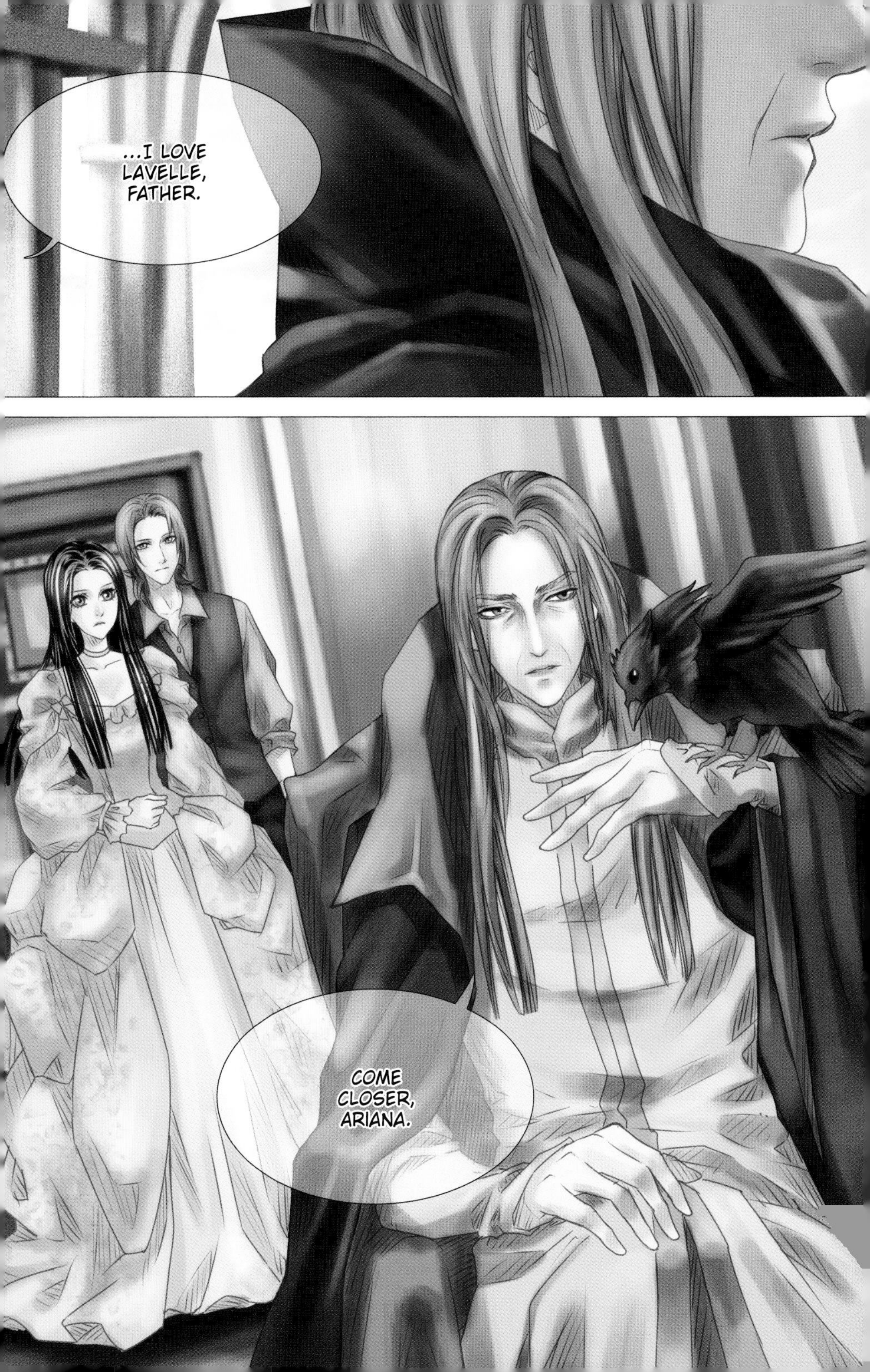
...I LOVE LAVELLE, FATHER.
COME CLOSER, ARIANA.

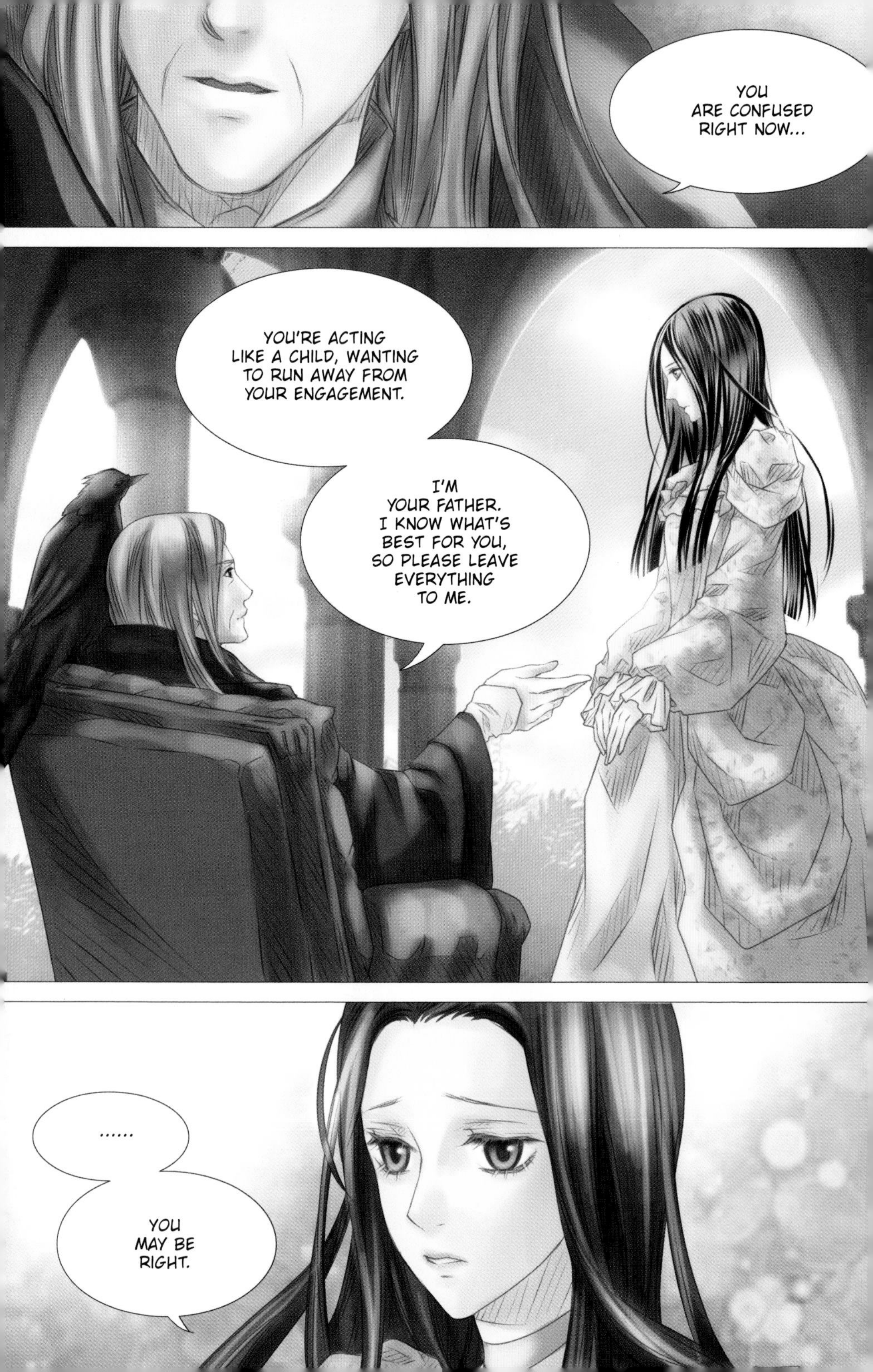
YOU ARE CONFUSED RIGHT NOW...
YOU'RE ACTING LIKE A CHILD, WANTING TO RUN AWAY FROM YOUR ENGAGEMENT.
I'M YOUR FATHER. I KNOW WHAT'S BEST FOR YOU, SO PLEASE LEAVE EVERYTHING TO ME.
......
YOU MAY BE RIGHT.

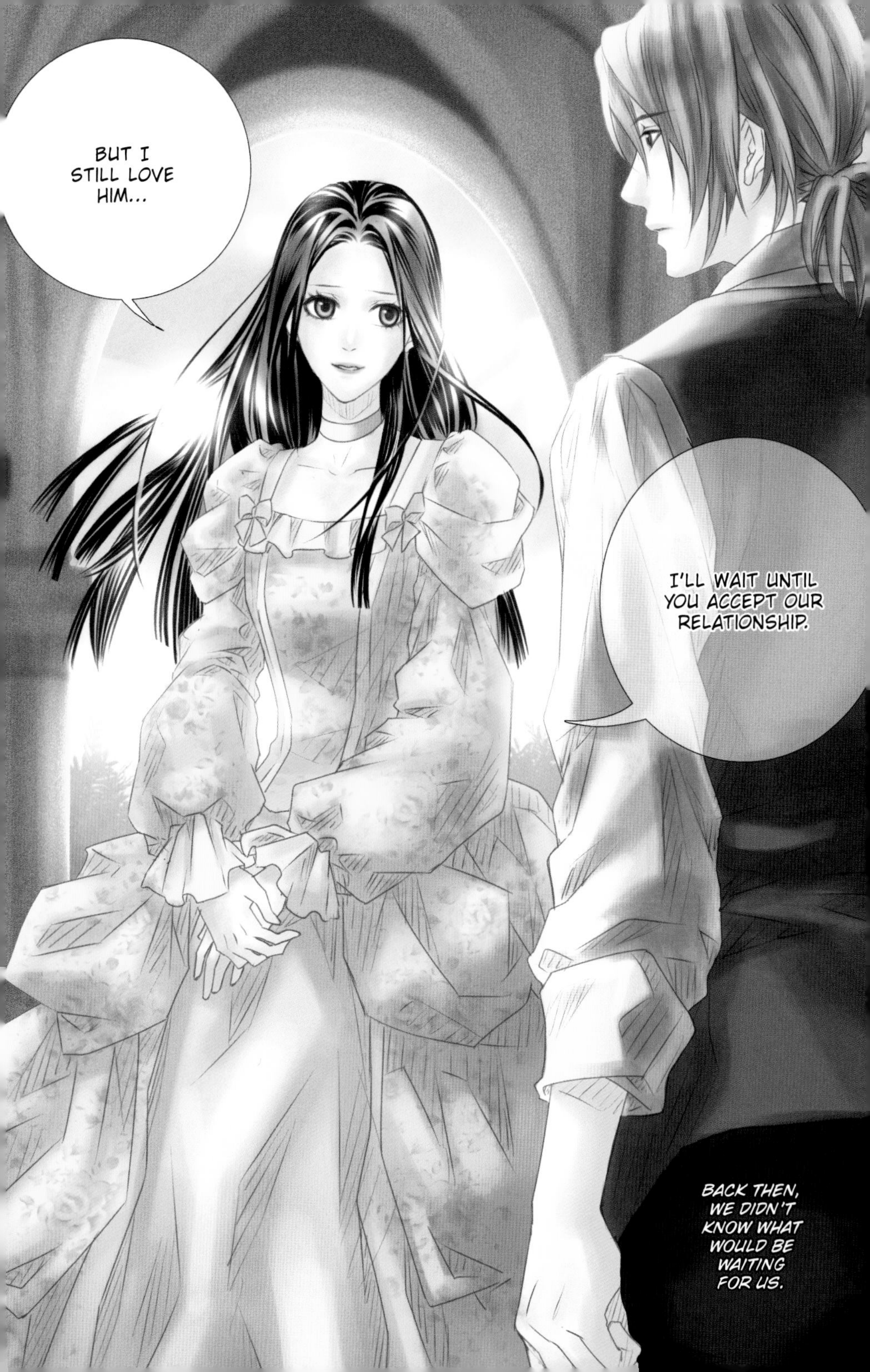
BUT I STILL LOVE HIM...
I'LL WAIT UNTIL YOU ACCEPT OUR RELATIONSHIP.
BACK THEN, WE DIDN'T KNOW WHAT WOULD BE WAITING FOR US.

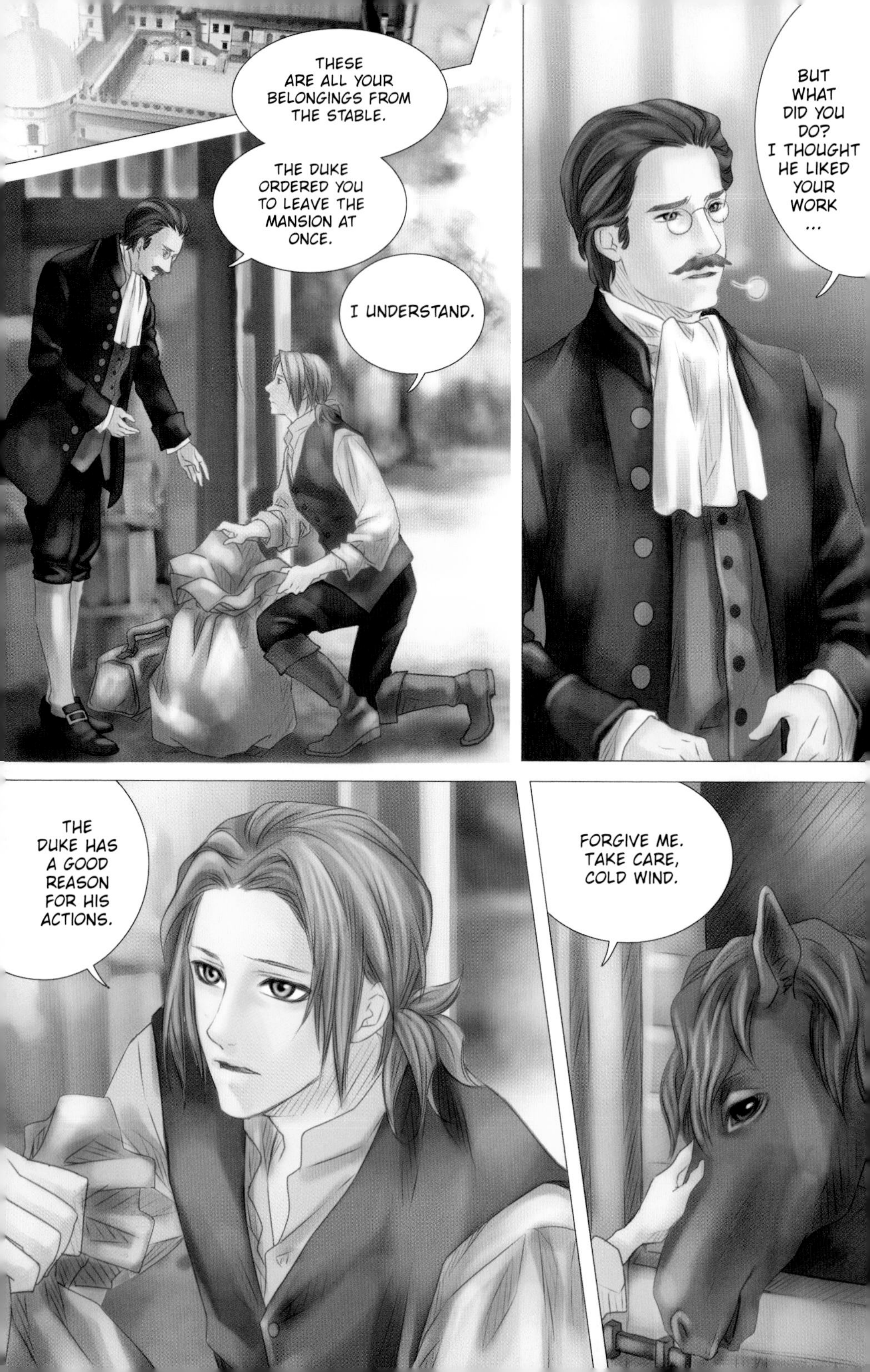
THESE ARE ALL YOUR BELONGINGS FROM THE STABLE.
THE DUKE ORDERED YOU TO LEAVE THE MANSION AT ONCE.
I UNDERSTAND.
BUT WHAT DID YOU DO? I THOUGHT HE LIKED YOUR WORK ...
THE DUKE HAS A GOOD REASON FOR HIS ACTIONS.
FORGIVE ME. TAKE CARE, COLD WIND.

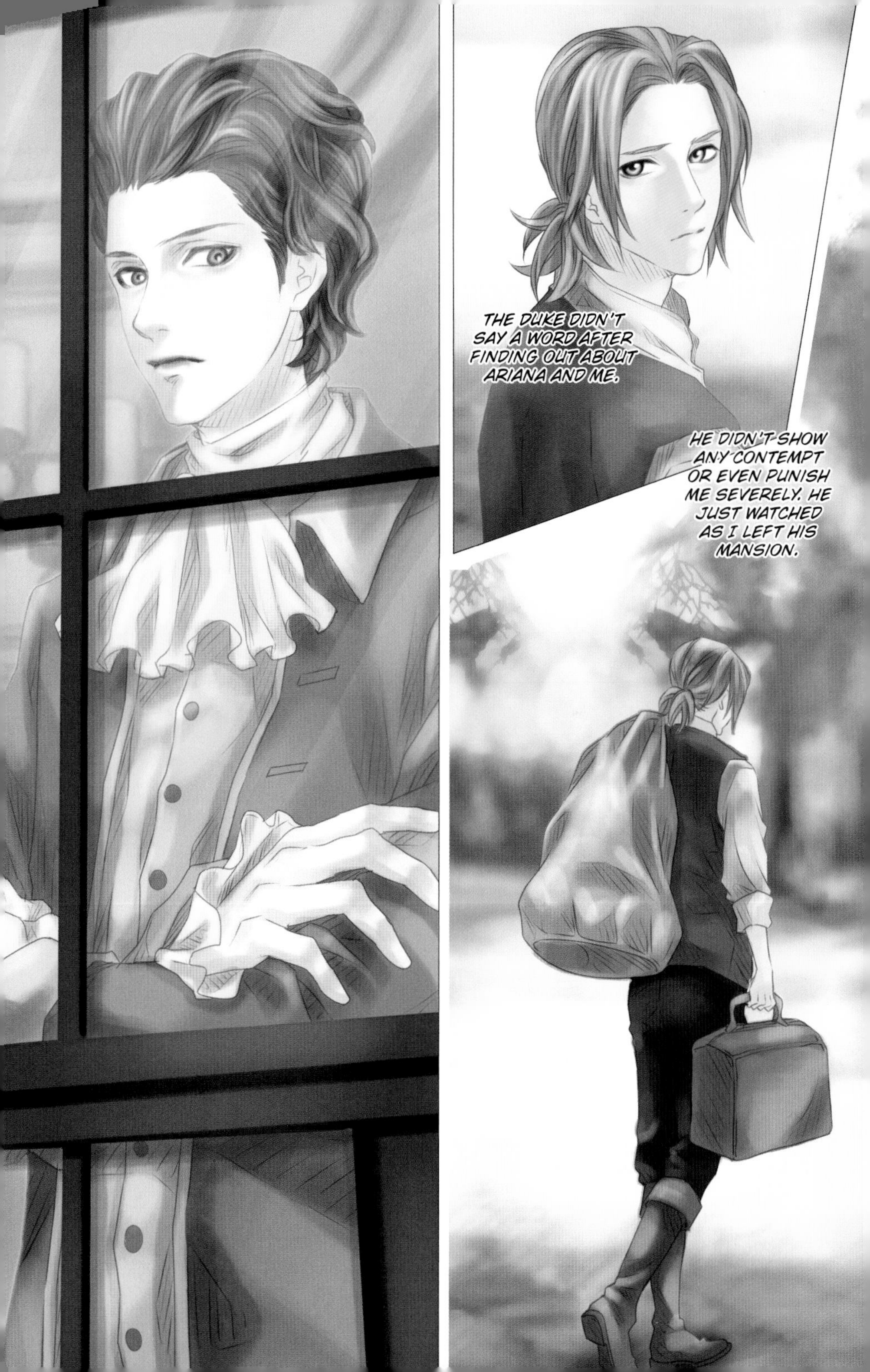
THE DUKE DIDN'T SAY A WORD AFTER FINDING OUT ABOUT ARIANA AND ME.
HE DIDN'T SHOW ANY CONTEMPT OR EVEN PUNISH ME SEVERELY. HE JUST WATCHED AS I LEFT HIS MANSION.

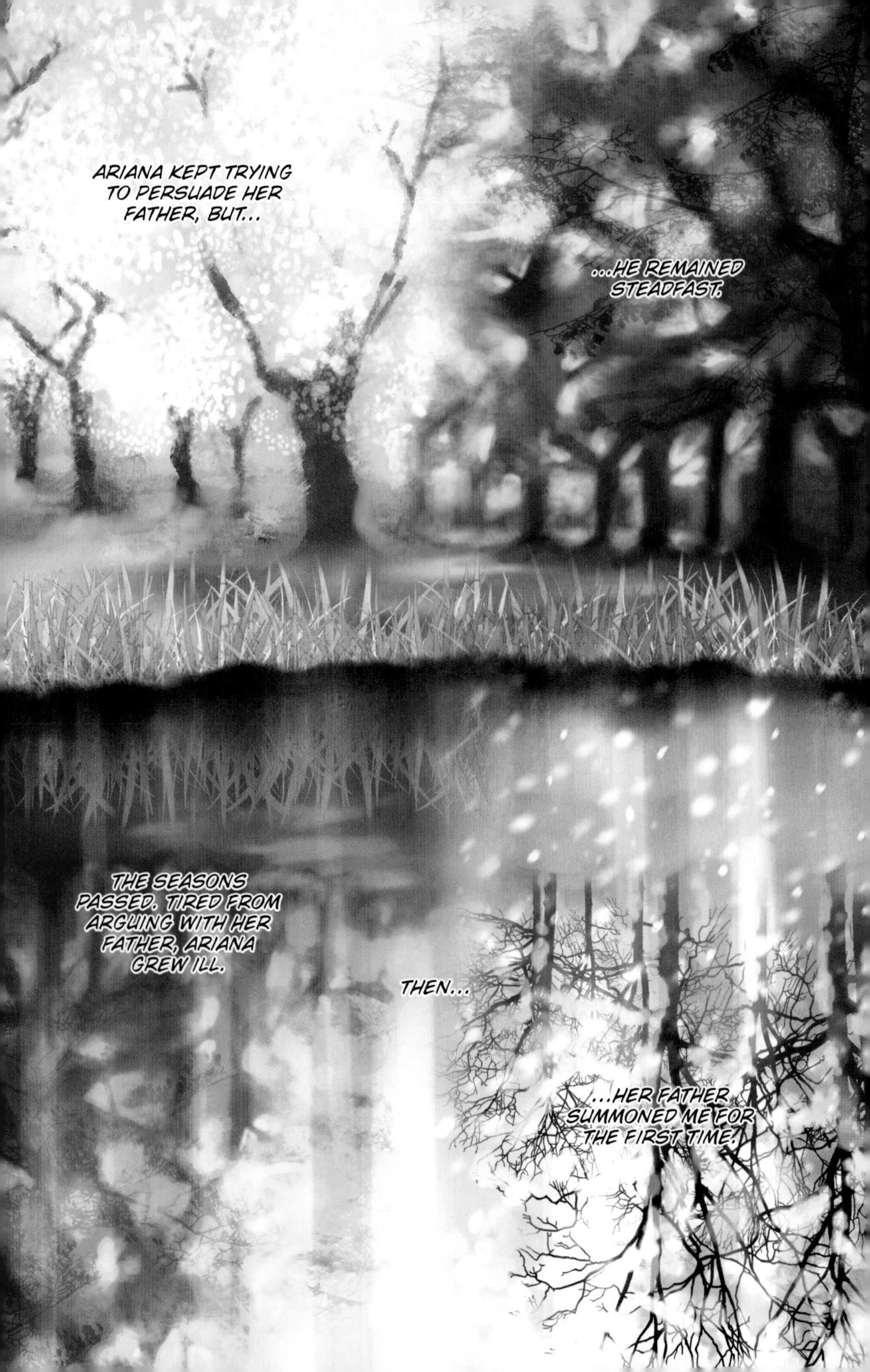
ARIANA KEPT TRYING TO PERSUADE HER FATHER, BUT...
...HE REMAINED STEADFAST.
THE SEASONS PASSED. TIRED FROM ARGUING WITH HER FATHER, ARIANA GREW ILL.
THEN...
...HER FATHER SUMMONED ME FOR THE FIRST TIME.

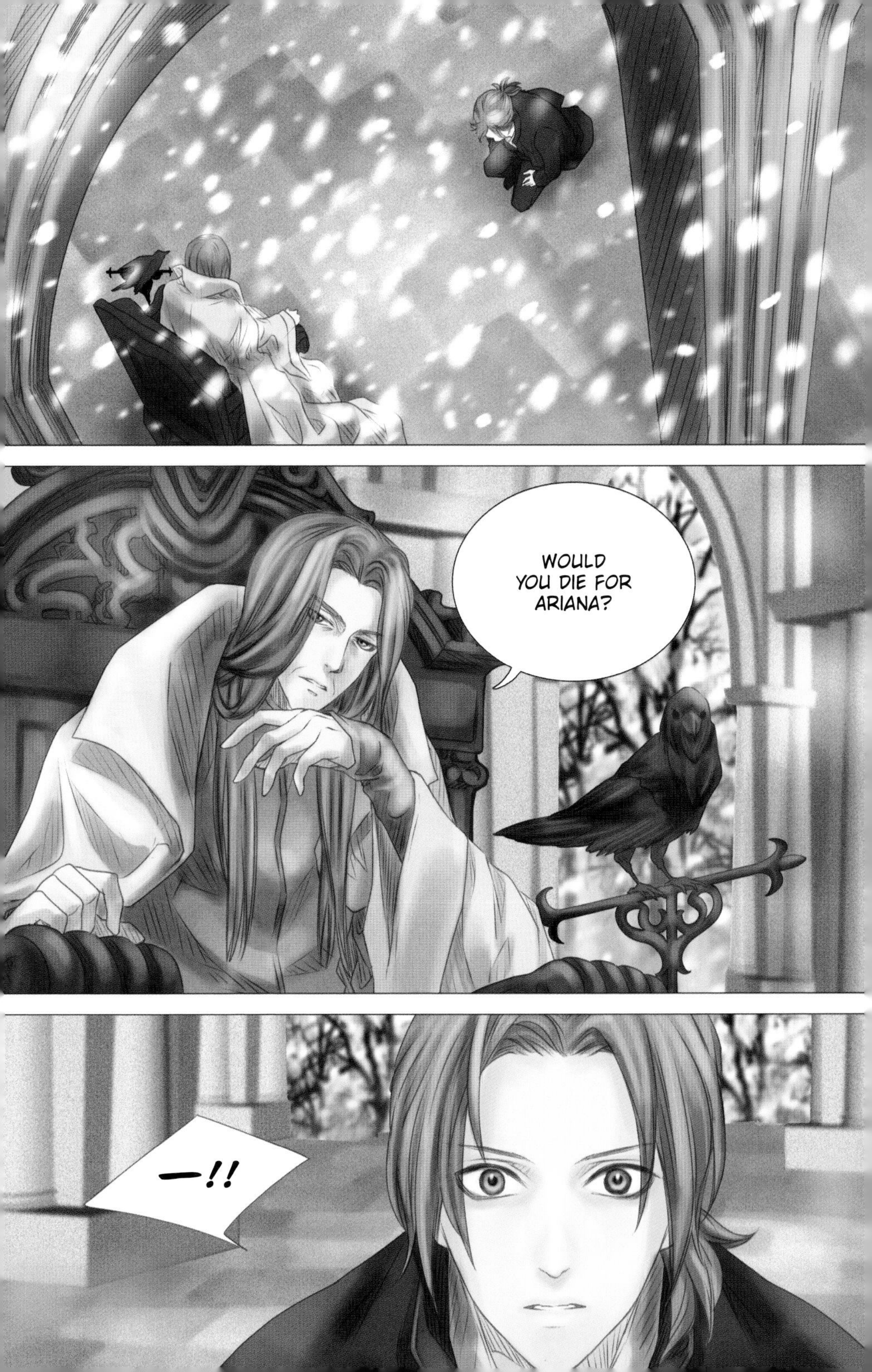
WOULD YOU DIE FOR ARIANA?
—!!

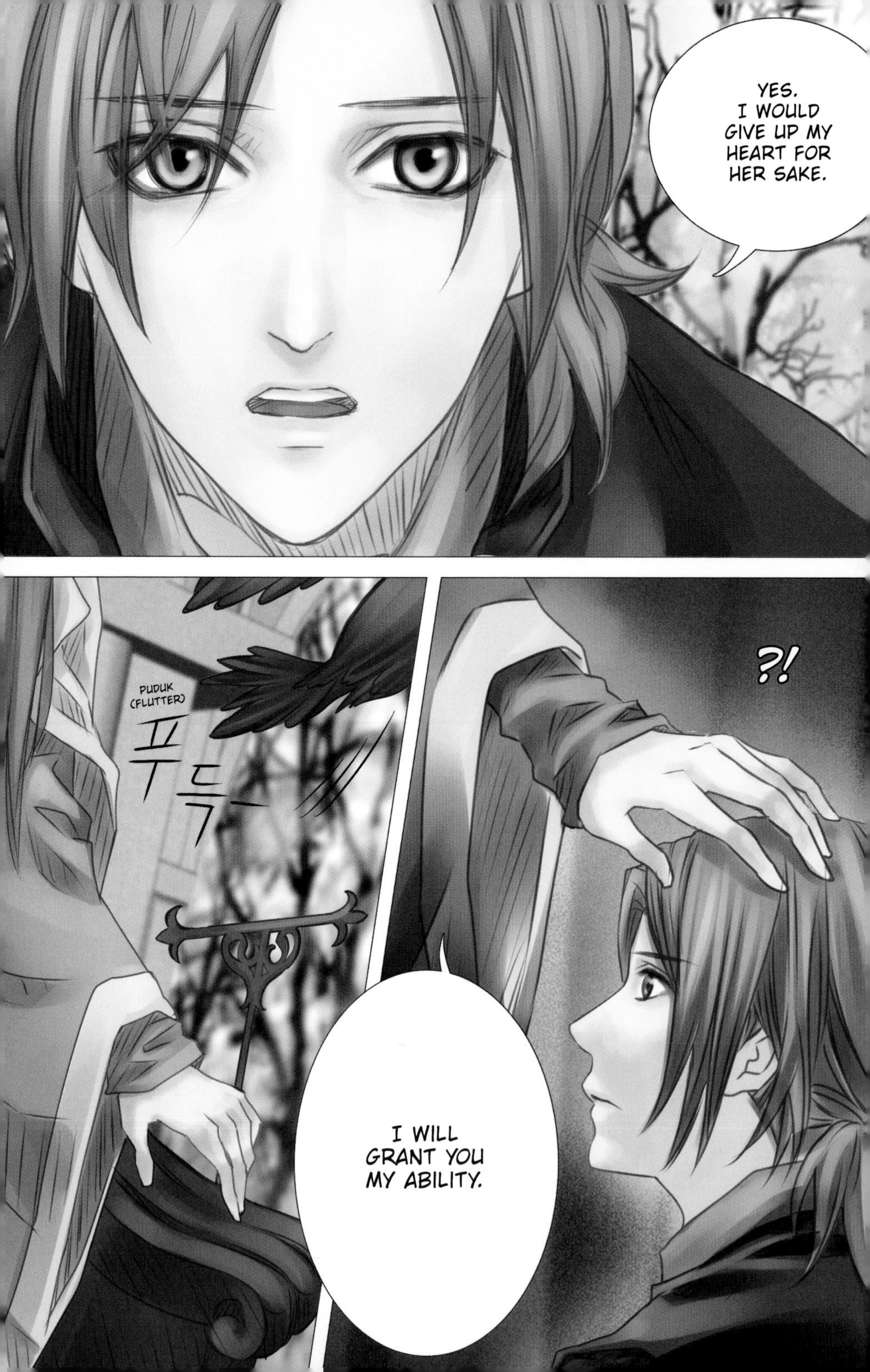
YES.
I WOULD
GIVE UP MY
HEART FOR
HER SAKE.
?!
PUDUK
(FLUTTER)
푸드득
I WILL
GRANT YOU
MY ABILITY.

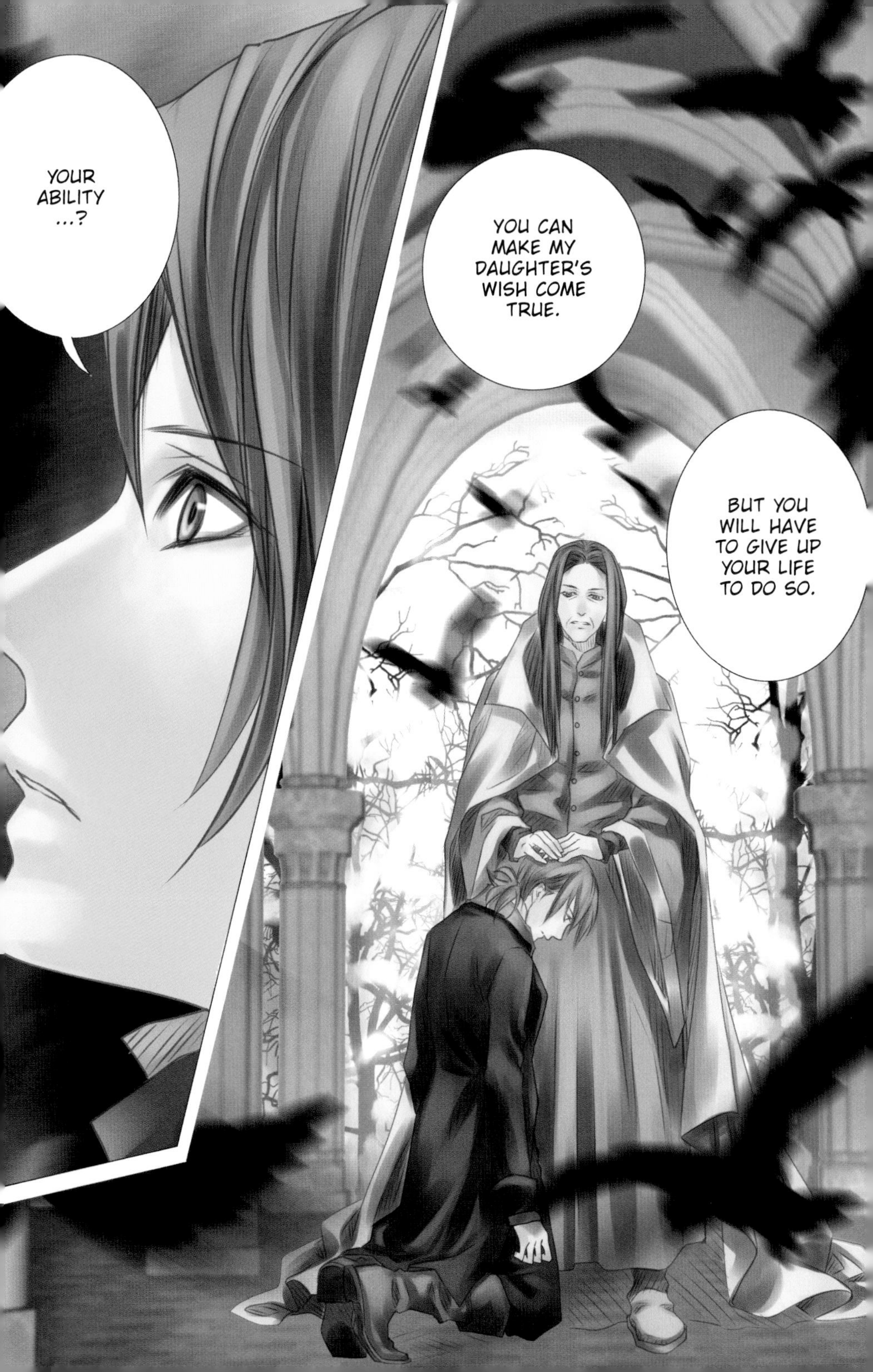
YOUR ABILITY ...?
YOU CAN MAKE MY DAUGHTER'S WISH COME TRUE.
BUT YOU WILL HAVE TO GIVE UP YOUR LIFE TO DO SO.

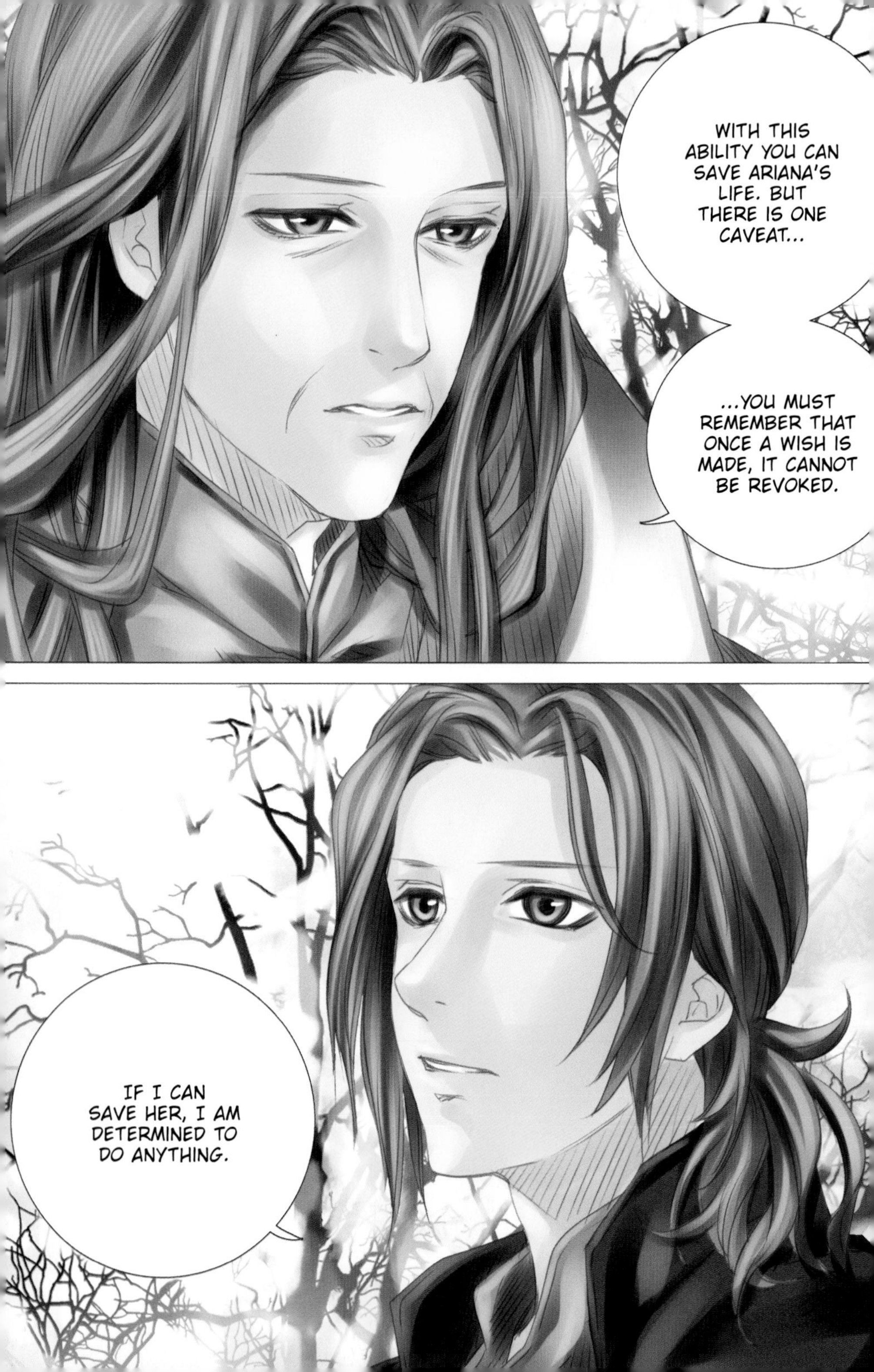
WITH THIS ABILITY YOU CAN SAVE ARIANA'S LIFE. BUT THERE IS ONE CAVEAT...
...YOU MUST REMEMBER THAT ONCE A WISH IS MADE, IT CANNOT BE REVOKED.
IF I CAN SAVE HER, I AM DETERMINED TO DO ANYTHING.

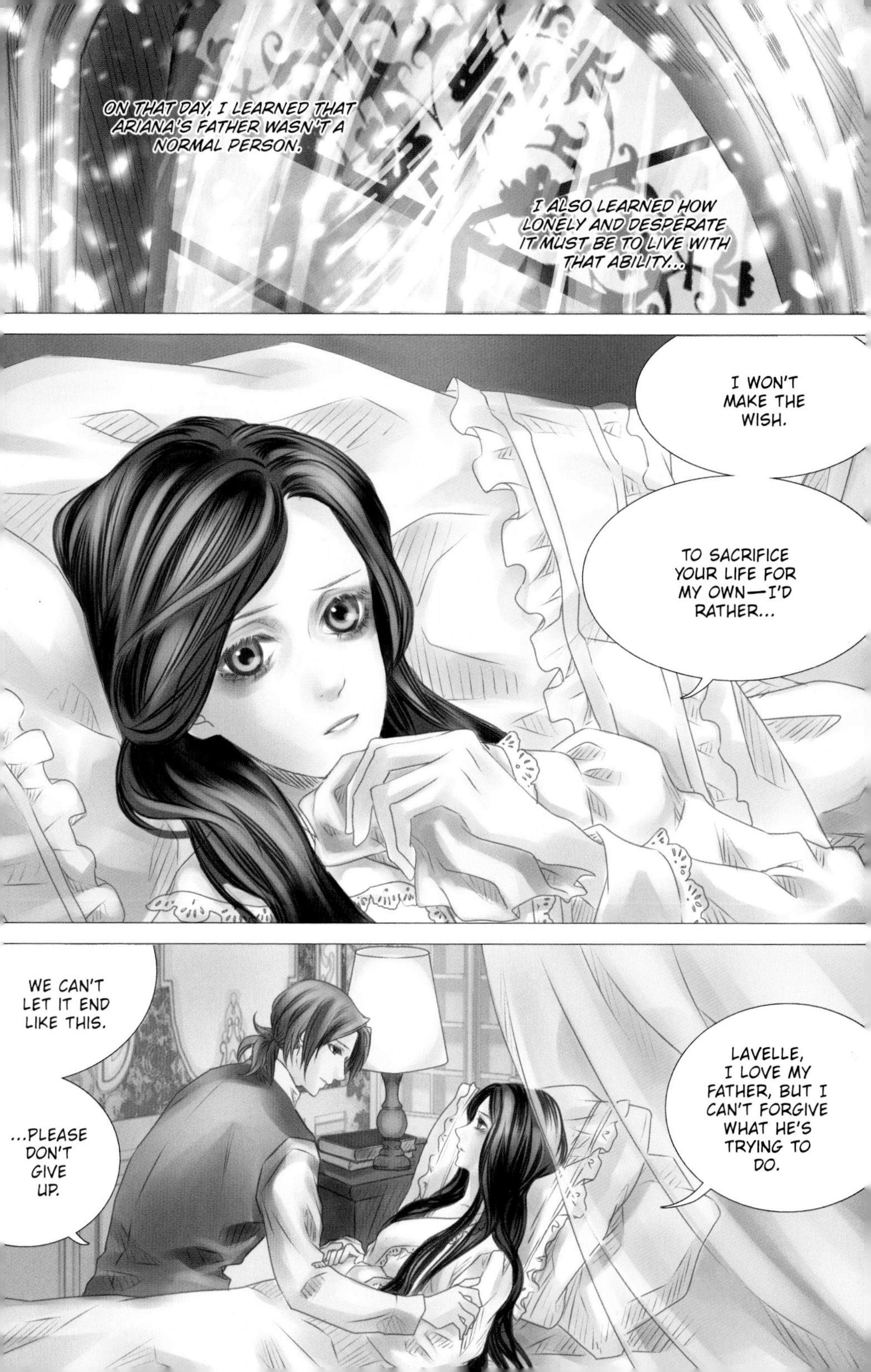
ON THAT DAY, I LEARNED THAT ARIANA'S FATHER WASN'T A NORMAL PERSON.
I ALSO LEARNED HOW LONELY AND DESPERATE IT MUST BE TO LIVE WITH THAT ABILITY...
I WON'T MAKE THE WISH.
TO SACRIFICE YOUR LIFE FOR MY OWN—I'D RATHER...
LAVELLE, I LOVE MY FATHER, BUT I CAN'T FORGIVE WHAT HE'S TRYING TO DO.
WE CAN'T LET IT END LIKE THIS.
...PLEASE DON'T GIVE UP.

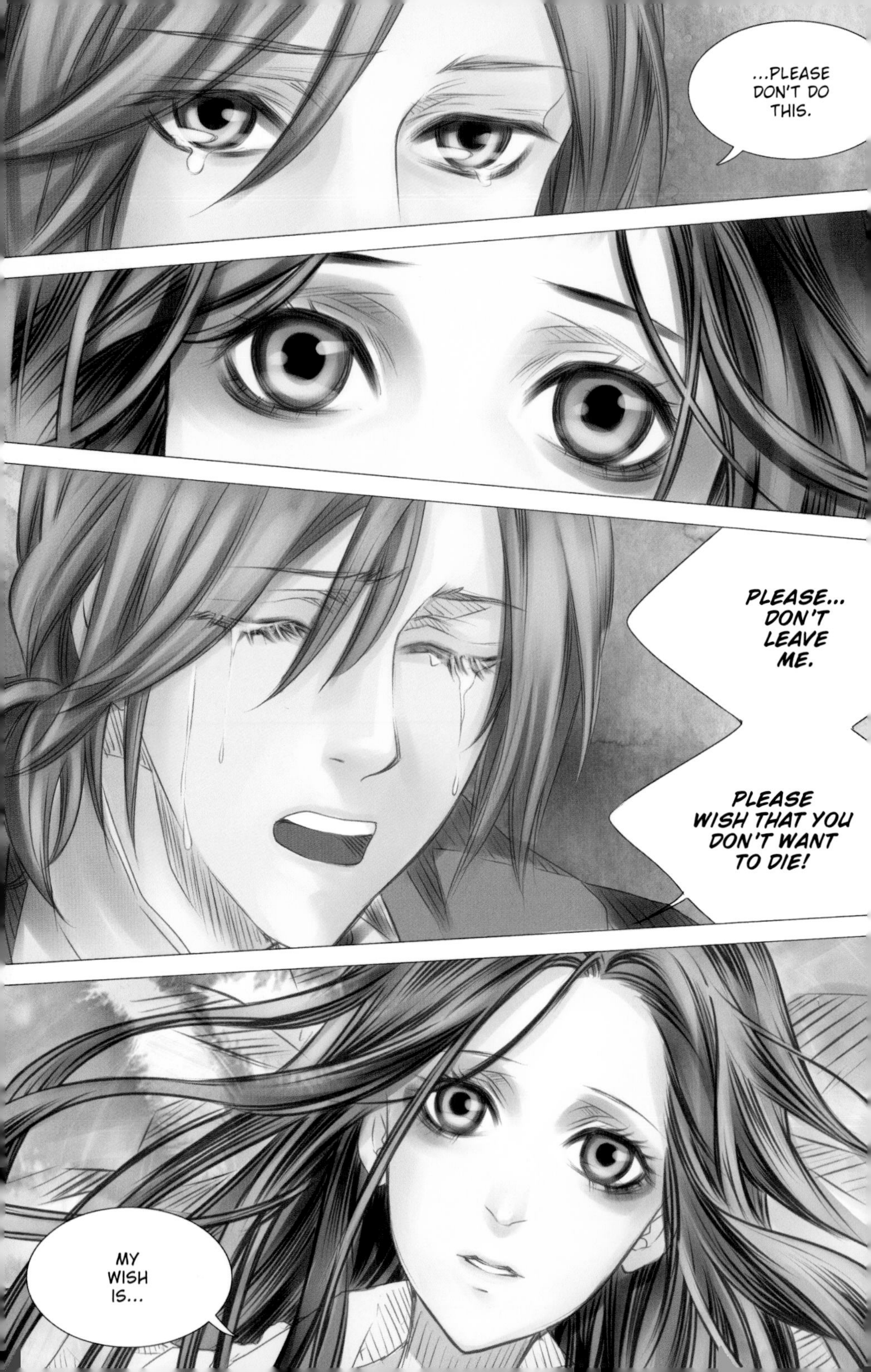
...PLEASE DON'T DO THIS.
PLEASE... DON'T LEAVE ME.
PLEASE WISH THAT YOU DON'T WANT TO DIE!
MY WISH IS...

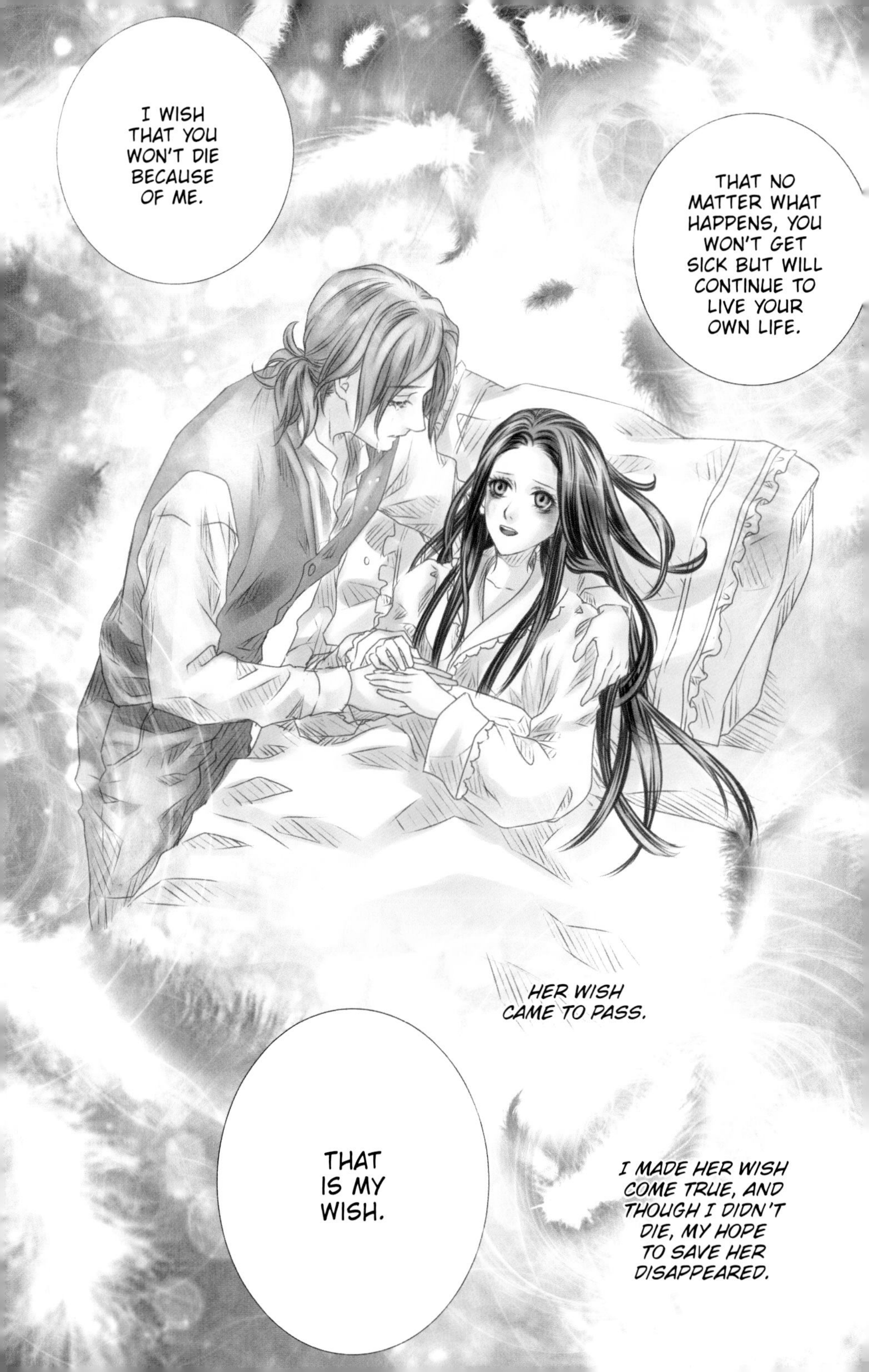
I WISH THAT YOU WON'T DIE BECAUSE OF ME.
THAT NO MATTER WHAT HAPPENS, YOU WON'T GET SICK BUT WILL CONTINUE TO LIVE YOUR OWN LIFE.
THAT IS MY WISH.
HER WISH CAME TO PASS.
I MADE HER WISH COME TRUE, AND THOUGH I DIDN'T DIE, MY HOPE TO SAVE HER DISAPPEARED.

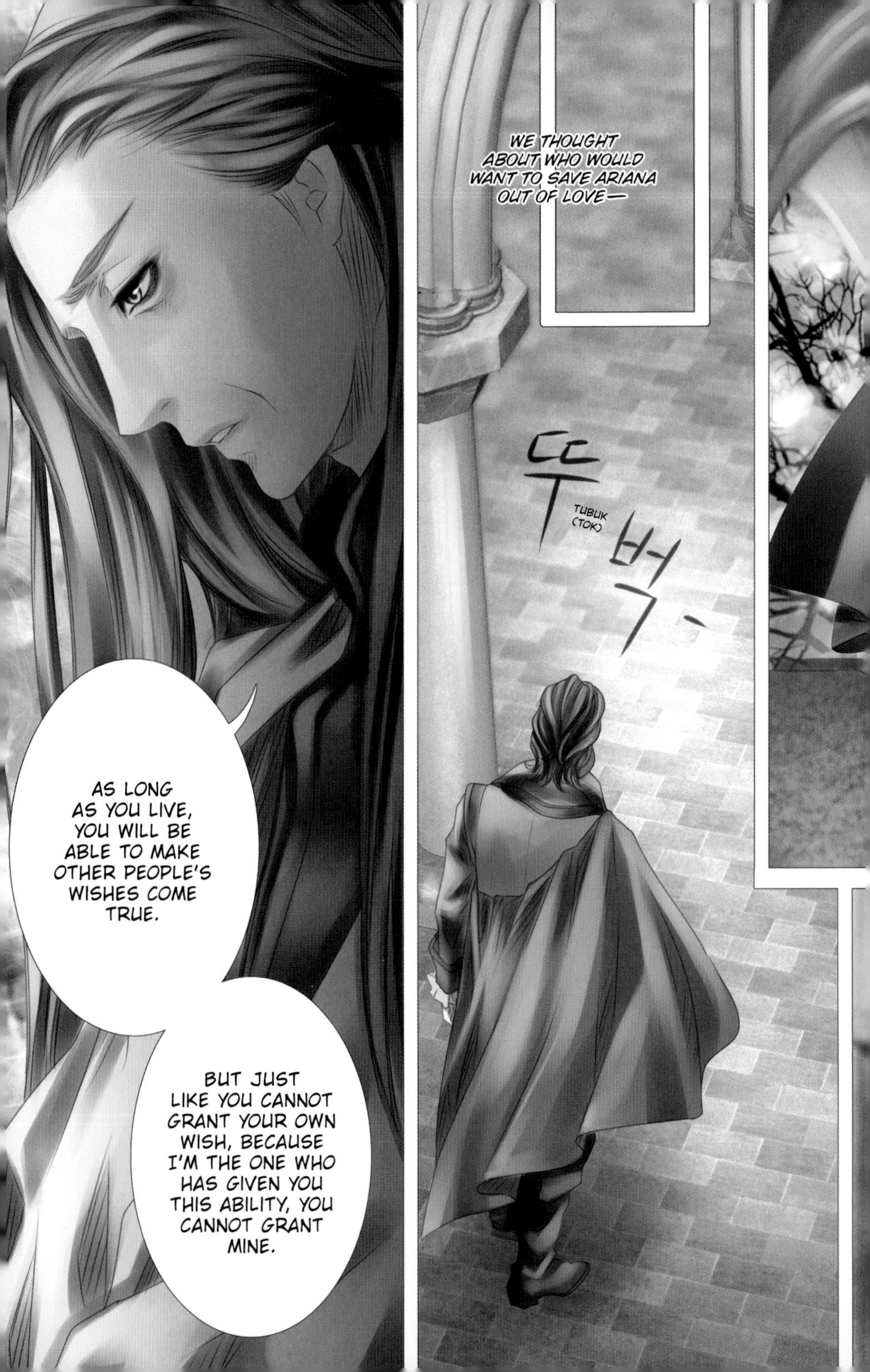
AS LONG AS YOU LIVE, YOU WILL BE ABLE TO MAKE OTHER PEOPLE'S WISHES COME TRUE.
BUT JUST LIKE YOU CANNOT GRANT YOUR OWN WISH, BECAUSE I'M THE ONE WHO HAS GIVEN YOU THIS ABILITY, YOU CANNOT GRANT MINE.
WE THOUGHT ABOUT WHO WOULD WANT TO SAVE ARIANA OUT OF LOVE—
뚜벅
TUBUK (TOK)

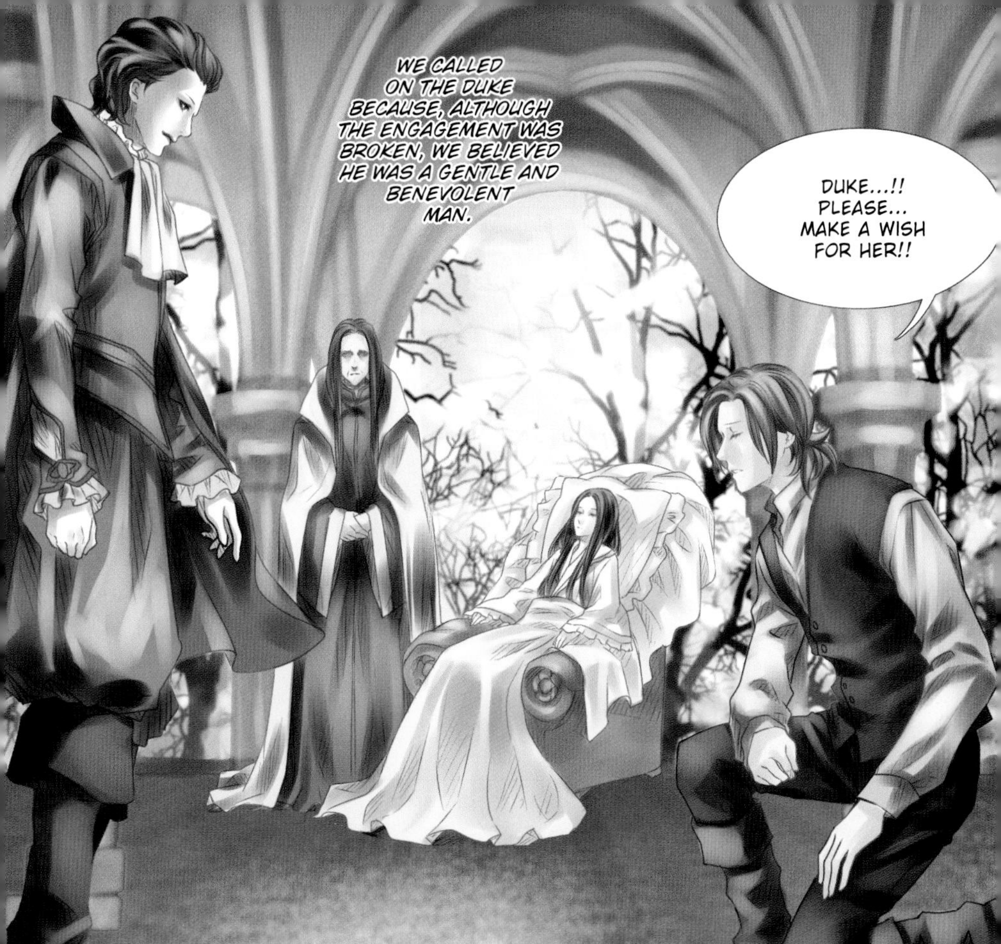
WE CALLED ON THE DUKE BECAUSE, ALTHOUGH THE ENGAGEMENT WAS BROKEN, WE BELIEVED HE WAS A GENTLE AND BENEVOLENT MAN.
DUKE...!! PLEASE... MAKE A WISH FOR HER!!

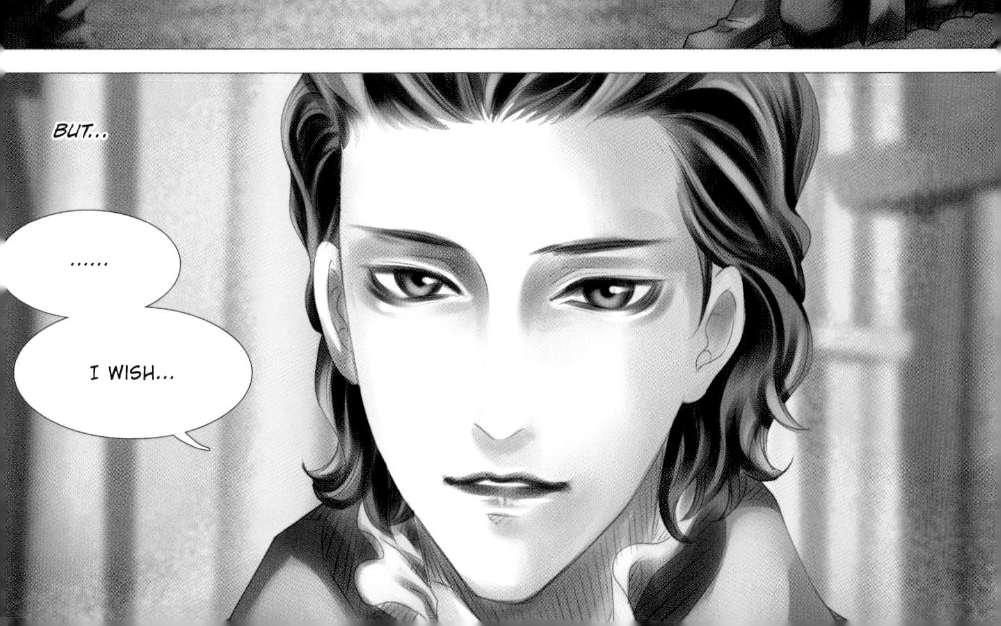
BUT...
......
I WISH...

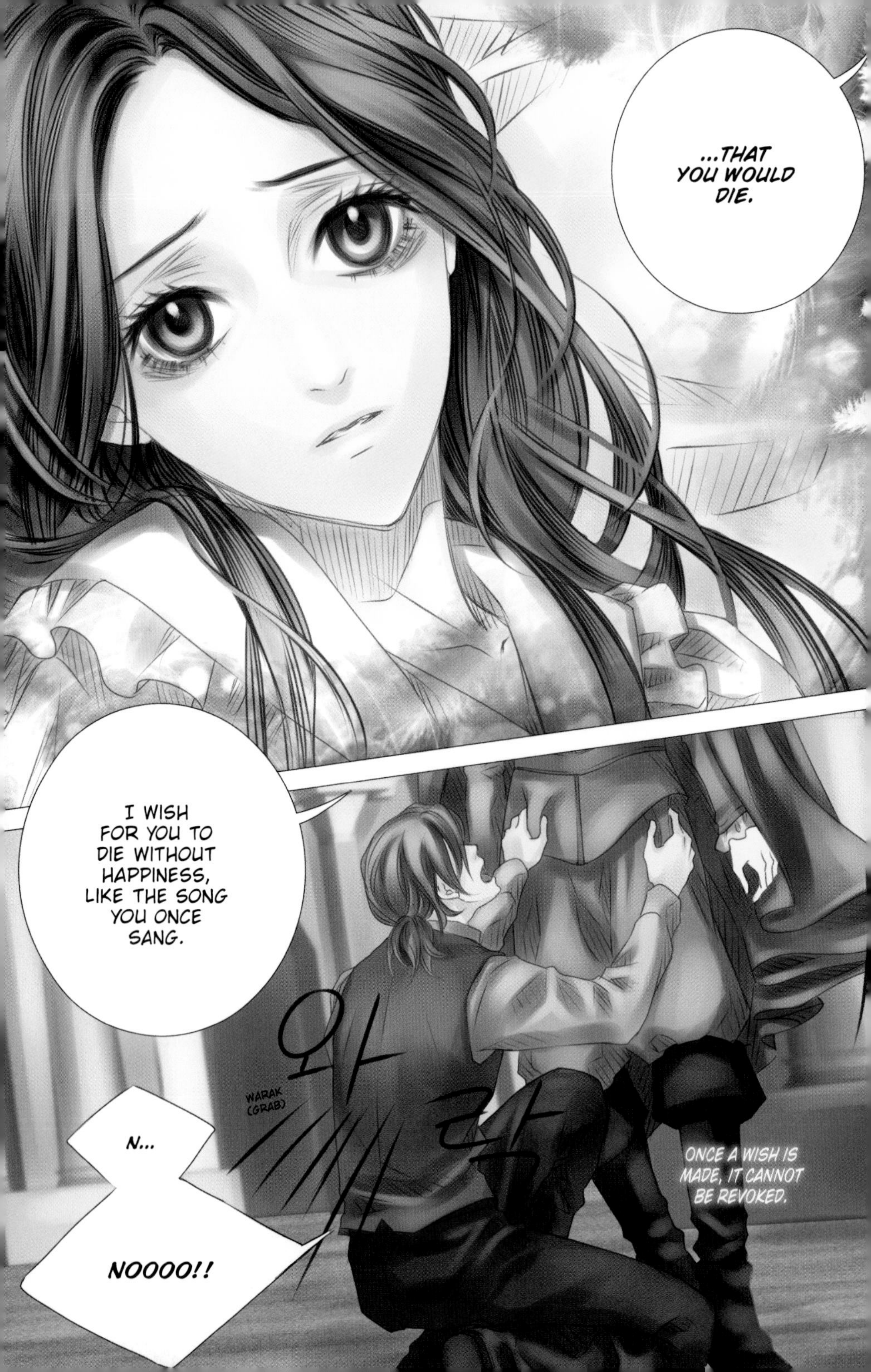
...THAT YOU WOULD DIE.
I WISH FOR YOU TO DIE WITHOUT HAPPINESS, LIKE THE SONG YOU ONCE SANG.
WARAK (GRAB)
N...
NOOOO!!
ONCE A WISH IS MADE, IT CANNOT BE REVOKED.

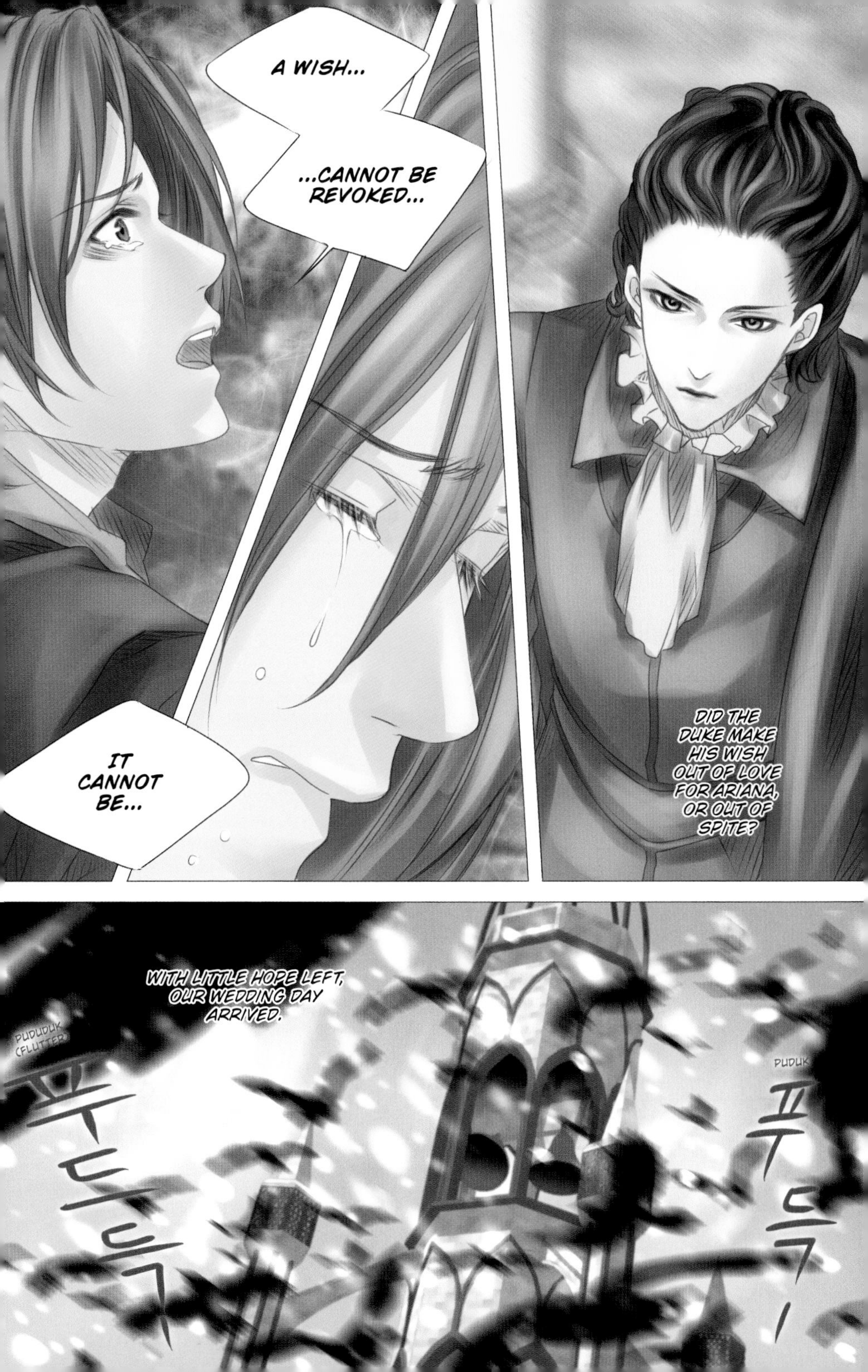
A WISH...
...CANNOT BE REVOKED...
IT CANNOT BE...
DID THE DUKE MAKE HIS WISH OUT OF LOVE FOR ARIANA, OR OUT OF SPITE?
WITH LITTLE HOPE LEFT, OUR WEDDING DAY ARRIVED.
PUDUDUK (FLUTTER)
PUDUK

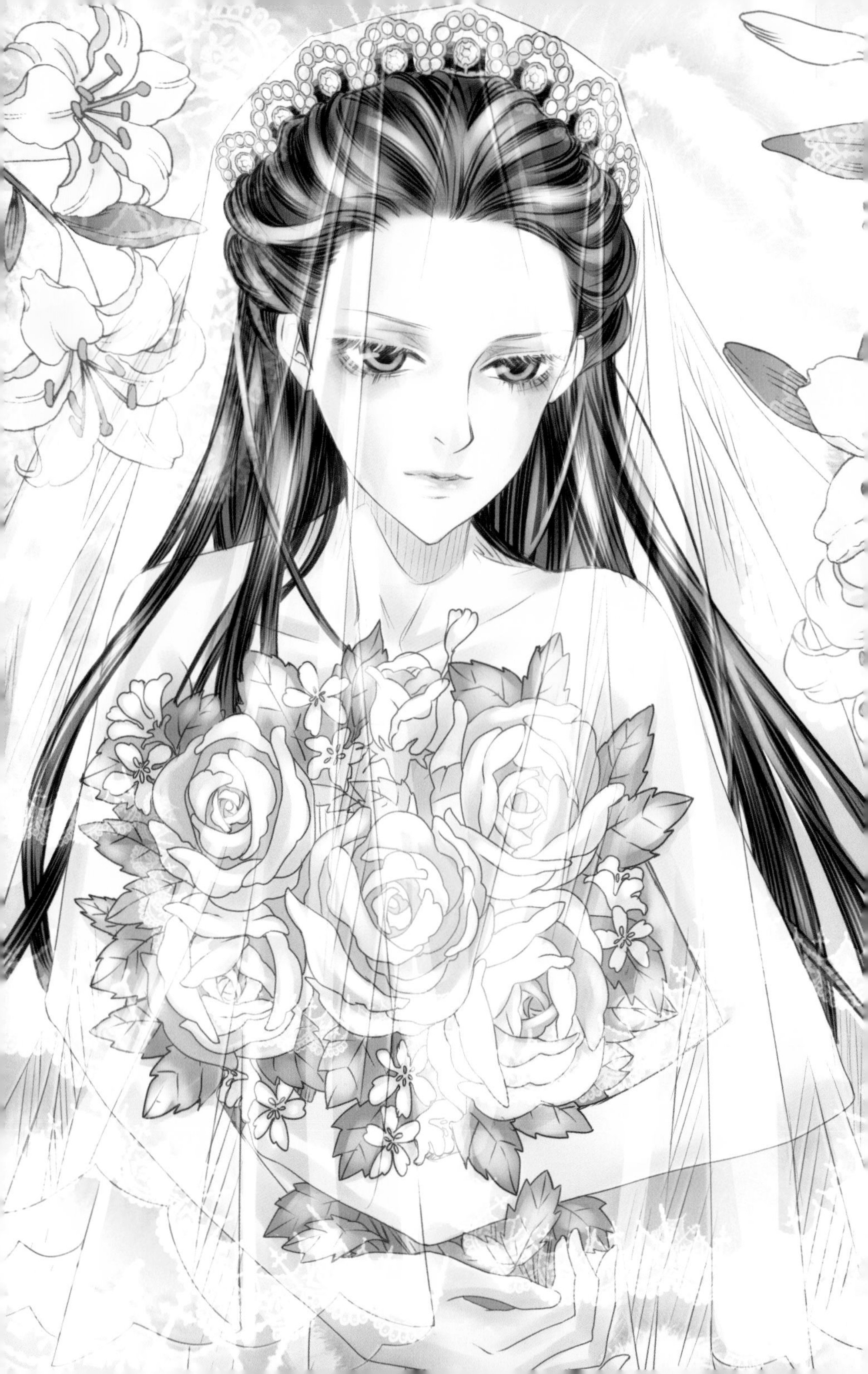

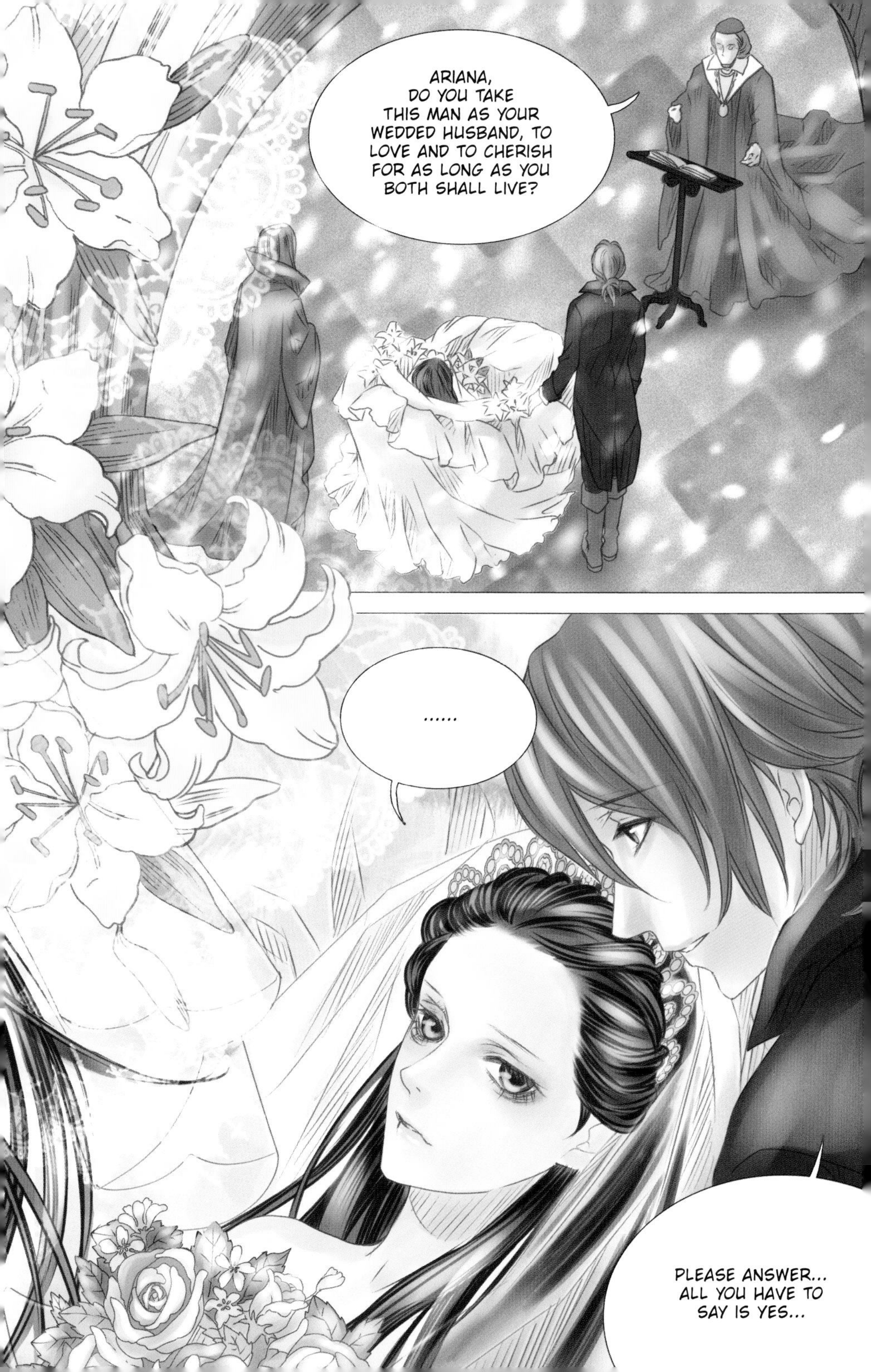
ARIANA, DO YOU TAKE THIS MAN AS YOUR WEDDED HUSBAND, TO LOVE AND TO CHERISH FOR AS LONG AS YOU BOTH SHALL LIVE?
......
PLEASE ANSWER... ALL YOU HAVE TO SAY IS YES...

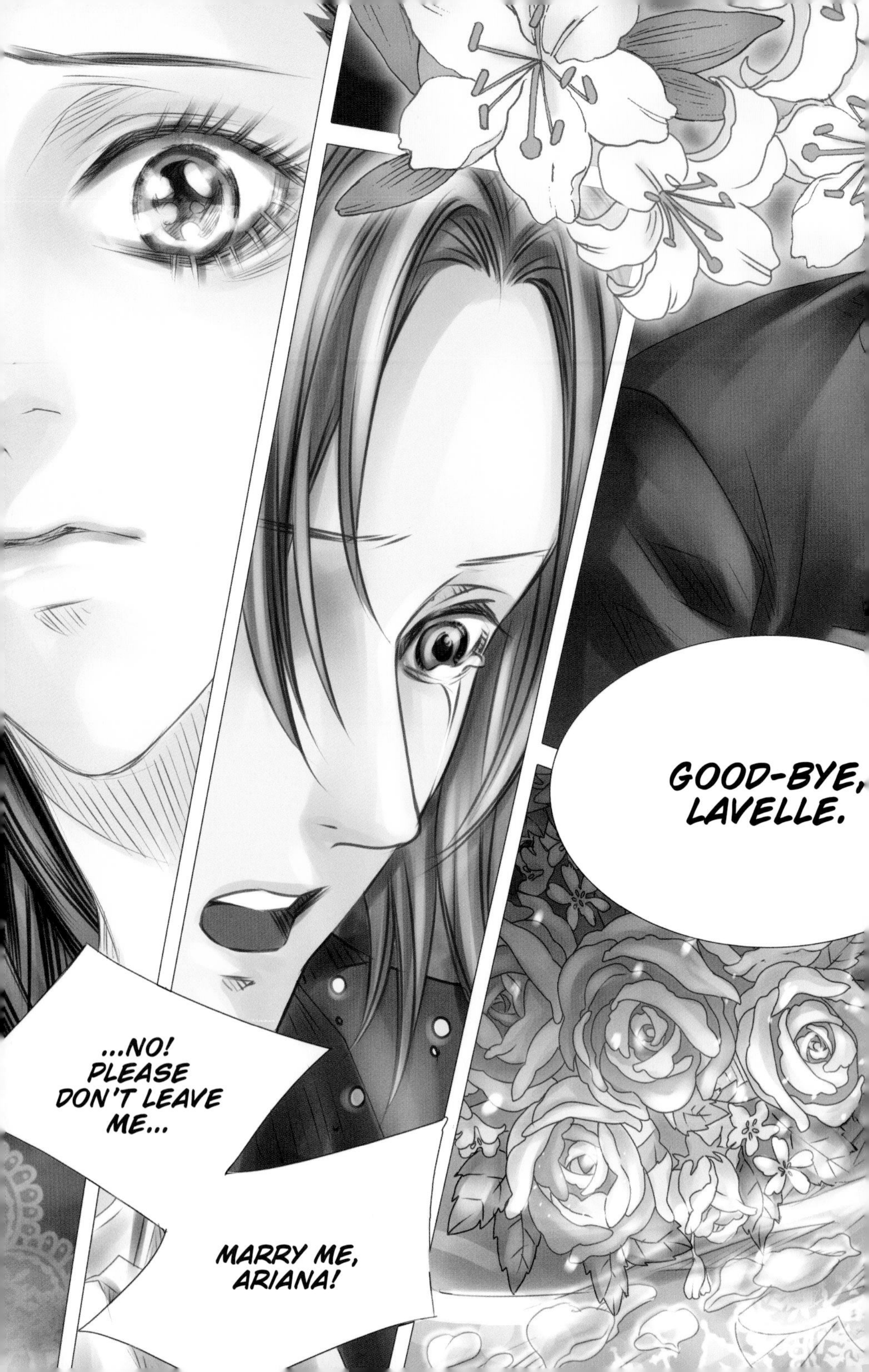
GOOD-BYE, LAVELLE.
...NO! PLEASE DON'T LEAVE ME...
MARRY ME, ARIANA!

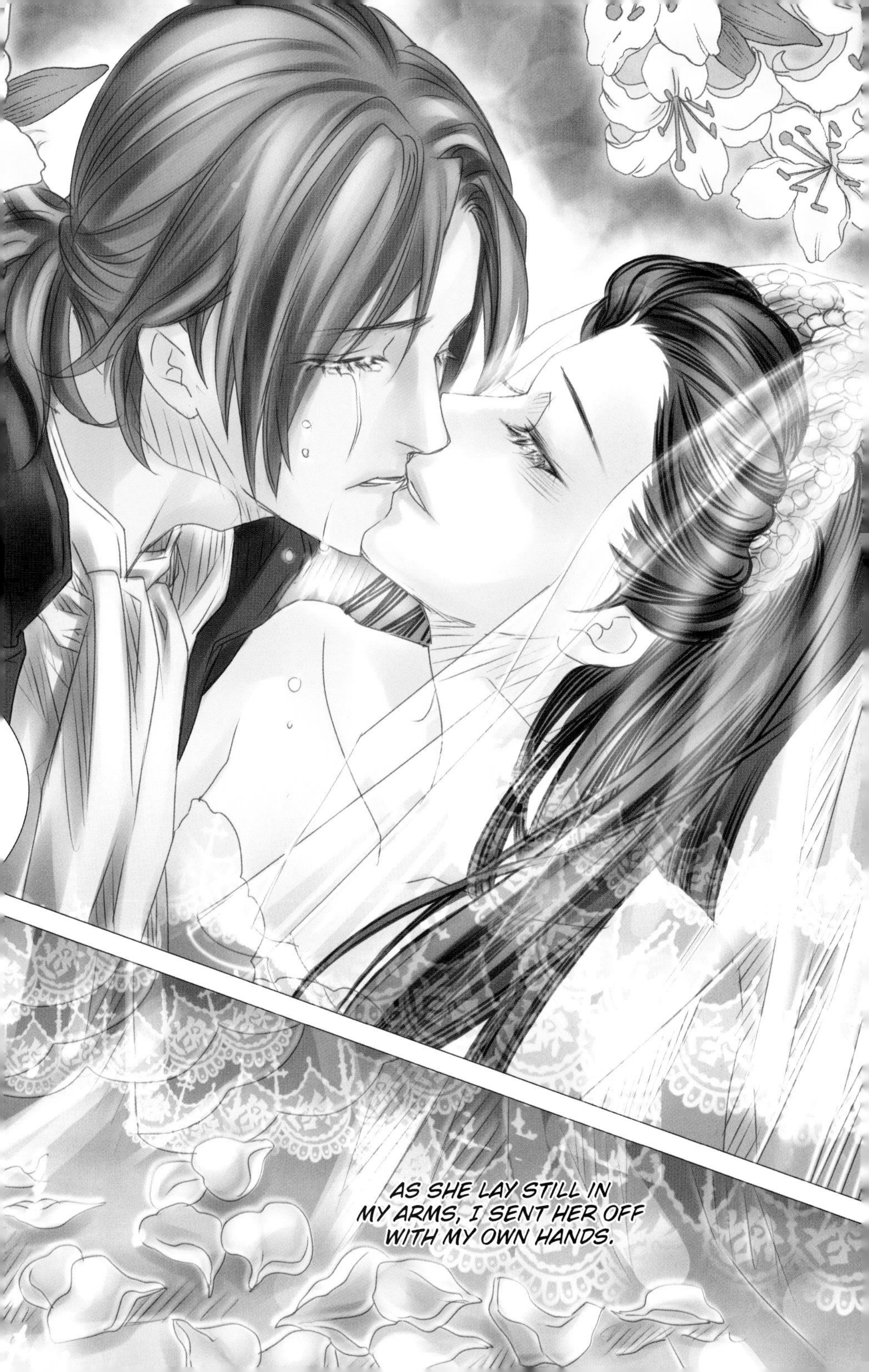
AS SHE LAY STILL IN MY ARMS, I SENT HER OFF WITH MY OWN HANDS.

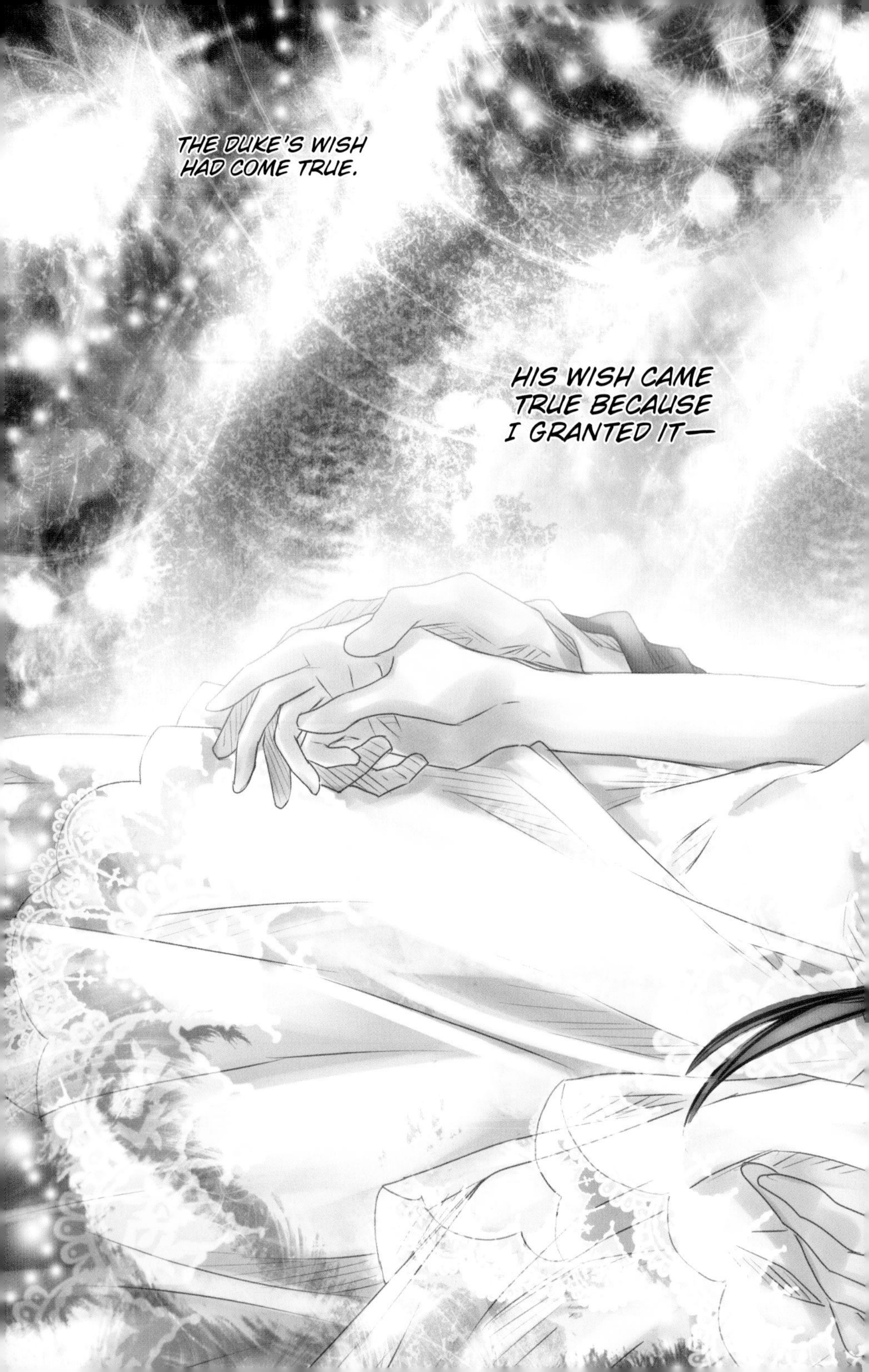
THE DUKE'S WISH HAD COME TRUE.
HIS WISH CAME TRUE BECAUSE I GRANTED IT—

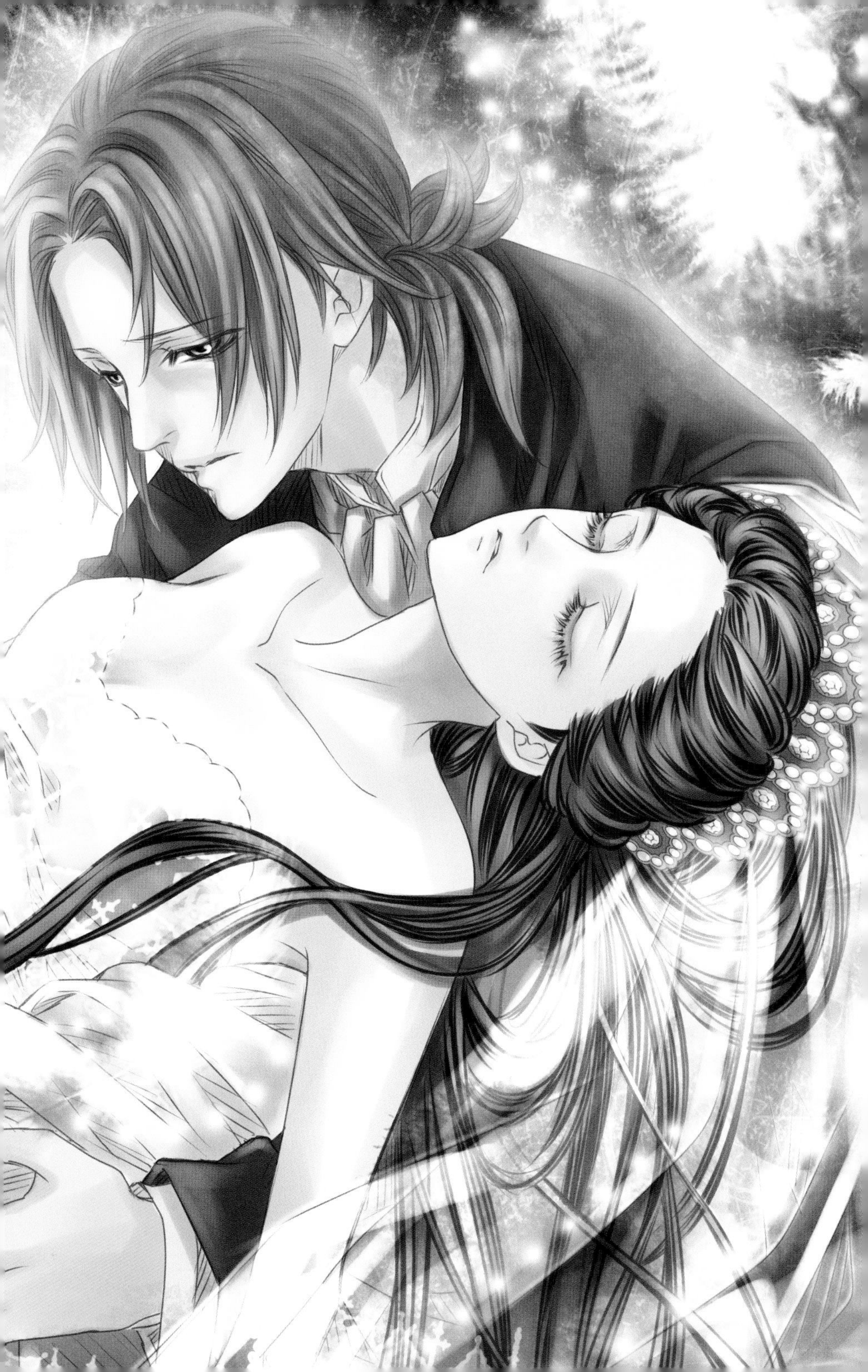

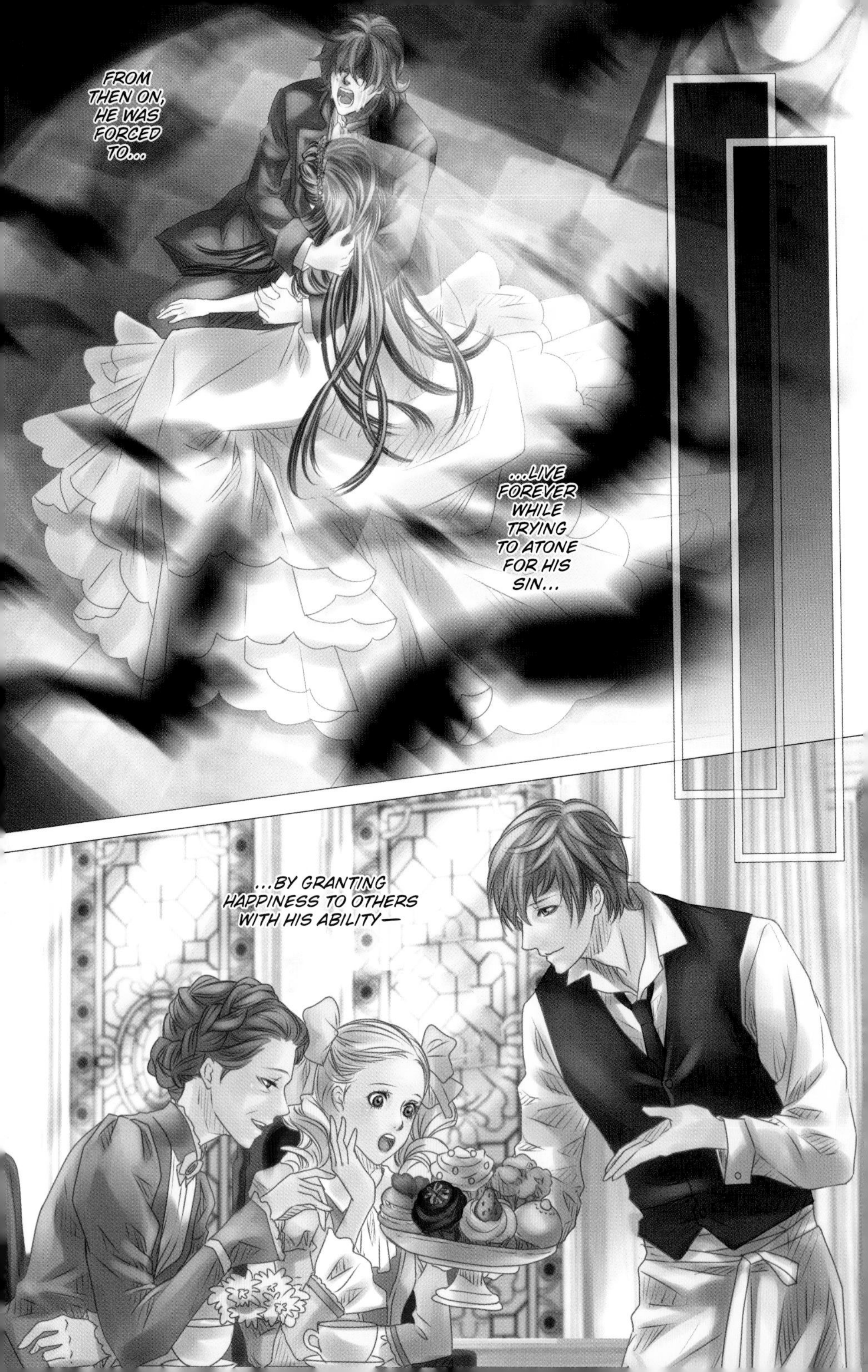
FROM THEN ON, HE WAS FORCED TO...
...LIVE FOREVER WHILE TRYING TO ATONE FOR HIS SIN...
...BY GRANTING HAPPINESS TO OTHERS WITH HIS ABILITY—

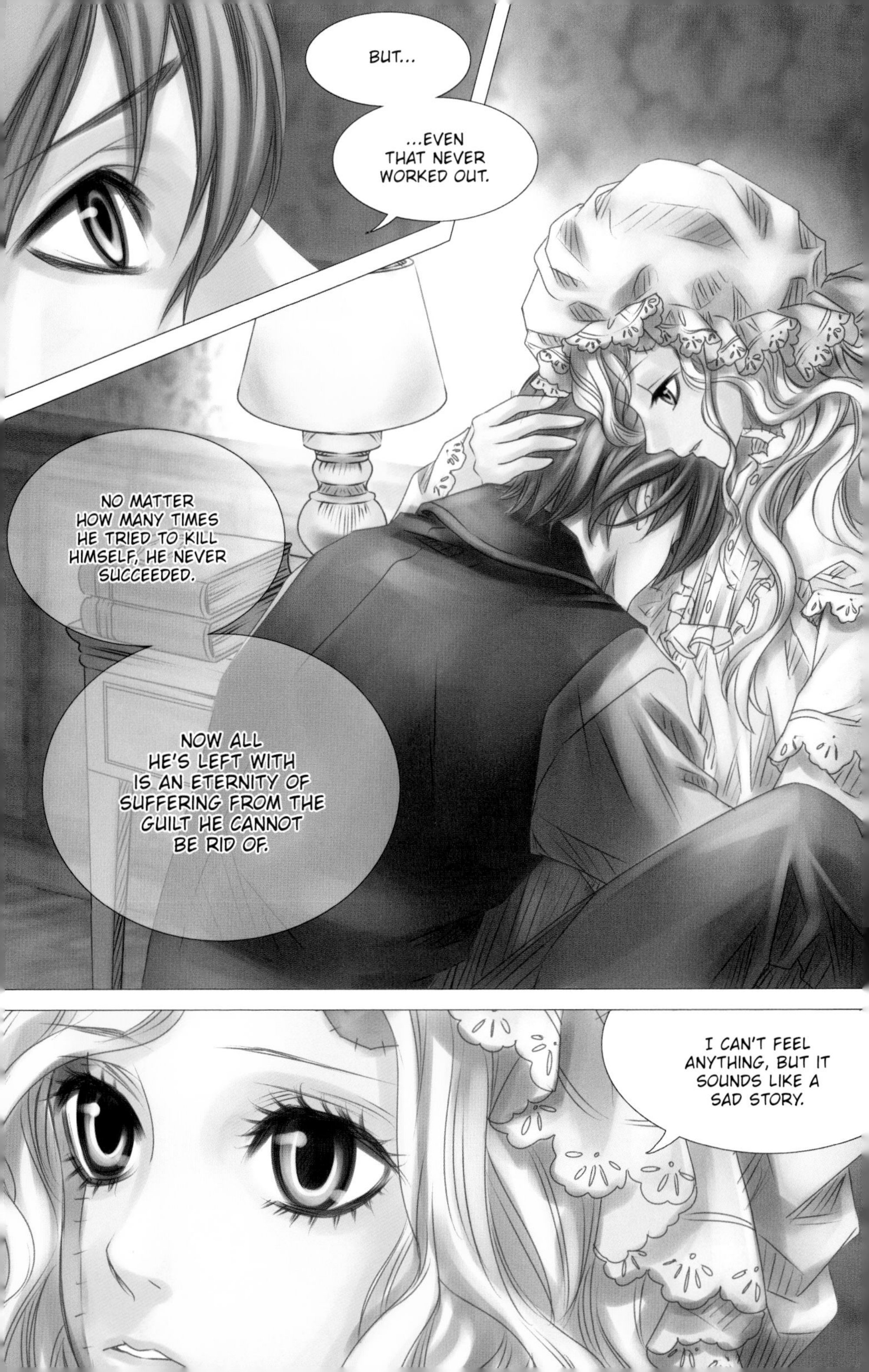
BUT...
...EVEN THAT NEVER WORKED OUT.
NO MATTER HOW MANY TIMES HE TRIED TO KILL HIMSELF, HE NEVER SUCCEEDED.
NOW ALL HE'S LEFT WITH IS AN ETERNITY OF SUFFERING FROM THE GUILT HE CANNOT BE RID OF.
I CAN'T FEEL ANYTHING, BUT IT SOUNDS LIKE A SAD STORY.

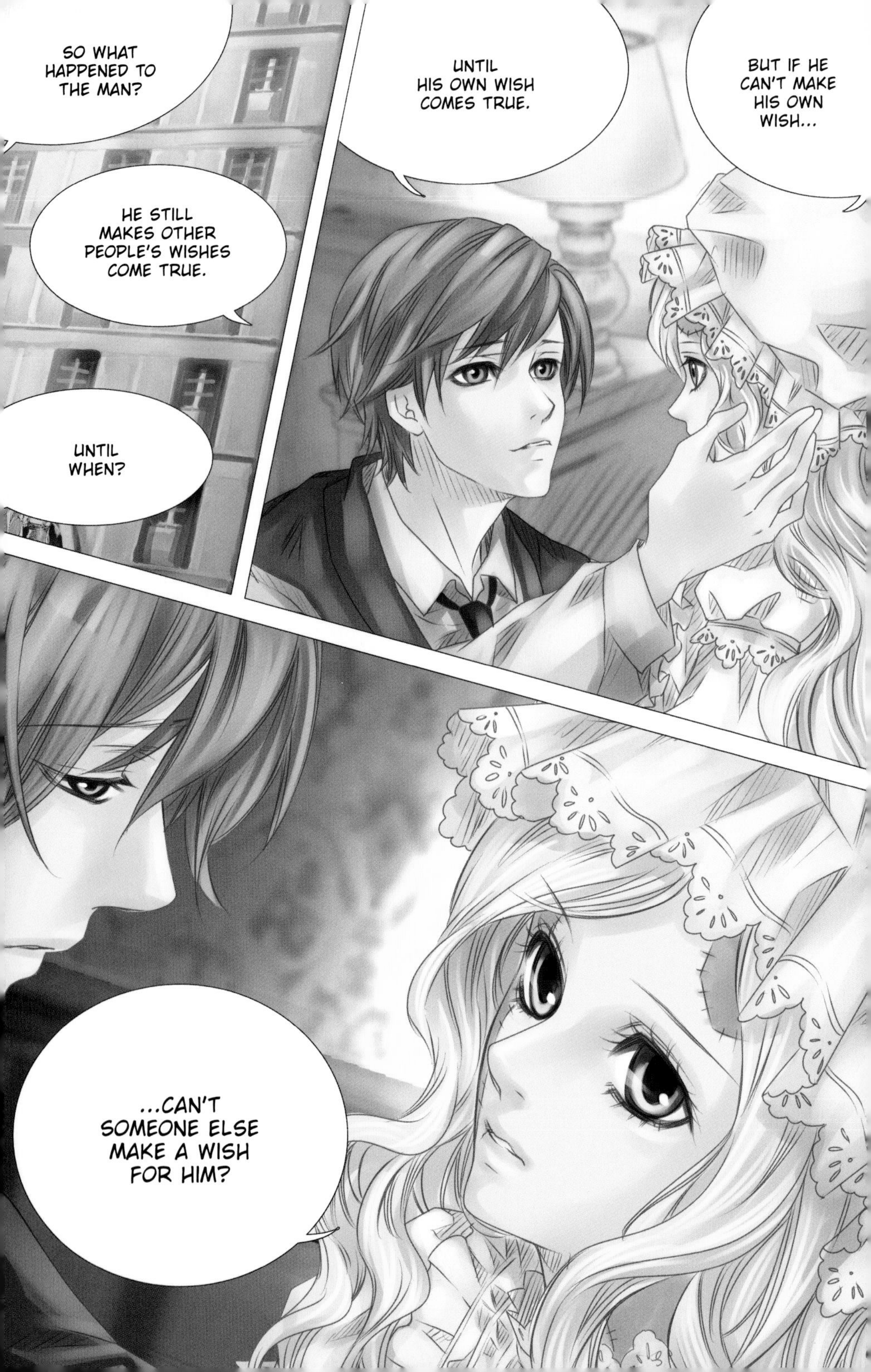
SO WHAT HAPPENED TO THE MAN?
HE STILL MAKES OTHER PEOPLE'S WISHES COME TRUE.
UNTIL WHEN?
UNTIL HIS OWN WISH COMES TRUE.
BUT IF HE CAN'T MAKE HIS OWN WISH...
...CAN'T SOMEONE ELSE MAKE A WISH FOR HIM?

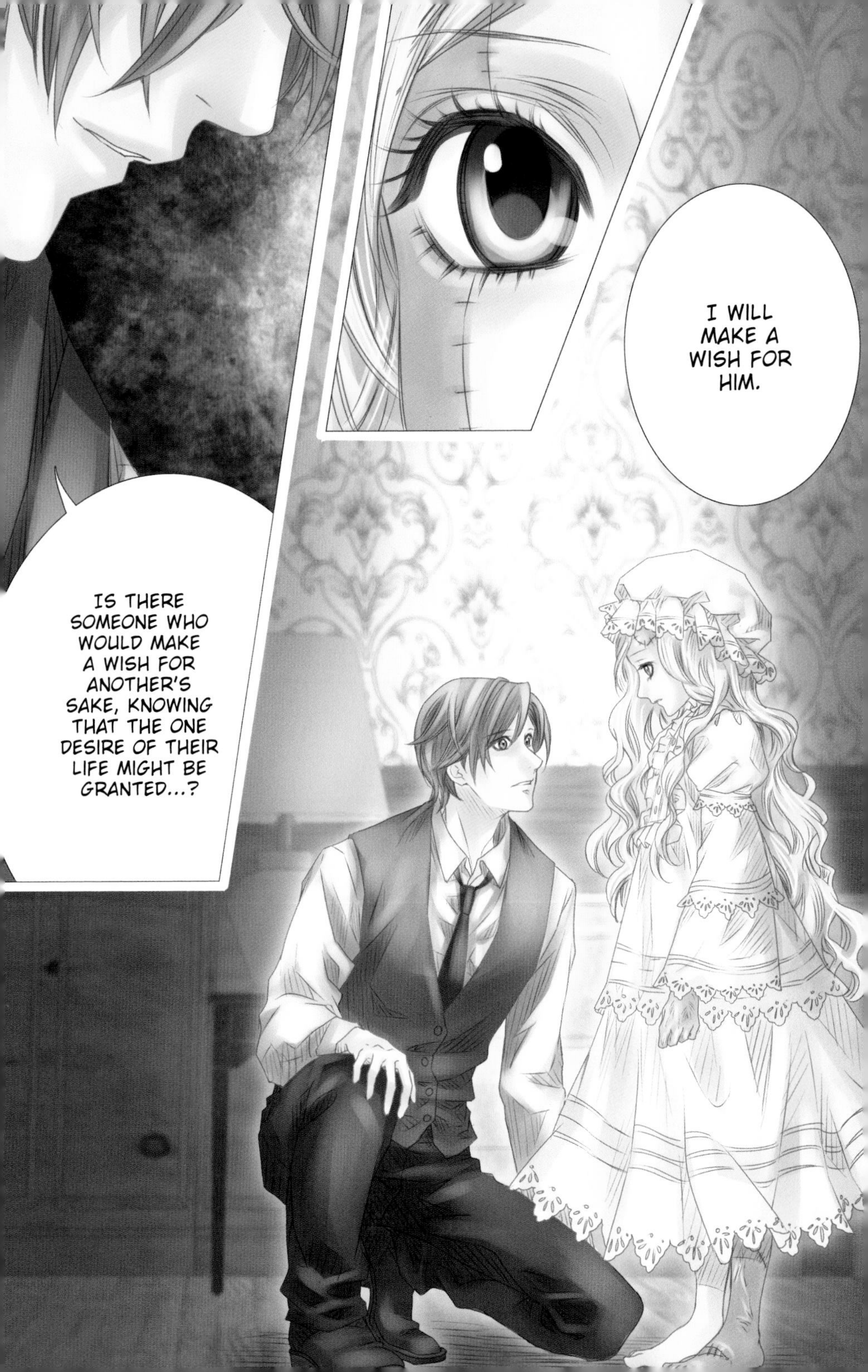
I WILL MAKE A WISH FOR HIM.
IS THERE SOMEONE WHO WOULD MAKE A WISH FOR ANOTHER'S SAKE, KNOWING THAT THE ONE DESIRE OF THEIR LIFE MIGHT BE GRANTED...?

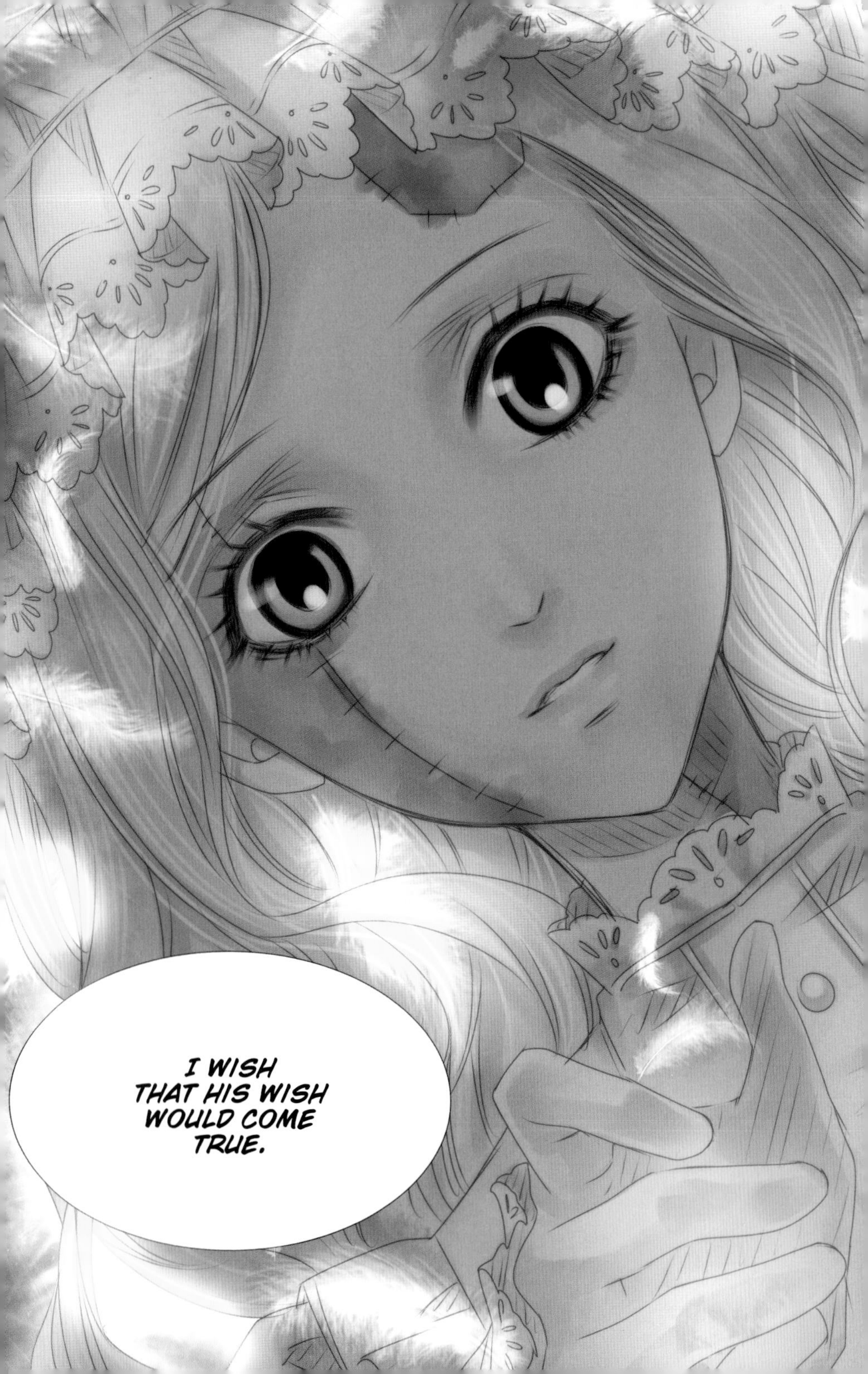
I WISH THAT HIS WISH WOULD COME TRUE.

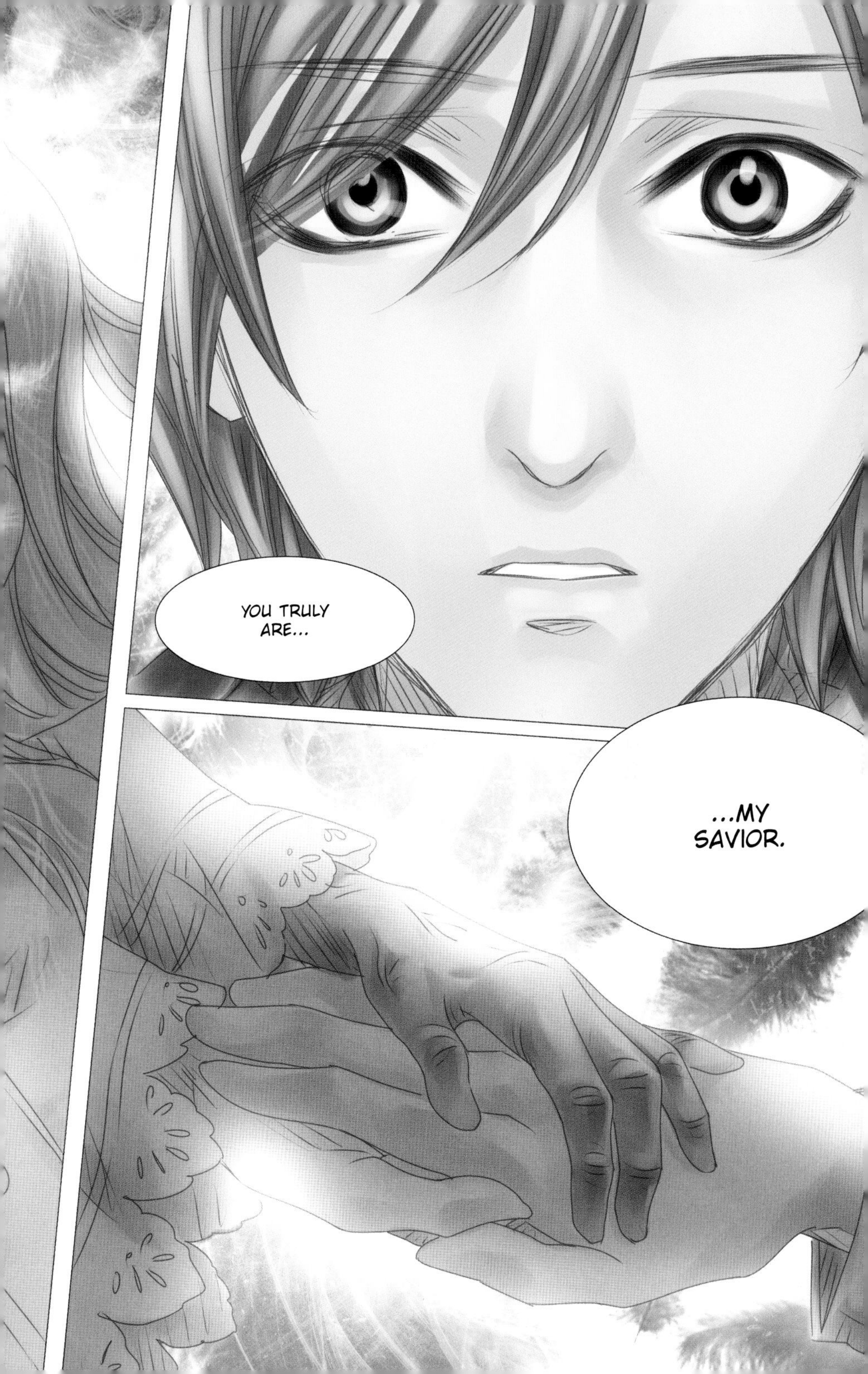
YOU TRULY ARE...
...MY SAVIOR.

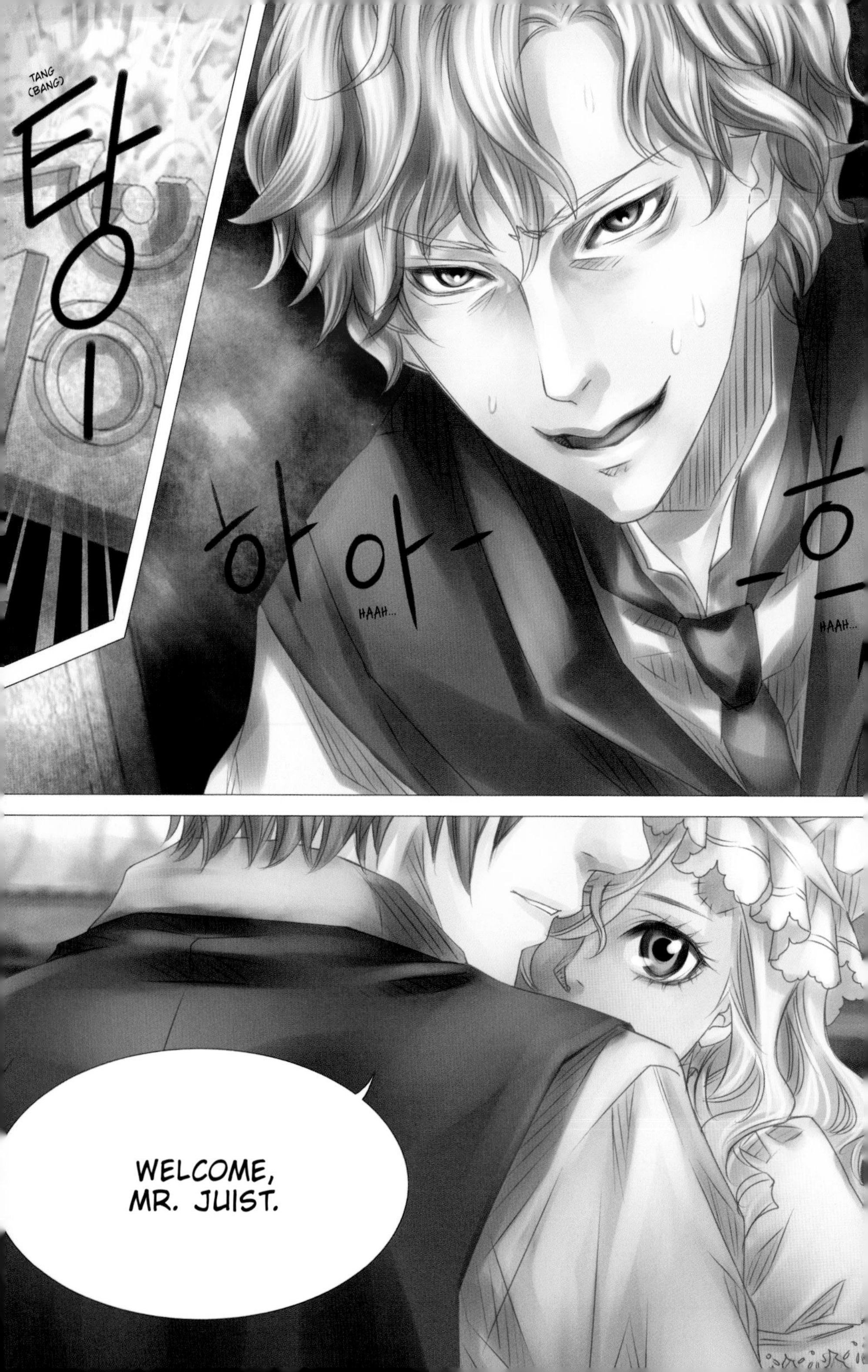
탕
TANG (BANG)
하아-
HAAH...
흐-
HAAH...
WELCOME, MR. JUIST.

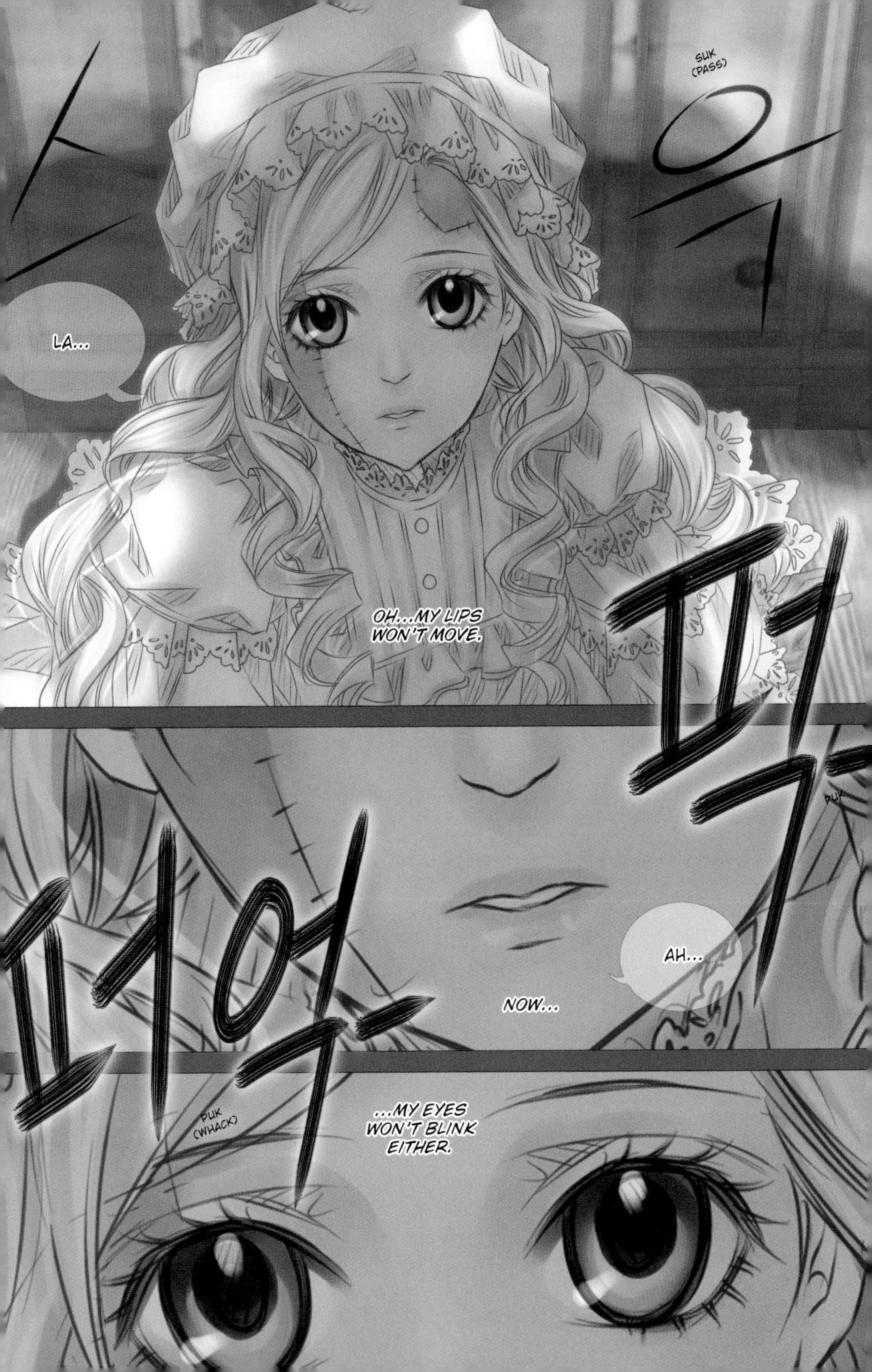

SUK (PASS)
LA...
OH...MY LIPS WON'T MOVE.
PUK
AH...
NOW...
PUK (WHACK)
...MY EYES WON'T BLINK EITHER.

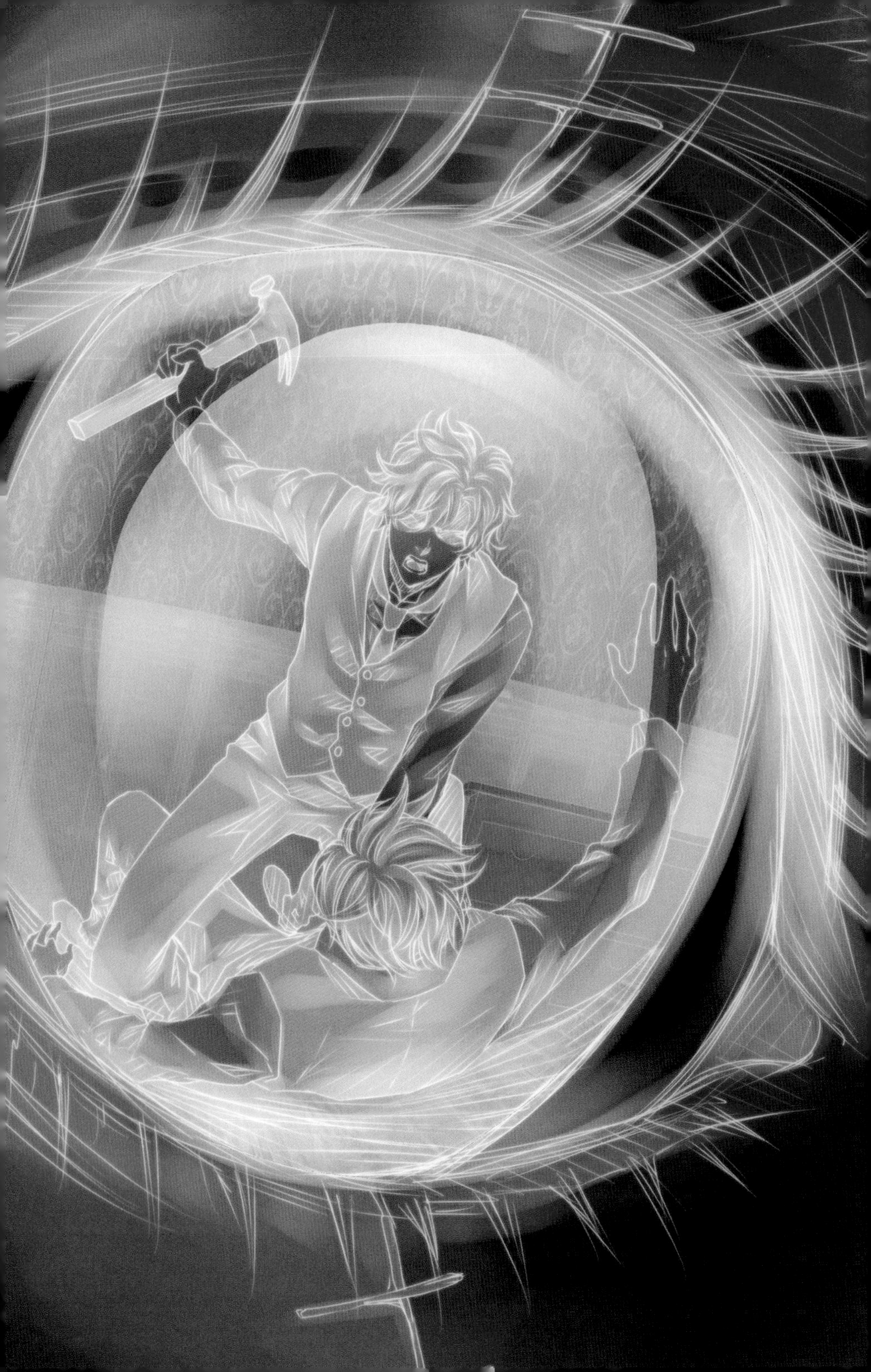

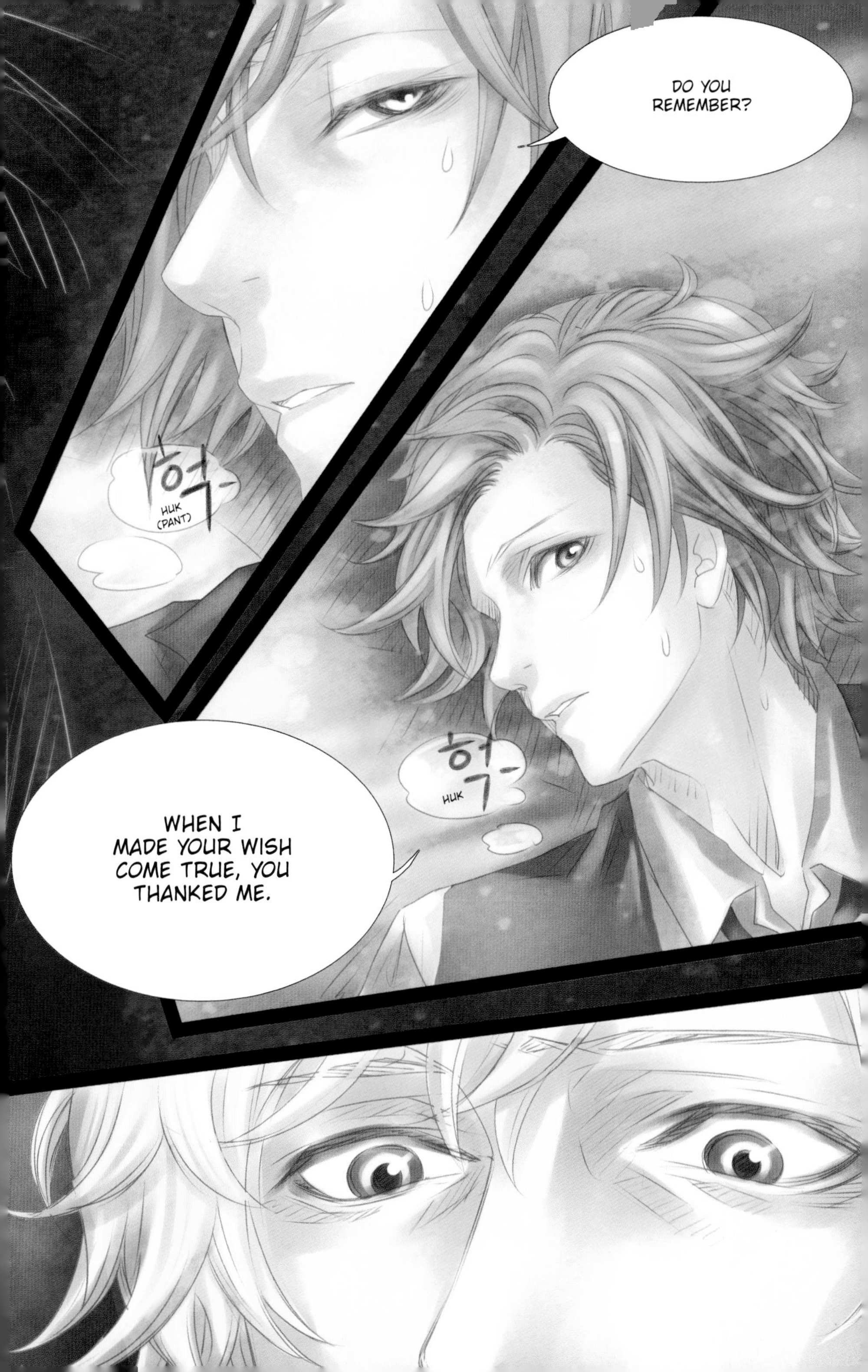
DO YOU REMEMBER?
헉
HUK (PANT)
헉
HUK
WHEN I MADE YOUR WISH COME TRUE, YOU THANKED ME.

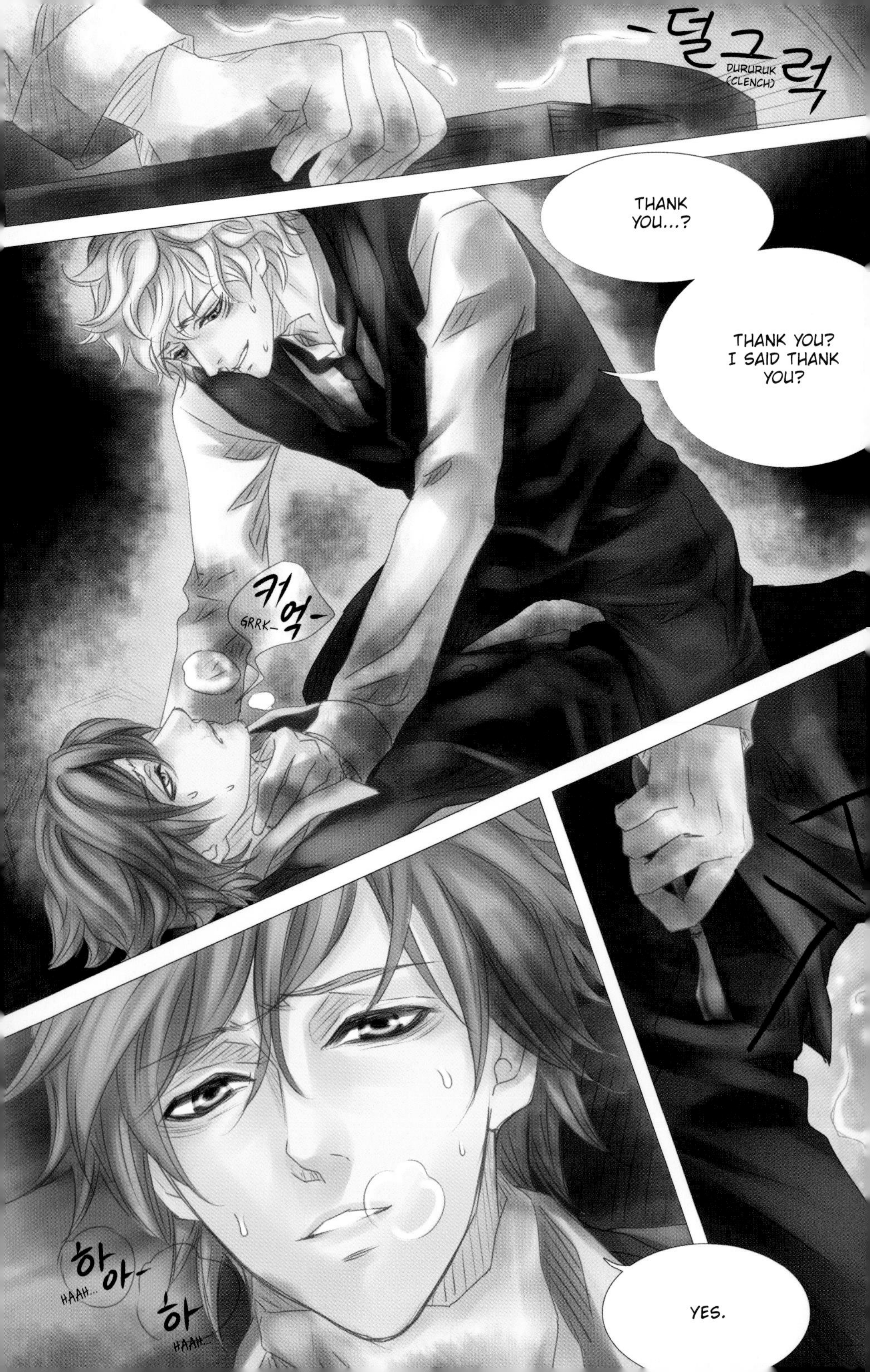

덜그럭
DURURUK (CLENCH)
THANK YOU...?
THANK YOU? I SAID THANK YOU?
커억-
GRRK-
하아-
HAAH...
하
HAAH...
YES.

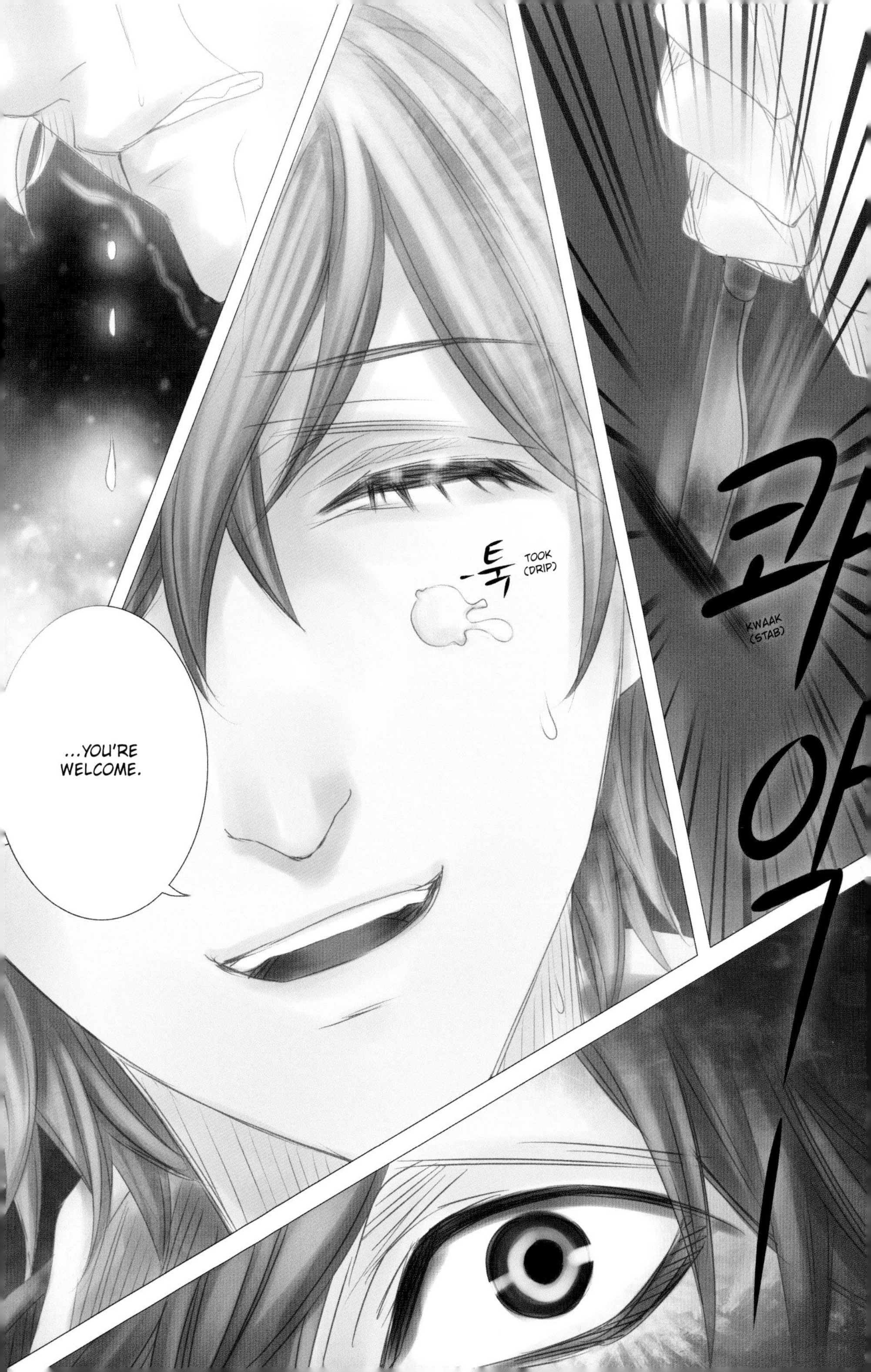
...YOU'RE WELCOME.
툭
TOOK (DRIP)
콰악
KWAAK (STAB)

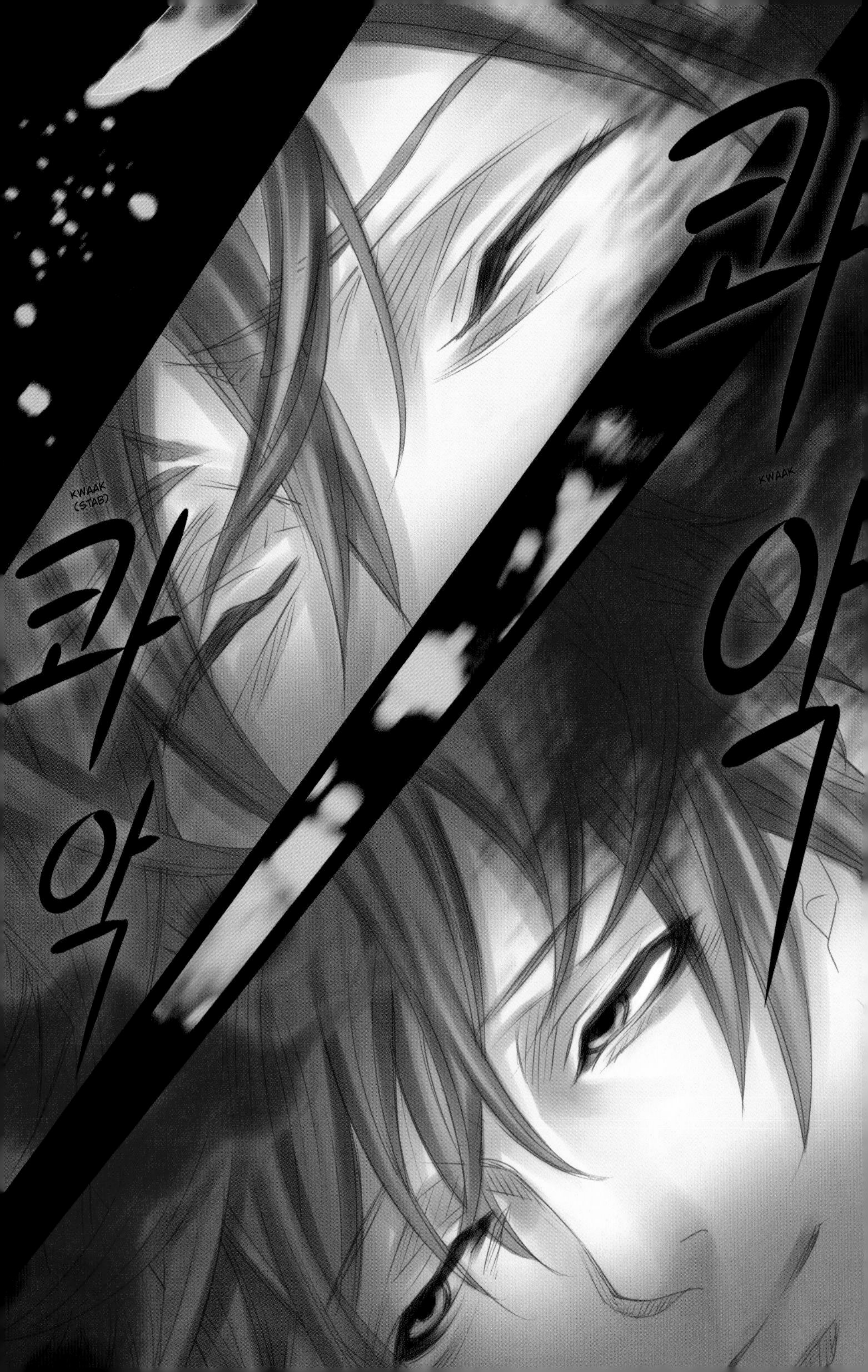
콰악
KWAAK
KWAAK
(STAB)
콰악

Void's Enigmatic Mansion

"

Why do you
look so sad?

"

"

It's because
your wish has been
granted, my child.

"

Void's Enigmatic Mansion

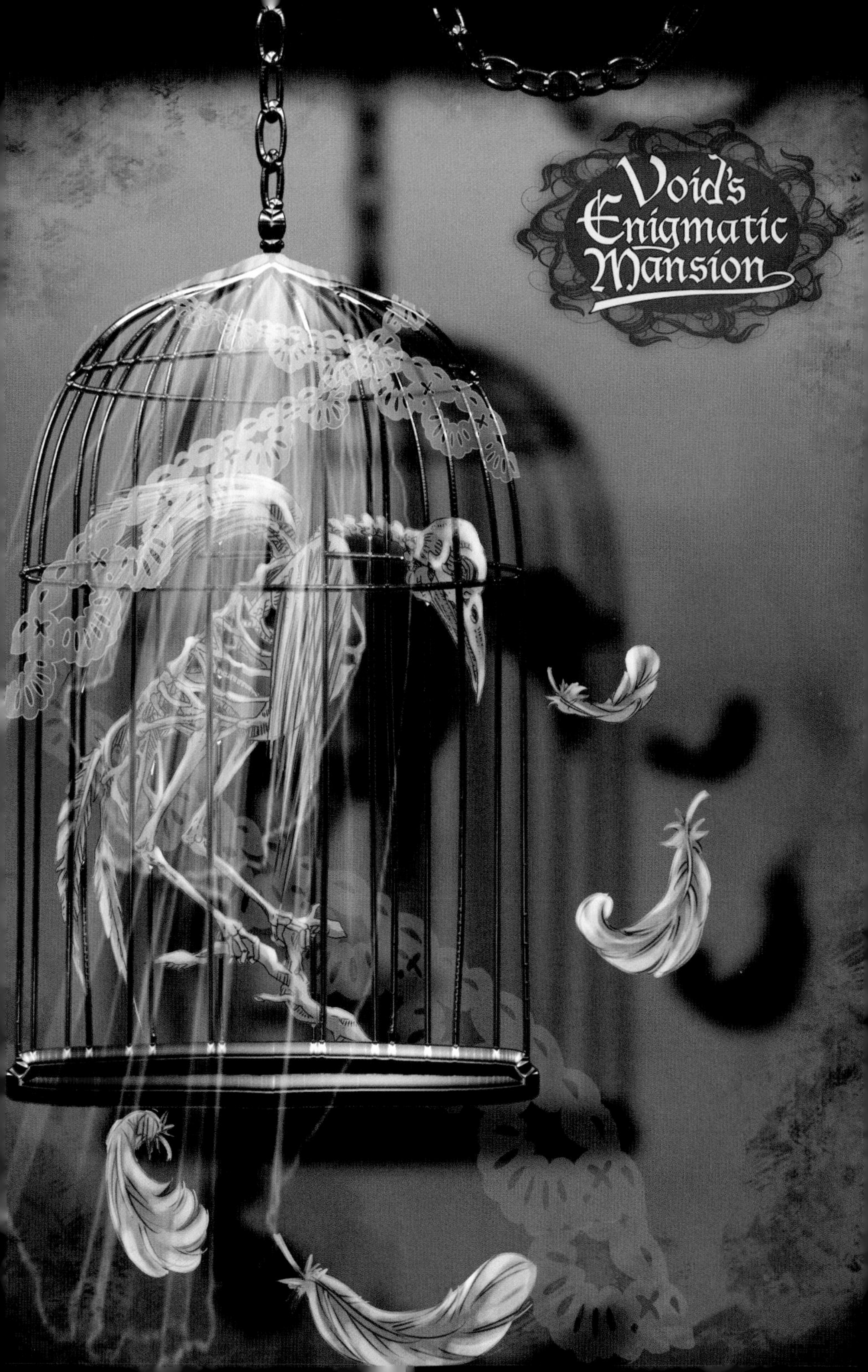
Void's Enigmatic Mansion

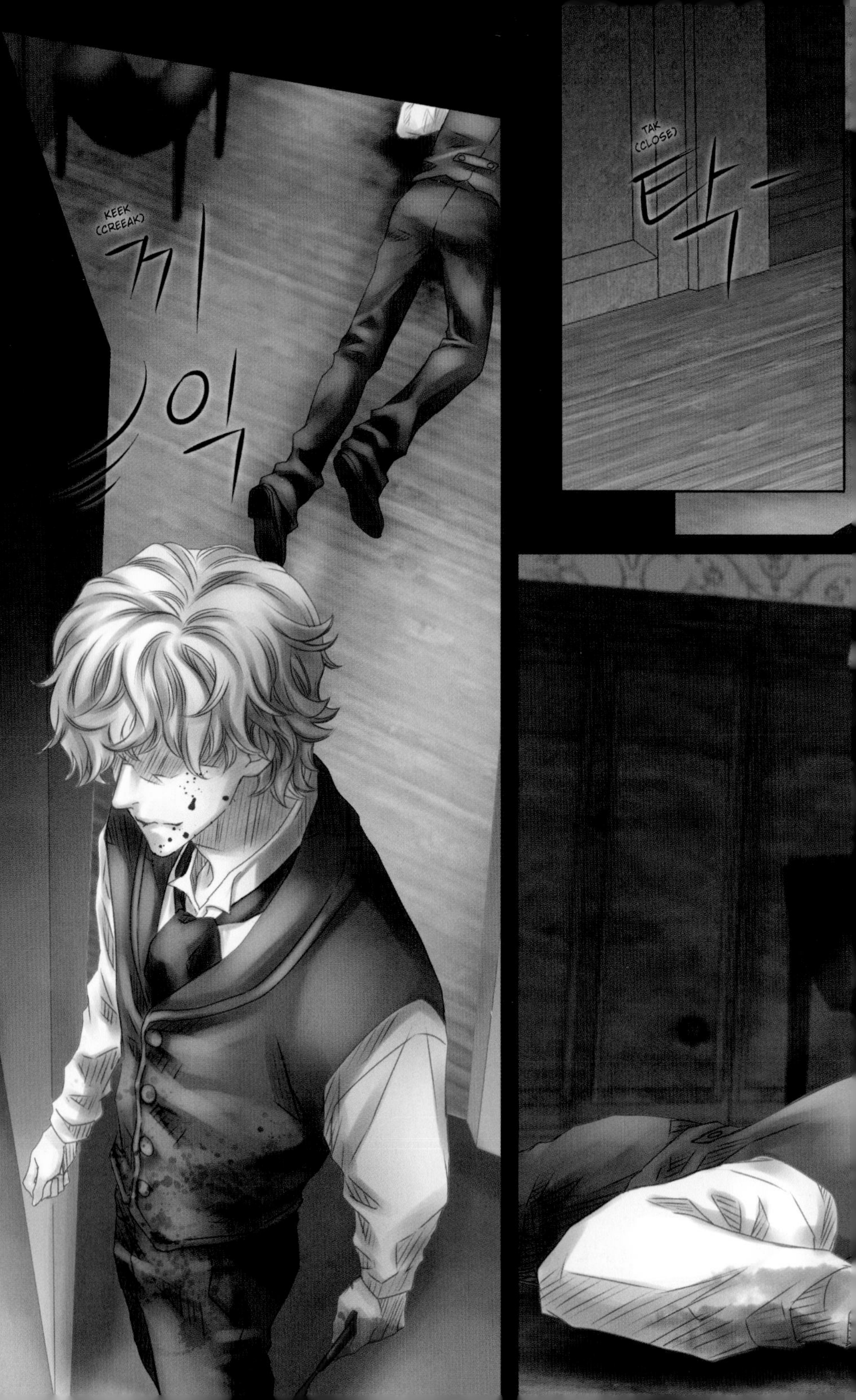
KEEK (CREEAK)
끼익
TAK (CLOSE)
탁

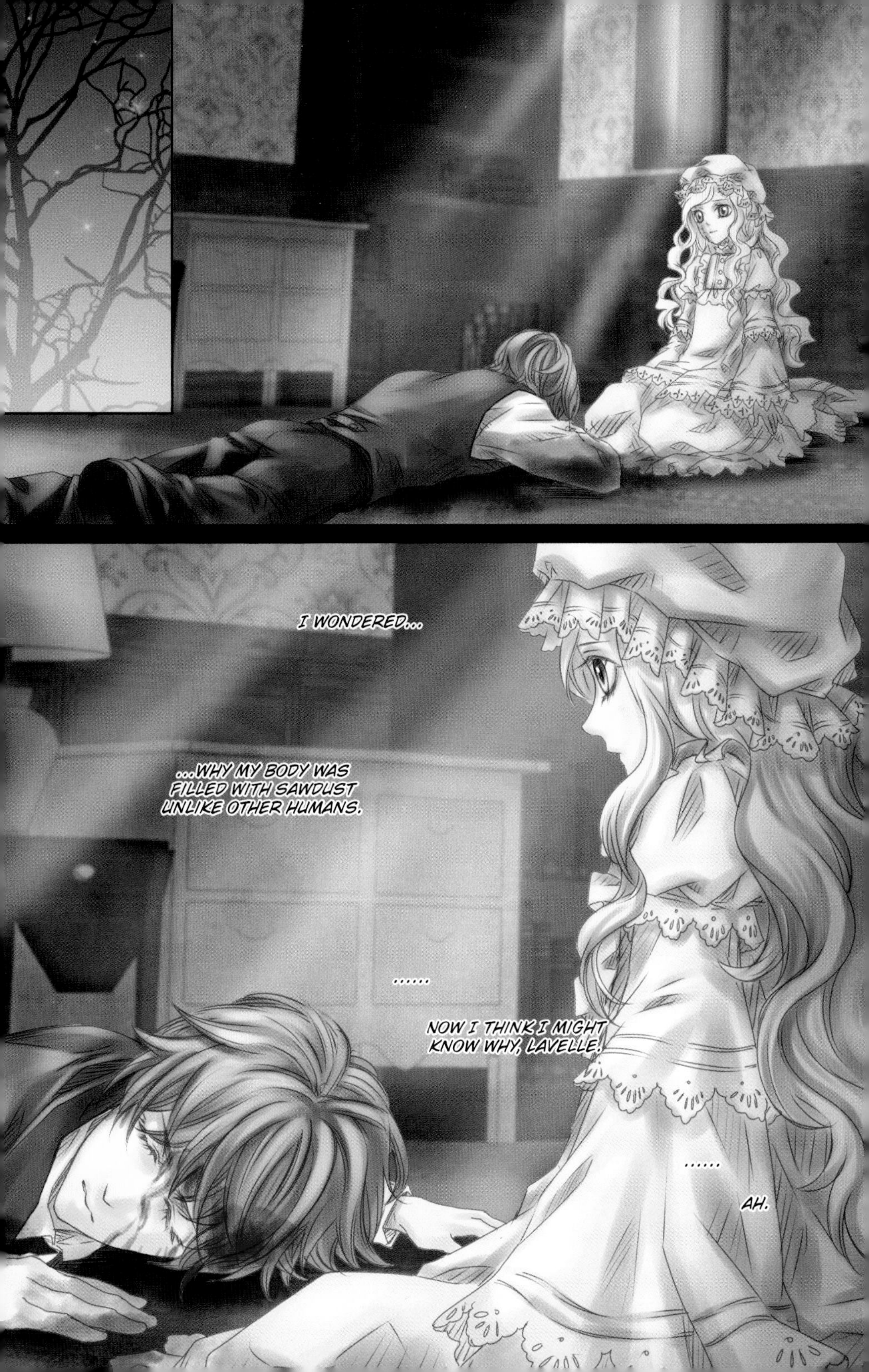
I WONDERED...
...WHY MY BODY WAS FILLED WITH SAWDUST UNLIKE OTHER HUMANS.
......
NOW I THINK I MIGHT KNOW WHY, LAVELLE.
......
AH.

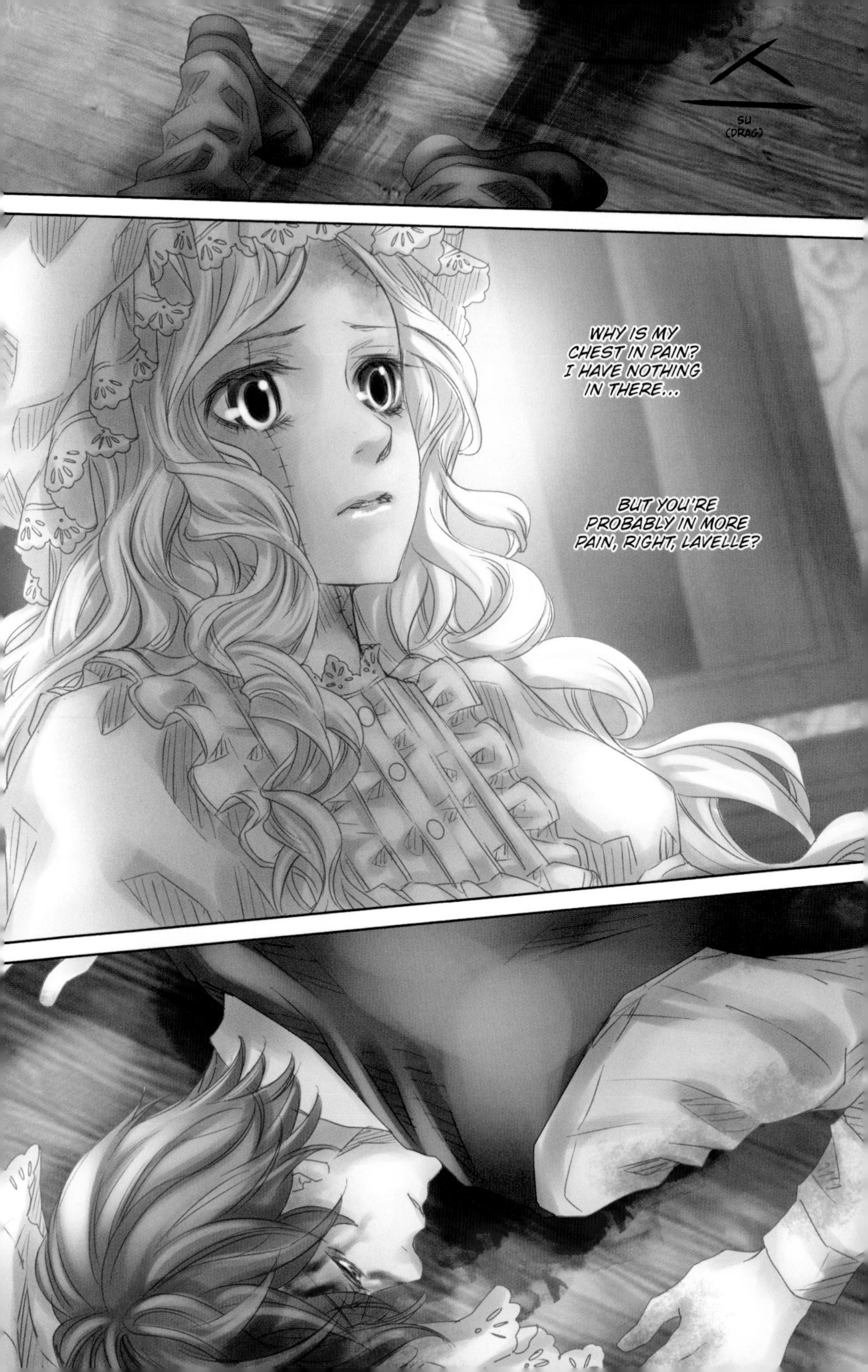
SU
(DRAG)
WHY IS MY CHEST IN PAIN? I HAVE NOTHING IN THERE...
BUT YOU'RE PROBABLY IN MORE PAIN, RIGHT, LAVELLE?

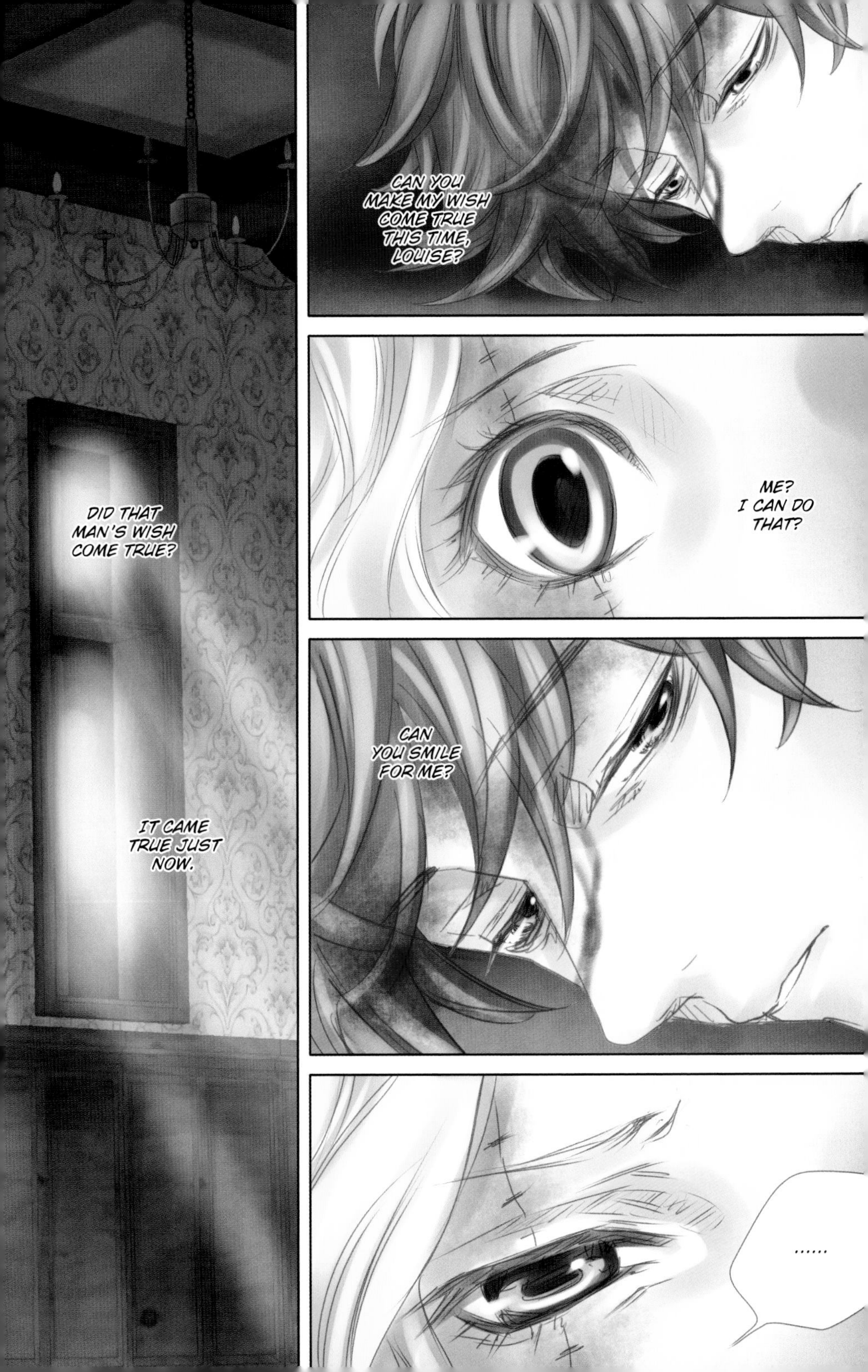
CAN YOU MAKE MY WISH COME TRUE THIS TIME, LOUISE?
ME? I CAN DO THAT?
CAN YOU SMILE FOR ME?
......
DID THAT MAN'S WISH COME TRUE?
IT CAME TRUE JUST NOW.

...I CAN'T.

IT'S OKAY.
THAT WAS
ENOUGH.

EVERYTHING
I DID WAS A SIN
EXCEPT CREATING
YOU...

과—악

KWAAK
(GRAB)

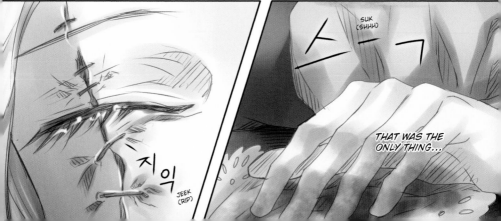

ㅅ—ㄱ

SUK
(SHHH)

지익

JEEK
(RIP)

THAT WAS THE
ONLY THING...

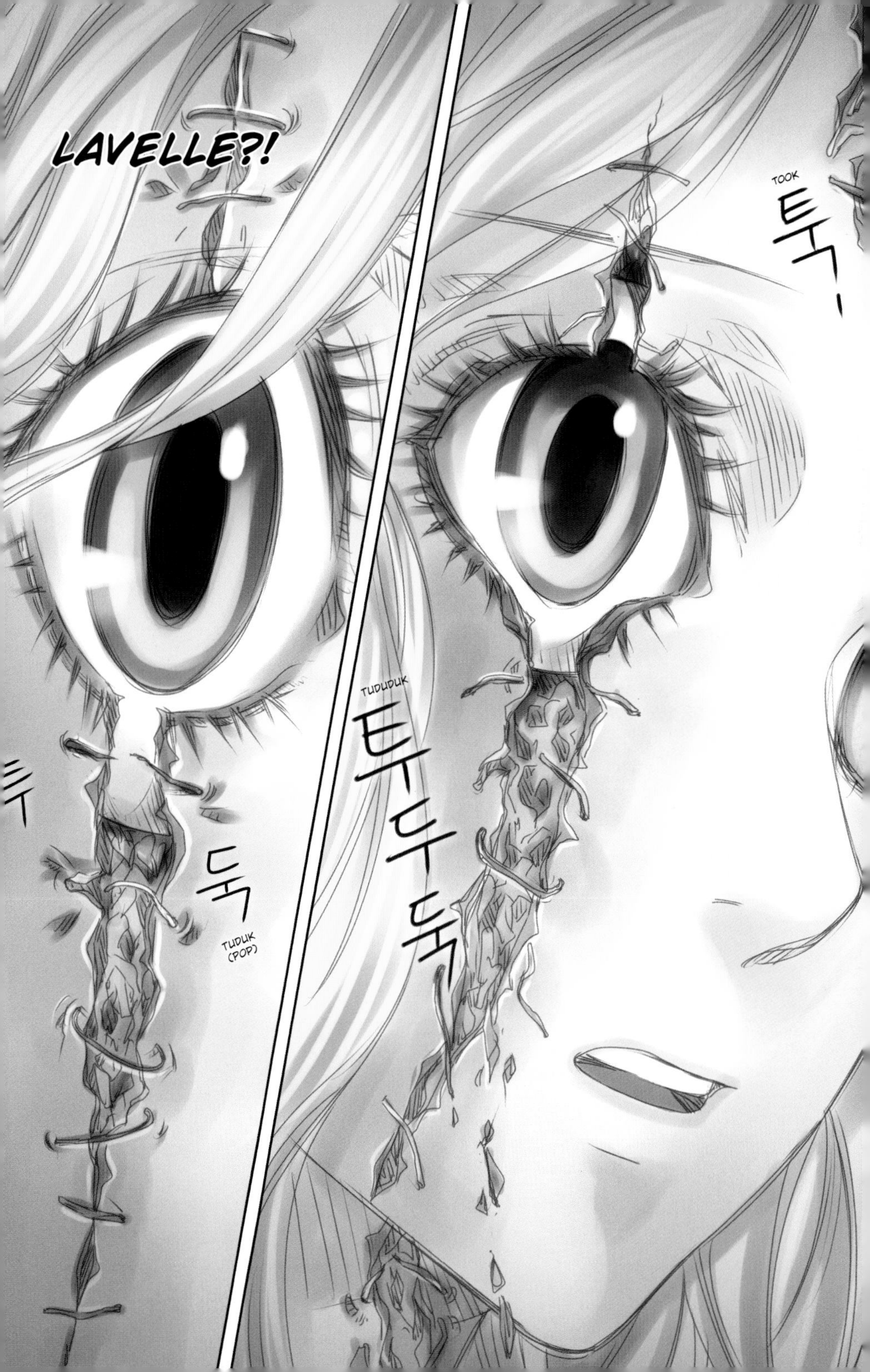

톡
TOOK
투두둑
TUDUDUK
LAVELLE?!
투둑
TUDUK (POP)

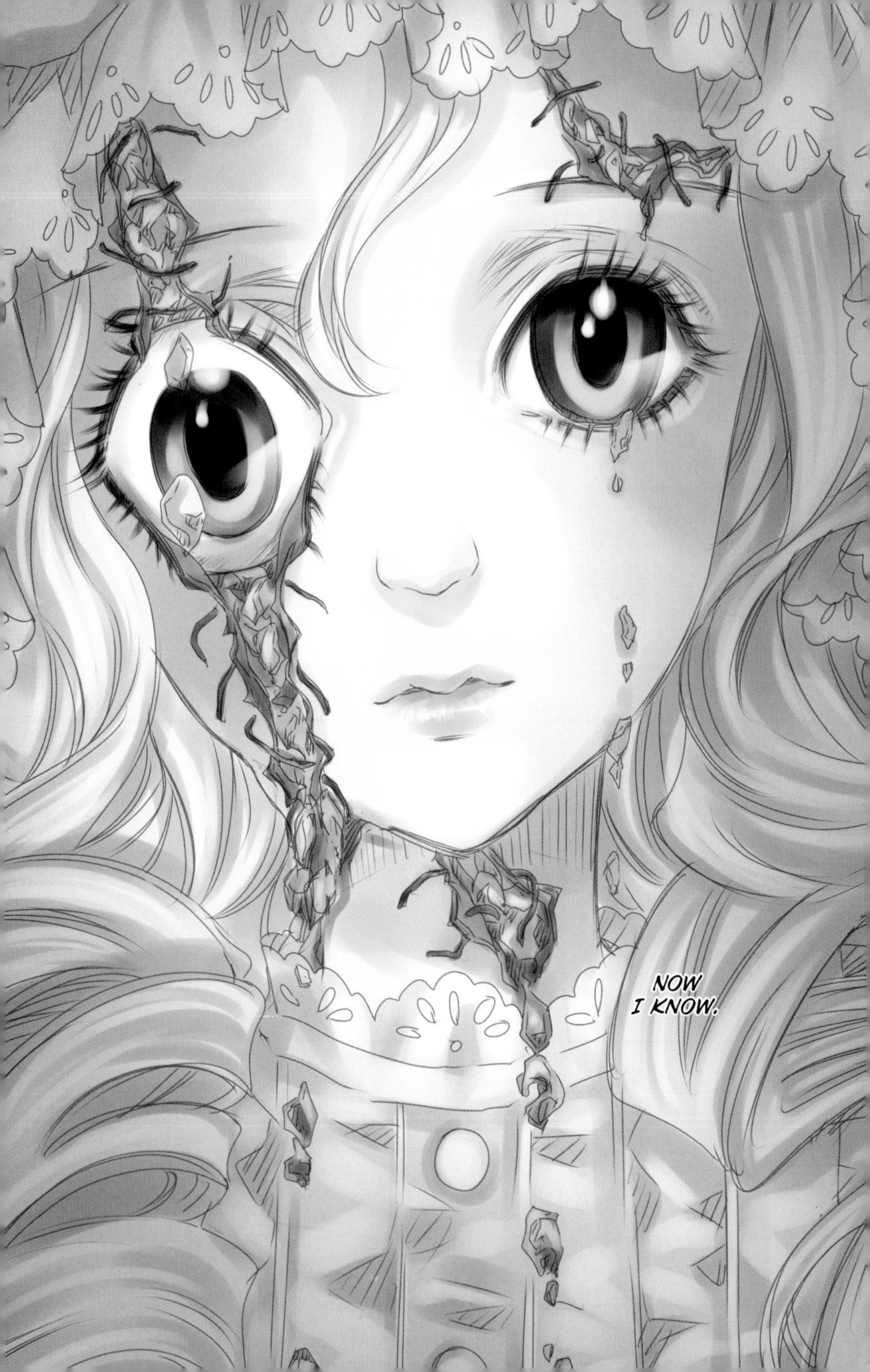
NOW I KNOW.

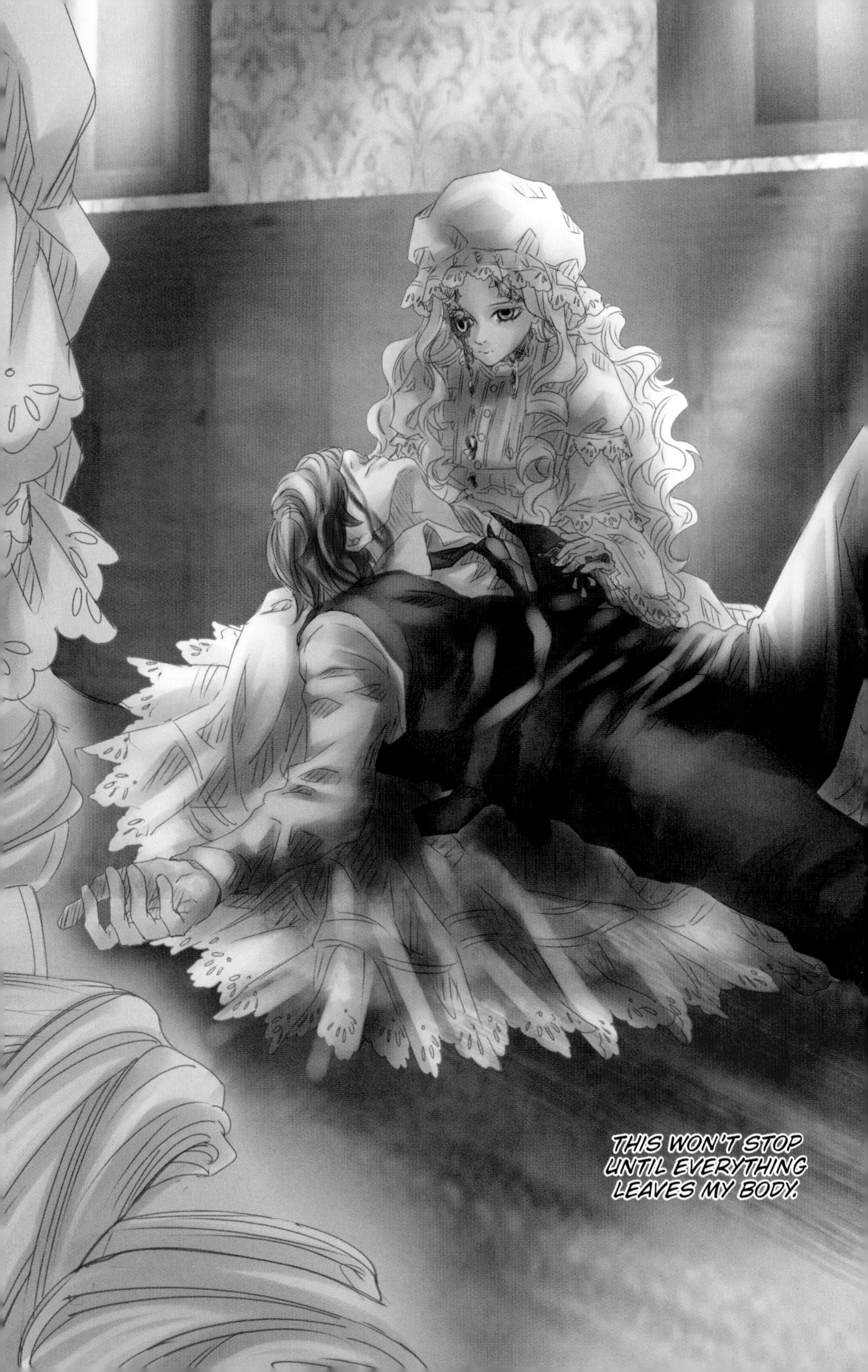
THIS WON'T STOP UNTIL EVERYTHING LEAVES MY BODY.

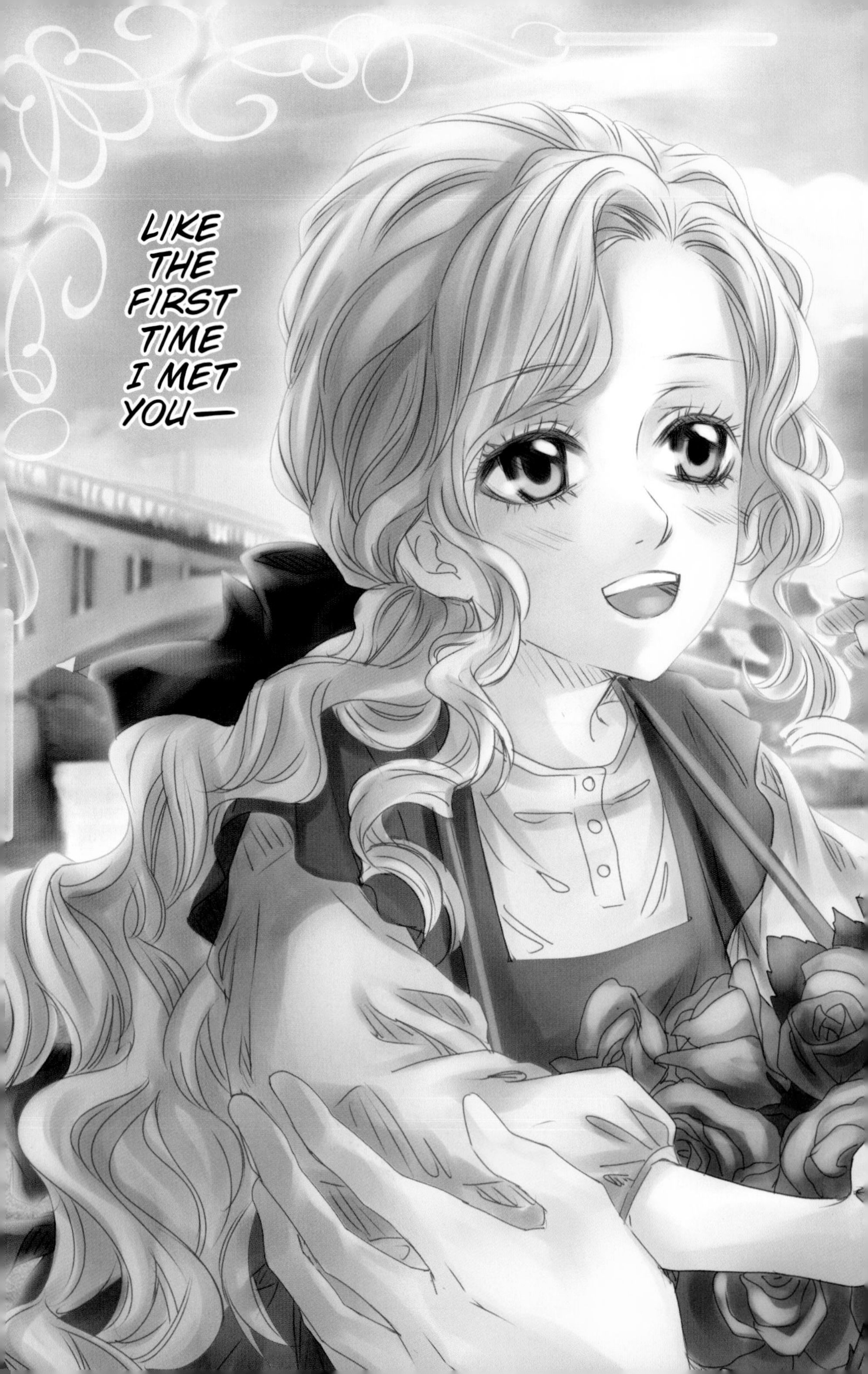
LIKE THE FIRST TIME I MET YOU—

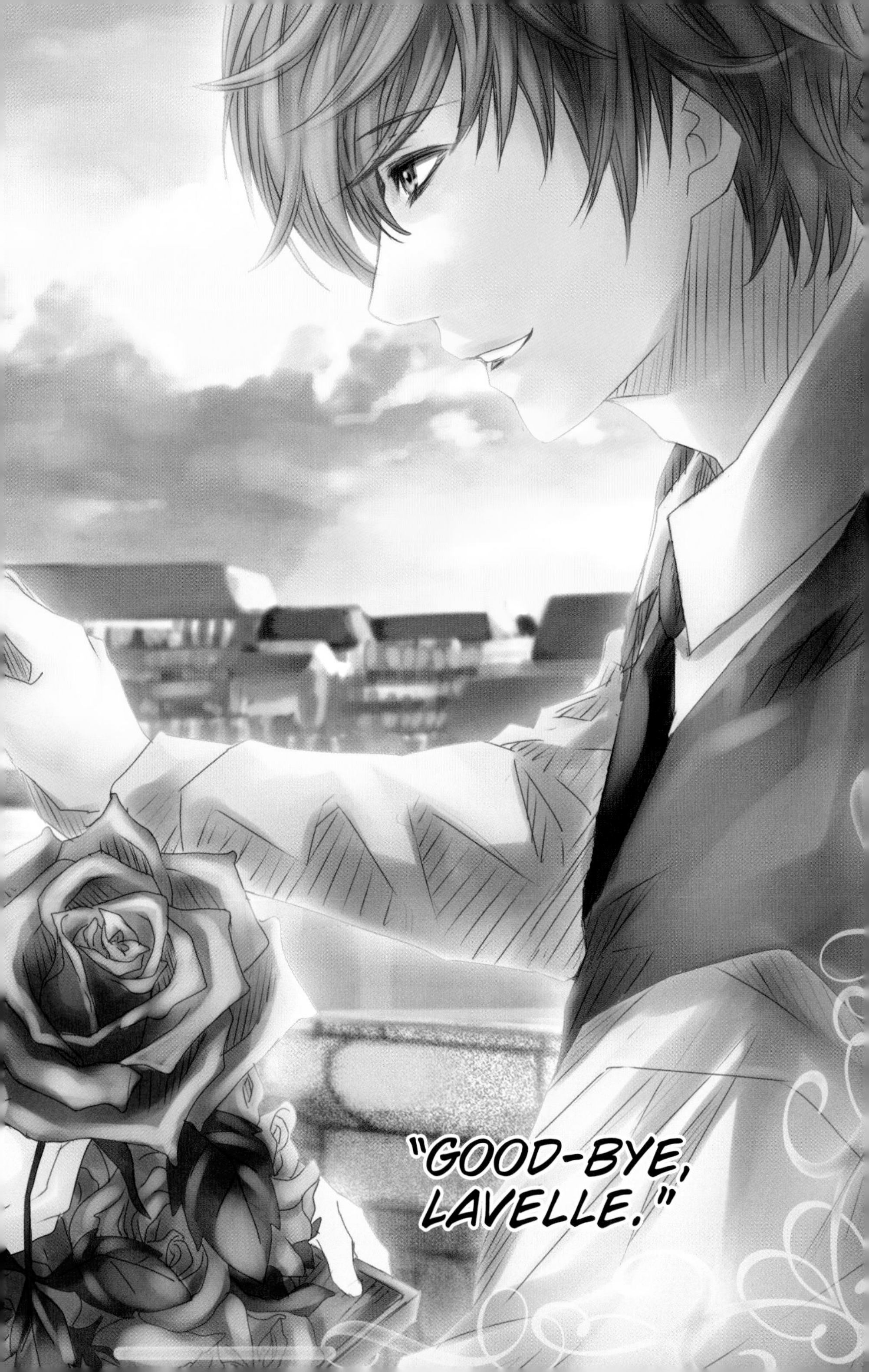
"GOOD-BYE, LAVELLE."

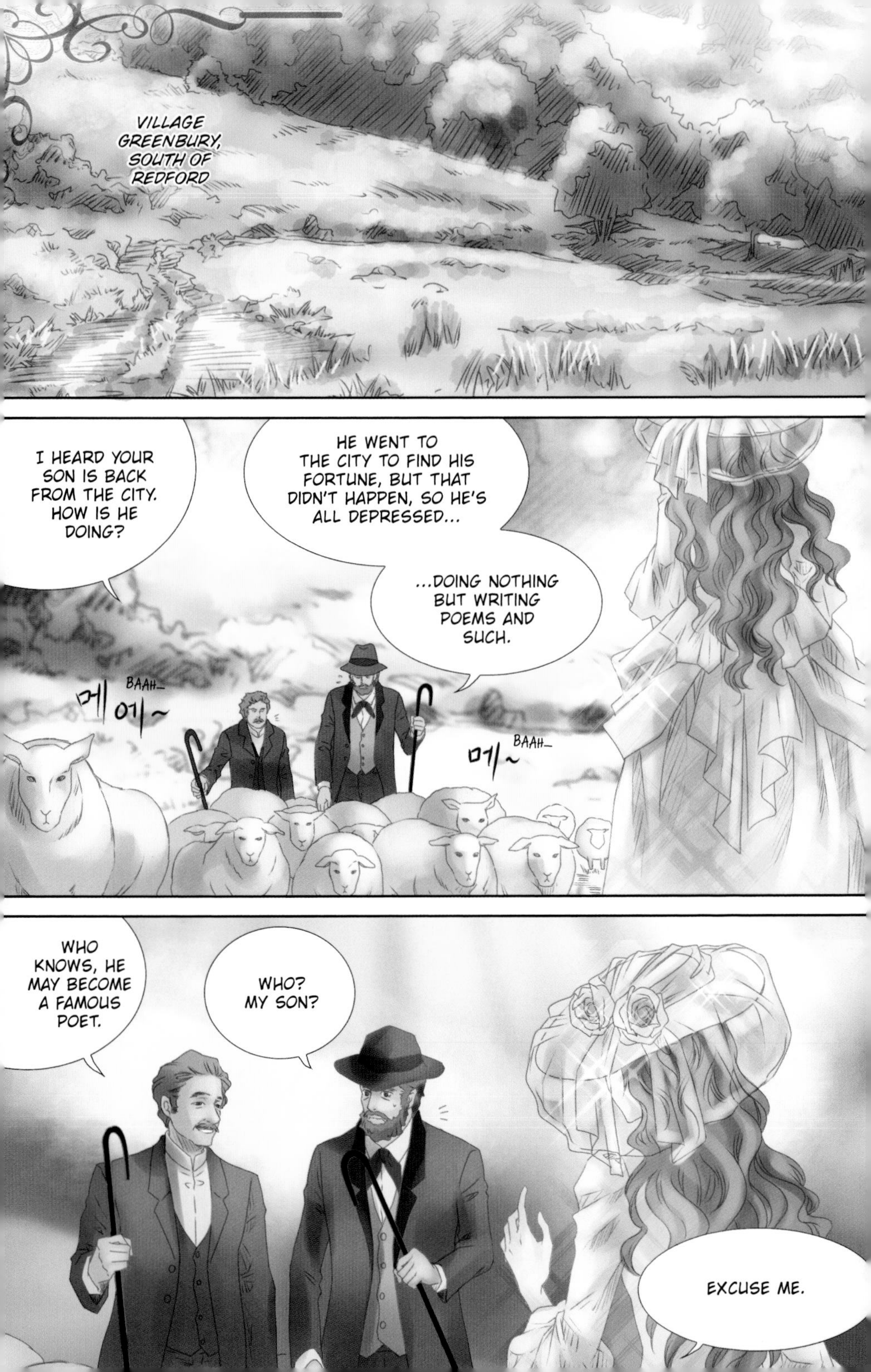
VILLAGE GREENBURY, SOUTH OF REDFORD
I HEARD YOUR SON IS BACK FROM THE CITY. HOW IS HE DOING?
HE WENT TO THE CITY TO FIND HIS FORTUNE, BUT THAT DIDN'T HAPPEN, SO HE'S ALL DEPRESSED...
...DOING NOTHING BUT WRITING POEMS AND SUCH.
메에~ BAAH_
메~ BAAH_
WHO KNOWS, HE MAY BECOME A FAMOUS POET.
WHO? MY SON?
EXCUSE ME.

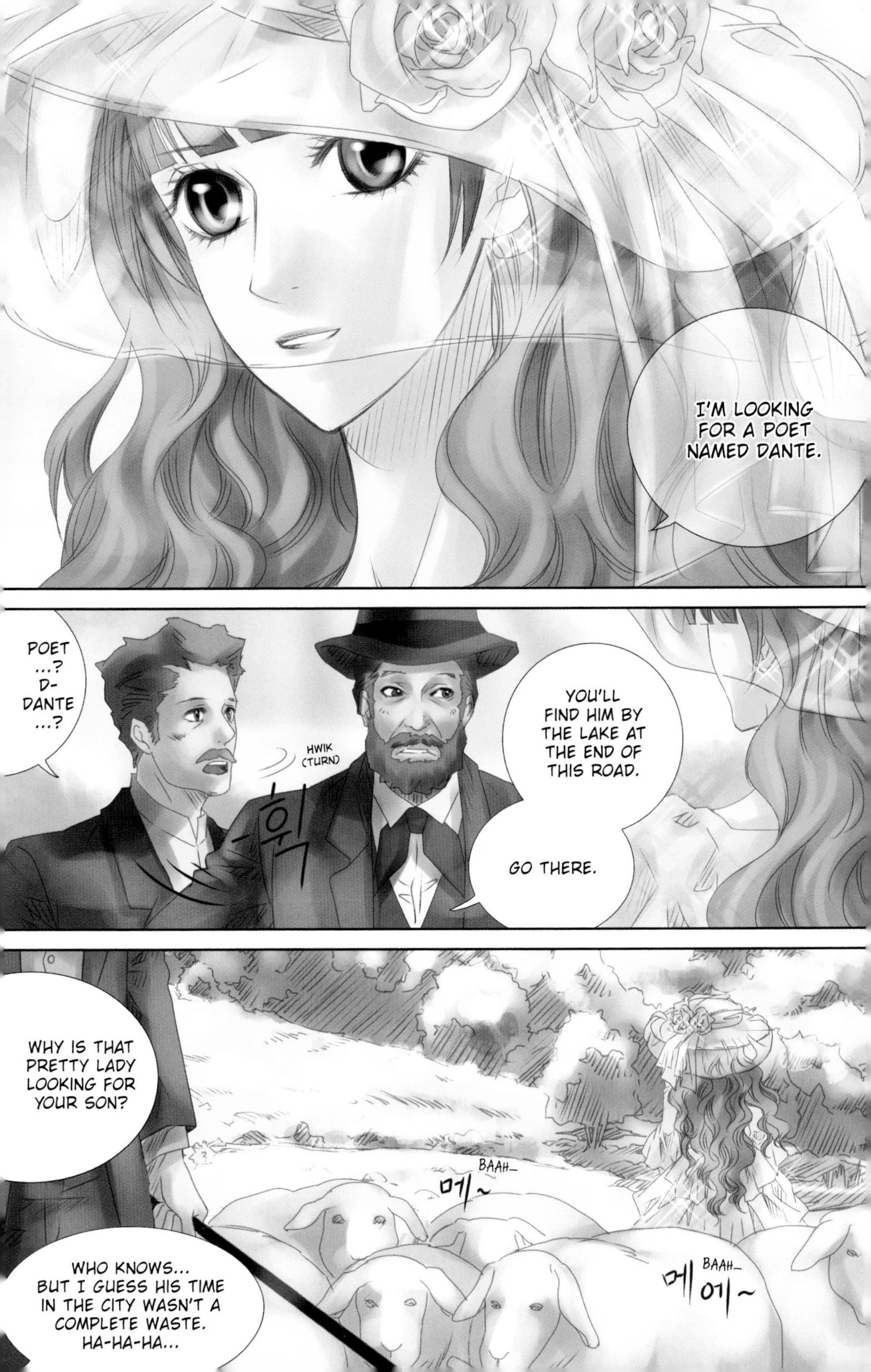
I'M LOOKING FOR A POET NAMED DANTE.
POET ...? D-DANTE ...?
HWIK (TURN)
휙
YOU'LL FIND HIM BY THE LAKE AT THE END OF THIS ROAD.
GO THERE.
WHY IS THAT PRETTY LADY LOOKING FOR YOUR SON?
BAAH_
메~
BAAH_
메에~
WHO KNOWS... BUT I GUESS HIS TIME IN THE CITY WASN'T A COMPLETE WASTE. HA-HA-HA...

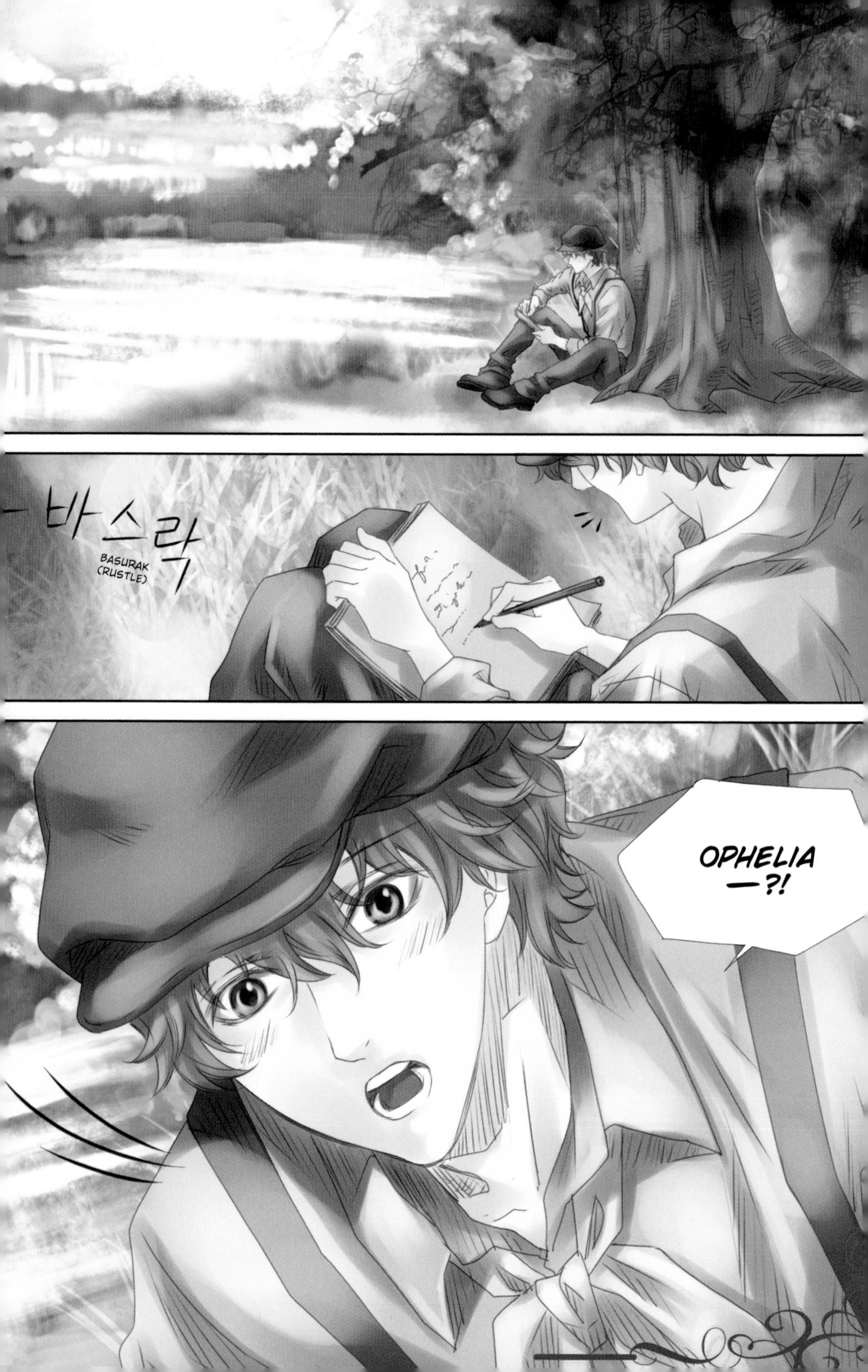
바스락
BASURAK (RUSTLE)
OPHELIA —?!

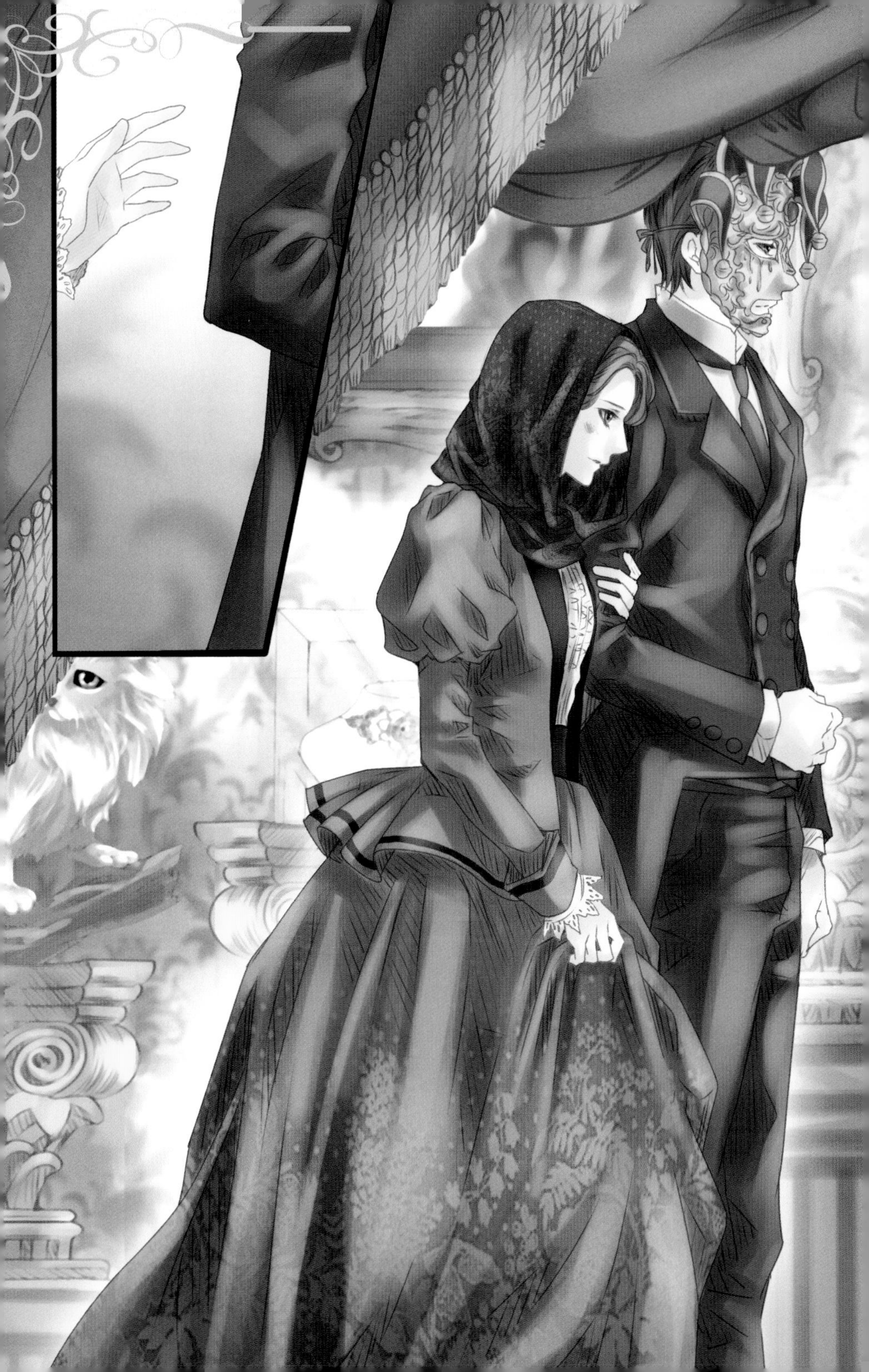

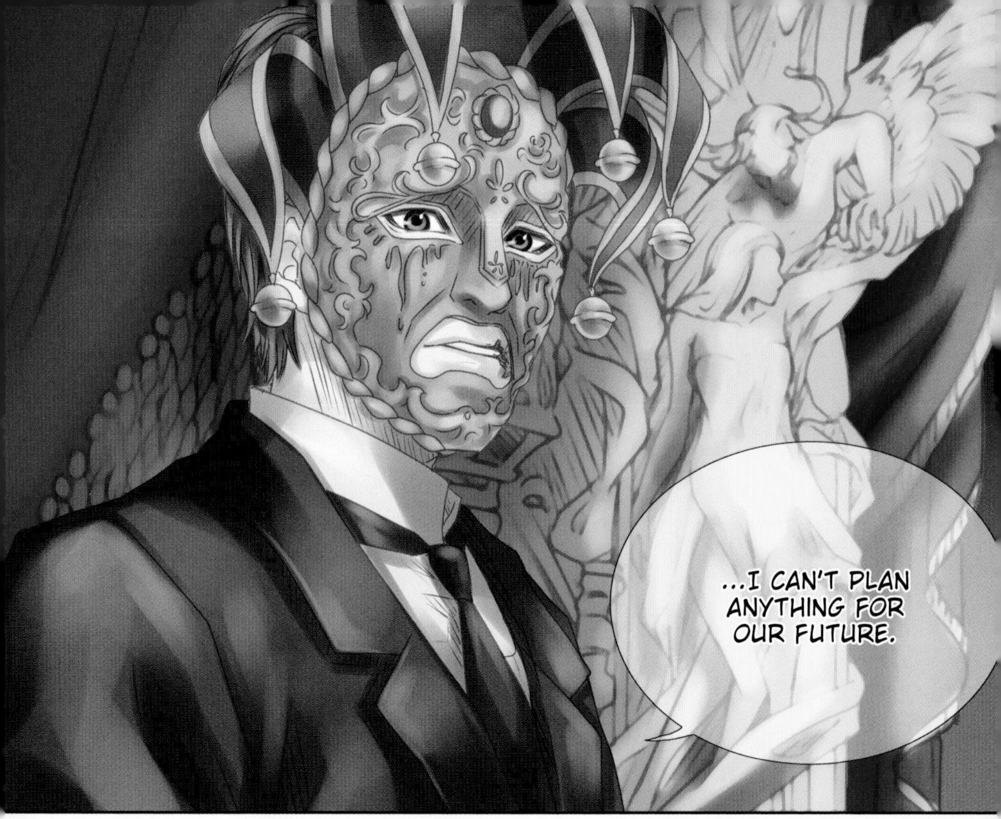
...I CAN'T PLAN ANYTHING FOR OUR FUTURE.

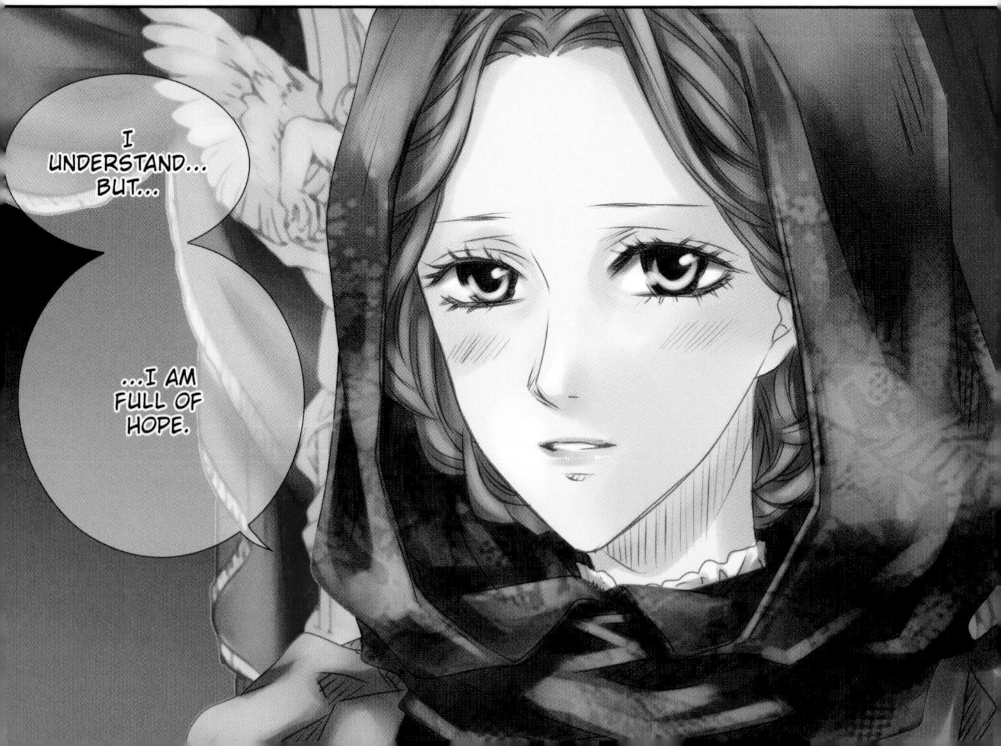
I UNDERSTAND... BUT...
...I AM FULL OF HOPE.

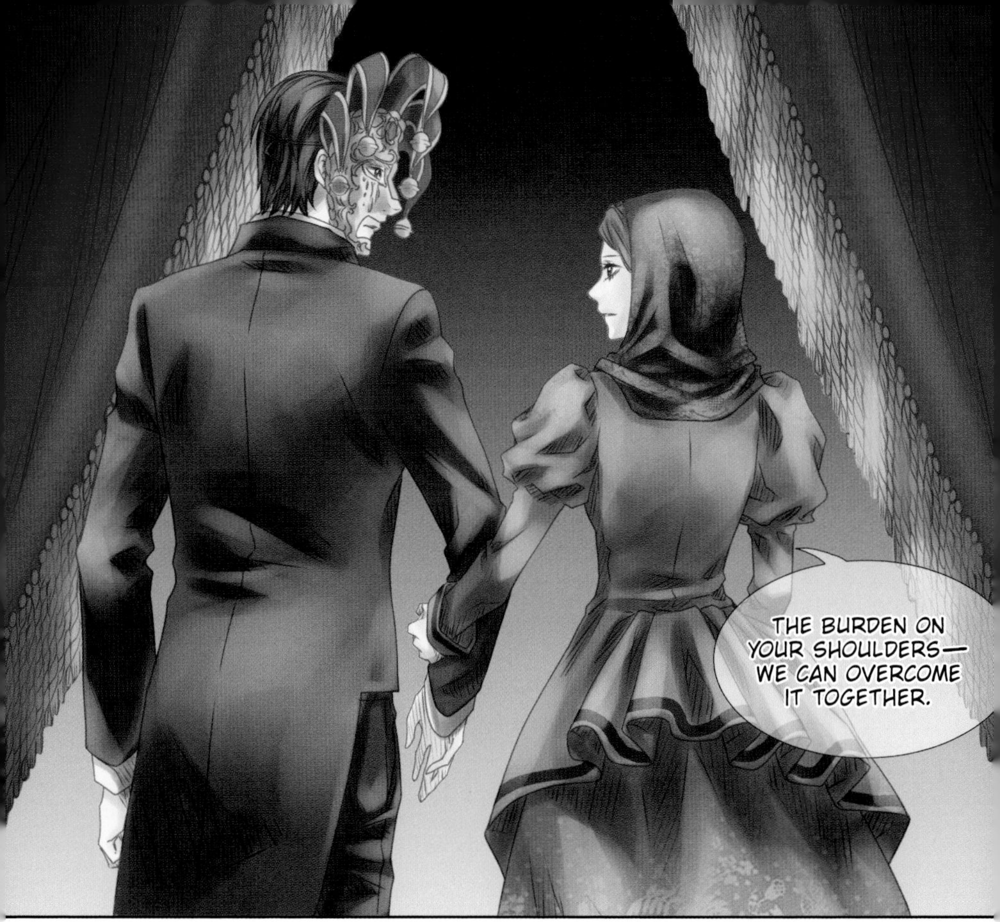
THE BURDEN ON YOUR SHOULDERS— WE CAN OVERCOME IT TOGETHER.

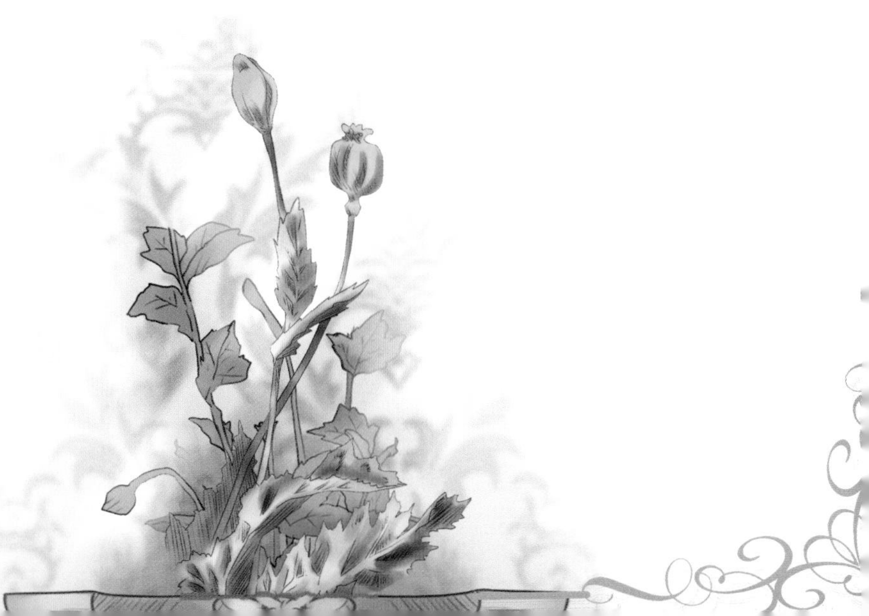

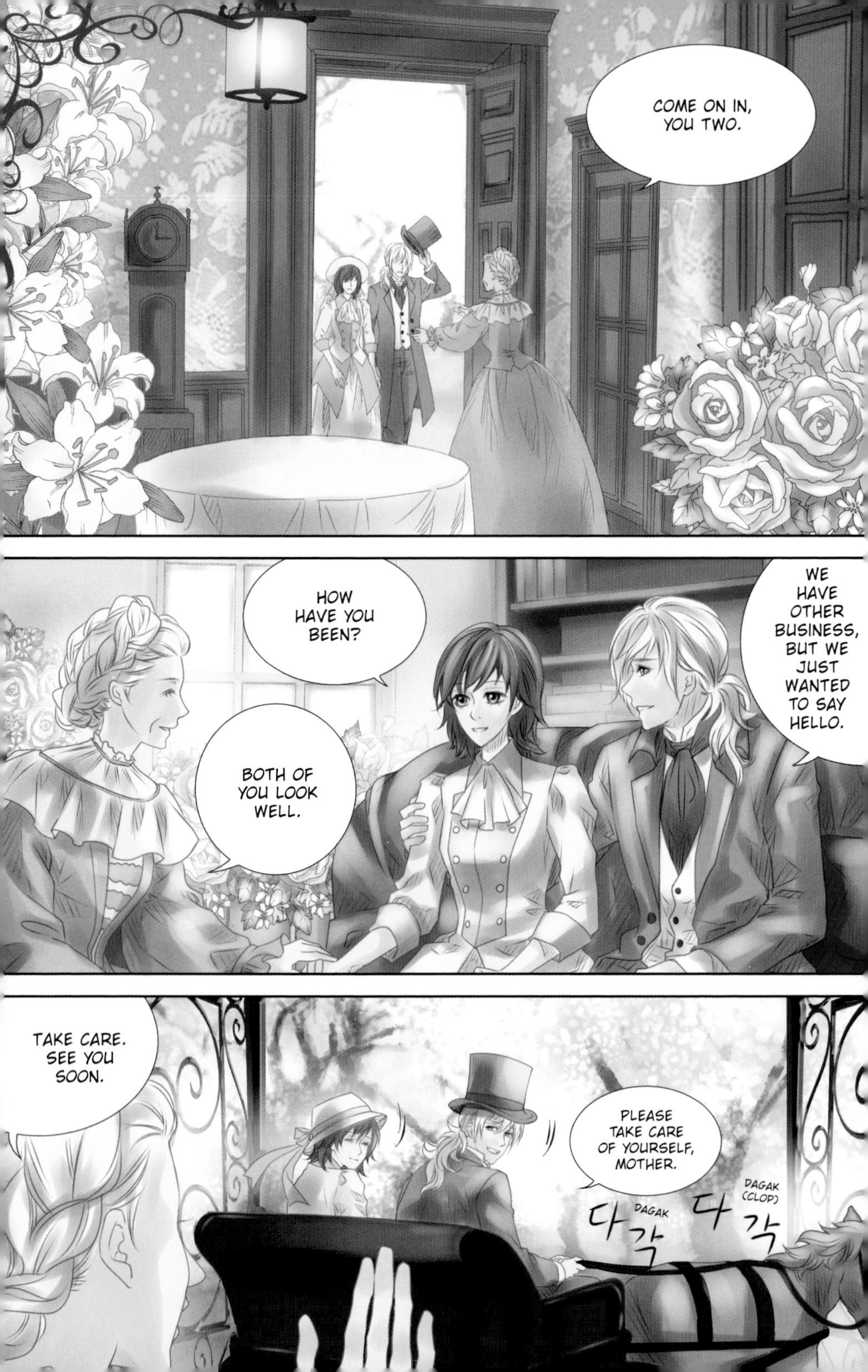
COME ON IN, YOU TWO.
HOW HAVE YOU BEEN?
WE HAVE OTHER BUSINESS, BUT WE JUST WANTED TO SAY HELLO.
BOTH OF YOU LOOK WELL.
TAKE CARE. SEE YOU SOON.
PLEASE TAKE CARE OF YOURSELF, MOTHER.
다각 DAGAK
다각 DAGAK (CLOP)

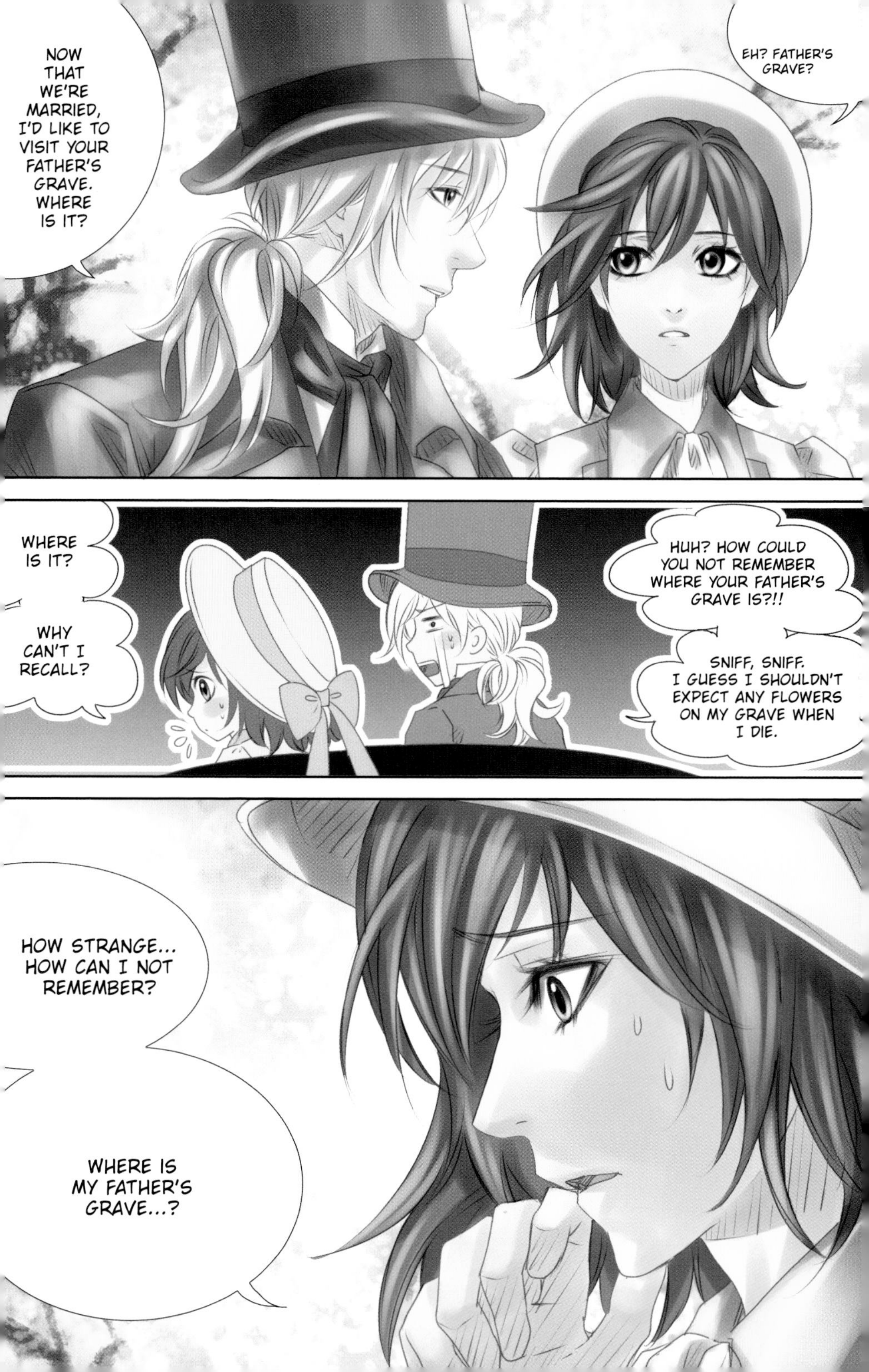
EH? FATHER'S GRAVE?
NOW THAT WE'RE MARRIED, I'D LIKE TO VISIT YOUR FATHER'S GRAVE. WHERE IS IT?
HUH? HOW COULD YOU NOT REMEMBER WHERE YOUR FATHER'S GRAVE IS?!!
SNIFF, SNIFF. I GUESS I SHOULDN'T EXPECT ANY FLOWERS ON MY GRAVE WHEN I DIE.
WHERE IS IT?
WHY CAN'T I RECALL?
HOW STRANGE... HOW CAN I NOT REMEMBER?
WHERE IS MY FATHER'S GRAVE...?

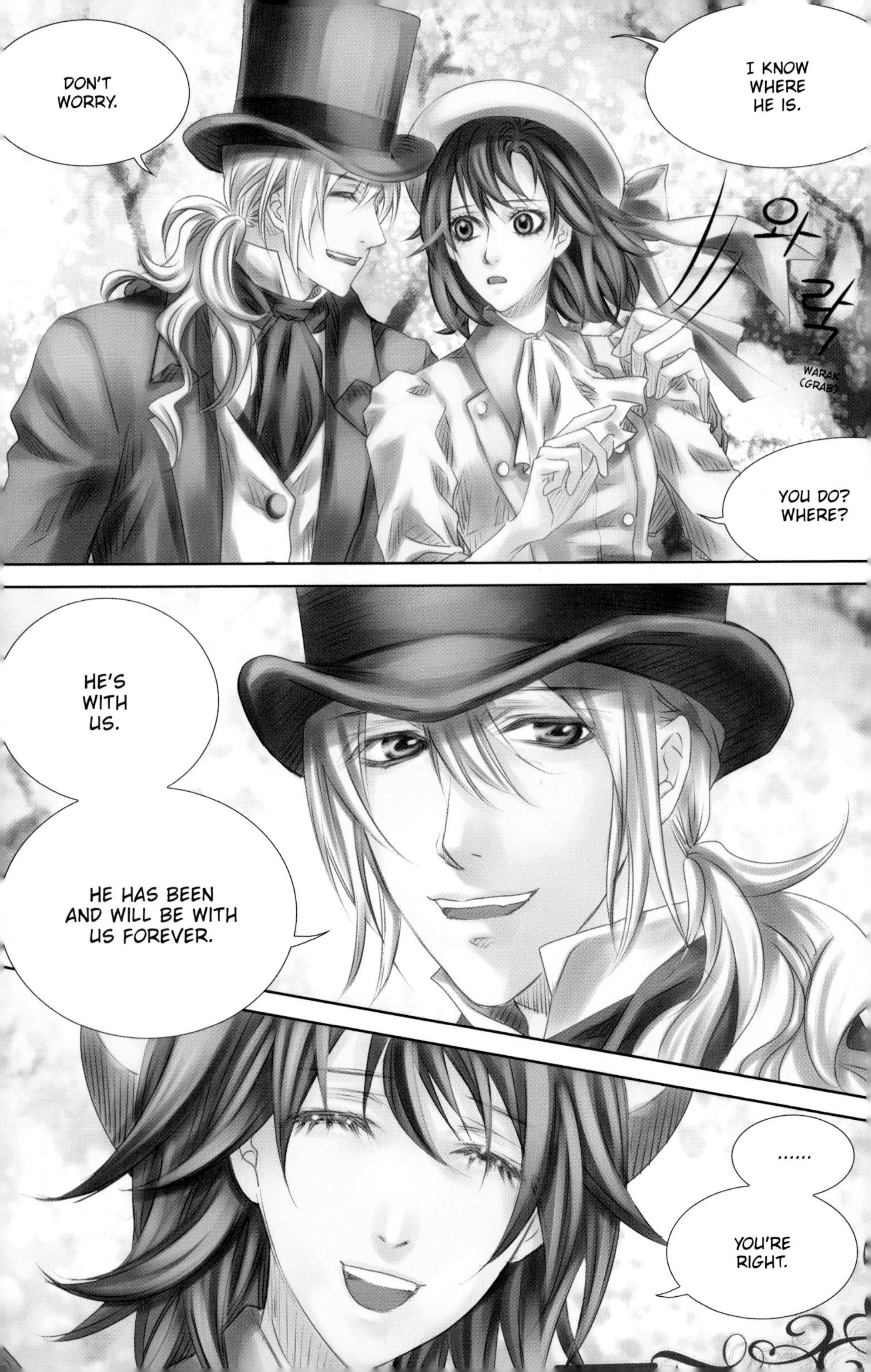
DON'T WORRY.
I KNOW WHERE HE IS.
와락
WARAK (GRAB)
YOU DO? WHERE?
HE'S WITH US.
HE HAS BEEN AND WILL BE WITH US FOREVER.
......
YOU'RE RIGHT.

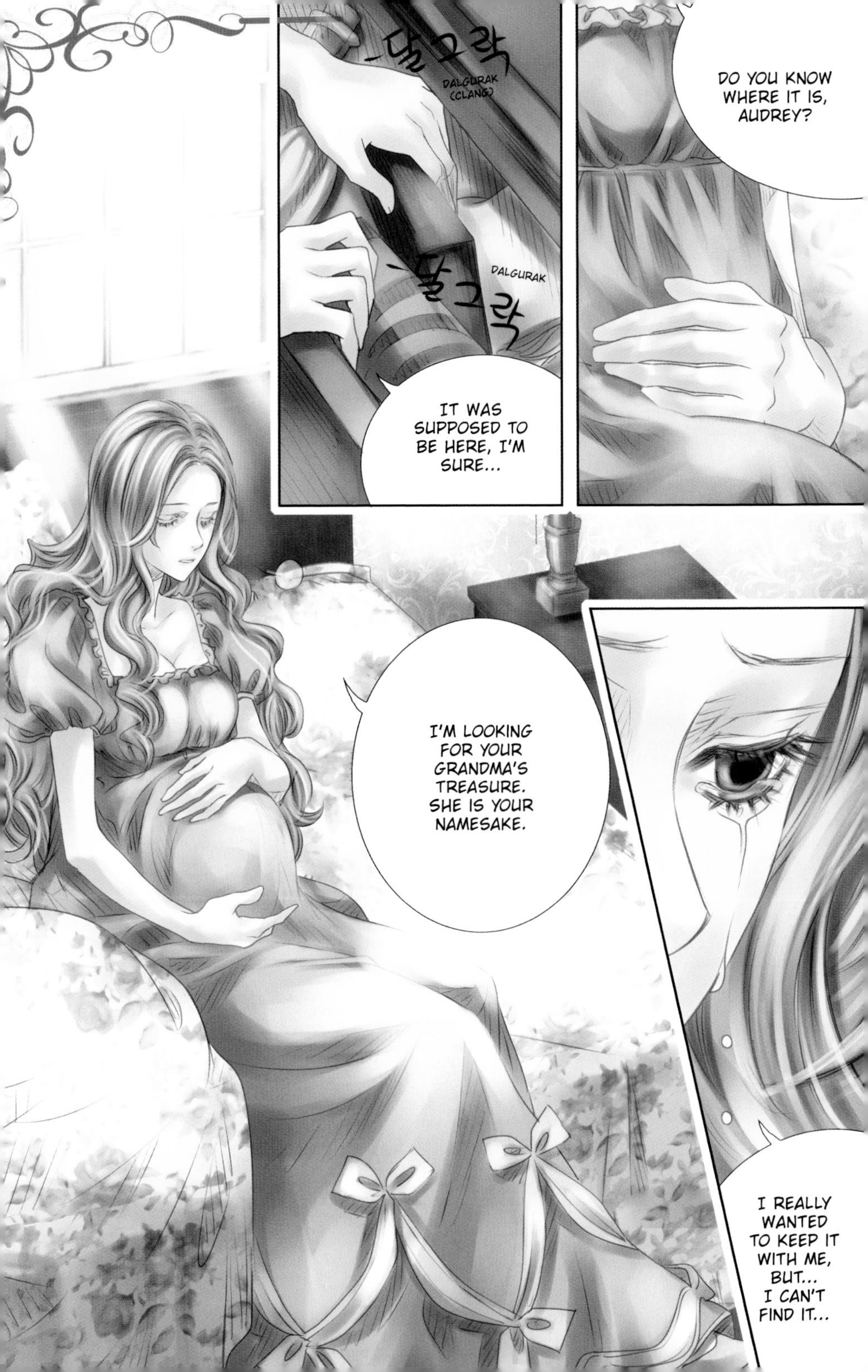

달그락
DALGURAK (CLANG)
달그락
DALGURAK
IT WAS SUPPOSED TO BE HERE, I'M SURE...
DO YOU KNOW WHERE IT IS, AUDREY?
I'M LOOKING FOR YOUR GRANDMA'S TREASURE. SHE IS YOUR NAMESAKE.
I REALLY WANTED TO KEEP IT WITH ME, BUT... I CAN'T FIND IT...

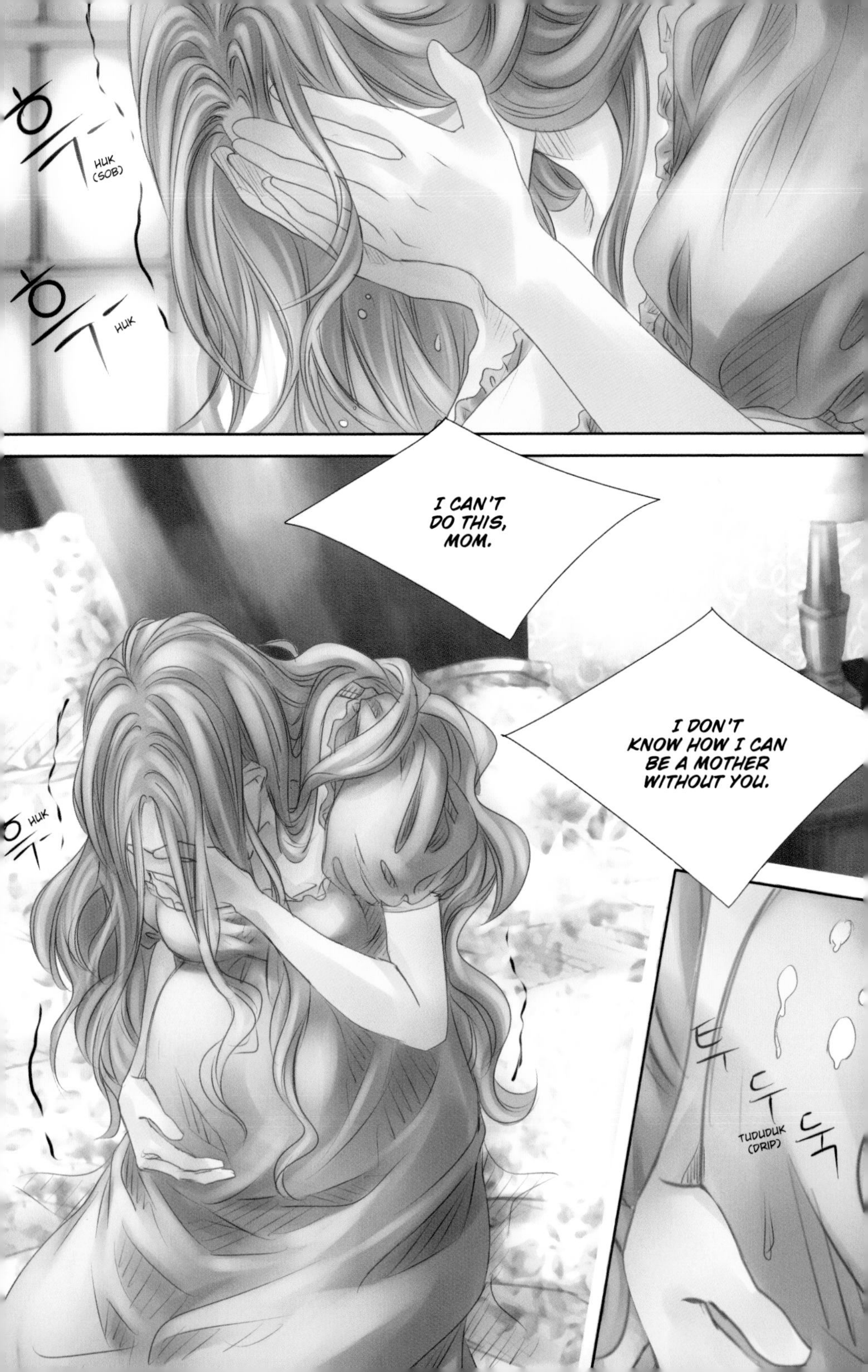
흐윽
HUK (SOB)
흐윽
HUK
I CAN'T DO THIS, MOM.
I DON'T KNOW HOW I CAN BE A MOTHER WITHOUT YOU.
흐윽
HUK
투두둑
TUDUDUK (DRIP)

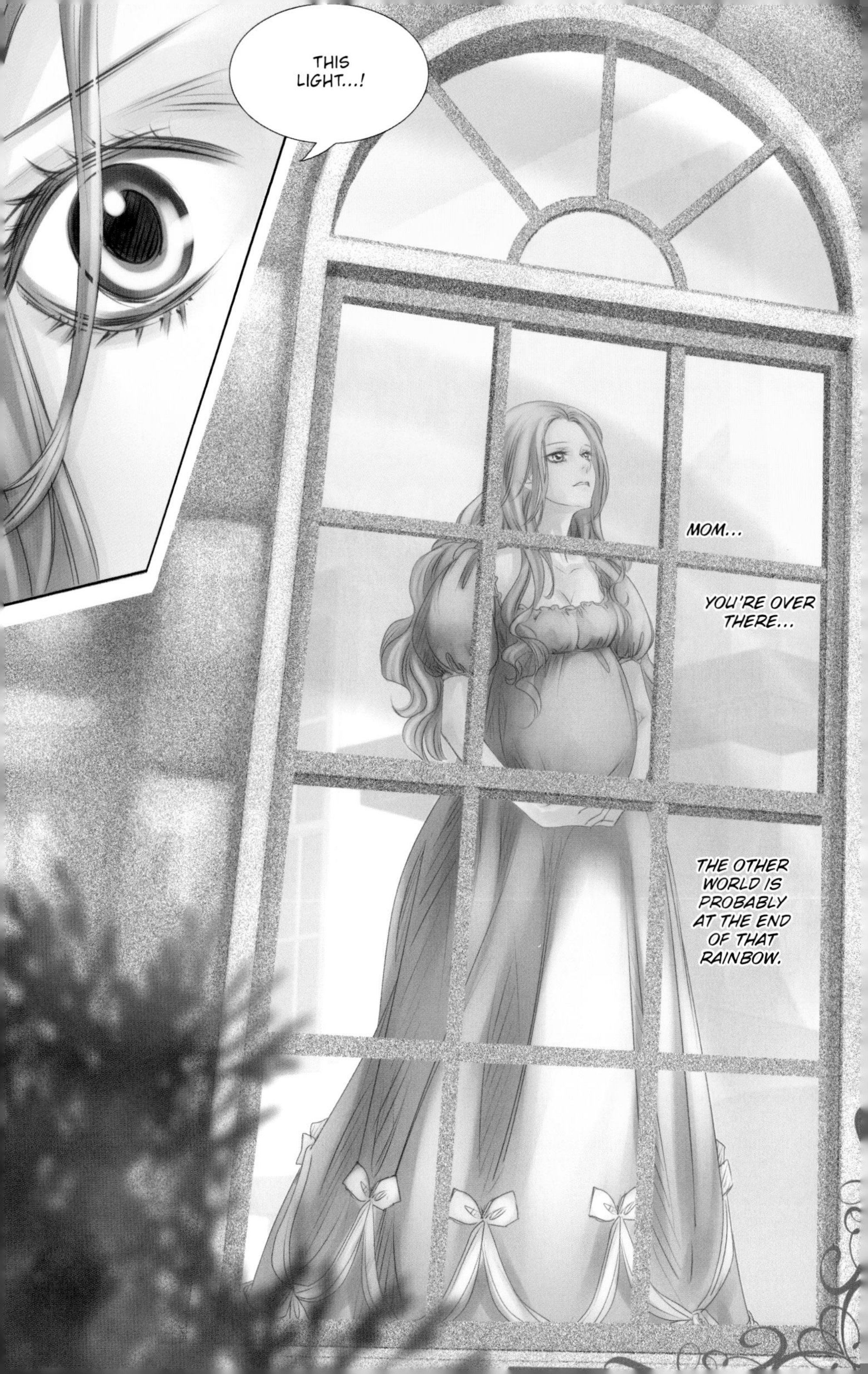
THIS LIGHT...!
MOM...
YOU'RE OVER THERE...
THE OTHER WORLD IS PROBABLY AT THE END OF THAT RAINBOW.

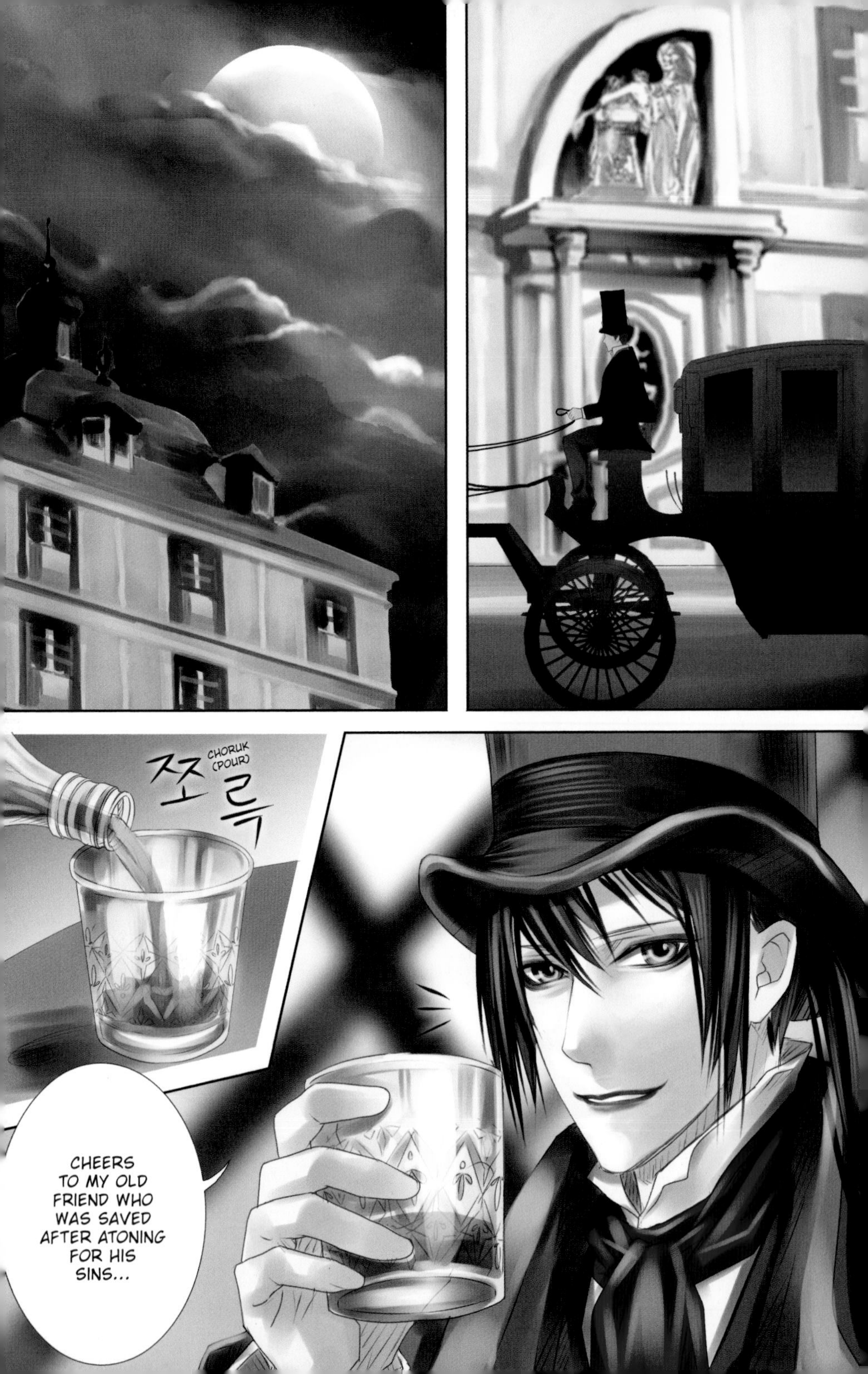

쪼르륵
CHORUK (POUR)
CHEERS TO MY OLD FRIEND WHO WAS SAVED AFTER ATONING FOR HIS SINS...

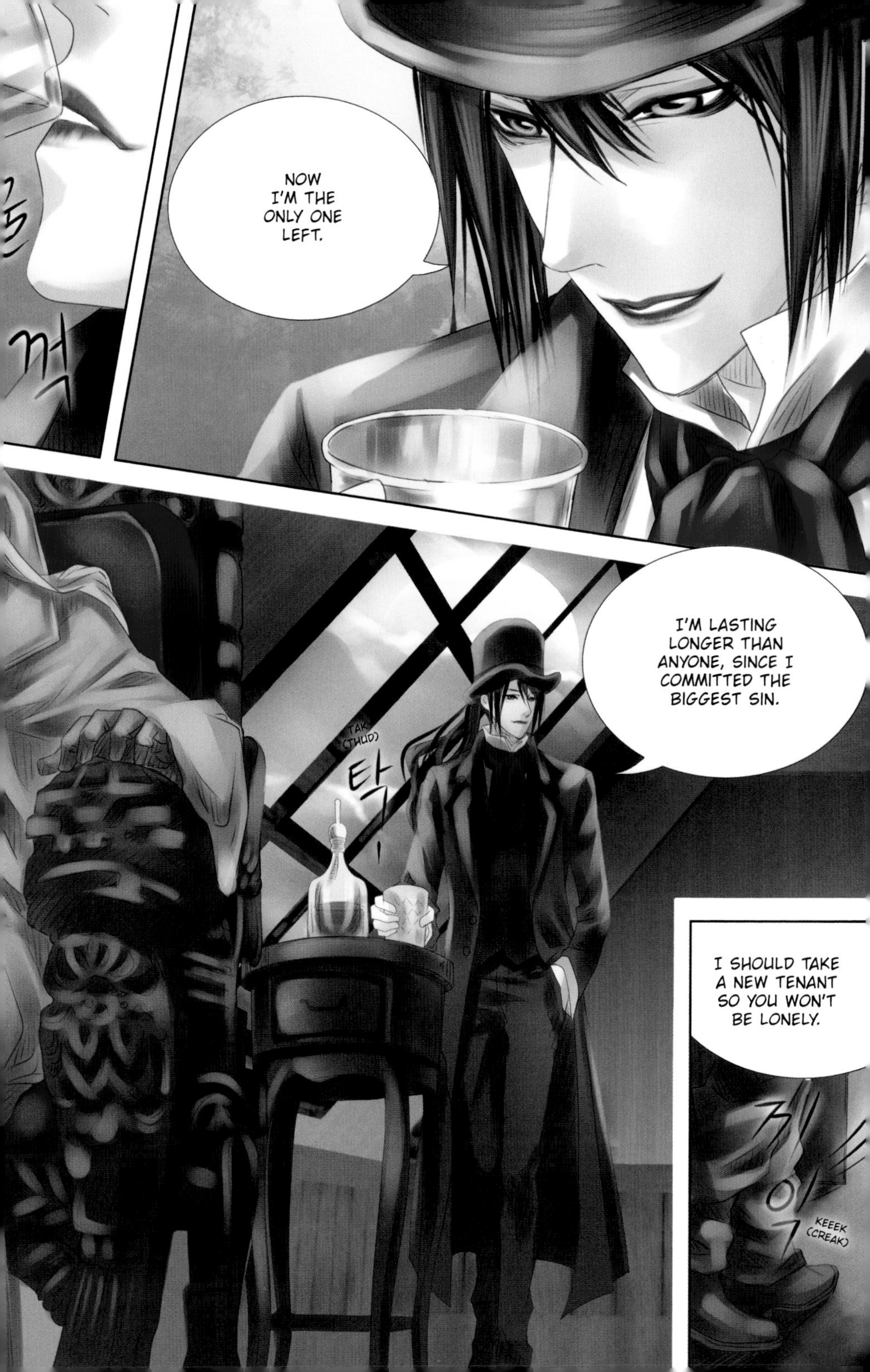

NOW I'M THE ONLY ONE LEFT.
I'M LASTING LONGER THAN ANYONE, SINCE I COMMITTED THE BIGGEST SIN.
TAK (THUD)
I SHOULD TAKE A NEW TENANT SO YOU WON'T BE LONELY.
KEEEK (CREAK)

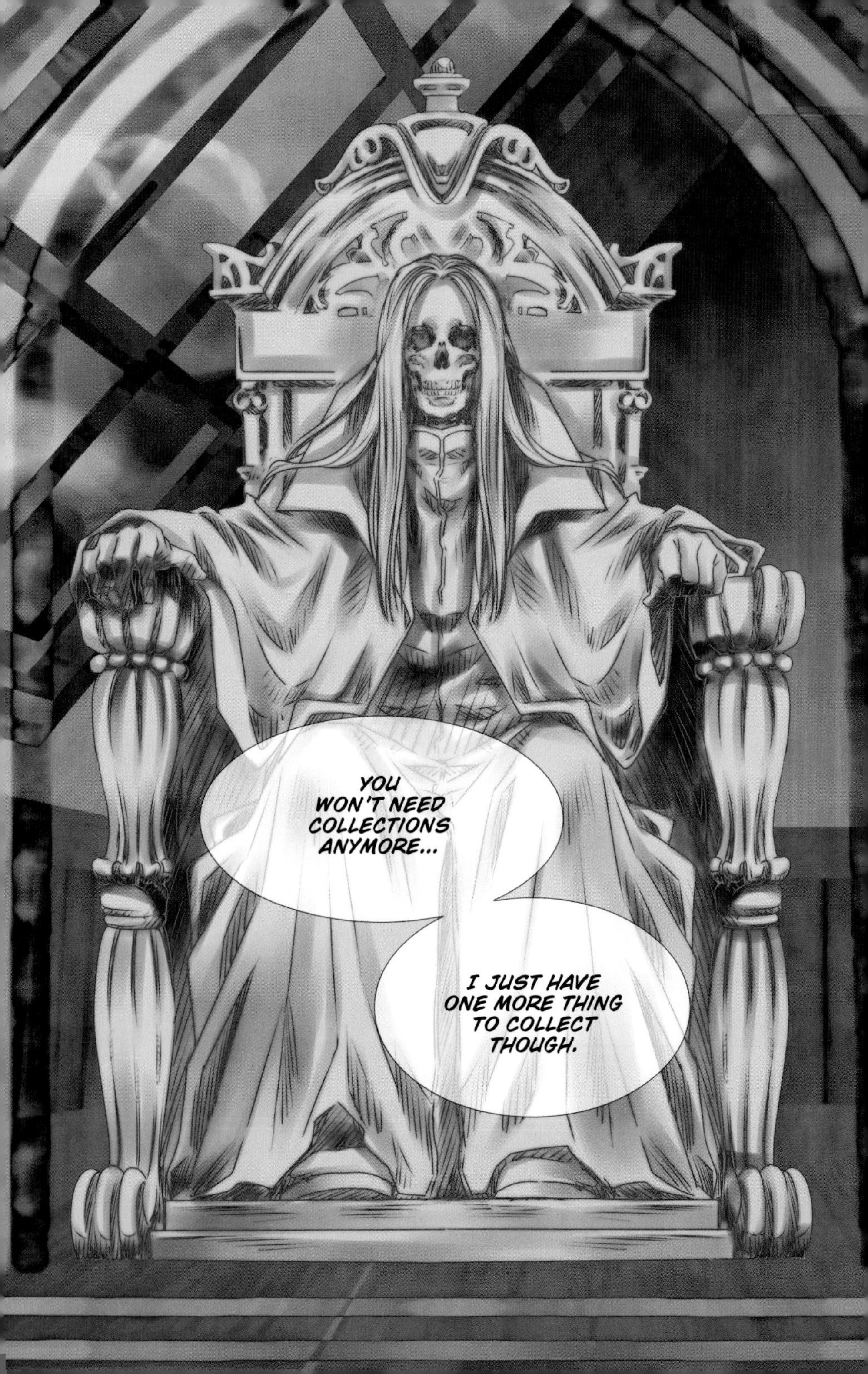
YOU WON'T NEED COLLECTIONS ANYMORE...
I JUST HAVE ONE MORE THING TO COLLECT THOUGH.

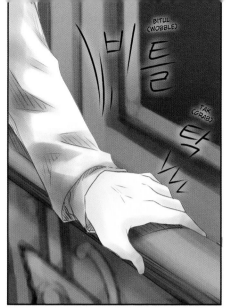

BITUL
(WOBBLE)

TAK
(GRAB)

I NEED
TO REST.

MY HEAD
HURTS
TOO...

NOW THAT MY
WORK IS DONE,
I NEED TO
CELEBRATE.

HEH...

HEH...

SUK

SUK
(WIPE)

TOOBUK
(TOK)

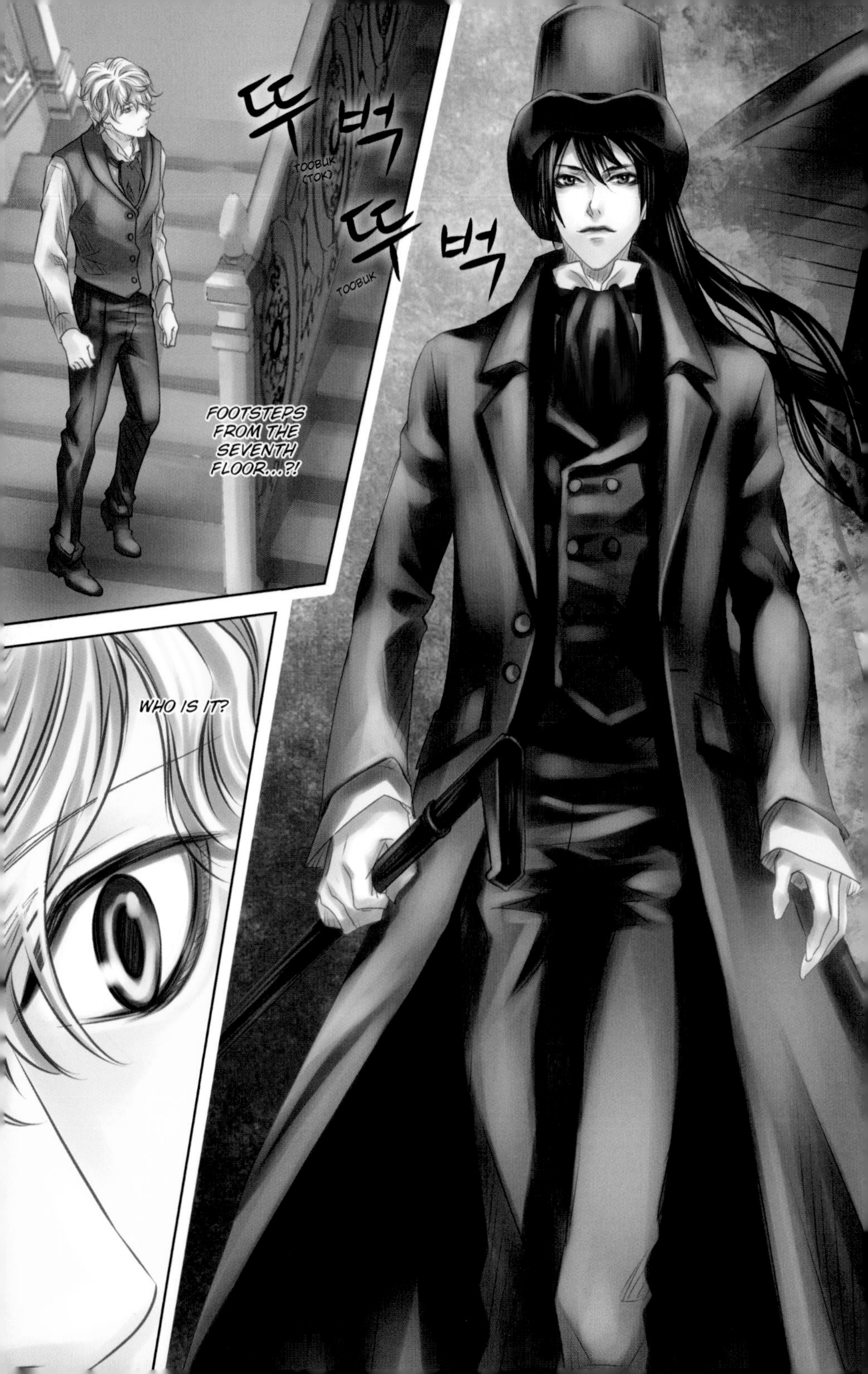
뚜벅
TOOBUK (TOK)
뚜벅
TOOBUK
FOOTSTEPS FROM THE SEVENTH FLOOR...?!
WHO IS IT?

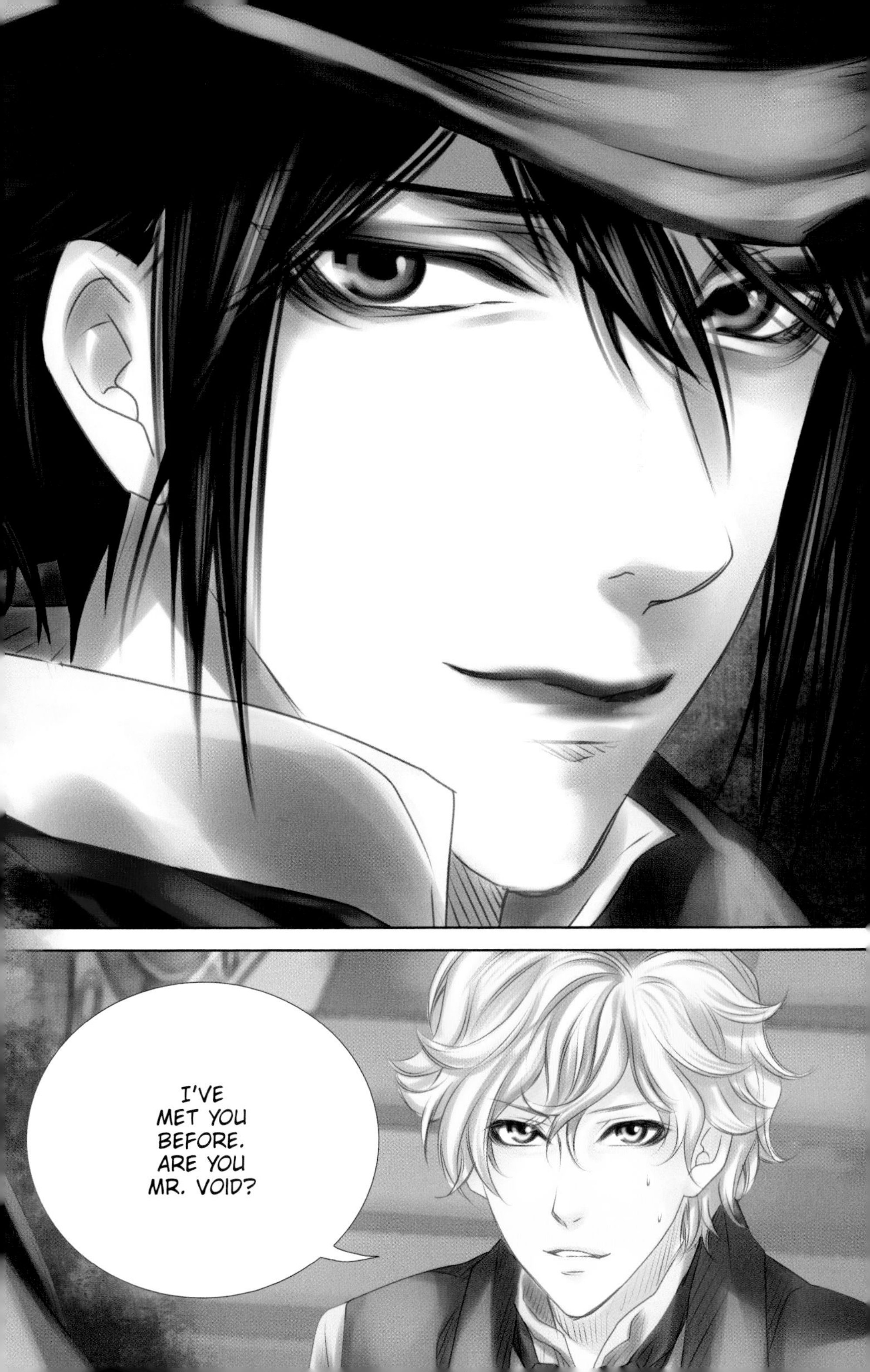
I'VE MET YOU BEFORE. ARE YOU MR. VOID?

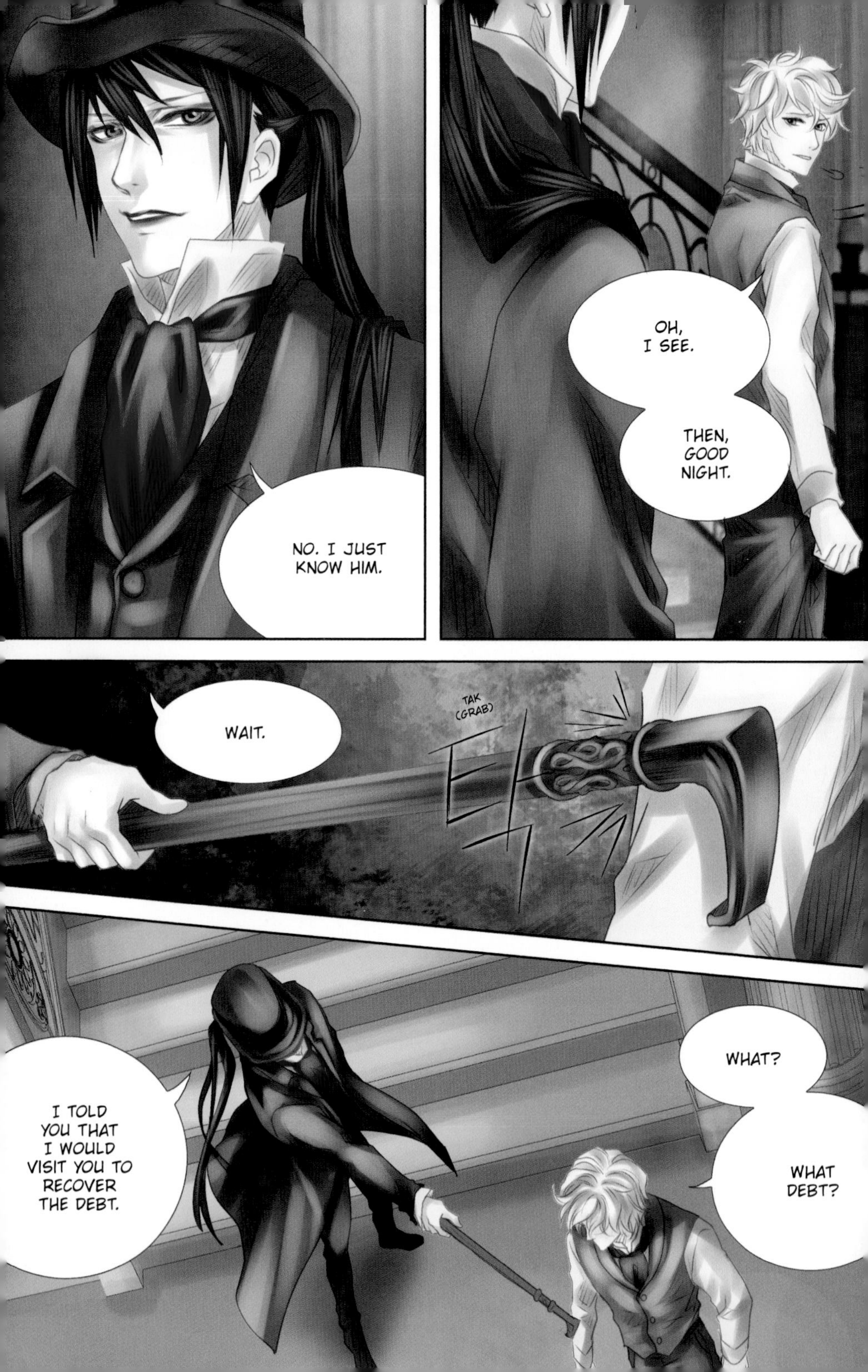
NO. I JUST KNOW HIM.
OH, I SEE.
THEN, GOOD NIGHT.
WAIT.
TAK (GRAB)
WHAT?
WHAT DEBT?
I TOLD YOU THAT I WOULD VISIT YOU TO RECOVER THE DEBT.

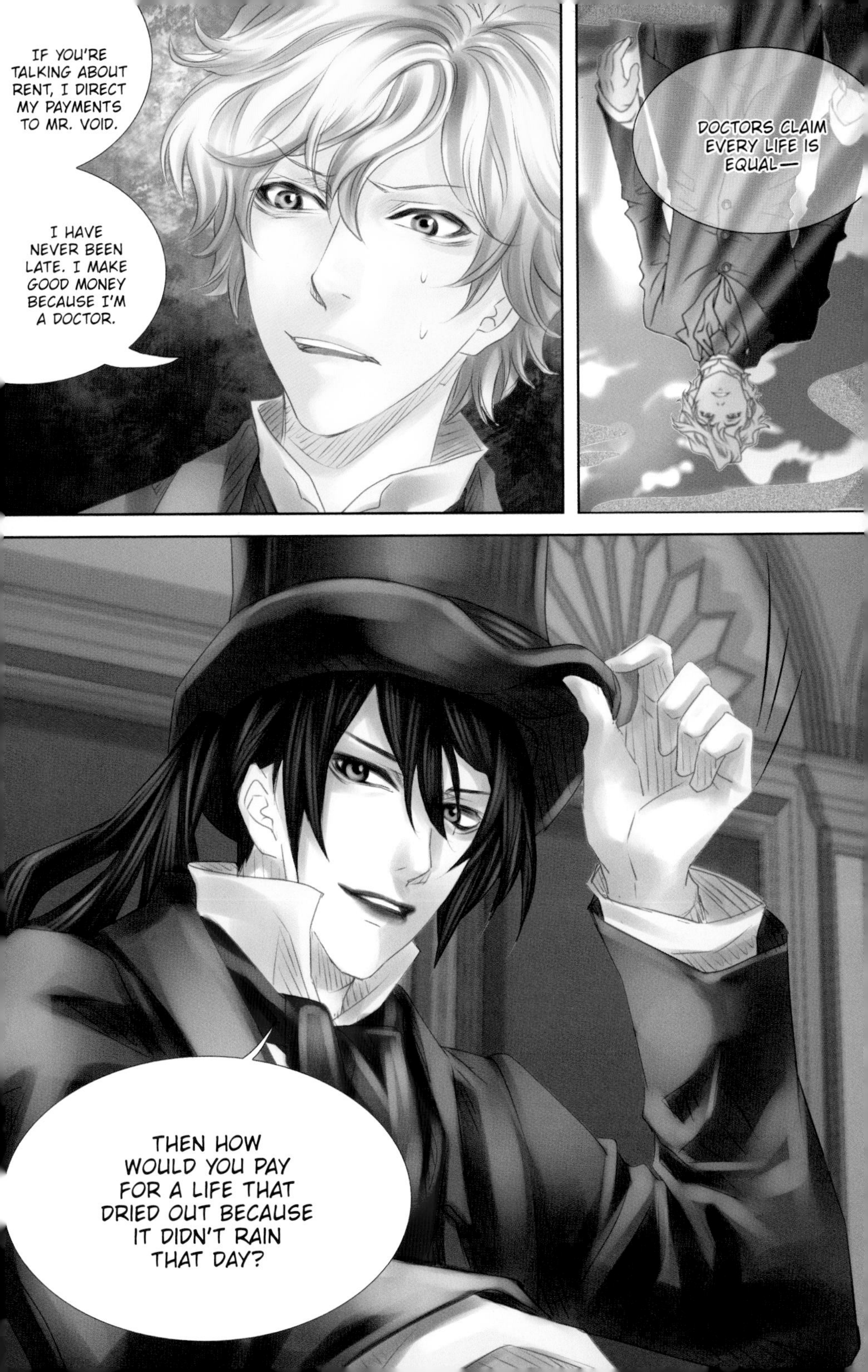
IF YOU'RE TALKING ABOUT RENT, I DIRECT MY PAYMENTS TO MR. VOID.
I HAVE NEVER BEEN LATE. I MAKE GOOD MONEY BECAUSE I'M A DOCTOR.
DOCTORS CLAIM EVERY LIFE IS EQUAL—
THEN HOW WOULD YOU PAY FOR A LIFE THAT DRIED OUT BECAUSE IT DIDN'T RAIN THAT DAY?

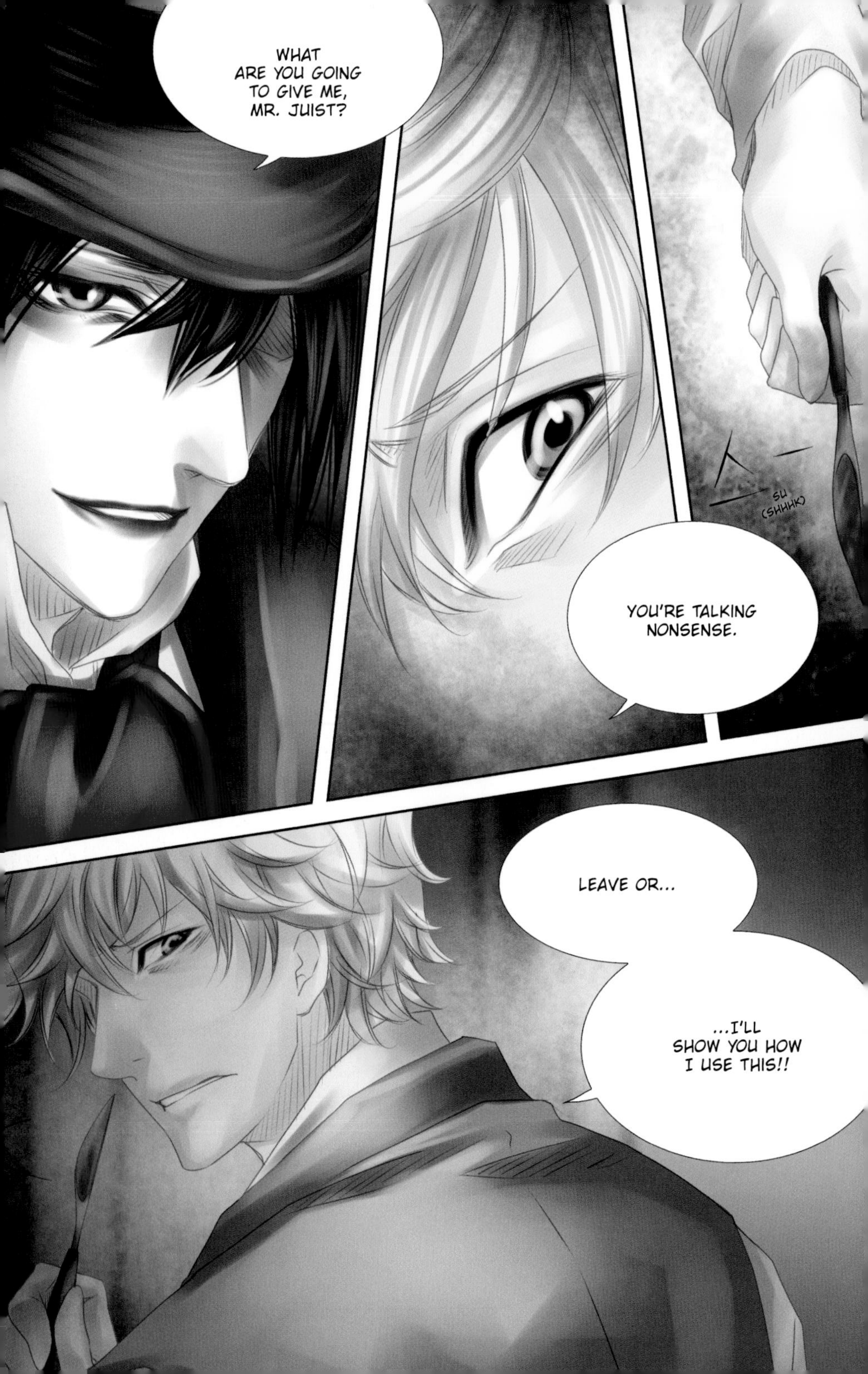
WHAT ARE YOU GOING TO GIVE ME, MR. JUIST?
SU (SHHHK)
YOU'RE TALKING NONSENSE.
LEAVE OR...
...I'LL SHOW YOU HOW I USE THIS!!

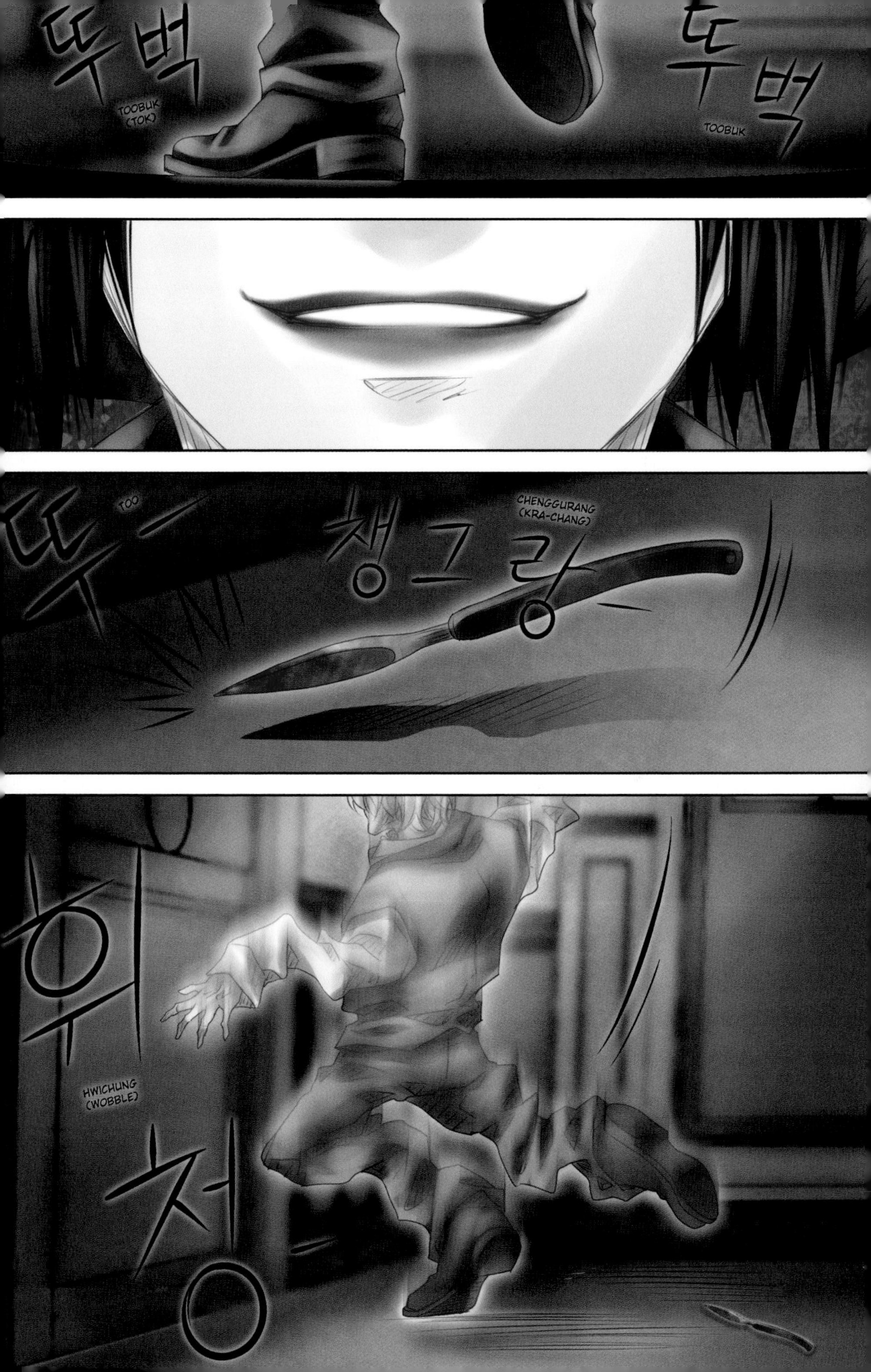
뚜벅
TOOBUK (TOK)
뚜벅
TOOBUK
뚜
TOO
챙그랑
CHENGGURANG (KRA-CHANG)
휘청
HWICHUNG (WOBBLE)

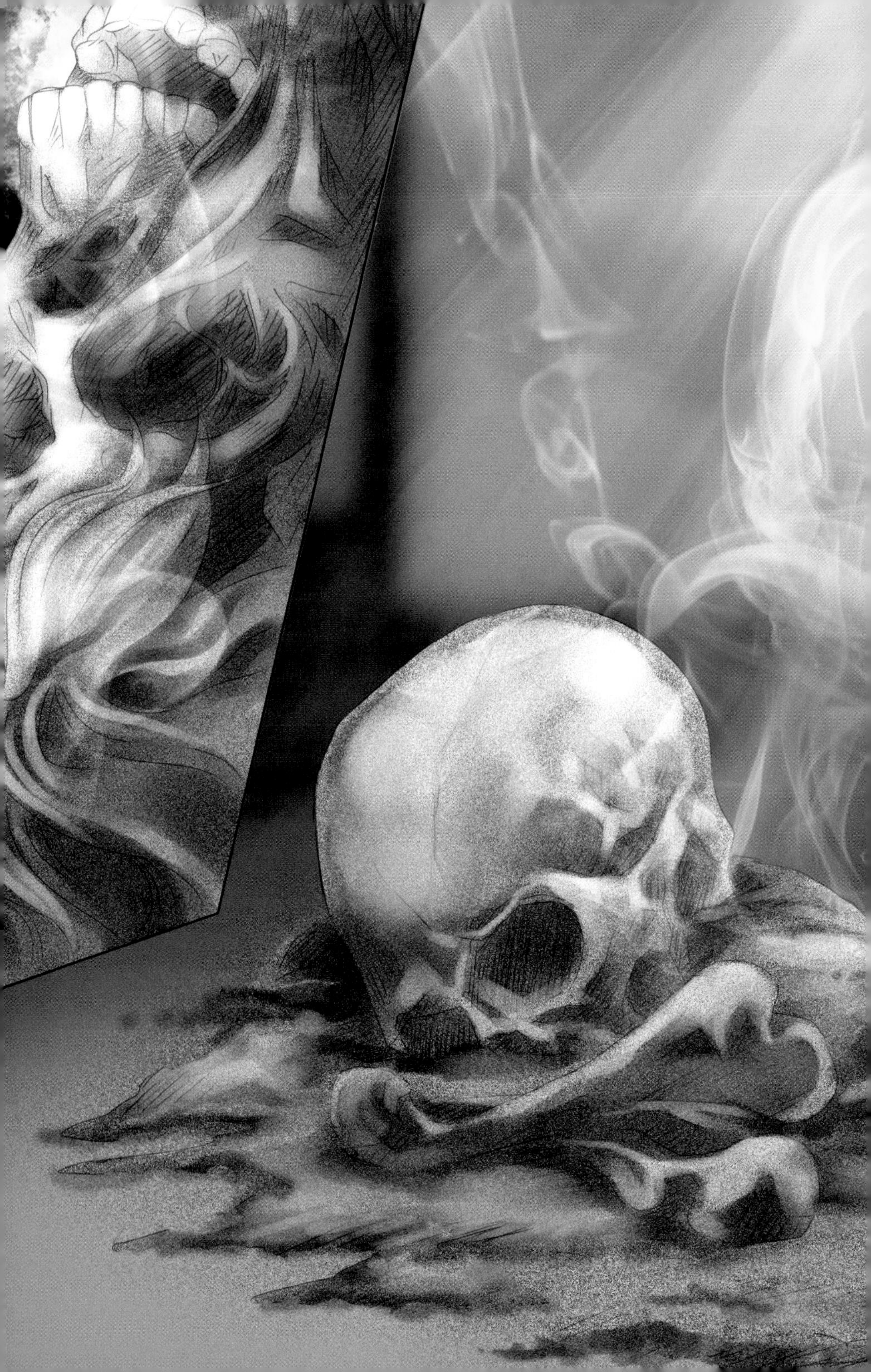

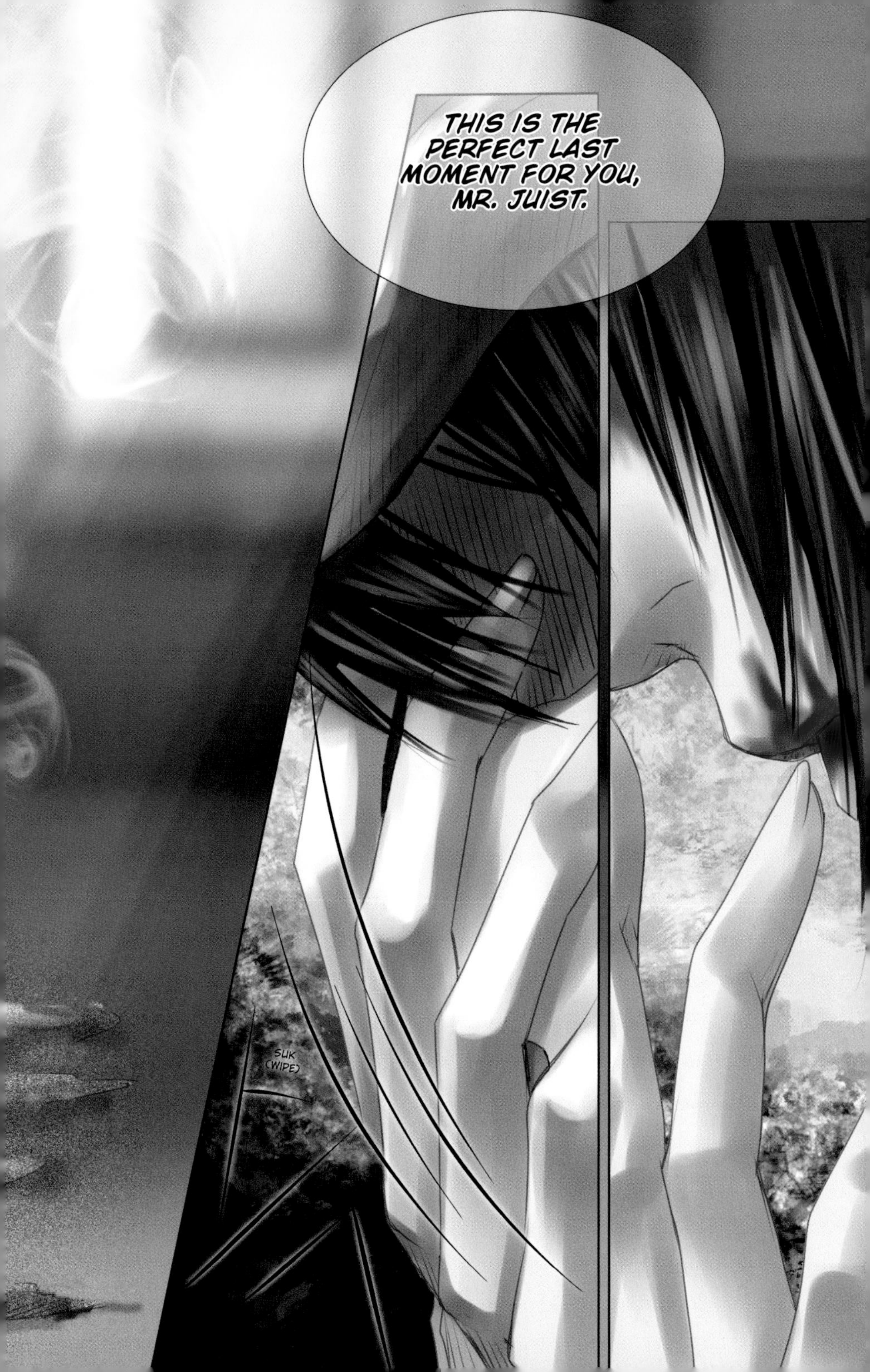
THIS IS THE PERFECT LAST MOMENT FOR YOU, MR. JUIST.
SUK (WIPE)

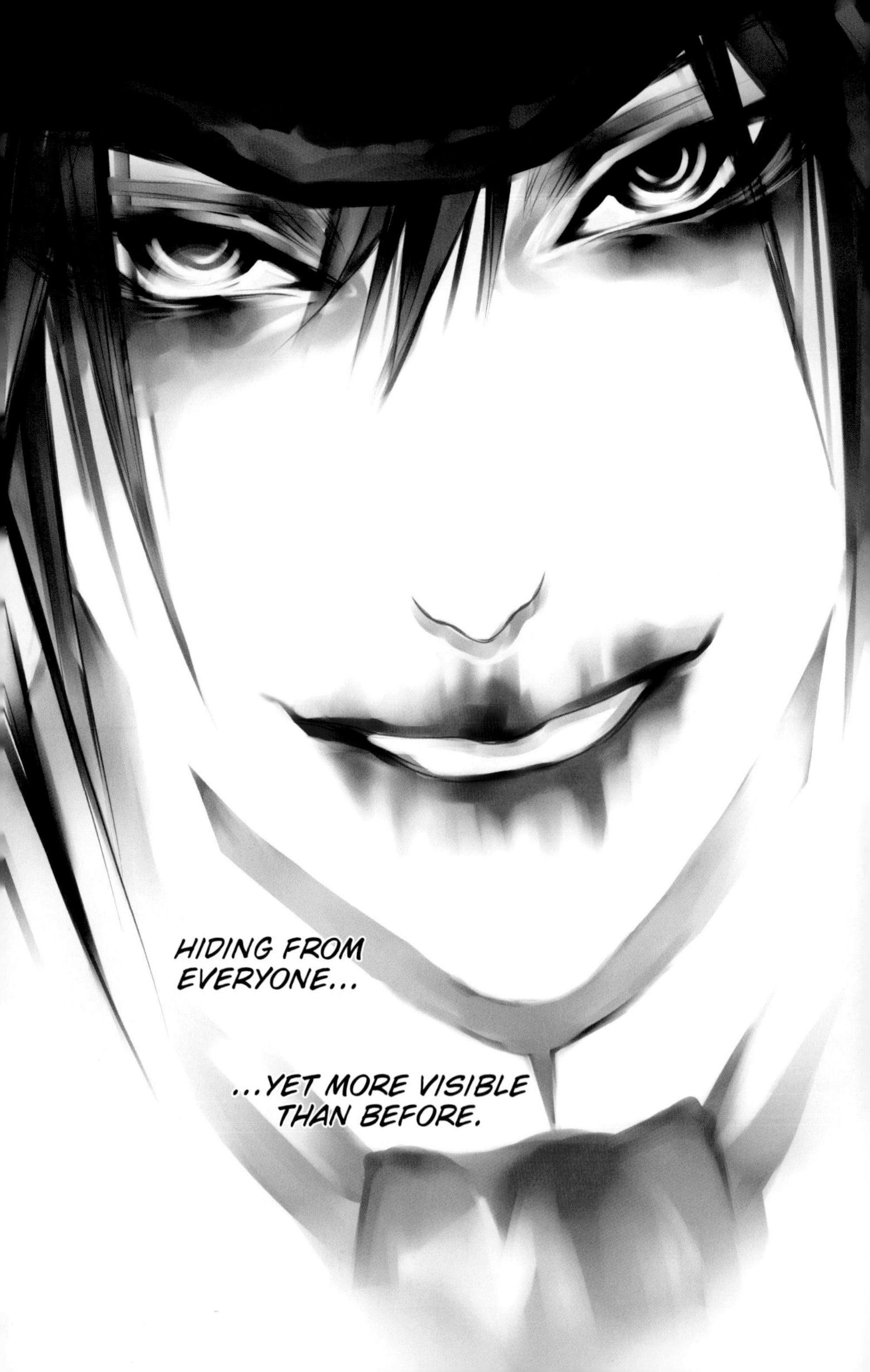
HIDING FROM EVERYONE...
...YET MORE VISIBLE THAN BEFORE.

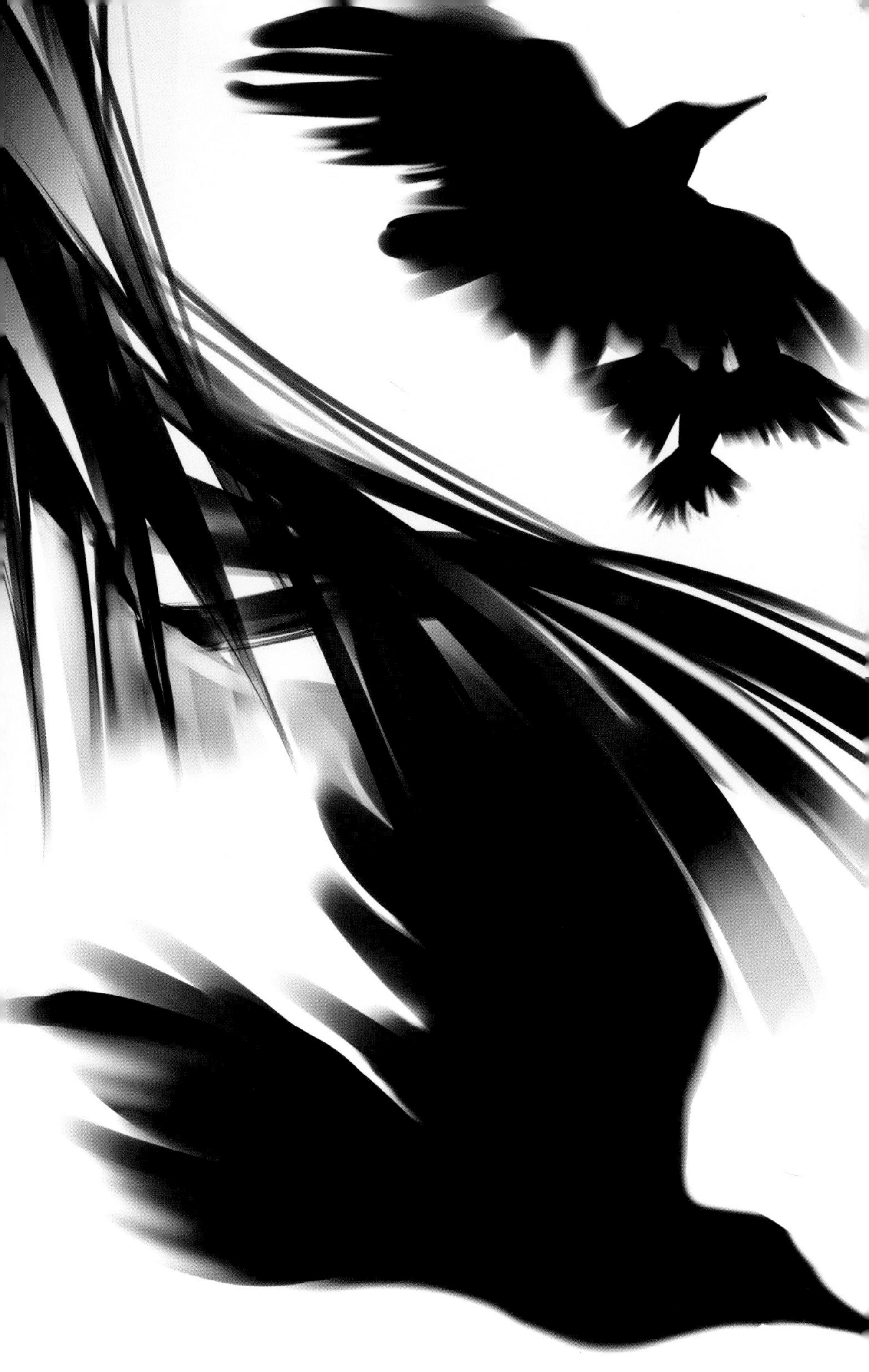

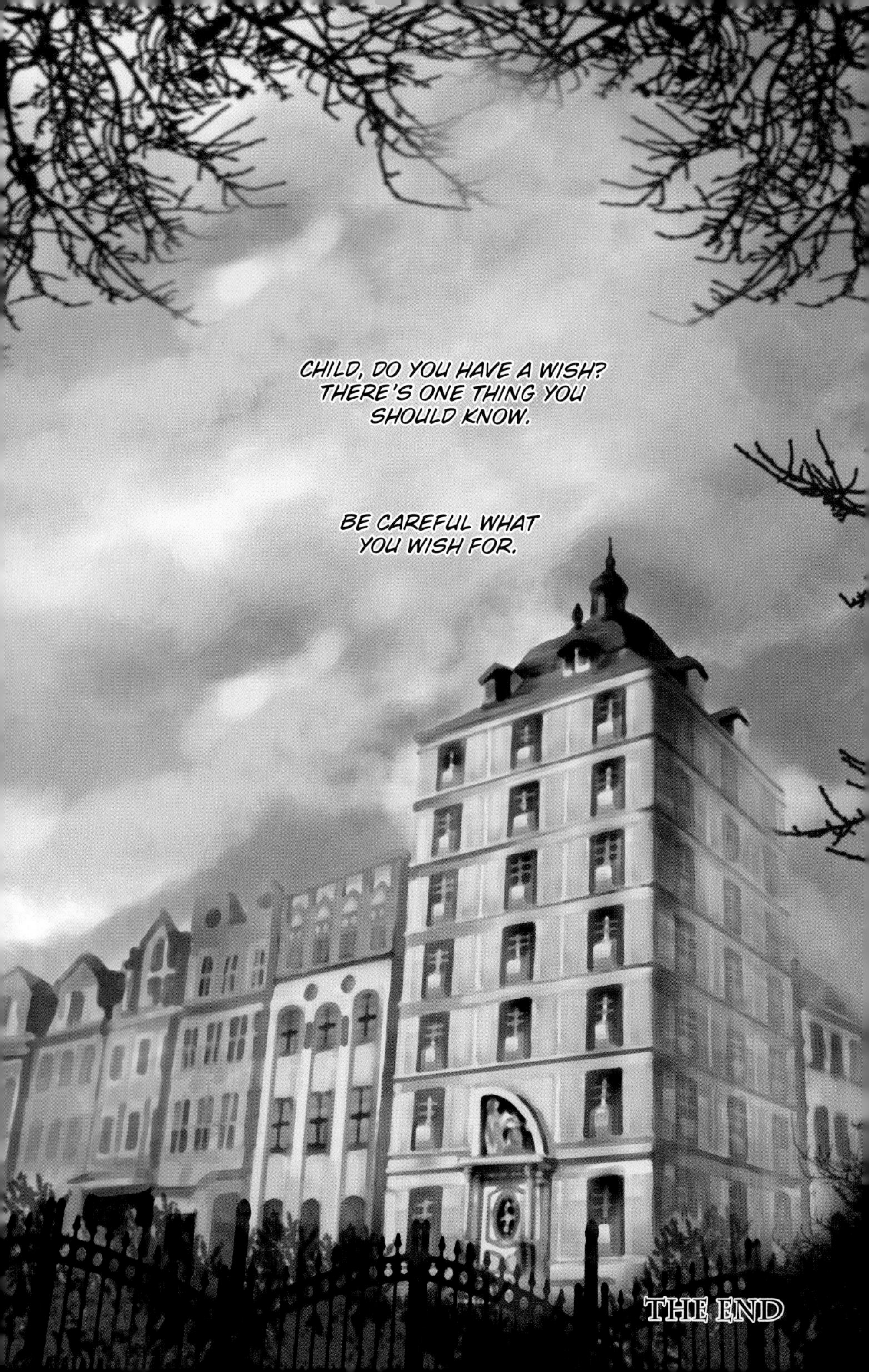
CHILD, DO YOU HAVE A WISH? THERE'S ONE THING YOU SHOULD KNOW.
BE CAREFUL WHAT YOU WISH FOR.
THE END

Void's Enigmatic Mansion

Void's Enigmatic Mansion

Visit artist HeeEun Kim's blog at http://blog.naver.com/kimnoran!

Void's
Enigmatic
Mansion

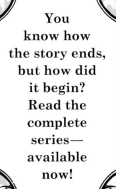

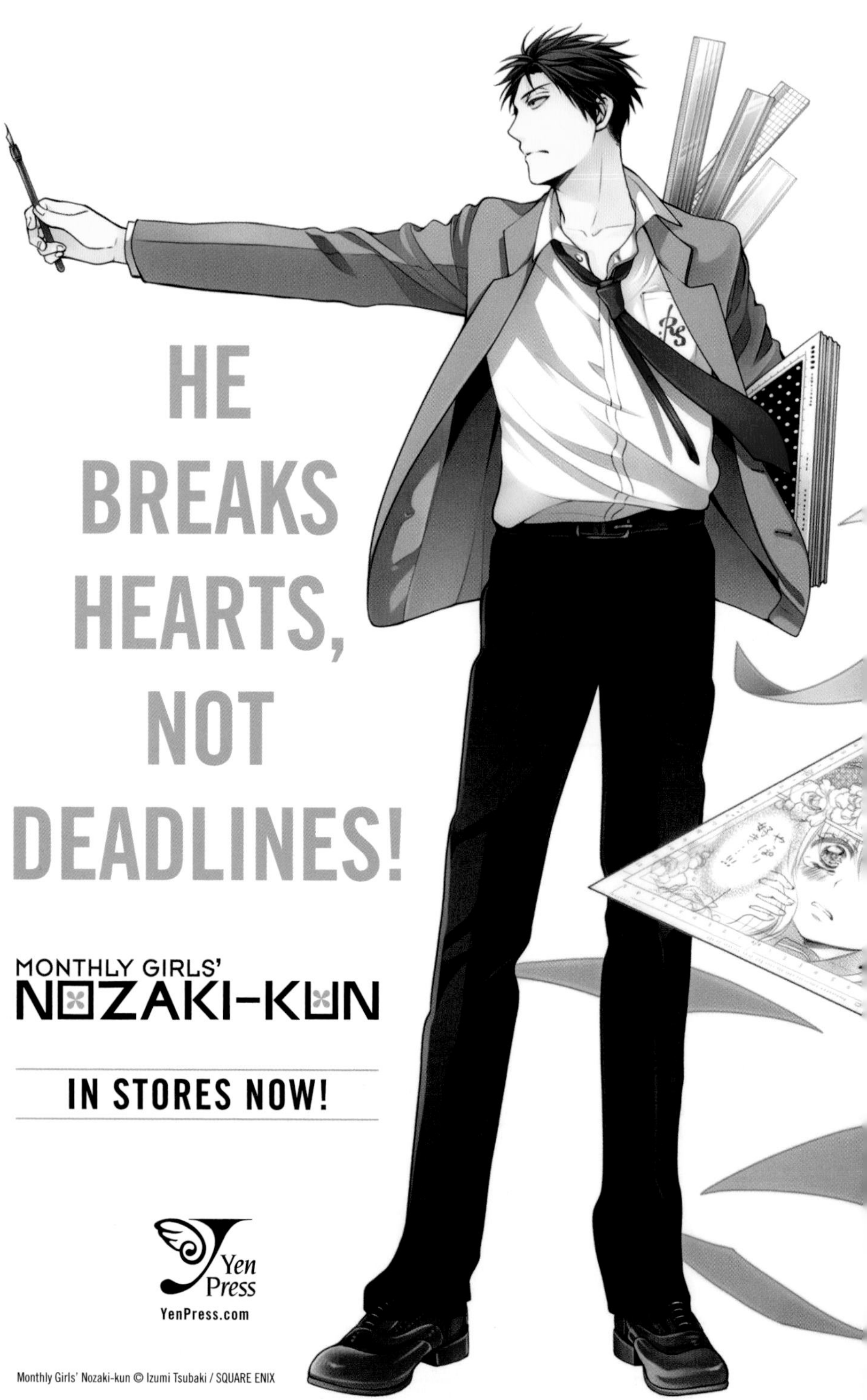
HE
BREAKS
HEARTS,
NOT
DEADLINES!
MONTHLY GIRLS'
NOZAKI-KUN
IN STORES NOW!
Yen Press
YenPress.com

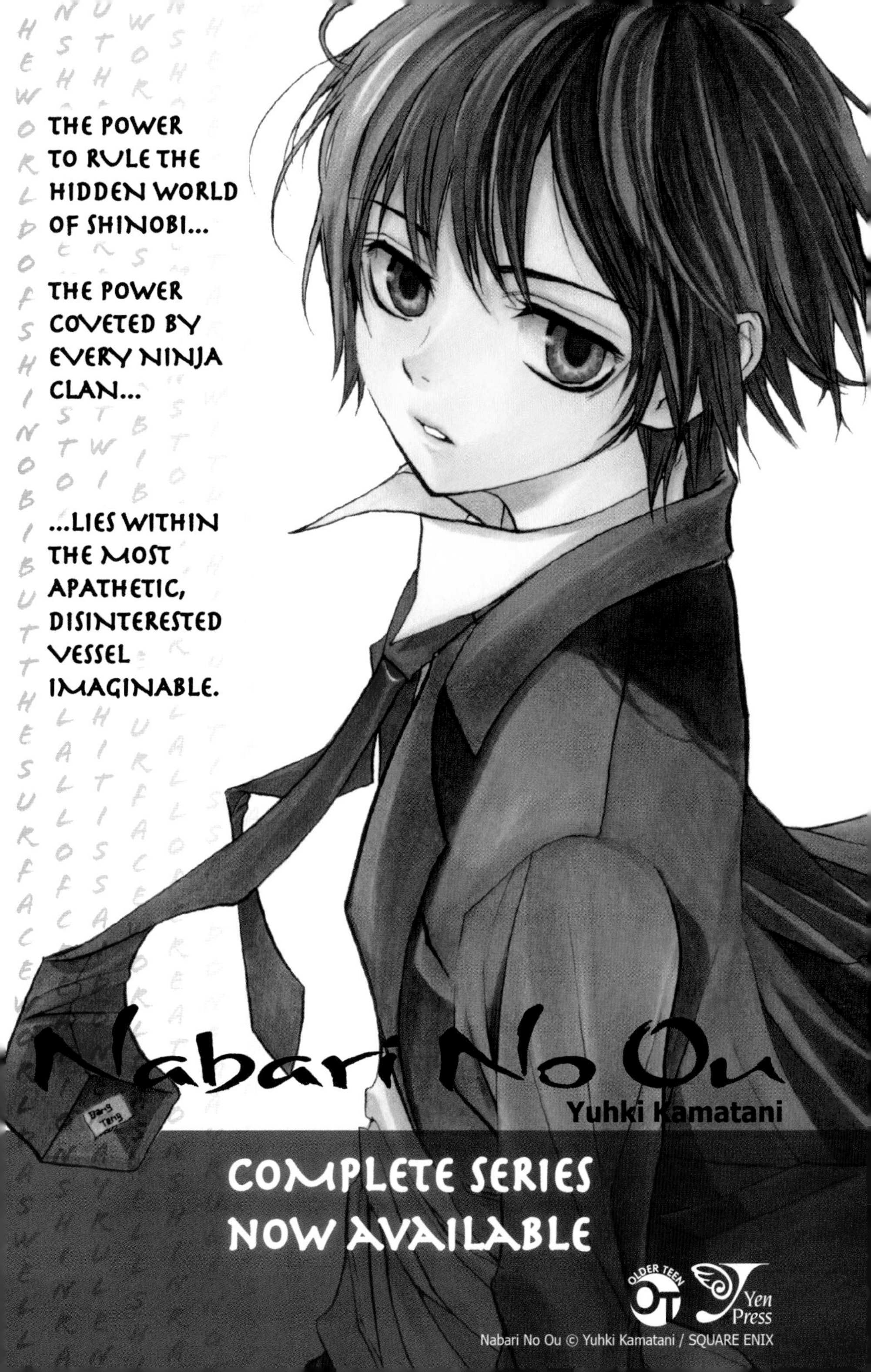
THE POWER TO RULE THE HIDDEN WORLD OF SHINOBI...
THE POWER COVETED BY EVERY NINJA CLAN...
...LIES WITHIN THE MOST APATHETIC, DISINTERESTED VESSEL IMAGINABLE.
Nabari No Ou
Yuhki Kamatani
COMPLETE SERIES NOW AVAILABLE
OLDER TEEN OT
Yen Press
Nabari No Ou © Yuhki Kamatani / SQUARE ENIX

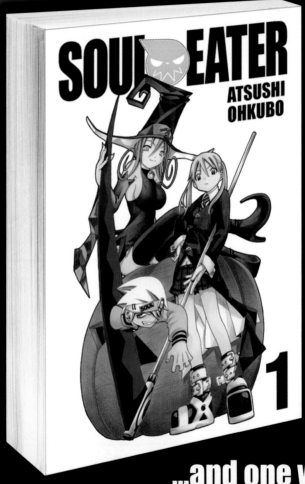

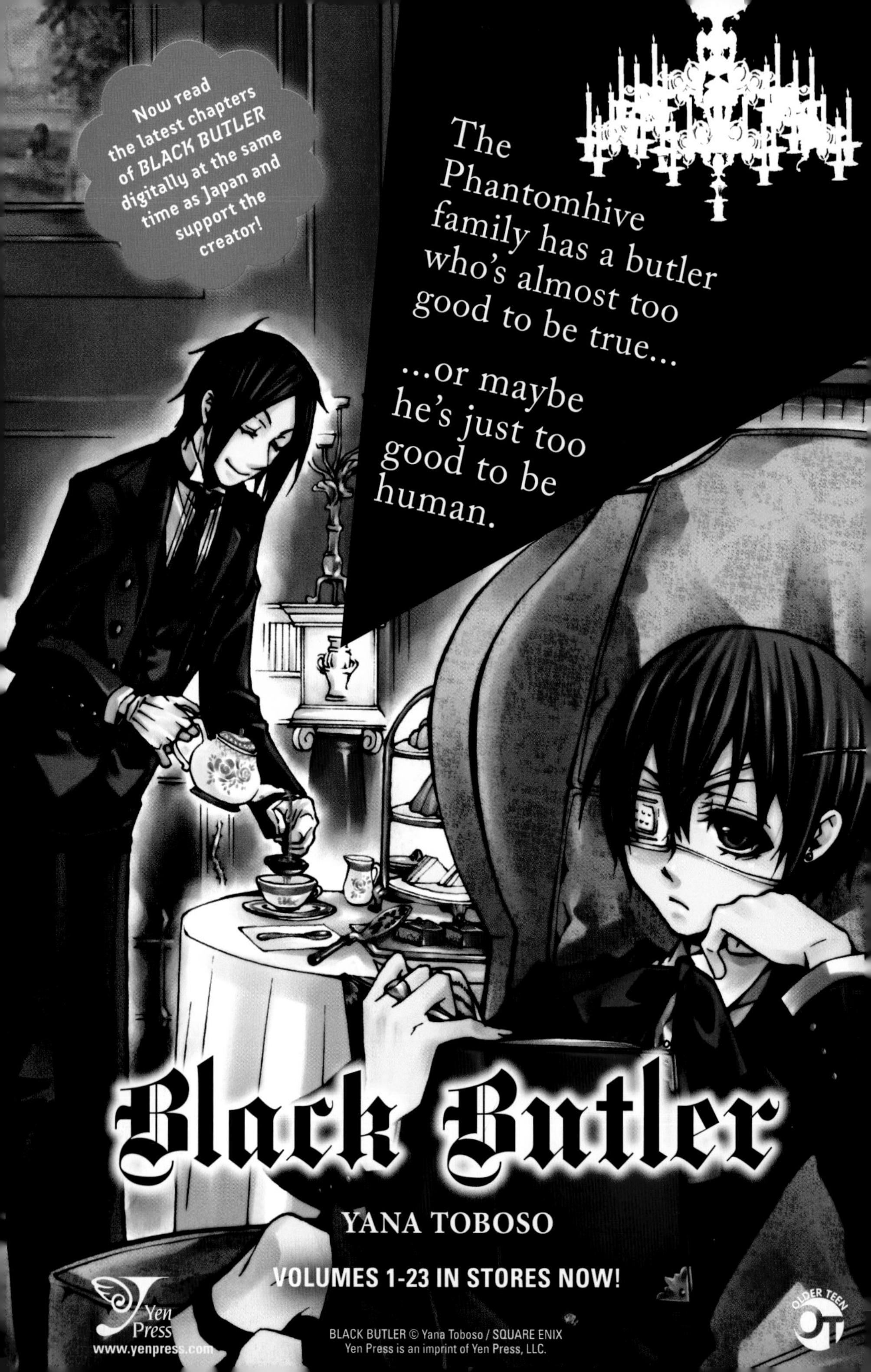
Now read the latest chapters of BLACK BUTLER digitally at the same time as Japan and support the creator!
The Phantomhive family has a butler who's almost too good to be true...
...or maybe he's just too good to be human.
Black Butler
YANA TOBOSO
VOLUMES 1-23 IN STORES NOW!
Yen Press
www.yenpress.com
OLDER TEEN
OT
BLACK BUTLER © Yana Toboso / SQUARE ENIX
Yen Press is an imprint of Yen Press, LLC.